Microsoft Dynamics 365 Enterprise Edition – Financial Management
Third Edition

Maximize your business productivity through modern financial management in Dynamics 365

Mohamed Aamer

BIRMINGHAM - MUMBAI

Microsoft Dynamics 365 Enterprise Edition – Financial Management
Third Edition

Commissioning Editor: Richa Tripathi
Acquisition Editor: Denim Pinto
Content Development Editor: Vikas Tiwari
Technical Editor: Madhunikita Sunil Chindarkar
Copy Editor: Safis Editing
Project Coordinator: Ulhas Kambali
Proofreader: Safis Editing
Indexer: Tejal Daruwale Soni
Graphics: Tania Dutta
Production Coordinator: Deepika Naik

First published: November 2013
Second edition: February 2015
Third edition: March 2018

Production reference: 1210318

Published by Packt Publishing Ltd.
Livery Place
35 Livery Street
Birmingham
B3 2PB, UK.

ISBN 978-1-78883-929-7

www.packtpub.com

My sincere thanks go to all the people who directly/indirectly taught, guided, supported, and advised me to build my personal profile.

I dedicate this book to the memory of my father, and my uncle, Hamza; both of them invested the seeds of concepts and beliefs in my brother and me, and now we are harvesting the fruits of it. I also dedicate this book to my older brother, Ramy, and my mother for their support and prayers. I would also like to thank my lovely wife, Fatema, who has given up so much of our personal life during the development of my career.

`mapt.io`

Mapt is an online digital library that gives you full access to over 5,000 books and videos, as well as industry leading tools to help you plan your personal development and advance your career. For more information, please visit our website.

Why subscribe?

- Spend less time learning and more time coding with practical eBooks and Videos from over 4,000 industry professionals

- Improve your learning with Skill Plans built especially for you

- Get a free eBook or video every month

- Mapt is fully searchable

- Copy and paste, print, and bookmark content

PacktPub.com

Did you know that Packt offers eBook versions of every book published, with PDF and ePub files available? You can upgrade to the eBook version at `www.PacktPub.com` and as a print book customer, you are entitled to a discount on the eBook copy. Get in touch with us at `service@packtpub.com` for more details.

At `www.PacktPub.com`, you can also read a collection of free technical articles, sign up for a range of free newsletters, and receive exclusive discounts and offers on Packt books and eBooks.

Contributors

About the author

Mohamed Aamer is a Escalation Engineer at Microsoft. In 2013, he was awarded AX MVP. He uses his time to support Microsoft premier customers and partners and is engaged in escalations. He is a Microsoft MCP and MCT. He has varied consultation experience in dealing with Microsoft partners and customers. He has carried out multiple implementations of AX in numerous capacities, such as solutions architect and lead consultant. Also, he achieved a top speaker award for Microsoft TechReady. He is a an author.

My sincere gratitude to people who have helped me in my career. Special thanks to Shaimaa Farid, Ashraf Abusen, Ashraf Ali, Mohamed Samy, Ahmed Kazem, Chandru Shankar, Jason Gumpert, Eva Del Pino, Arijit Basu, and Murray Fife. Also, I want to thank AX MVPs for their contribution to the community.

About the reviewer

Wendy Rijners is a consultant at Microsoft. Over the years, Wendy has worked for several customers who use Dynamics ERP solutions. Since 2011, she has been focused on retail, in combination with Dynamics AX, Dynamics 365 Finance and Operations, and Dynamics 365 Retail, and has been involved in multiple retail implementations.

Packt is searching for authors like you

If you're interested in becoming an author for Packt, please visit `authors.packtpub.com` and apply today. We have worked with thousands of developers and tech professionals, just like you, to help them share their insight with the global tech community. You can make a general application, apply for a specific hot topic that we are recruiting an author for, or submit your own idea.

Table of Contents

Preface

The essential foundation of the Enterprise Resource Planning (ERP) implementation is the financial part, which is considered the backbone of the implementation. The implementation team from the partner side and customer side should ensure that the financial module is well structured and designed. This book provides a broad guide to Microsoft Dynamics 365 for Finance and Operations financial management fundamentals for parties involved in the implementation project, with considerations of the business rationale behind functions, basic setups, configurations, transactions in action, and examples of real-life scenarios.

Who this book is for

This book is intended for application consultants, technical consultants, solution architects, in addition to controllers, CFOs, key users, and other professionals who are involved in the Microsoft Dynamics 365 for Finance and Operations implementation project. Basic knowledge of financial terms, concepts, and Microsoft Dynamics 365 for Finance and Operations terminology is required.

Each company has its unique business model, organizational policy, and requirements. This leads to unique challenges for ERP implementation. While going through this book, you may encounter recommendations, guidelines, and experiences I gained from my work experience; however, you may need to adopt the recommendations as per your requirements, based on the particular project size, timeline, business organization structure, and industry.

What this book covers

Chapter 1, *Getting Started with Microsoft Dynamics 365 for Finance and Operations*, explains the ERP concept, integration of modules, the financial posting mechanisms in Microsoft Dynamics 365 for Finance and Operations, the role of consultant in implementation team, Microsoft Dynamics Sure Step implementation methodology, Microsoft Dynamics Lifecycle Services, and the Microsoft Dynamics 365 for Finance and Operations user interface.

Chapter 2, *Understanding the General Ledger*, explains the usage of main accounts, control points, and the Microsoft Dynamics 365 for Finance and Operations shared financial data concept. It also gives you a practical insight into opening balance tips and month-end closing procedures. In addition, it covers newly introduced features, such as global the general journal, financial period close.

Chapter 3, *Exploring Financial Dimensions*, focuses on financial dimensions features in Microsoft Dynamics 365 for Finance and Operations, its practical utilization, and its reporting. In addition, it covers the financial dimension's posting mechanism in transaction documents.

Chapter 4, *Understanding Sales Tax*, focuses on the sales tax mechanism in Microsoft Dynamics 365 for Finance and Operations, then covers the integration of sales tax with other modules. In addition, it covers the sales tax and withholding tax configurations, controls, and transactions. Finally, it explores the tax declaration process.

Chapter 5, *Working with Currencies*, focuses on multi-currency capabilities of Microsoft Dynamics 365 for Finance and Operations, cover the setup, mechanism, and daily transactions. Then cover the triangulation currency handling. Finally, it discusses the foreign currency revaluation on sub ledgers and the general ledger.

Chapter 6, *Understanding Accounts Payable Basics and Controls*, focuses on integrating accounts payable with other modules, vendor master data, and vendor controls.

Chapter 7, *Exploring Accounts Payable Transactions*, focuses on accounts payable transactions, vendor invoices, payment, and prepayment. In addition, it covers global vendor invoices, and the vendor settlement mechanism in Microsoft Dynamics 365 for Finance and Operations.

Chapter 8, *Understanding Accounts Receivable*, focuses on integrating accounts receivable with other modules, the customer transactions, sales invoices, free text invoices and its correction, in addition to customer controls and basic master data.

Chapter 9, *Understanding Cash and Bank Management*, will help you understand the cash and bank management module integration, controls, the bank reconciliation process, and then cover the bank facility function, in addition to working with checks.

Chapter 10, *Functioning of Cash Flow Management*, focuses on the integration points between cash flow management and other modules in Microsoft Dynamics 365 for Finance and Operations, providing the basic setups, configuration, and cash flow transaction.

Chapter 11, *Exploring Budgeting,* focuses on the budget capabilities in Microsoft Dynamics 365 for Finance and Operations and basic budget configuration, and then covers the budget planning process and budget control feature. Finally, it discusses budget management in actions.

Chapter 12, *Working with Intercompany Accounting,* covers intercompany features in Microsoft Dynamics 365 for Finance and Operations characteristics. Then it focuses on configuration, setups, and transactions.

Chapter 13, *Working with Consolidation and Elimination,* covers consolidation and elimination characteristics in Microsoft Dynamics 365 for Finance and Operations. Then it explores the consolidation and elimination configuration, setup, and process.

Chapter 14, *Working with Cost Management,* covers the inventory costing model in Microsoft Dynamics 365 for Finance and Operations and provides information about inventory cost setups and configuration, inventory reconciliation with general ledger, recalculation, and closing.

Chapter 15, *Exploring Fixed Assets,* focuses on the integration of fixed assets with other modules and their transactions. Exploring, fixed assets acquisition, depreciation, disposal, and finally fixed asset statement.

Chapter 16, *Exploring Financial Reporting and Analysis,* will help you to find out the reporting needs at early stages of the implementation project and what sides you should consider during the project's life cycle. It also explores Microsoft Dynamics 365 for Finance and Operations inquiry forms and SQL Reporting Services (SSRS) reports, in addition to financial reporting capabilities.

To get the most out of this book

Before you start reading this book, you'll need to have a test environment of Microsoft Dynamics 365 for Finance and Operations, Enterprise edition with demo data, in order to practice what you have learned.

Download the example code files

You can download the example code files for this book from your account at www.packtpub.com. If you purchased this book elsewhere, you can visit www.packtpub.com/support and register to have the files emailed directly to you.

You can download the code files by following these steps:

1. Log in or register at www.packtpub.com.
2. Select the **SUPPORT** tab.
3. Click on **Code Downloads & Errata**.
4. Enter the name of the book in the **Search** box and follow the onscreen instructions.

Once the file is downloaded, please make sure that you unzip or extract the folder using the latest version of:

- WinRAR/7-Zip for Windows
- Zipeg/iZip/UnRarX for Mac
- 7-Zip/PeaZip for Linux

The code bundle for the book is also hosted on GitHub at https://github.com/PacktPublishing/Microsoft-Dynamics-365-Enterprise-Edition-Financial-Management-Third-Edition. We also have other code bundles from our rich catalog of books and videos available at https://github.com/PacktPublishing/. Check them out!

Download the color images

We also provide a PDF file that has color images of the screenshots/diagrams used in this book. You can download it here: https://www.packtpub.com/sites/default/files/downloads/MicrosoftDynamics365EnterpriseEditionFinancialManagementThirdEdition_ColorImages.pdf.

Conventions used

There are a number of text conventions used throughout this book.

CodeInText: Indicates code words in text, database table names, folder names, filenames, file extensions, pathnames, dummy URLs, user input, and Twitter handles. Here is an example: "Mount the downloaded WebStorm-10*.dmg disk image file as another disk in your system."

Bold: Indicates a new term, an important word, or words that you see onscreen. For example, words in menus or dialog boxes appear in the text like this. Here is an example: "In order to view all the main account categories, navigate to **General ledger** | **Chart of accounts**| **Accounts** | **Main account categories**."

Warnings or important notes appear like this.

Tips and tricks appear like this.

Get in touch

Feedback from our readers is always welcome.

General feedback: Email `feedback@packtpub.com` and mention the book title in the subject of your message. If you have questions about any aspect of this book, please email us at `questions@packtpub.com`.

Errata: Although we have taken every care to ensure the accuracy of our content, mistakes do happen. If you have found a mistake in this book, we would be grateful if you would report this to us. Please visit `www.packtpub.com/submit-errata`, selecting your book, clicking on the Errata Submission Form link, and entering the details.

Piracy: If you come across any illegal copies of our works in any form on the Internet, we would be grateful if you would provide us with the location address or website name. Please contact us at `copyright@packtpub.com` with a link to the material.

If you are interested in becoming an author: If there is a topic that you have expertise in and you are interested in either writing or contributing to a book, please visit `authors.packtpub.com`.

Reviews

Please leave a review. Once you have read and used this book, why not leave a review on the site that you purchased it from? Potential readers can then see and use your unbiased opinion to make purchase decisions, we at Packt can understand what you think about our products, and our authors can see your feedback on their book. Thank you!

For more information about Packt, please visit `packtpub.com`.

1
Getting Started with Microsoft Dynamics 365 for Finance and Operations

The **Enterprise Resource Planning** (**ERP**) application is a must for companies, irrespective of whether they are a small or big enterprise; it is a tool that gives visibility to management regarding the enterprise's performance on all levels. People should be familiar with the ERP concept, no matter who implements the solution or uses it (definitely, the level of detail varies between the user and the consultant, but the core is common). This chapter covers the following topics:

- Understanding ERP characteristics
- Discovering the ERP implementation team
- Exploring key intentions for ERP implementations
- Understanding the ERP module's integrations
- Exploring ERP and reporting
- Posting types in Microsoft Dynamics 365 for Finance and Operations
- Exploring common terms used in ERP implementations
- Exploring the Microsoft Dynamics Implementation Methodology – Sure Step
- Exploring Microsoft Dynamics **Lifecycle Services** (**LCS**)
- Looking at the Microsoft Dynamics 365 for Finance and Operations user interface

Understanding ERP characteristics

ERP is a mission-critical application for business, as day-to-day activities rely on this application where the end users enter transactions and the management is able to monitor the business performance on a daily basis and take decisions within a proper time period. The ERP application has different characteristics from any other application, and these characteristics are mentioned in the Wikipedia definition:

> *"A business management software-usually a suite of integrated applications-that a company can use to collect, store, manage, and interpret data from many business activities."*

From this definition, ERP is an integrated application. In the past, each business area had its own application, and this led to the creation of isolated islands for each department in the same organization; these cost the organization time, effort, and money. This led to a lack of accurate information, which directly affects management decision making, because of the unavailability or redundancy of information; for example, a customer account in accounts receivable (Finance department) is different from a customer code in the Sales department, so the management can't identify the customer's balance. With ERP, the data is unified, controlled, and classified. This gives the company the ability to transform this data into information that helps in the decision-making process. In the modern world, the deployment of ERP has been moved to the cloud as a reaction to rapid customer business needs; the cloud provides the opportunity for business to respond to business scalability, reliability, and agility. The ERP application has taken its position in cloud technology, and we are witnessing an evolving revolution, and we contributing to it.

Discovering the implementation team

It is important for companies that want to implement ERP to understand that its implementation is not an easy task and it requires dedication, investment, and a professional partner. For example, **Value Added Reseller (VAR)**, which has a consulting team experienced in implementing ERP, preferably has a partner that is an expert in the customer industry. On top of that, the customer should have a close engagement between management, key users, and end users during the implementation project. The implementation team is considered to be the key success factor for the ERP implementation.

The following diagram illustrates the ERP implementation team that consists of **Subject Matter Experts** (**SMEs**) and **key users** from customer- and partner-side applications and technical consultants. This team works together closely during the implementation, where the customer representatives (**SMEs** and **key users**) deliver the business requirements (that is, what they are expecting from ERP), with the consulting team that bridges the gap between the business requirements and the implemented application. This comes through several workshops via analysis, design, development, and testing. Microsoft plays a role in the implementation life cycle; the **FastTrack team** from Microsoft is a customer program that works on the implementation from the beginning to ensure safe onboarding for the customer to the cloud solution.

In order to check the full FastTrack service offering, you can go to `https:/ /fasttrack.microsoft.com/dynamics`.

The Microsoft **Support team** works directly with partners and customers on support requests, and there is also a newly introduced team which is responsible for service requests that are related to the production environment:

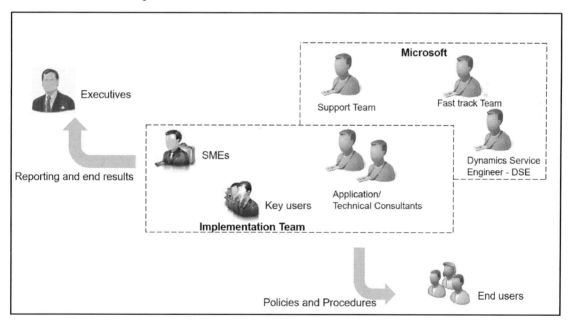

The implementation team should focus on two types of internal client: business executives and end users. Each client has a different perspective of the ERP implementation, and the implementation team should consider their requirements during the implementation life cycle. The executives' management focuses on reporting and end results, and the implementation team delivers policies and procedures to end users, who then operate the final product, which is the ERP application.

Responsibilities and motivation of an ERP consultant

Application consultant, functional consultant—the job title differs from one company to another, but whatever the title is, the person doing this job around financial and ERP software is considered as the middleman between the application and the technology, as well as having the key role of driving the adoption of a new technology by the business. The application consultant can start their career after graduation from university; they can major in business administration, finance, or information systems, if it covers a subject related to business.

Alternatively, the application consultant can start working in other fields. Some people start out as an accountant, procurement agent, commercial agent, or even sales representative. I do not consider it a career shift; I consider it as an advance in your career path. In other words, it is capitalizing on previous experience.

Traditionally, consulting skills are divided into two main areas: the **business side**, which is related to business aspects, and the **technical side**, which is related to the technicality of ERP. Then, there is a more general **soft skills** set that all application consultants need, as they spend most of their time in discussions, workshops, and training, related to business.

Some of the key skills that a company should look for in an application consultant, broken down into **business side**, **technical side**, and **soft skills**, are highlighted in the following diagram:

Business Side	Technical Side
• Business knowledge in business domains Vertical or Horizontal	• Understanding application flow of information
•Understanding business process cycles	•Understanding ERP integration
• Understanding business integration	• Understanding ERP implementation life cycle

Soft Skills	
Communication skills	Leadership skills
Presentation skills	Project Management skills
Business writing skills	Technical writing skills

Application consultants have a very important role in the ERP implementation project, as they are involved in implementation tasks and activities. Microsoft Dynamics Sure Step has defined the application consultant role during implementation phases. It is a long and broad list of tasks, and this range of tasks is what I believe keeps most application consultants motivated and satisfied with their jobs. The challenges are always changing and the career path offers many opportunities to develop new skills.

Exploring key intentions of ERP implementations

Enterprises that intend to implement Microsoft Dynamics 365 for Finance and Operations Enterprise edition pursue a variety of common benefits from ERP, but in most projects there are no well-defined benefits that the organization's management agreed on, and no roadmap to help them accomplish those intentions. It is vital to plan an ERP implementation carefully. In the sections that follow, we will look at the key objectives of ERP implementation.

An organization can have a legacy system and manual business processes, and they need to be unified by one single integrated application to manage, operate, and control the business areas and deliver reports to management, as shown in the following diagram:

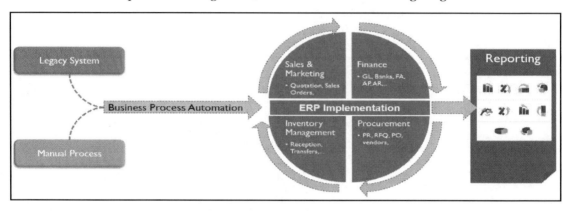

Enterprises that have decided to implement ERP should be coordinating together with a consulting partner specializing in Microsoft Dynamics 365 for Finance and Operations. The customer and partner should plainly outline the objectives of the ERP solution as early as possible in the diagnostic phase. They can replace the legacy system and reduce manual business processes by automating the business processes using the ERP solution in organization departments. Samples of ERP implementation intentions are as follows:

- **Business process**: This comprises the following:
  - Business process automation
  - Streamlined business process in cross-function operations
  - Unified business process across holdings and subsidiaries
  - Single point of contact for reducing redundant data within departments
- **Controlling**: This comprises the following:
  - Segregation of duties and data access privileges
  - Advanced workflow and approval matrix ceiling
  - Tracking the actual costs against budgeted
  - Inventory tracking and cost control
- **Decision support**: This comprises the following:
  - Real-time and ad hoc reports for all organization levels
  - Dynamic and dimensional reports
  - Key Performance Indicators and indicator dashboard

Understanding the ERP module's integration

The core objective of running a business is making a profit, which requires making revenue that covers the costs and adding a margin to secure a profit. The core role of management is to achieve this profit; the ERP application gives the management the necessary business insights to monitor business performance.

Microsoft Dynamics 365 for Finance and Operations manages and controls day-to-day transactions that occur in the company; these transactions are transformed into financial information that represents the key component of financial statements (balance sheet and income statement), which are expenditure and income; in other words, cash out and cash in. All these are shown in the following diagram:

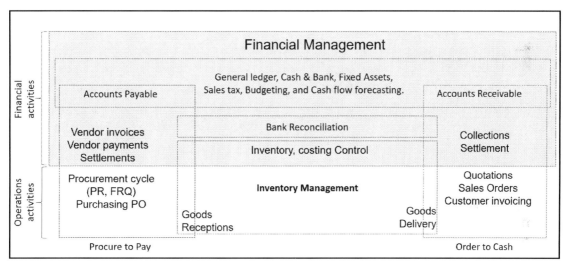

The cash to cash cycle entails two core cycles, which are commonly known as **procure-to-pay** and **order-to-cash**. The first cycle covers the expenditure part (cash out), that is, every aspect related to vendor management, procurement management, purchasing management, product reception, and vendor invoices, payment, and settlement. The second cycle covers the revenue part (cash in), that is, every aspect related to customer management, sales management, product delivery, customer invoices, collection, and settlement. These activities could be distinguished by **financial activities**, that is, every aspect related to finance and accounting activities, and **operations activities**, that is, every aspect related to the company's daily operations of the supply chain.

Microsoft Dynamics 365 for Finance and Operations enables the module's integration when relating transactions to each other and can automatically inherit information from one and pass it to another after adding additional information, along with generating automatic financial entries in the general ledger and control points to monitor transactions. There is integration between the Microsoft Dynamics 365 Finance and Operations modules, where production modules are integrated with the inventory module, the warehouse management module and the sales and marketing module, in addition to the procurement and sourcing module.

The project module is integrated with the inventory module, the sales and marketing module, the accounts receivable modules, the procurement and sourcing modules, and the accounts payable module. This book focuses on core financial module and its integrations with operational activities.

Procure-to-pay

The procure-to-pay cycle links the following business functions that are accountable for company expenditure:

- Procurement
- Purchasing
- Warehousing *Product Reception*
- Financial
    - Accounts payable
    - Bank management

The procure-to-pay cycle manages and controls the business processes of procuring the needed materials, receiving them, and paying to the vendor. There are specific documents to handle these business processes.

Financial transactions related to this cycle are product receipts, vendor invoices, payments, and settlements. The other documents relate to operations activities.

Product receipts

A product receipt represents the physical reception of products in the company warehouse. This increases the physical quantities in the inventory and reduces the quantity of the remainder in the Purchase Order, in addition to changes in the inventory value according to the inventory valuation method.

Invoice

The vendor sends a Purchase Order invoice either along with product reception, or after product reception. Recoding the vendor invoice to reflect the company's liabilities to the vendor results in an increase in the open vendor balance. Microsoft Dynamics 365 for Finance and Operations supports the company's internal control of vendor invoices by matching the invoice with the Purchase Order and the invoice amount.

It can be either three-way matching or two-way matching. A **three-way match** is for a product purchases when comparing the Purchase Order quantity against the quantities in the vendor invoice. And comparing the purchase prince in the purchase order against the invoice amount. A **two-way match** is for services when comparing the Purchase Order amount against the invoice amount, vendor service invoices that are not related to a Purchase Order, and recoding the vendor service invoice to reflect the company's liabilities to the vendor.

Payment

Vendor payment processing reduces the company liability to vendors. The payment can be an advanced one, attached to a specific Purchase Order, or independent of other Purchase Orders; it is usually the responsibility of the accounts payable section in the Finance department.

Settlement

The settlement processing involves settling open invoices against payments. This process affects vendor statements by decreasing open vendor invoices, increasing closed vendor invoices, and aging as well.

Order-to-cash

The order-to-cash cycle joined the following business functions that are accountable for a company's revenues:

- Sales
- Warehousing *Product Issuance*
- Finance
    - Accounts receivable
    - Bank management

This cycle manages and controls the business processes of sales activities, customer orders, delivering goods, and collection from the customer. There are specific documents to handle these business processes: sales orders, the issuing process by packing slip, and finally the invoice document.

The related financial transactions to this cycle are packing slips, invoices, collection, and settlement. The other documents relate to operations activities.

Packing slips

A packing slip represents the physical issuance of products from the company warehouse. This decreases the physical quantities in the inventory and reduces the quantities remaining in the sales order.

Invoice

After the delivery of goods or services to the customer, the sales team issues a customer invoice, increasing the customer open invoices. This affects the customer statement and customer aging, in addition to revenue recognition and the cost of goods sold.

Payment

The customer payment process represents a transaction of the required amount of money from the customer, whether it is against an open invoice or advanced payment collection.

Settlement

The settlement process settles the open invoices against collection. This process affects the customer statement, reducing the number of open customer invoices and increasing the number of closed customer invoices and aging.

Understanding the cloud offering

Information technology before the cloud operated on-premises data centers, where the company takes care of every single aspect of the hardware, infrastructure, security, and maintenance operations. The company was responsible for procuring the hardware servers, installing and configuring them, and executing regular maintenance for upgrade and batching, in addition to safeguarding the information in the company data center. With cloud technology, companies can reduce a lot of expenses, time, and effort, where the vendor provides all required hardware, infrastructure, security and maintenance operations against subscriptions. Microsoft Cloud over Microsoft Azure technologies offers three different models and these will depend on the customer needs. The first option is **Software as a Service (SaaS)**, the second is **Platform as a Service (PaaS)**, and the third is **Infrastructure as a Service (IaaS)**. The following diagram illustrates the difference between each offering along with the traditional on-premises offering:

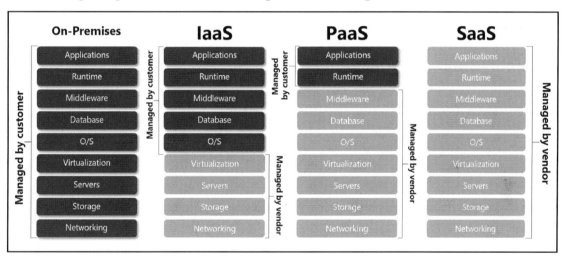

If we look at the previous diagram from left to right, with the on-premises option the customer manages everything from the application to the lowest networking aspects. Moving to IaaS, the customer here manages the application, database and operating system, but the vendor will take care of the core infrastructure work storage, networking, and servers. In PaaS, the scope of the customer narrows to merely being responsible for the application, and runtime, with the rest of the stack being managed by the vendor. SaaS is the final offering where the vendor manages the whole stack of the application, and the customer is only consuming application usage. Microsoft Dynamics 365 for Finance and Operations is available on the SaaS model, and on-premises.

Exploring ERP on the cloud

The ERP application moved to the cloud in response to the business needs of global reach accessibility, agility, scalability, and standardization. The cloud offering changed the game for ERP, shifting deployments from local on-premises servers to cloud data centers, managed by specialized professionals. The customer no longer needs to procure, operate, and maintain the hardware, infrastructure, and security. The cloud gives the customer the room to direct infrastructure resources, money, and manpower to business-related activities that impact customer efficiency.

Decision makers should think differently when it comes to an ERP-on-the-cloud decision. There are three main pillars that should be considered whenever a company has this discussion on the table:

- **Total cost of ownership**: A cloud ERP is accessed via a web browser from anywhere using any PC, rather than on-premises deployment, which requires building your own data center and infrastructure. The initial investment of the cloud ERP is lower than the on premises, which requires upfront investment. The time to deploy the environment on the cloud is a great deal faster than on premises; it is an automated process and is monitored by Microsoft.
- **Upgrades and maintainability**: Upgrades are smoother than ever; it is an automated process initiated from Dynamics LCS and monitored by Microsoft engineers. Of course, the customer has the ability to do the upgrade on his own on a **user acceptance test (UAT)**, or a development environment for testing purposes.
- **Performance and accessibility**: Performance was one of the most challenging tasks when designing on-premises ERP and, based on the customer business requirements, this may increase the cost and the hardware performance trade-off. With the on-cloud version, this is not a challenging task but it may be tricky to identify a reasonable deployment which fits the customer's needs.

The benefits of cloud ERP are evolving and it is being developed and enhanced over time. Currently, customers have the ability to scale their Microsoft Dynamics 365 for Finance and Operations as per their business needs, by adding additional users, additional hardware to cover the peak times, and then reducing it whenever it needed.

End users access the application from a web browser or mobility devices, such as smartphones and tablets. With the cloud offering, customers who have global operations have no need to worry about the consistency of their ERP deployment across all regions.

Exploring ERP and reporting

The main principles of reporting are reliability of business information and the ability to produce the right information, at the right time, for the right person. Reports that analyze ERP data in a meaningful way represent the output of the ERP implementation; it is considered as the cream of the implementation, the next level of value that the solution owners should aim for. This ideal outcome results from building all reports based on a single information source, the ERP solution where the business is recording all transactions on a daily basis.

As shown in the following diagram, organizational reporting levels are divided into the following three main layers:

- Operational management
- Middle management
- Senior management

Each level has a different perspective on report usage, irrespective of whether it is tactical/short term usage or strategic/long term usage, and a different opinion on report complexity:

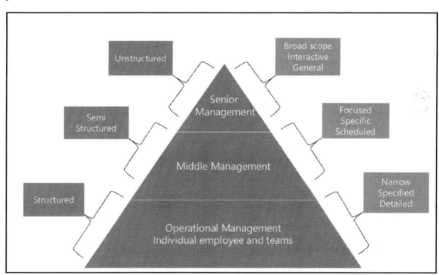

The dimensional characteristic of information is divided into two dimensions; the first is scope of information and the second is types of decision making.

Information scope defines the required level of detail for each managerial level. Typically, the scope can be described as follows:

- **Narrow, specified, and detailed**: This is the first layer of the information scope for the operational management level. Clerks or supervisors in this level typically receive information relevant to their particular subunit. They require a narrow scope for reports, with details to the lowest level of information (transactional level) and specific to the daily operational work.
- **Focused, specific, and scheduled**: This is the second layer of the information scope for the managerial level. Managers at this level typically receive summarized information. They require reports with a scope focused on aggregate and summarized transactional information. These reports cover specific periods: weekly, monthly, quarterly, half yearly, and yearly.
- **Broad, interactive, and general**: This is the third layer of the information scope and is the highest level for top management. They require reports with a broader scope to get more comparisons, actual versus budget, period comparisons, and KPIs, in addition to aggregated reports that cover specific monthly, quarterly, half yearly, and yearly performance.

The type of decision making used by an organization is another dimension of reporting analysis. Typically, decision-making styles can be described as follows:

- **Structured**: This is a repetitive and routine decision-making style and is best used in the operational layer. This style requires reports that are considered static.
- **Semi-structured**: This is a mix between the structured and unstructured decision-making style and is best used in the middle management layer. This style requires reports that are considered static or dynamic.
- **Unstructured**: This style is used by decision makers at the executive level, who must provide judgment, evaluation, and business insight to evaluate the overall business performance. This style requires reports that are considered dynamic.

Posting types in Microsoft Dynamics 365 for Finance and Operations

In Microsoft Dynamics 365 for Finance and Operations, there are two ways to post transactions to general ledger accounts. The first type is through the posting profile, which represents the integration point between the general ledger and subledgers, and it generates entries automatically, according to the posting profile setup. The second type is journal entries that post directly to ledger accounts, and or automatic entry generation through the posting profile if the journal used to post to subledger. The two ways are explained in detail as follows:

- **Manual entry journal posting**: The journal model in Microsoft Dynamics 365 for Finance and Operations is a journal header that contains voucher lines, in which the default data in the journal name (header) is copied into voucher lines such as currency and sales tax, which can be changed in the voucher line. Every subledger has its own journal name based on the transaction type.

- **Automatic entry – posting profile**: This is the integration point between subledgers (fixed assets, payables, inventory, banks, receivables, project, and production) and the general ledger. It is a set of ledger accounts that are used in generating the automatic ledger entry in which a transaction occurred. It is possible to select different ledger accounts for each type of subledger transaction. Microsoft Dynamics 365 for Finance and Operations offers flexibility in posting profile setups:

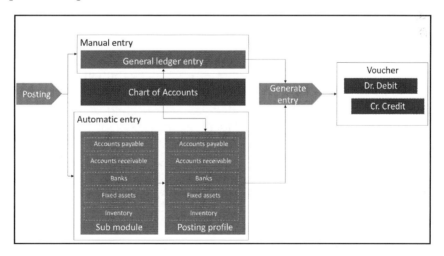

The voucher line can be a ledger account, vendor account, customer account, fixed asset, bank, or project. If the selected account is an option other than the ledger account, the subledger posting profile will directly post to the ledger account.

Exploring common terms in ERP implementations

There are some common terms that are used in all the phases of ERP implementation. These terms describe a specific task or activity during the implementation life cycle, and they are as follows:

- **Provisioning**: This process requests the creation of a new machine/environment of Microsoft Dynamics 365 for Finance and Operations.
- **Configuration**: This process identifies which options will be activated (checked) according to customer requirements and this will be followed in the day-to-day business (module parameters).
- **Setup**: This process sets up the data within the application, identifying how to group it according to customer requirements, vendors, items, and the chart of accounts.

Microsoft Dynamics 365 for Finance and Operations gives flexibility to be adopted into business needs by personalizing the application, modifying it, or customizing it. This is described as follows:

- **Personalization**: Personalizations or enhancements are small changes that occur in the application to fit customer requirements, such as rearrangement of form fields, wide company enhancements, or user-based. Enhancements deliver more usability to operational *data entry* users.
- **Modification**: Modifications are medium to large changes that occur in the application to fit customer requirements, such as changing a field's property to make it mandatory, setting a default value for a checkbox in a transaction form instead of making the user select it every time, and developing document validations. It can also be wide company modifications. The purpose of these modifications is to have more control over application options and behavior rather than module parameters.

- **Customization**: Customizations are the largest changes occurring in the application to fit customer requirements, such as changes in an application's business logic and calculations, changes in a module's integration concepts and posting profile, and developing new modules that are not covered in the standard application modules. Although customization is not recommended in ERP implementation, the purpose of customization is to cover a critical business need to be handled by the application. Always try to minimize the size of customizations.

Microsoft Dynamics 365 for Finance and Operations has a new concept of customization which is **extensions**.

Exploring the Microsoft Dynamics implementation methodology – Sure Step

Veteran ERP consultants understand how to execute an implementation project. They can call on their years of experience to design a new project that will have a good chance at success. When the next generation of consultants joins the team, these practices will be passed along, even if there is no process in place to manage the knowledge transfer. Many implementation consultants can probably recall their own experience learning *the way it's always been done* at their early jobs.

Consulting companies can apply their own implementation methodology based on previous projects, and there is no problem with this as long as the company achieves its objectives and satisfies its customers. The company should also be committed to continuously improving its own methodology and building on it by experience.

However, there is a range of problems with an implementation methodology based on transferring the senior consultant's knowledge and experience to the next class of junior consultants. Such informal or small-scale approaches will lead to variances in implementation approach between different consultants, even in the same company, and it can create differences from one project to another, even for the same consultant. To add to the risk, a consulting firm that depends on consultants to provide an implementation methodology is exposed to a loss of creditability with their customers, if the consultant is changed and the new consultant has his own approach.

Alternatively, there is an implementation methodology built up by an experienced organization where information and data have been gathered from a range of experienced implementers and based on the best practices from a broad range of previous projects and experiences across a range of business domains and client types. That organization is, of course, Microsoft, and the methodology is Microsoft Dynamics Sure Step.

Microsoft brought Sure Step to the Microsoft Dynamics market in 2007 and has recently launched its online version. The common question from implementers is: why do we need a standard implementation methodology for ERP when we have our own?

At a high level, there are common phases of an ERP implementation project, but the depth and complexity of each phase depend on the nature of the project itself. The procedure to execute the project will depend on the consulting firm and its approach in project execution, as well as its style in managing customers. The phases are diagnostic, analysis, design, development, deployment, and operation. The key characteristics of the Microsoft Dynamics Sure Step methodology are as follows:

- It covers the main implementation project phases, activities, tasks, documents templates, and output.
- It minimizes consultant effort to stop reinventing the documentation and templates.
- It not only covers the implementation phases (analysis, design, development, deployment, and operation), but also takes into consideration sales and presales activities in the diagnostic phase.
- It is aligned with other Microsoft methodologies such as **Microsoft Delivery Methodology (SDM)**, **Microsoft Solution Selling Process (MSSP)**, and **Microsoft Solution Framework (MSF)**. This gives it a variety of guidance built on Microsoft methodologies.
- It is designed especially for Microsoft Dynamics products (such as AX, NAV, SL, GP, and CRM).
- It complies with **Project Management Institute (PMI)** methodologies (scope management, time management, cost management, resource management, risk management, quality management, and procurement management).
- It includes a huge collection of templates and documents according to phase activity and shows the integration between phases and activities.
- It contains implementation project type customization (Enterprise, Standard, Rapid, Agile, and Upgrade).

Exploring Microsoft Dynamics Lifecycle Services

Microsoft Dynamics **Lifecycle Services, LCS**, is the heart of the Microsoft Dynamics 365 for Finance and Operations implementation. It is the starting point of the implementation and it is the platform you use to manage, maintain, monitor, upgrade, and search for known reported issues in the knowledge base. Microsoft has announced LCS tools to help partners and customers be more engaged in the Microsoft Dynamics 365 for Finance and Operations implementation project. LCS is a cloud-based solution that provides the required tools to let a customer collaborate with a partner and Microsoft in planning, managing, and operating the implementation project. It is mandatory for Dynamics 365 for Finance and Operations implementation. Microsoft Dynamics LCS helps customers and partners have predictable, repeatable, and manageable implementations. LCS is built on Microsoft Azure technologies, and this gives the opportunity to utilize Azure capabilities in data insights used in environment telemetry for monitoring. Through LCS, the customer can smoothly migrate data/customization between environments. In addition to that, the knowledge base which directly feed by Microsoft in issue search.

 The Microsoft Dynamics LCS URL is `https://lcs.dynamics.com/`.

Each implementation project should have at least three environments: production, **user acceptance test (UAT)**, and development. The customer/partner does not have direct access to the production environment machine and soon the UAT; the only team eligible for accessing the Dynamics 365 for Finance and Operations production environment is the Microsoft **Dynamics Service Engineers (DSE)** team.

The Microsoft Dynamics LCS offers an assortment of services as follows:

- **Business process modeler**: This is the tool to design, store, and retrieve business process flowcharts, and it gives the ability to identify gaps in the application during the analysis phase, where a business process could be moved from one project to another, and can be used as a training assistance for end users.
- **Subscription estimator**: This is the tool to evaluate customer subscription requirements for the current version of Dynamics 365 Finance and Operations.
- **System diagnosis**: This helps system administrators monitor and understand the health of one or more Microsoft Dynamics 365 for Finance and Operations environments.
- **Issue search**: This is used to search for product issues, and determine whether an issue has been resolved, is open, or has a workaround; otherwise the user needs to report it to Microsoft for further investigation.

Looking at the Microsoft Dynamics 365 for Finance and Operations user interface

Microsoft Dynamics 365 for Finance and Operations revealed significant changes in its user interface, making it more user-friendly and easy-to-use for complex business transactions, in addition to the richness in accessing the application through the web interface via laptop, tablet, or mobile.

Microsoft Dynamics 365 for Finance and Operations is linked to the Azure active directory where all system users are registered and which will be used as the base for logging into Dynamics 365 for Finance and Operations.

The web client is the most commonly used interface accessed by users from their PC or laptop. There are changes in the interface concept, where we have a newly introduced dashboard, workspaces, and their components. The Microsoft Dynamics 365 for Finance and Operations web client interface structure is illustrated in the following diagram:

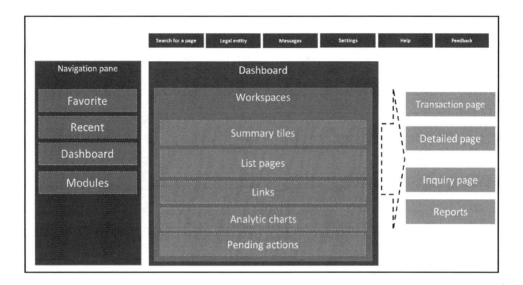

The Microsoft Dynamics 365 for Finance and Operations default dashboard is shown in the following screenshot:

The default dashboard consists of workspaces as per the security roles of the user, a navigation bar in a hidden mode, a menu bar that contains legal entities, a search box for forms, a messaging center, feedback, settings, and help. In addition, it contains a calendar, which represents the session date, and on the bottom left there is a section showing the work items assigned to the user.

The shortcut to go to the default dashboard is *Ctrl + Shift + Home*.

The main workspace is divided into the following sections:

- **The address bar**: The address bar or breadcrumb that provides access to Microsoft Dynamics 365 for Finance and Operation companies, from searching forms, the message center; it also provides feedback, settings, help, support and ideas is as follows:

The user can navigate to the company by pressing on the arrow icon or key in the company name, as shown in the following screenshot:

The shortcut to choose a legal entity is *Ctrl + Shift + O*.

The user can navigate to favorites, recent, workspaces, and modules by clicking on the hamburger icon on the right to open the Navigation Pane; the user also has the option to pin the Navigation Pane open, as shown in the following screenshot:

- **Navigation search**: The bar contains the navigation search box to look for forms instead of accessing it using the normal Navigation Pane. This helps with productivity; the end user does not need to memorize the menu paths, as they key in the full name or partial name from the form name and the search will filter it, as shown in the following screenshot:

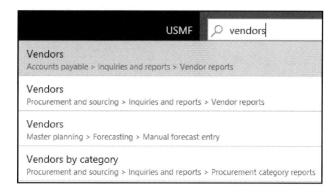

The bar contains the Message Center icon on the right-hand side, as shown in the following screenshot:

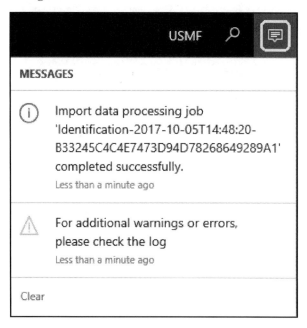

The shortcut to view system messages is *Ctrl+ Shift + F7.*

The bar also contains the Feedback icon on the right-hand side, as shown in the following screenshot:

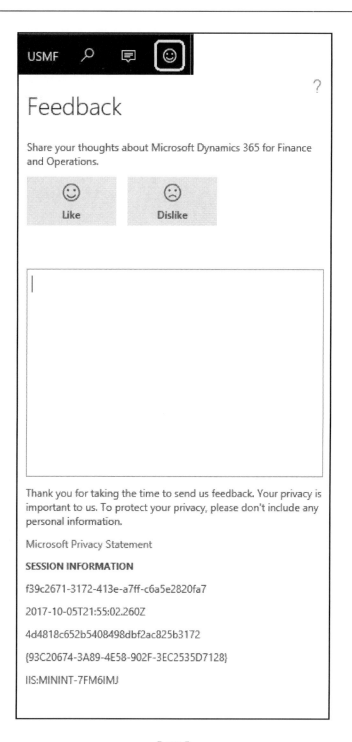

The bar also contains the Settings icon on the right-hand side, which contains **User options**, a **Task recorder**, a **Mobile app**, **Trace**, and **About**, as shown in the following screenshot:

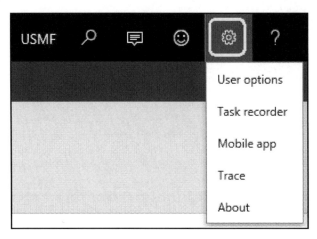

The bar also contains the Help icon on the right-hand side, which has **Help**, **Support**, and **Ideas**, as shown in the following screenshot:

- **The Favorites menu**: This is the upper part of the Navigation Pane. The **Favorites** menu contains commonly used submenus and is personalized per user. Each user can add his/her favorites. In order to add menus to **Favorites**, go to the Menus pane and navigate to **General ledger | Journal entries**. Mark the star besides **General journals**, as shown in the following screenshot:

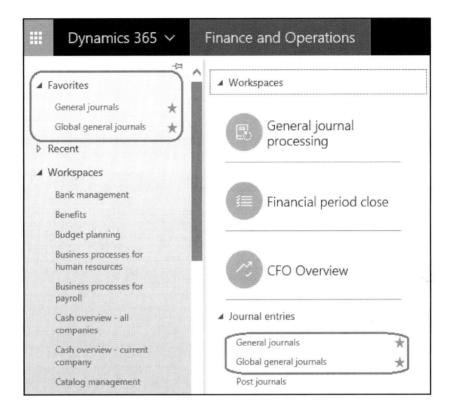

- **The Content pane**: The Content pane in Microsoft Dynamics 365 for Finance and Operations is where the user can access forms, list pages, reports, and setup. As shown in the following screenshot, the Content pane may look different from module to module but it has the following main sections in common:
  - Master data setups such as vendors' master data, customer master data, and charts of accounts
  - **Journals**: This represents access to module journals to create and post journal transactions
  - **Inquiries**: This represents access to modules reporting in the form style
  - **Reports**: This represents access to printable reports that can be shown on the screen or printed in a hard copy
  - **Periodic**: This represents access to periodic jobs that are being run on a monthly or weekly basis

- **Setup**: This represents access to module setups and configuration:

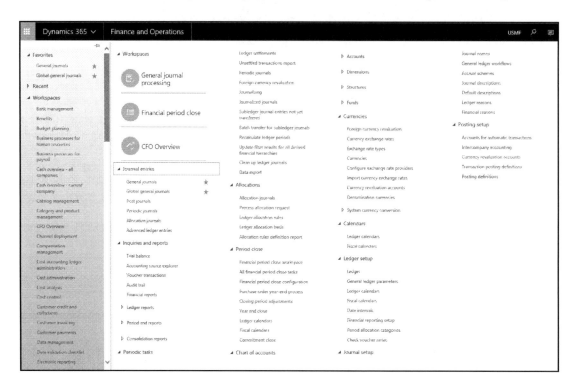

- **The list page**: The list page, as shown in the following screenshot (all vendors), shows the vendor list. The user can create a new record from the list page by pressing *Ctrl + N*, editing an existing record, and/or posting daily transactions:

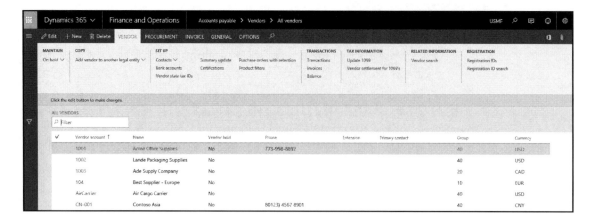

- The list page has the following characteristics:

  - **The Action pane**: The Action pane consists of the action buttons for executing a specific task or activity, as shown in the following screenshot. This is similar to the Microsoft Office ribbon. The user has the option of docking the Action pane so it remains visible, hidden, or accessible when hovering the mouse over.

  - **The search box in the Action pane**: The search box is a quick way of finding an action the user wants to execute on a selected record, as shown in the following screenshot:

    The search can be executed by keying in part of the action name and then choosing from the filtered list, or entering the full action name.

  - **Export to Excel**: The export to Excel option is used for exporting data from the grid to Microsoft Excel:

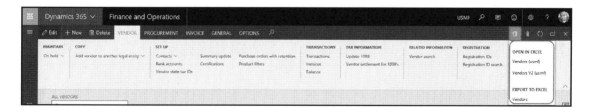

The export could be exporting a data entity or exporting the exact grid view.

- **Attachments**: This is to attach files to the selected record so they can be retrieved by other users.

- **Refresh the grid**: This refreshes grid content instead of refreshing the whole web page; remember it is a web-based client, but on the other hand it is a business application and we need to retain the productivity of business users:

The shortcut to refreshing grid content is *Shift + F5*.

The grid checkboxes are used for multiple selections of records, as shown in the following screenshot:

The user can use grid selection to export specific records to Excel (non-data entity export).

- **Grid filtration**: The grid filtration option looks for a specific record; the user can search by selecting columns in the grid, as shown in the following screenshot:

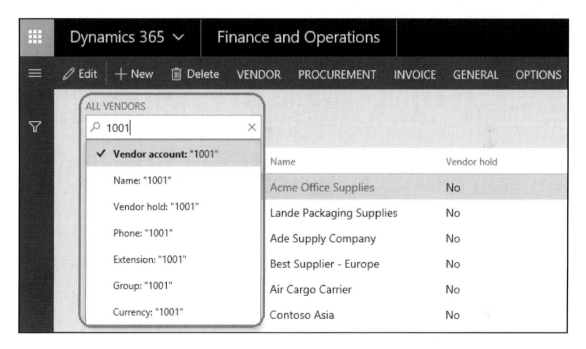

Also, there is a filtration option, which the user can use to look for a record based on the selected search criteria:

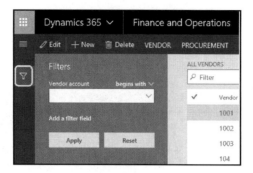

- **The fact box**: The fact box is a new component, introduced in a previous version of Dynamics 365 for Finance and Operations to display summarized information about the selected record, as shown in the following screenshot:

- **The fast tab**: This consists of a group of fields. The fast tab replaces the regular tabs on the form and also displays some summary fields, as shown in the following screenshot:

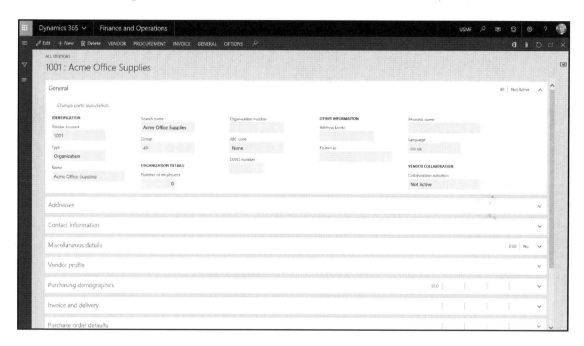

- **Workspaces**: Workspaces are activity-oriented pages that are designed to increase a user's productivity by providing information that answers the targeted user's most pressing activity-related questions, and allows the user to initiate their more frequent tasks. Access to the various workspaces depends on the roles that users have in the organization. Much of the list and **business intelligence (BI)** content from the old Role Center pages is exposed on workspaces. To navigate to a workspace, you can click a tile on the dashboard, click a link in the Navigation Pane, or find the workspace using the navigation search feature:

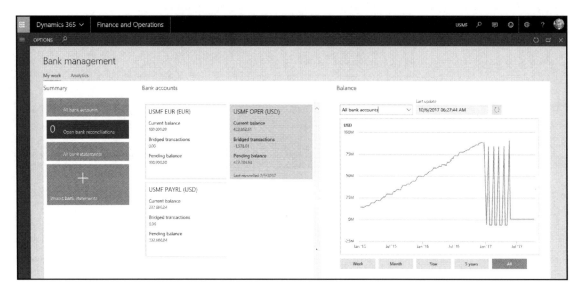

- **Tiles**: Windows 8 introduced the concept of tiles, and you will see them used in the client. A tile is a rectangular button that behaves like a menu item button. It is used to navigate to or open pages. In addition, tiles can display relevant data, such as counts or **Key Performance Indicators (KPIs)**. A tile can include images that provide the user with additional visual context.

Summary

In this chapter, we discussed the introduction of ERP and its main characteristics of modules integration, with the general ledger at a high level (it will be covered in detail in the next chapters), and posting types in Microsoft Dynamics 365 for Finance and Operations. We also explored the ERP implementation team and the role of the application consultant in an implementation project. Then, we covered the cloud offering, ERP on the cloud, and then covered ERP reporting levels and needs, after which we moved on to the Microsoft implementation methodology, Sure Step, and LCS, and explored the interface of Microsoft Dynamics 365 for Finance and Operations.

In the next chapter, we will cover the general ledger, main account types, classifications, and control points. We will also explore the practices in the financial implementations of Microsoft Dynamics 365 for Finance and Operations.

2
Understanding the General Ledger

The **chart of accounts (COA)** is the backbone of **Enterprise Resource Planning (ERP)**. It is a part of the financial module, which is the foundational module of ERP. It is a list of categorized ledger accounts (known as main accounts in Microsoft Dynamics 365 for Finance and Operations) that is used by an organization to record all financial transactions, and it depends on the nature of the organization's business. The COA of manufacturing companies differs from trading companies, service companies, and so on. This chapter covers the following topics:

- Understanding the COA
- Classifying main accounts
- Controlling main accounts
- Understanding shared financial data
- Understanding financial management in action
- Opening balance
- Performing daily transactions
- Closing procedure

Understanding the COA

The classified skeleton of a main account is the responsibility of the controller from the customer side and the application consultant from the partner side, who bridges the application capabilities to the customers' requirements. This activity is designed in the analysis and design phases and deployed in the deployment phase.

Main accounts are at the core of financial reporting and include the trial balance, balance sheet, income statement, working capital, and cash flow. The starting point in building COAs is identifying the financial reporting requirements to ensure that all classification levels and categories are captured in Microsoft Dynamics 365 for Finance and Operations. The quality of reports build on the details that are captured during data entry and will be reflected in the quality of reporting.

Classifying main accounts

The first classification of main accounts in Microsoft Dynamics 365 for Finance and Operations is the type, which represents the nature of the ledger account, that is, is it a balance sheet account or profit and loss account? The following figure shows an example of a balance sheet and an income statement that contains the profit and loss account:

Balance Sheet	Income Statement
Assets	**Revenues**
Fixed Assets	Sales Revenue
Fixed Assets	Sales Returns
Accumulated Depreciation	*Total Revenues*
Total Fixed Assets	Cost of Goods Sold
Current Assets	*Gross Profit*
Banks	**Operating Expenses**
Inventory	Manfacturing Expenses
Total Current Assets	Selling and marketing Expenses
Total Assets	Administration Expenses
Liabilities & Owner Equities	Depreciation Expenes
Current Liabilities	*Total Operating Expense*
Accounts Payable	Interest Income
Accruals	*Net Operating Profit*
Total Current Liabilities	**Net Income**
Long Term Liabilities	
Notes Payable	
Total Long Term Liability	
Owners' Equity	
Retained Earnings	
Total Owners' Equity	
Liabilities & Owner Equities	

A balance sheet report represents the assets, liabilities, and owner's equity at specific date, and is also known as the company's financial position. This report's balances are accumulated during the lifetime of the company.

An income statement represents the revenues, expenses and resulting net income or net loss for a specific period, and is also known as the operational results for a specific period. This report's balances are reset to 0 each year. In the year-end transaction, the balances are rolled up in the retained earnings account.

Microsoft Dynamics 365 for Finance and Operations classifies main account types into two main groups. The first group is **transactional accounts**, where all financial transactions are recorded. The second group is **reporting accounts**, which is used to report and classify caption totals, as shown in the following figure:

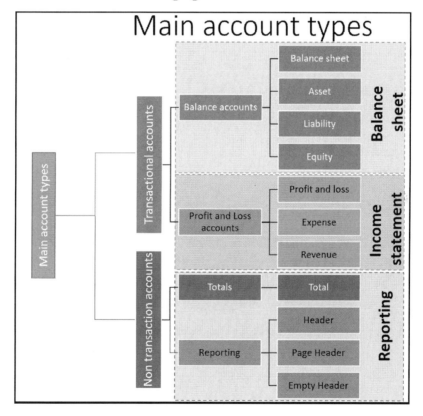

The transactional accounts, which carry posted transactions on the application, maintain a record of all the data related to the transaction. This includes the main account number, amount, transaction side (debit/credit), currency, transaction text, and transaction type, in addition to original documents (that generate this entry), and who posted the transaction.

These classifications help at the reporting level and are considered as the first classification layer for main accounts.

In order to view all the main account types, navigate to **General ledger | Chart of accounts | Accounts | Main accounts**. Click on **Edit**, go to the **General** fast tab, and then go to the **Main account type** combobox.

Reporting type: This is used in financial statement reporting for Brazil only.
Common type: This is used only for China.

Using transactional accounts

Transactional accounts represent the primary classification of the main accounts. They are divided into two main groups: balance accounts and profit and loss accounts.

Balance accounts

The first classification type of transactional accounts is balance accounts, which represent the balance sheet report components.

The balance in a balance account is calculated from the day the account opened till the date of reporting. In the year-end transaction, the closing voucher is transferred to the opening balance of the account.

Balance accounts have the following three classifications that represent their nature:

- **Assets**: This represents the resources that are owned by the organization and are used to carry out business activities, such as producing a product
- **Liabilities**: This represents the claims against assets; for example, the obligations of borrowing money to acquire machines, or products
- **Equity**: This represents the claim on total assets; it is equal to total assets minus total liabilities

Profit and loss accounts

The second classification of transactional accounts is profit and loss accounts, which represents the **income statement** report components.

 The balance of profit and loss accounts are reset to 0 each year. In the year-end transaction, the balances are rolled up in the retained earnings account.

Profit and loss accounts have two classifications that represent the nature of accounts: expense and revenue. The expense accounts represent the costs of assets that are consumed in the process of generating revenue; it is the actual or expected cash outflow. The revenue accounts represent the results from sales; it is the actual or expected cash inflow.

The following screenshot illustrates the main account type. To access this form, navigate to **General ledger** | **Chart of accounts** | **Accounts** | **Main accounts**. Click on **Main account**, then click on **Edit**, and then on the **General** fast tab:

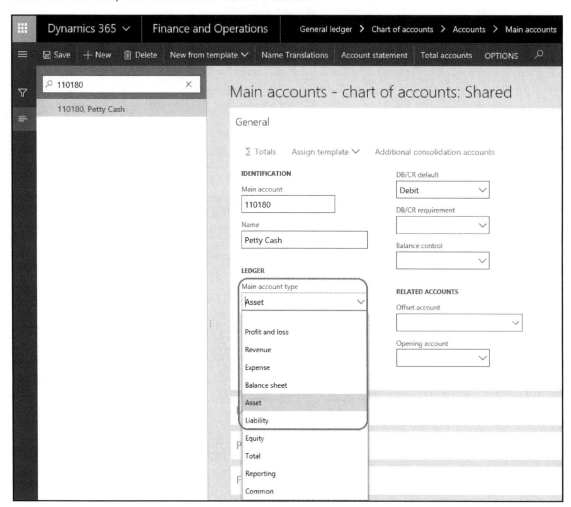

Using nontransactional accounts

Nontransactional accounts represent the financial reporting presentation, and are divided into two main types: **totals** and **reporting**. None of the transactions are allowed to be posted on these accounts.

Totals

Totals are used to sum up the caption or subcaption range of main accounts to give a quick overview of an account's balance; the following screenshot illustrates the setup of the total account type:

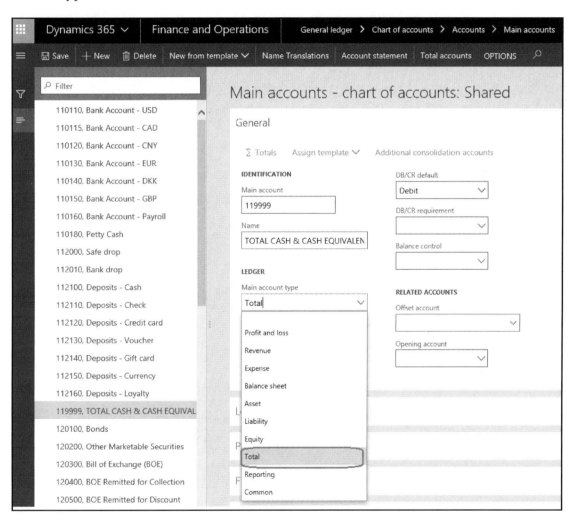

The total of accounts is managed through an account interval form in order to identify the range of main accounts that will be included in the summation. Go to **General ledger** | **Chart of accounts** | **Accounts** | **Main accounts**, then select main account with **Total** type. Then the **Totals** option will be activated, as shown in the following screenshot:

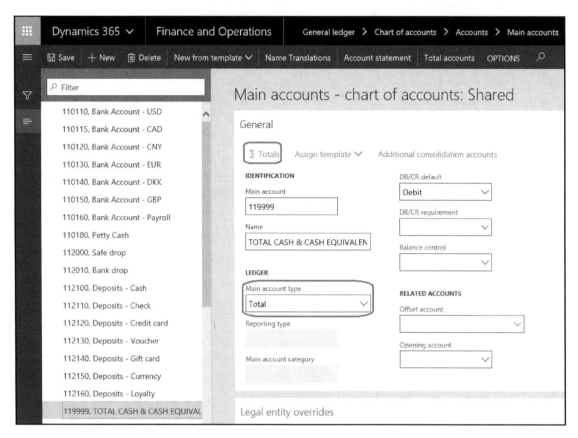

After clicking on **Totals**, the account interval form will open, which is where you enter the main accounts value in the **From value** and **To value** fields. In addition to that, there is an option to invert the sign, as shown in the following screenshot. Then create a new line by clicking **New** or pressing *Alt + N:*

 If there are subtotal accounts, they are neglected in the grand total. Do not worry—there are no duplications in the calculation of totals.

Main account categories

Main account categories represent a second level of classification and are used as a grouping layer for the main accounts. The main account category is used for reporting and in cubes for business intelligence.

 More than 50 ledger account categories are provided by default.

In order to view all the main account categories, navigate to **General ledger** | **Chart of accounts** | **Accounts** | **Main account categories**. The following screenshot shows the **Main account category** screen:

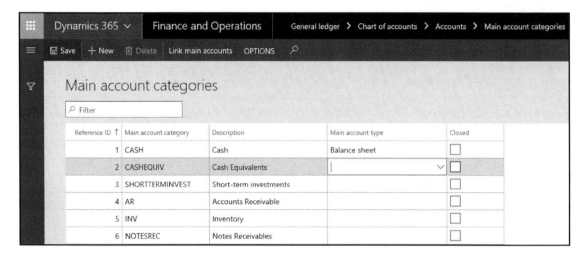

If the **Closed** checkbox is checked, that particular **Reference ID** value cannot be selected in the main account form. It is better to serialize the reference IDs in the logical order of reporting levels, so that they can be used as a sorting identifier.

The following screenshot illustrates the account category link to the main account; you can see **Link main accounts**, this opens the dialog where the user can link the main account to an account category:

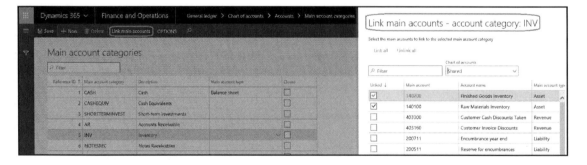

The following screenshot illustrates the main account; you can see the **Main account category** field under the **Ledger** fast tab:

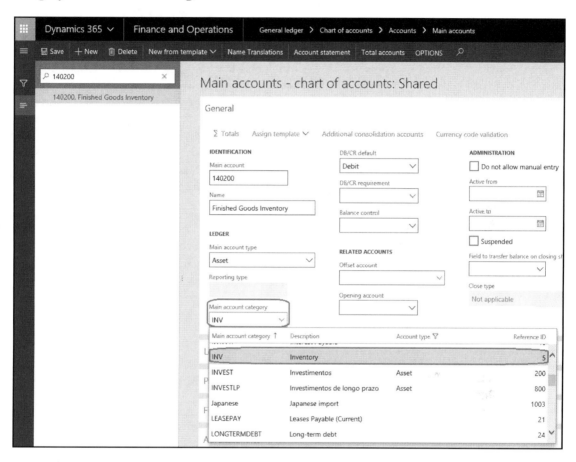

Controlling the general ledger

In the following section, we will discuss the major control point of the general ledger module. Focusing on two perspectives, the first is controlling the main accounts, and the second is general ledger parameters. These controls gives the controller the ability to have an oversight of the execution of daily transactions.

Controlling the main accounts

As seen in the following figure, Microsoft Dynamics 365 for Finance and Operations offers three main groups of controls over the main accounts. The first is specific to debit and credit controls, the second to account administration, and the third to posting validation:

Debit/credit controls

The **debit/credit controls** group is divided into three subgroups: the first is **debit/credit default**, the second is **debit/credit requirements**, and the third is **balance control**.

Debit/credit default

Every main account has a normal accounting side, be it debit or credit. The financial controller can prefer to let Microsoft Dynamics 365 for Finance and Operations suggest to the accountants the side of the main account (whether it is debit or credit), and give the user the option to move to the other side, according to the transaction.

For example, the cash account is proposed to be on the debit side; this is recommended for fresh accountants. For experienced accountants, they can decide whether it is required to change the side of the account as per transaction needs. The following screen illustrates the debit/credit option, to access the main accounts form, go to **General ledger** | **Chart of accounts** | **Accounts** | **Main accounts:**

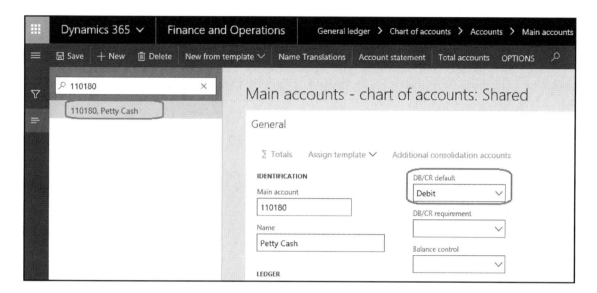

During the processing of a transaction, the cursor moves to the side that is configured in the debit/credit default (when the *Tab* key is pressed), as shown in the following screenshot. You can access it by navigating to **General ledger** | **Journal entries** | **General journals** and creating a new journal, then by clicking on **Lines**:

Also you can use the search box in the header bar to access **General journals** or add it to **Favorites**.

Debit/credit requirements

Every main account has a normal accounting balance, be it debit or credit, and this main account is debited or credited. The financial controller can prefer to get Microsoft Dynamics 365 for Finance and Operations to control specific main accounts in order to prevent end users from shifting the entry side of the main account. For example, the rent account should always be debited against the bank account.

The following screenshot shows the debit/credit requirements of a main account:

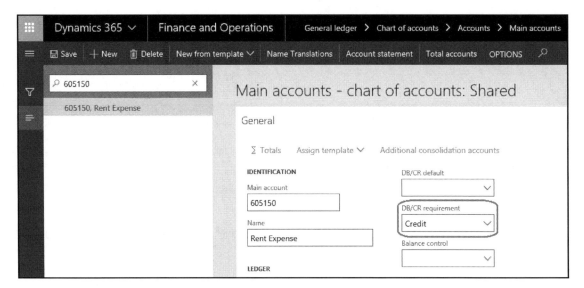

The main account configuration is **Credit**. The accountant attempts to enter transactions in the debit side, as you can see in the following screenshot, it illustrates the message details while validating or posting the transaction. You can access **General journal** by navigating to **General ledger** | **Journal entries** | **General journals** and creating a new journal, then clicking on **Lines**:

Balance control

Every main account has a normal accounting side, be it debit or credit. If the balance contradicts this norm, it indicates a concern and should be outlined, then investigated. The financial controller can have preferences to get Microsoft Dynamics 365 for Finance and Operations to control a specific main account's balance, in order to prevent any balance issues. For example, bank accounts should always be on the debit side. If it is on the credit side, it indicates an issue. As shown in the following screenshot, **Balance control** prevents this from happening:

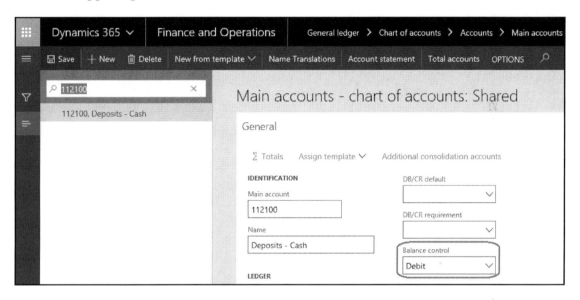

If the balance control is broken during the processing of a transaction, an error message bar window will pop up displaying the message: **A requirement for credit balance is selected for account #####, but this is violated by voucher #####**. This could be examined from **General ledger** | **Journal entries** | **General journals** and creating a new journal, then clicking on **Lines**.

The main account's configuration in balance control is **Debit**. The current balance of the main account is a debit of **100.00**. The current transaction credits the main account by **-101.00**. So the difference is **-1**.

While posting the entry, Microsoft Dynamics 365 for Finance and Operations certifies the main account's balance control configuration and then calculates the current balance. The difference is shown in a message window, as shown in the following screenshot. You can access **General journal** by navigating to **General ledger** | **Journal entries** | **General journals** and creating a new journal, then clicking on **Lines**:

Using account administration

The main account administration is divided into three main groups. The first group is **Do not allow manual entry**, the second is **Activation dates**, and the third is **Accounts suspension**.

Do not allow manual entry

The integrity between the general ledger and sub-ledger is an essential factor in ERP. It is characterized in the main accounts and sub-ledgers. The sub-ledger should guarantee that all posted transactions to the general ledger are from the submodules' end. Microsoft Dynamics 365 for Finance and Operations controls the main accounts; this does not allow any direct transactions to be posted to the main account. This means that any transaction affecting a main account must be posted throughout the submodules posting the profile. This checkbox is **Do not allow manual entry**.

On the other hand, there are other accounts that accept manual entries, such as the accounts that are not related to any sub-ledger and post transactions directly to these accounts. The following screenshot illustrates the control of **Do not allow manual entry**, to access the main accounts form go to **General ledger | Chart of accounts | Accounts | Main accounts**:

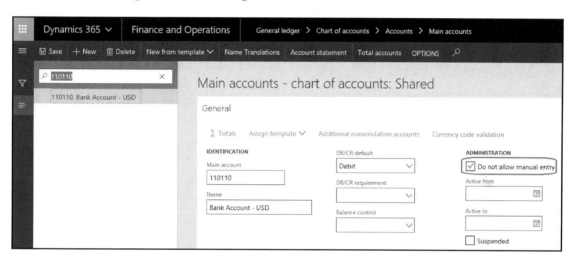

During the processing of a transaction, if an accountant wants to select a main account and this account is configured as **Do not allow manual entry**, an **Infolog** window will pop up that will display **Value (account #####) is not allowed for manual entry. Enter another value**. In other words, this means *select another account*; this is shown in the following screenshot:

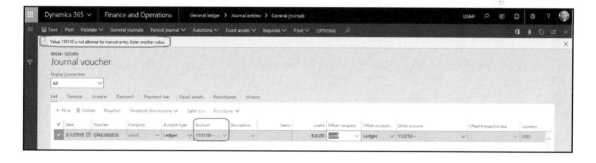

Activation date

The activation date is commonly used for newly created accounts (which will be active for operations at a future date) and in another scenario for main accounts (which can be deactivated after a specific period), as shown in the following screenshot:

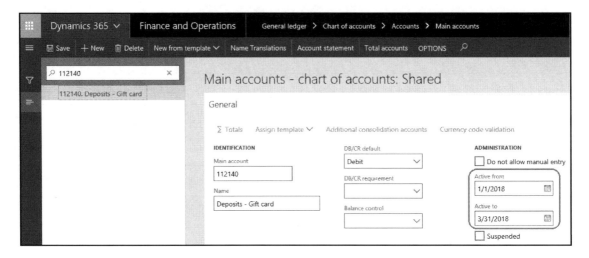

If an accountant wants to work with a main account, but it has not been a day since its activation, a message bar will pop up during the processing of a transaction that will display **Main account ##### is not active for the following account structure #####**, as shown in the following screenshot:

Suspending account

The suspending account is used in cases where there is an account that requires to be stopped from an operation, as it will not be used any more. As shown in the following screenshot, there is a control to suspend an account from operational posting:

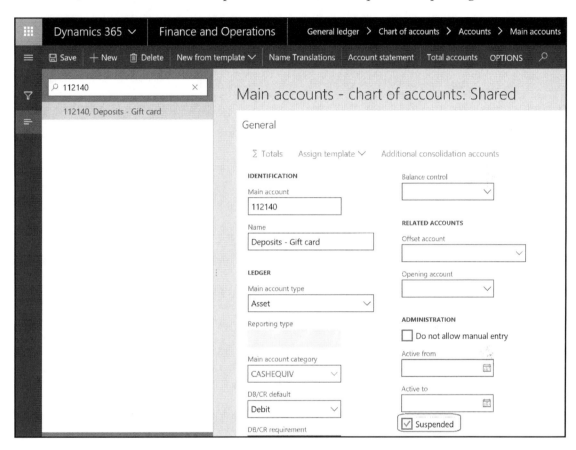

During the processing of a transaction, if an accountant selects a main account that is suspended, a message window will pop up that will display **Main account ##### is closed**, as shown in the following screenshot:

Using posting validation

Posting validation is divided into three main groups. The first group is **currency control**, the second is **user control**, and the third is **posting type control**.

Currency control

The financial controller can prefer to get Microsoft Dynamics 365 for Finance and Operations to control specific currencies, in order to stop transactions in other currencies in the main account.

For example, the controller requires the Egyptian bank main account to only accept transactions in Egyptian pounds, **EGP**, and prevents it from posting any transaction with a different currency, as shown in the following screenshot:

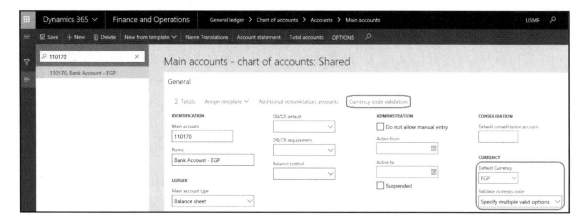

The **Validate currency code** options are as follows:

- **Optional**: This field is not authenticated at the time of posting. This is the default setting.
- **Required**: This field (provided by Microsoft Dynamics 365 for Finance and Operations) checks whether the field is filled in for posting.
- **Specify single valid option**: This field (provided by Microsoft Dynamics 365 for Finance and Operations) examines whether the field is completed for posting and that the value matches the value specified in the main account.
- **Specify multiple valid options**: This field verifies that the field is filled in with one of the values that are defined on the **Currency code validation** button.

 The **Currency code validation** button is only activated if the selected validation is a **Specify multiple valid options**.

During the processing of a transaction, if an accountant changes the currency, a warning bar will pop up that will display the message: **The currency for account ##### is not valid**, as shown in the following screenshot:

User control

Every main account might have a posting constraint per user. The financial controller can prefer to get Microsoft Dynamics 365 for Finance and Operations to control specific accounts for certain end users who are permitted to post transactions on these main accounts, by navigating to **General ledger** | **Chart of accounts** | **Accounts** | **Main accounts**. Click on **Main account**, then click on **Edit**, and then go to the **Posting validation** fast tab:

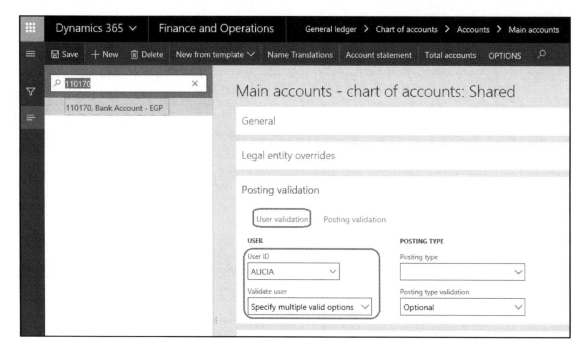

 User validation is only activated if the selected validation is a **Specify multiple valid options**.

During the processing of a transaction, if an unauthorized accountant tries to post a transaction on the main account, a warning bar will pop up that will display **You are not authorized to use account** #####, as shown in the following screenshot:

Posting type

The **Posting type** validation is a control that is used to stop posting on a specific type of transaction of the main account, as shown in the following screenshot:

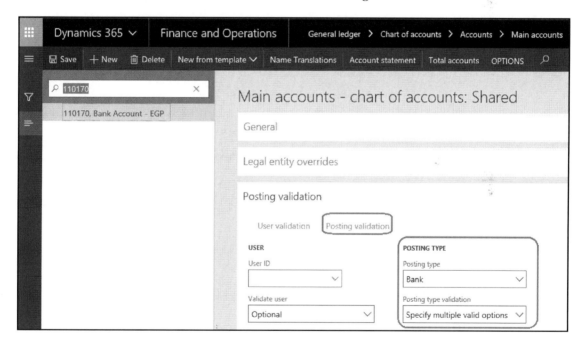

During the processing of a transaction, if a transaction breaks the posting type of the main account, a warning bar will pop up that will display **The posting type for account ##### is not valid**, as shown in the following screenshot:

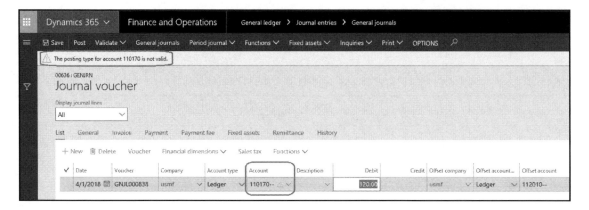

General ledger parameters

The general ledger parameters represent the broad setting of how the system should handle the general ledgers controls—module parameters are company specific settings. These are introduced in the following figure, and will be explored in depth in the next section. We will explore general controls, and accounting rules:

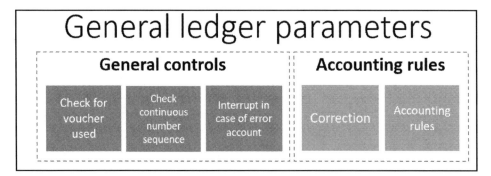

General controls

General controls consist of three subgroups: check for voucher used, check continuous number sequence, and interrupt in case of error account.

Check for voucher used

This control oversees the voucher number sequence and has an option to check whether the voucher number has been used before or not. There are then four different action options, as shown in the **General ledger parameters** screenshot, which you can access from **General ledger** | **Ledger setup** | **General ledger parameters**:

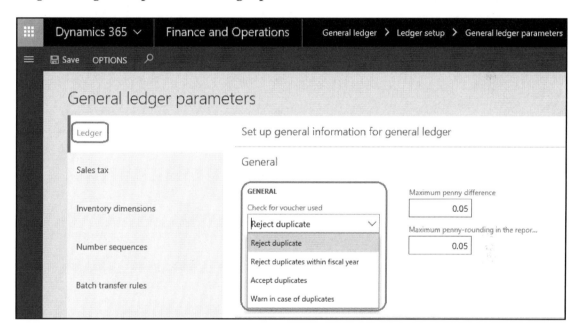

The four options are:

- **Reject duplicate**: The system will prevent you using the same voucher again
- **Reject duplicates within fiscal year**: The system will prevent you using the same voucher again within the same fiscal year, in the next fiscal year the voucher number could be used
- **Accept duplicates**: The system will allow you to reuse the same voucher number
- **Warn in case of duplicates**: The system will allow to reuse the same voucher number but will warn the user

The recommended option is to reject duplicates. In cases where the customer business requires you to accept duplicate options, it should be very well analyzed, and verified by the customer finance team, as it may cause reporting issues in future.

Check continuous number sequence

The **Check continuous numbers** sequence option verifies that the number sequences that generate vouchers in the ledger are set to continuous, as shown in the following screenshot of **General ledger parameters**:

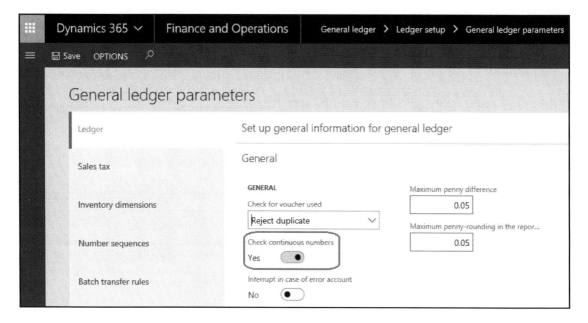

The number sequence setup from **Organization administration** | **Number sequences** | **Number sequences**, the continuous option is illustrated in the following screenshot:

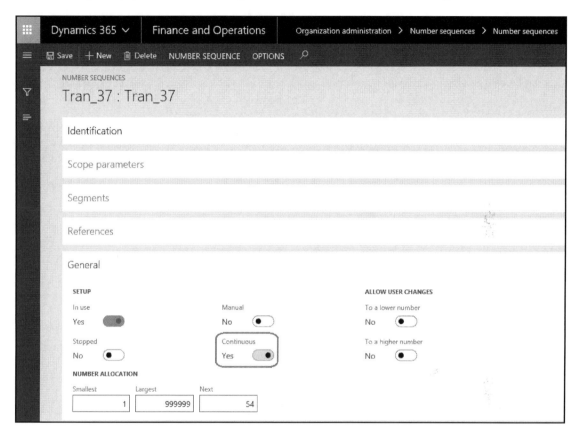

Interrupt in case of error account

The **Interrupt in case of error account** option allows the system to interrupt updates to automatic transactions, with a message when the error account is used in the posting process.

Accounting rules

The accounting rules contain two points, the first being the correction and how reversal transactions are posted, and the accounting rules to use.

Correction

This option controls the presentation on the reversal transaction. If this option is selected as **Yes** for transaction reversals, a debit transaction is reversed by adding a minus debit transaction, and a credit transaction is reversed by adding a minus credit transaction. The credit side will be eventfully positive sign as shown in the transaction screenshot. When you reverse a customer or vendor transaction by using a correction, the connected ledger transactions are also reversed by using corrections. This is known as **Storno reversal**.

The following screenshot illustrates the correction control set as **Yes**:

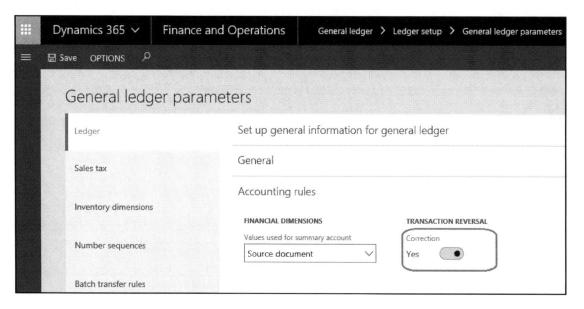

The following screenshot shows a reversal voucher transaction presentation where the correction control is set as **Yes**:

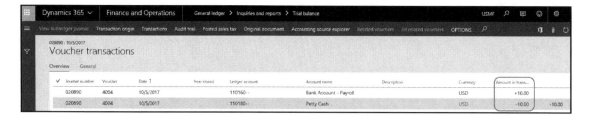

The following screenshot shows a reversal voucher transaction presentation where the correction control is set as **No**:

Accounting rules

Activate **Use posting definition** to be used for transaction types that are defined in the transaction posting definition form. The posting profiles and posting definitions could be used together, in order to enable the **Commitment accounting** options. The following screenshot illustrates the warning message shown after activating **Use posting definition**:

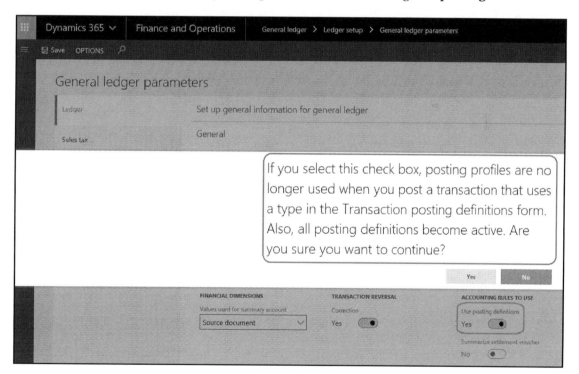

Understanding shared financial data

Since the previous version of Microsoft Dynamics 365 for Finance and Operations, Microsoft has introduced a new concept called **shared financial data**, which reduces the effort and time of deployment in a multiple-company environment and operational maintenance. A group of companies can share the same chart of accounts, currencies, and dimensions—this decreases the operation time. For example, a new main account will be available to all companies. The following figure explains the concept of shared financial data in detail:

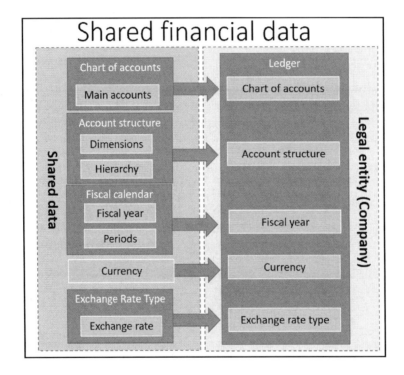

The financial data that will be shared between the companies is as follows:

- **Chart of accounts (COA)**: This contains the main account, the COA could be one shared COA between all legal entities, or a COA for one legal entity or group of legal entities. This is all dependent on customer requirements, and the nature of the business. It is a trade-off decision, if subsidiaries decide to maintain separate chart of accounts instead of using one shared COA.

- **Account structure**: This contains the applicable dimensions of the main accounts. This could be shared across legal entities, a group of legal entities or a single account structure to a single legal entity.
- **Fiscal year**: This contains the start date and end date of the fiscal year and the period's management. If all legal entities have the same fiscal year requirement, it is recommended you use the shared fiscal year between all legal entities.
- **Currencies**: This represents the default currency and reporting currency.
- **Exchange rate type**: This sets the monthly exchange rate for foreign currencies and the default budget exchange rate.

To access the ledger window, navigate to **General ledger** | **Ledger setup** | **Ledger.** The following screenshot shows the Microsoft Dynamics 365 for Finance and Operations ledger:

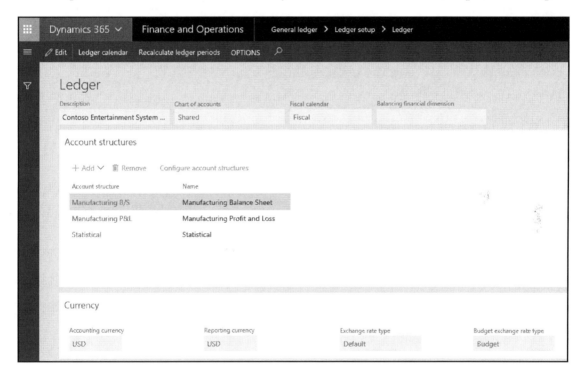

For the customer who will use a shared COA for all legal entities, and each legal entity has internal requirements for the main account, Microsoft Dynamics 365 for Finance and Operations gives you the ability to do an override on the main accounts per each legal entity. In the next section, we will walk-through the legal entity override options for the main accounts. To access the legal entity overrides, go to **General ledger** | **Chart of accounts** | **Accounts** | **Main accounts**, then move to the **Legal entity overrides** fast tab. The following screenshot shows the available override options. The override could be the suspension of a particular main account, an activate date, allocation terms, and an exchange rate type:

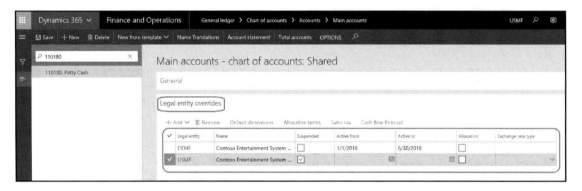

The following screenshot illustrates the financial dimension override per legal entity. This gives the option to specify the default dimensions, for an account; to access the default financial dimensions go to **General ledger** | **Chart of accounts** | **Accounts** | **Main accounts**, then move to the **Legal entity overrides** fast tab. After adding a legal entity, go to **Default dimensions**.

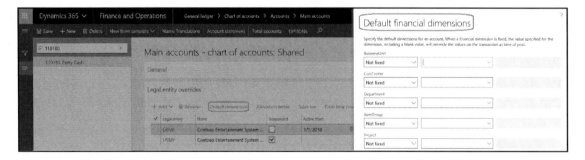

Enterprises may have subsidiaries in many countries that use shared COA. In such a scenario, you can use the multi-language capabilities in Microsoft Dynamics 365 for Finance and Operations. This enables the translation of the client interface, including menus and data translation.

In this section, we will focus on the translation of the shared COA functionality; this enables the translation of the client interface, including menus and data translation.

In my example, a company has two subsidiaries in one instance. The first legal entity is in the USA, and the second is in Italy. The COA is identical across legal entities, and each legal entity is required to have the COA in their own language:

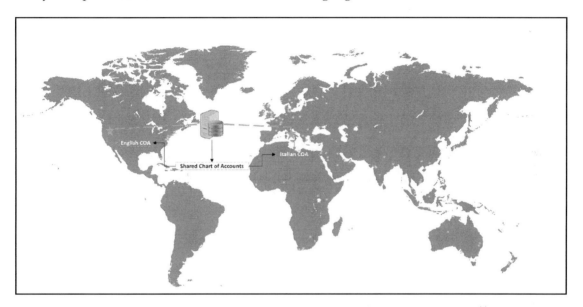

 In a real-life scenario, you must also consider specific regulations from each country that relate to a COA.

The following example will demonstrate how to use the multi-language functionality in Dynamics 365 to fulfill the scenario presented previously. In order to fulfill these requirements and demonstrate it in a proper way:

- Firstly, use the shared COAs across legal entities (USA and Italy). The shared COA language is English.
- Secondly, use the translation functionality in the COA.
- Thirdly, add another user to set the language interface.

The following diagram illustrates the basic concept of the shared COA, the use of translation functionality, and user language:

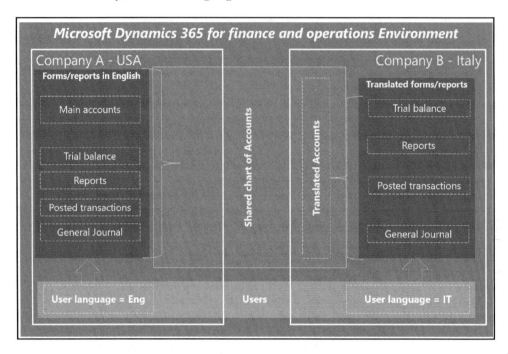

The following screenshot illustrates the main account translation option; to access this form, go to **General ledger** | **Chart of accounts** | **Accounts** | **Main account**, then select your main account (110180 is used in this example). Select the **Name Translations** button:

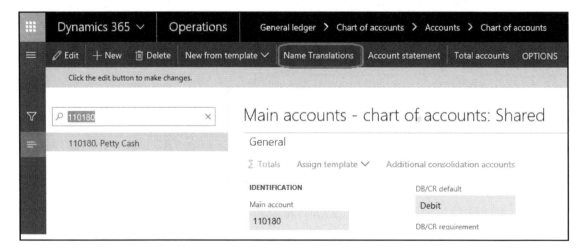

In the **Text translations** form, select the language and add the translation text:

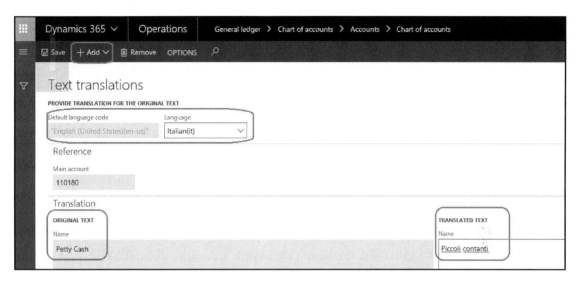

Go to **System administration** | **Users** | **Users**, then select **User** and move to **User options**, and move to **Preferences** under **Options**. Then move to the **Language and country/region preferences** fast tab and change the language to **IT (Italian)**:

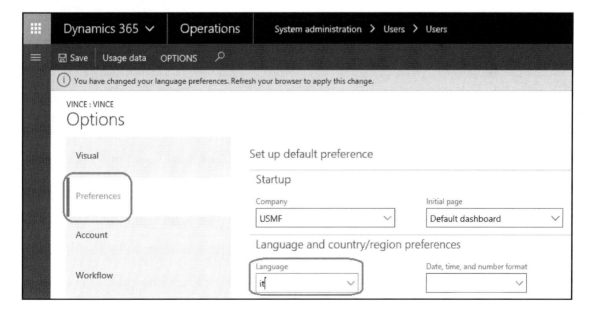

Changing the user options will result in menus being translated into Italian. To see this change, go to **General ledger** | **Journal entries** | **General journal**. Create and post a general journal entry from the Italian interface. Note the account name is shown in Italian:

The posted transaction details are shown in Italian, as shown here:

The following example shows what the translation looks like on a ledger transaction report (**General ledger** | **Journal entries** | **General journals**). Select the posted journal and go to **Lines,** then select **Print** and select **Voucher**:

 The translations that you create are displayed everywhere that a main account name is displayed, except on the main account list.

The following screenshot demonstrates the multi-language functionality with the **Trial Balance** page. To access this page, go to **General ledger | Inquiry and reports | Trial balance**:

Understanding financial management in action

Here, we will look at the process of financial management through the opening balance and various daily transactions.

Opening balance

When a company migrates to Microsoft Dynamics 365 for Finance and Operations from a legacy ERP solution, one of the important data migration tasks is the creation of opening balances in the new system. This process is moving the financial balance to Dynamics 365 for Finance and Operations, which represents the base of organization financial reporting, so that the opening balance must be executed properly to ensure it is audit-compliant and matches customer reporting requirements.

The opening balance building blocks consist of four main blocks, which are customer requirements, sub-ledgers, trial balance, and validation and reconciliation:

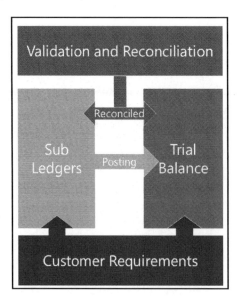

- **Customer requirements**: Identifying customers' business to-be relates to sub-ledgers posting profile setup, design of COA and financial reporting dimensions, in addition to master data mapping between legacy systems and Dynamics 365 for Finance and Operations.
- **Sub-ledgers**: The sub-ledgers are vendors, customers, banks, fixed assets, and items. The sub-ledgers are linked to the COA through the posting profile setup.
- **Trial balance**: The trial balances (general ledger accounts) consist of the balance sheet and income statement accounts. Balance sheet accounts represent the balance sheet report, which denotes the company financial position. Balance accounts move their balances from one year to another. Profit and loss accounts, which represent the income statement results and do not move to another year, are the base of the income statement report, which denotes the operational result for a specific period.
- **Validation and reconciliation**: The balance of sub-ledgers (vendors, customers, banks, fixed assets, and items) must equal the balance of the corresponding general ledger accounts (trial balance), with respect to the financial dimensions (business units, department, and purpose) balance, if it is used through submodules. The controllership and consulting team should finalize the validation of the design and deployment of the financial dimensions and the account structure that is required to be activated, before posting the opening balance.

In order to ensure accuracy in your Microsoft Dynamics 365 for Finance and Operations opening balances, it is important to take a systematic approach during the implementation phases begun in the analysis phase and moving from the design phase to the development and deployment phase. The following approach of the opening balance upload is divided into three main activities. The first activity consists of planning and designing the opening balance tasks, identifying master data changes between the legacy system and Dynamics 365 for Finance and Operations by performing master data mapping, agreeing on the opening balance posting date, and assigning roles and responsibilities. The second activity is executing the migration of data for trial balances and sub-ledgers. The third activity is the validation and reconciliation of the general ledger, sub-ledger, and financial dimensions.

In this section, we will lay out the process and the elements involved in creating new opening balances in Microsoft Dynamics 365 for Finance and Operations:

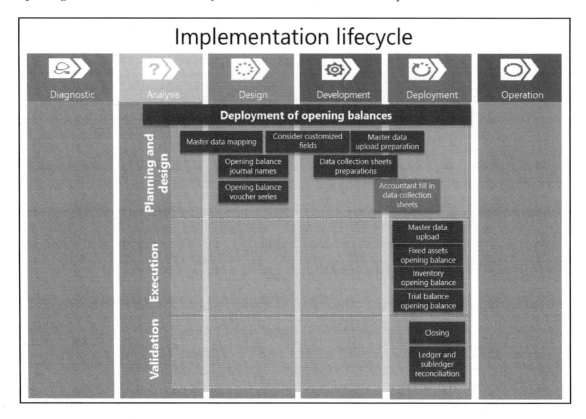

Planning and design

The planning and design of the opening balance began at the analysis phase of the implementation and extended to the design, development, and deployment phases. It is important to allocate separate workshops to discuss the opening balance plan, execution process, validation points and identification of tasks along with responsibilities:

- The master data that will be loaded to Dynamics 365 for Finance and Operations should be mapped to legacy system data. This will take place if the data structure will be changed between the two systems. That said, this task should be considered mainly in the design phase, but it is recommended that you begin it in the analysis phase by capturing the customer requirements and identifying whether the data structure will be changed. This is required to maintain high levels of coordination between the controllership and consulting team, including finalization of the mapping between the old COA (legacy system) and the new COA, in addition to customers, vendors, banks, fixed assets, and inventory coding structure.
- Customer requirements that include customizations that may involve the opening balance should be considered.
- Customer requirements that include analysis by financial dimension should be considered in the opening balance upload of sub-ledgers and trial balance.
- The master data preparation will involve the COA, banks, fixed assets, financial dimensions, vendors, customers, and inventory items.
- The consulting team should ensure the setup of the required fields in the data collection template they will use to upload the opening balance.
- The accountant who will fill in the opening balance data collection sheet must understand the fields and how they will fill it in.
- Create a separate journal name under the general ledger journal and voucher number sequence for easier tracking.
- Create separate journal names under inventory management (movement journal) and voucher number sequence for easier tracking.
- If adjustments are needed for the opening balance, use the same journal name and voucher.
- Agree with the customer the modules that will be involved in the opening balance.
- Agree with the customer on the opening balance date. This decision, depending on the customer, may be the first of the fiscal year where they finalize and close the fiscal year transactions, report it, and then start a fresh fiscal year based on the closing balances of the previous one. The customer may need to start the opening balance at the beginning of a quarter, which is similar to the fiscal year activities but without closing the profit and loss account. The third scenario is to post the opening balance in the middle of the month, and this is the most challenging scenario, where you identify a cut-off date in middle of month and upload the previous day's balances in addition to open transactions such as purchase orders/sales orders.

It is important during the planning of the opening balance to explain to the customer how the execution will be done. The execution mechanism of the opening balance is based on keeping a high level of integrity between the general ledger and sub-ledgers, in other words, the posting to general ledger should be through the sub-ledger posting profile instrument; avoid separating their uploads as much as you can to avoid audit integrity issues that may pop up after Go-Live. The posting of sub-ledgers' (accounts payable, accounts receivable, banks, fixed assets, and inventory) opening balances should be done through corresponding submodules.

As illustrated in the following diagram, the trial balance accounts are divided into two groups: the first group represents the accounts that are posted through posting profiles (accounts payable, accounts receivable, banks, fixed assets, and inventory), and the second group represents the non-posting profile accounts that we directly post to it:

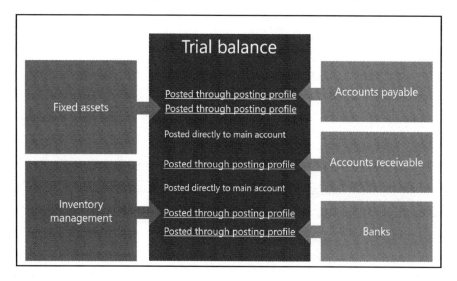

Execution

The opening balance is executed in three phases. This breakdown helps in managing and controlling each phase separately. The first phase represents the fixed assets opening balance acquisition and depreciation, the second phase represents the inventory opening balance, and the third phase represents the trial balance opening balances, which consists of accounts payable, and receivable, banks, and non-posting profile accounts:

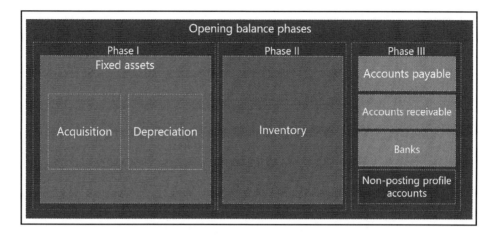

Before starting the execution of the opening balance, the implementation team should ensure the foundation is done properly; in the next section, we will cover the required foundations of the opening balance:

- Carry out the master data upload of the COA, financial dimensions, vendors, customer, banks, fixed assets and inventory items, in addition to inventory dimensions, and warehouses
- Completely configure the account structure, and advanced rules if required
- Set up the accounting currency, and reporting currency
- Set up currencies, and the used exchange rate for the opening balance
- Set up the posting profiles for the sub-ledgers (accounts payable, accounts receivable, banks, fixed assets and inventory)

Related to the foundation, a bridge account will be needed that is used in the fixed asset, and inventory opening balance entry. The bridge account is used to balance the posted entries of assets, and inventory; the balance of the bridge account is temporary till it is reversed in the trial balance posting. In other words, the use of a bridge account is to keep the double entry basis of posting assets, and inventory transactions.

In the following section, we will illustrate the high level of execution mechanisms from the accounting entries perspective for the three phases. The fixed asset phase is divided into two separate tasks:

- The first task is posting the asset acquisition
- The second task is posting the fixed asset depreciation

The posted opening balance of the fixed asset account is generated directly from the fixed asset submodule, and the acquisition entry is balanced by the bridge account (this amount will be reversed when posting the trial balance entry). The posted opening balance of the accumulated depreciation account is generated directly from the fixed asset submodule, and the depreciation entry is balanced by the bridge account (this amount will be reversed when posting the trial balance entry).

In the inventory opening balance, the posted opening balance of the inventory account is generated directly from the inventory submodule, and the movement entry is balanced by the bridge account (this amount will be reversed when posting the trial balance entry).

The third phase covers the posting of the opening balance of accounts payable, accounts receivable, banks, and the rest of the accounts (non-posting profile accounts) in addition to the reversal of the bridge account balances, which are generated from the fixed asset and inventory phase. The concept of the opening balance posting is to ensure that the balance sheet accounts that represent submodules should be posted from the submodule. The following diagram illustrates the posting of bridge accounts from submodules, and these bridge accounts are reversed in the trial balance, in addition to the posting of which represents submodules:

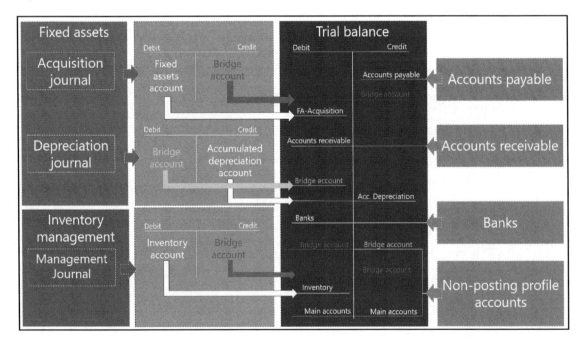

Fixed assets opening balance

The fixed assets opening balance phase has some specific considerations. To ensure accurate fixed asset opening balance, it is recommended you take into consideration the following points:

- Accurately collect the fixed assets register information: actual acquisition date, service life, current net book value, and depreciation remaining periods.
- To ensure the accuracy of fixed assets calculations, it is recommended you let the calculation be done by the fixed assets submodule in Microsoft Dynamics 365 for Finance and Operations.
- Also, consider the fixed assets that are acquired in a foreign currency, and modify the acquisition entry with the currency and the exchange rate.

The Go-Live of the fixed assets may be included in the first wave of the implementation, or it may be that the Go-Live is included in the second wave of the implementation; this is based on the agreement with the customer. On the other hand, the opening balance date may be at the beginning of the fiscal year, or it may be in the middle of the year:

	First wave of the implementation	Second wave of the implementation
Beginning of fiscal year	• The balance of fixed assets, and accumulated depreciation accounts will be posted from fixed asset sub-module. • Create fiscal periods for old fixed assets to post the acquisitions in the actual dates. • Post fixed assets depreciation up to the current year (opening balance date). • Post fixed assets transactions in the last day of the prior year. • Ensure the posting profile will post to fixed asset, accumulated depreciation, and bridge account. • The balance of bridge account will be reversed in trial balance entry.	• The balance of fixed assets, accumulated depreciation accounts already posted in the trial balance in the first wave of the implementation. • The opening balance entry of acquisition use the acquisition account as offset account to reverse the effect of original opening balance. • The opening balance of depreciation use the accumulated depreciation account as offset account to reverse the effect of original opening balance. • The fixed asset sub-module and general ledger reconciliation requires effort to ensure the accuracy.

Middle of the fiscal year	• The depreciation should be run in two separate tasks.
	  - The first task represents the depreciation of prior years, the entry will use accumulated depreciation against bridge account.
	  - Then second task represents the depreciation of the current on-going fiscal year, the entry will use accumulated depreciation against depreciation expense account.	

In the following section, we will discuss the two scenarios of the fixed assets Go-Live in the first wave, and the second wave of the implementation.

Migrating the fixed assets in the first wave is the recommended approach where Microsoft Dynamics 365 for Finance and Operations will take care of the whole fixed assets calculations when it comes to the depreciation amounts and remaining depreciation periods without interference. This approach ensures the highest accuracy; on the other hand, it will require efforts to create old periods which only carrying fixed assets acquisition and depreciation transactions. This approach is considered as mimicking fixed asset historical transactions. The generated entries will be the acquisition account against the bridge account, and the accumulated depreciation account against the bridge account. In the case where the opening balance is in the middle of the fiscal year, the posting of depreciation should be divided into two separate tasks, as the posting of the depreciation of the current year should be linked to the accumulated depreciation and depreciation expense itself, and the bridge account will be used only against accumulated depreciation for the years prior to the current fiscal year:

Pros	Cons
Accuracy of the opening balance since it is depending on the system logic and avoid any manual interference. Fixed assets sub module and general ledger integrity. Since posting of balance sheet accounts are done through posting profile.	Opening periods which will carry fixed asset transactions (depend on the oldest asset the customer has)

Migrating the fixed asset opening balance in the second wave could be an implementation decision, considering that the opening balance of the acquisition account, the accumulated depreciation account, and the depreciation expenses are already posted with the trial balance of the first wave. Then, in the course of posting the opening balance of the submodule, this will generate entries debit, and credit acquisition account this considered a reversal of posted opening balance in trial balance, and use voucher number indication in the submodule and GL reconciliation. The depreciation entry will be posted to the accumulated depreciation account as a debit and credit, which will reverse the accumulated depreciation posted balance in the trial balance first wave:

Pros	Cons
Distribute the Go-Live effort in two phases, this gave time to project team to focus in each phase.	Fixed assets sub module and general ledger reconciliation requires effort to ensure they are tied up.

Also, there are two options for the posting date of the fixed assets: whether to post the acquisition entry in the actual acquisition date and run the depreciation over all periods, or post the acquisition and the depreciation entry in the opening balance date.

The first approach requires the identification of the oldest acquisition date of assets to identify your very first period date in the upload sheet set service life, depreciation periods, and depreciation periods remaining; the system will then take care of the calculations from acquisition to monthly depreciation. Also, if there is any known adjustment (acquisition/depreciation), it is recommended that it is posted with its transactions type:

Pros	Cons
Accurate and smooth fixed asset operations	Needs effort to arrange, setup, and execute transactions of prior years.

The second approach is posting the fixed assets acquisition and depreciation at opening balance date, which requires manual interference to update the fixed asset book actual values for acquisition, depreciation periods, and the remaining depreciation periods:

Pros	Cons
Eliminate the effort in creating previous periods	Required manual interference to update asset data (acquisition date, depreciation run date, depreciation periods remaining) which may create issues in the future. The system will consider opening balance transaction as Acquisition amount, so there any adjustment posted in past years they system will not consider it.

Inventory opening balance

The inventory opening balance phase has some specific considerations; to ensure an accurate inventory opening balance, it is recommended you take into consideration the following points:

- Accurately collect the inventory information items, sites, warehouse, and inventory dimensions, if any
- Item costs and the used valuation method
- Item groups and posting profiles

Use the inventory movement journal to post opening balance to add quantity to inventory, and the generated entry will post to inventory balance sheet account, against bridge account.

Ledger and sub-ledger opening balances

The opening balances of the general ledger and the sub-ledger are uploaded together. The sub-ledger (vendors and customers) posting profiles should be assigned to the opening balance. This is important to ensure posting for vendors and customers whether to post to summary account or advance account.

The opening balance for open invoices could be posted in separate lines in the same entry using the invoice number, due dates, and discounts, if any. In addition to that, sub-ledger posting profiles (vendor, and customers) who have balances in a foreign currency should be considered along with the exchange rate.

If the opening balance is in a period that will be included in the next sales tax settlement, and the customer wants to use the tax settlement process, tax information should be assigned to opening balance transactions.
The bank's opening balance should be reconciled afterward to be considered in the next reconciliation.

Performing daily transactions

The daily transactions section covers the functionalities that help end users with their daily work, which facilitates the entry process and thereby saves time and effort.

As seen in the following figure, there are five main functionalities: **Ledger account alias**, **Recurring entries**, **Save voucher**, **Global general journal** (which is a new functionality delivered in Microsoft Dynamics 365 for Finance and Operations), and **Excel integration**:

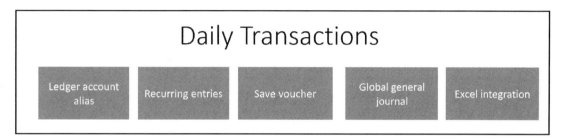

The ledger account alias

The ledger account alias is a function that can be utilized for non-financial users who are not aware of the structure of a COA and the requirements to input data for a financial transaction. The main account aliases give the option to enter a predefined code for every combination of main accounts, along with the financial dimensions. It is an alternative, manually selecting an individual dimension combination for every transaction. This is a usability function.

To access the account alias window, navigate to **General ledger** | ;**Chart of accounts** | **Accounts** | **Ledger account alias**, as shown in the following screenshot:

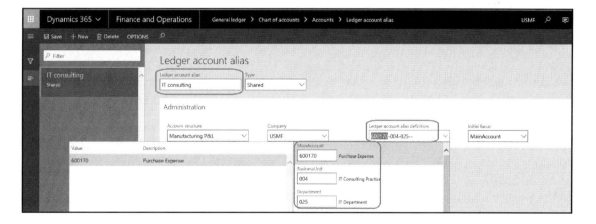

To access the general journal window, navigate to **General ledger** | **Journal entries** | **General journal** | **Lines**. In the **Account** column, enter the defined ledger account alias and click on the combobox; it filters to the entered alias and shows the account's structure as well:

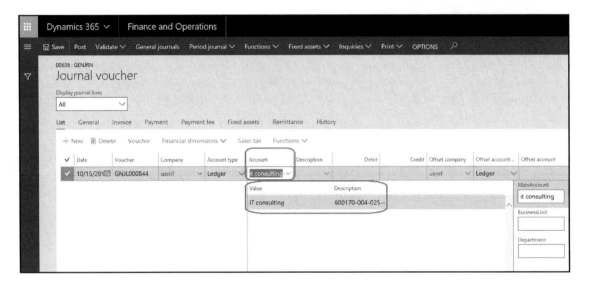

Then, select the alias description. It will be populated in the **Account** column with the account structure combination. The mouse cursor will be on a segment that has been specified in the **Initial focus** field in the setup form.

Recurring entries

Recurring entries are generally used for frequent transaction entries, such as rentals and subscriptions. The accountant is able to create a periodic journal and generate an entry based on the transaction periods that are already set up.

In order to create a recurring entry (for example, for rent), you have to create a periodic journal name. For this, navigate to **General ledger** | **Journal setup** | **Journal names** and create a journal name with the **Journal type** field as **Periodic**. The following screenshot shows **Periodic** in the **Journal type** field:

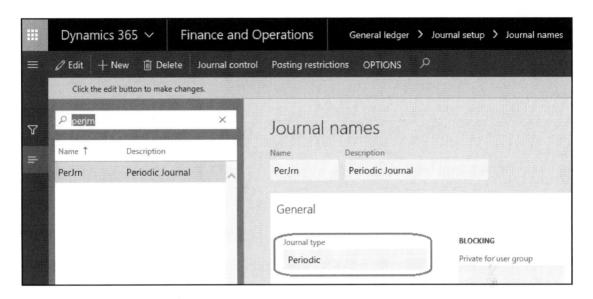

Then, as shown in the following screenshot, set the periodic journals for rent to be posted every month. For this, navigate to **General ledger** | **Journal entries** | **Periodic journals**; here, the periodic journal form opens up. Create a new journal entry by pressing *Ctrl + N*, and then click on **Lines**. In the lines form, enter the date, account type, account, debit of credit side, and offset account.

The **Unit** (whether days, months, or years) and **Number of units** fields set the recurring times of the transaction. For the rent example, select **Vendor** in **Account type** and the vendor ID and enter the amount in the credit side. Set the suitable offset main account. The **Unit** field is **Monthly** and **Number of units** is **1**, which means it will recur every month, as shown in the following screenshot:

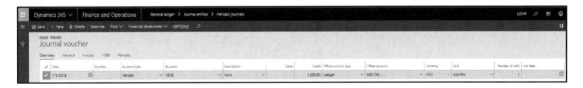

To execute a recurring transaction, navigate to **General ledger** | **Journal entries** | **General journal** and create a new journal by pressing *Ctrl + N*. Then, click on **Lines**. In the journal voucher form, go to the **Periodic journal** menu and select **Retrieve journal**. In the open dialog box, enter **End date** as 1/31/2018 and select a periodic journal name, as shown in the following screenshot:

Copy: The periodic transaction will be kept in the periodic journal, where it can be used in the future.

Move: The periodic transaction will be removed from the periodic journal.

The result of this process retrieves the periodic transaction in the journal line, as shown in the following screenshot. It also shows the next usage for the period journal, which will be in **2/1/2018,** in our example:

Saving a voucher

Saving a posted voucher and retrieving it in a new voucher is generally used for a long transaction entry.

To access the **Save voucher** window, navigate to **General ledger | Journal entries | General journal,** then select **Posted transactions,** and click **Lines**. In the voucher line, select **Functions** and select **Save voucher template**. Then select a posted transaction to be saved. The options for saving are in **Percent** or **Amount**, as shown in the following screenshot:

In order to create a new voucher in a newly created journal, click on **Functions** and then click on **Select voucher template**, as shown in the following screenshot:

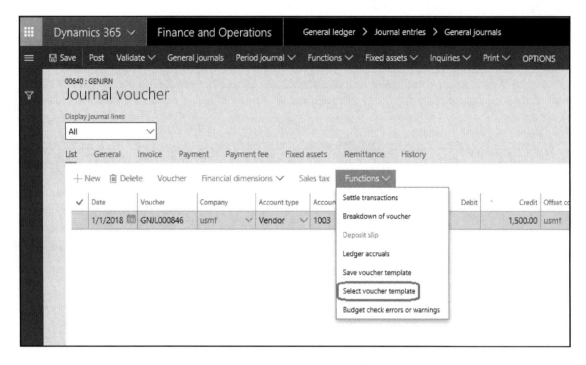

Microsoft Dynamics 365 for Finance and Operations will show all the saved vouchers in headers and lines, displaying both sides of the transaction. A particular voucher will create a new unposted voucher.

Global general journal

The global general journal is a newly introduced feature in Microsoft Dynamics 365 for Finance and Operations. It gives the ability to move between legal entities general journal without switching the legal entity. It increases the productivity of GL accountants who work across all legal entities.

In order to access the Global general journal, go to **General ledger** | **Journal entries** | **Global general journals**, as shown in the following screenshot. A user logged in to USMF and can see other companies journals:

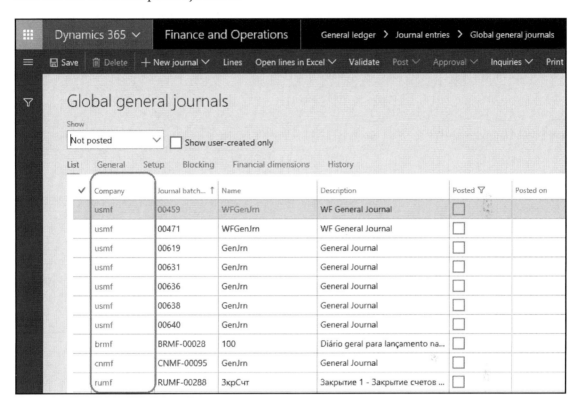

Excel integration

Microsoft Excel is still one of the most favorite applications for accountants, and there is a direct integration between Microsoft Dynamics 365 for Finance and Operations and Microsoft Excel. The end user can open journal entries in Excel, edit them, then publish the journal back to Microsoft Dynamics 365 for Finance and Operations.

Go to **General ledger** | **Journal entries** | **General journal**, then **Lines**, then add the required information date, main account, offset account, and amount. Then move to Excel integration and select **General journal line entry**, as shown in the following screenshot:

In the dialog shown in the following screenshot, select **Download**:

Microsoft Excel will open up, as illustrated in the following screenshot, and it will require you to **Enable editing,** and may request your credentials at first time login:

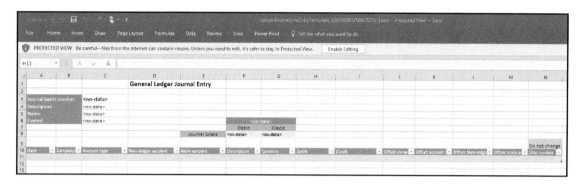

 Microsoft Excel will take time retrieving metadata.

Microsoft Excel retrieves the data from the journal line, and as shown in the following screenshot, the accountant can add more lines and publish the journal to the system:

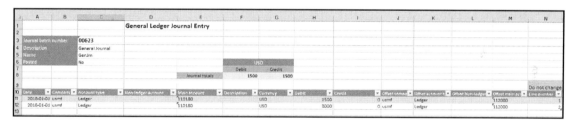

From the right-hand corner, the user will find the **Publish** button, as shown in the following screenshot:

It will take a while till Excel publishes the data to Dynamics 365 for Finance and Operations. This depends on the size of the entry.

As shown in the following screenshot, the journal has been updated:

The closing procedure

The closing procedure is a common practice at organizations to finalize monthly transactions and report monthly financial reporting. The procedure varies from one company to another, but it has common steps between company departments.

The finance controllership department is responsible for the closing procedure, where accountants follow up with the operations department to confirm that they have posted the monthly transactions in the ERP. The following figure explains the closing procedure in detail:

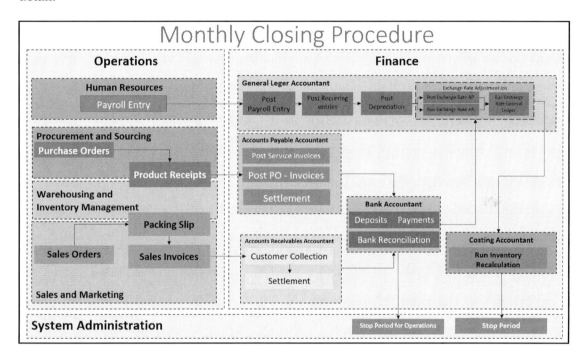

All the departments in a company are involved in the monthly closing process. The **human resources** department calculates the payroll and generates the payroll entry to be validated and posted by the general ledger's accountant.

The **procurement** department ensures that they have confirmed all purchase orders to be received at the warehouse and the warehouse keeper confirms receiving them, as it affects the inventory quantities and values. On the other side, the accounts payable accountants match and post purchase order invoices as well as service invoices. They then execute payments of due invoices that are related to the closing month.

The **sales** department verifies that they have confirmed all sales orders to be delivered to the customer and issues sales invoices accordingly, which generates the revenue and cost of goods sold. In the **finance** department, the accounts receivable accountant posts the customers' collections and settlements.

During this time, the fiscal period is stopped for all operations to prevent any further operational entries in that month and only the financial team is allowed to post the financial adjustment entries.

The general ledger's accountant posts the recurring entries such as rental and accruals. So, first run the fixed assets depreciation and exchange rate adjustment for sub-ledgers (accounts payable and accounts receivable), and then run the exchange rate adjustments for the general ledger.

The costing accountant runs the inventory recalculation to adjust the average cost of inventory items and adjusts the sold quantities by the proper cost. They stop the fiscal period after finalizing the inventory calculation.

The financial period close is a newly introduced feature in Microsoft Dynamics 365 for Finance and Operations. The following diagram illustrates the main elements of the financial period close feature:

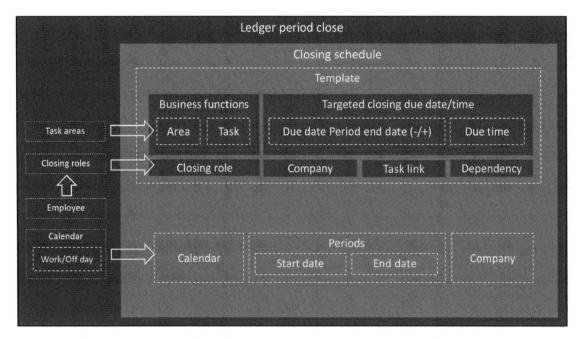

The following screenshot illustrates the financial period close workspace:

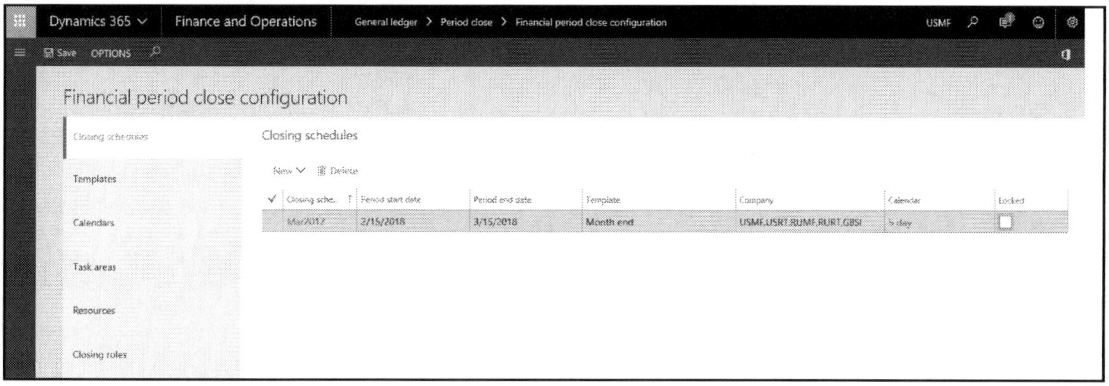

In the following section, we will walk-through the elements of the financial period close.

Closing schedules

You use a closing schedule to assign a financial close template to a specific financial period that must be closed. The tasks from the template are then automatically generated for the specified period, and the new closing schedule is added to the workspace. When you create a new closing schedule, the **Period end date** field is used to determine the actual due dates for the closing tasks, based on the relative due date that is assigned in the financial close template.

Assign the calendar appropriate for the closing schedule, to indicate the working days to be used in task scheduling. If you don't define a specific calendar, the task due dates will use all the days of the week.

You must also define the companies that will be associated with the closing schedule. If template tasks are assigned to multiple companies, separate tasks will be created for each company that is in the closing schedule and assigned to the template task.

After a closing schedule is completed, select the **Closed** option for it. The task history will still be available from the **All financial period close tasks list** page, but the closing schedule will be removed from the workspace. After a closing schedule has been marked as **Closed**, you won't be able to add tasks to it, edit tasks, or remove tasks from it.

The following screenshot illustrates the closing schedules. Navigate to **General ledger** | **Period close** | **Financial period close configuration**, then select **Closing schedules**:

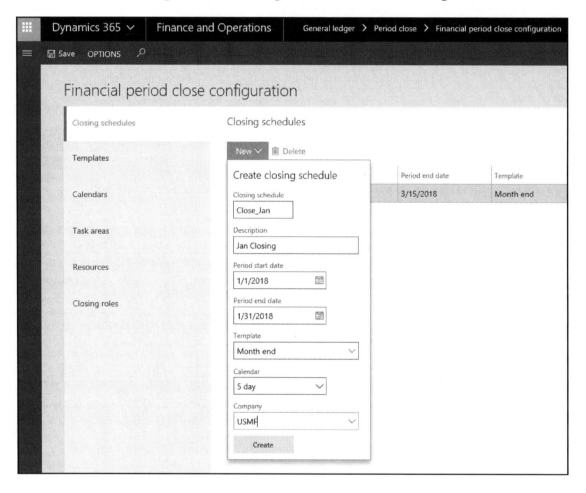

Templates

You use a financial close template to define all tasks that are part of a closing process. A closing task is a recurring work effort that is assigned to an individual to complete as part of each closing process. In the template, a relative due date must be defined for each closing task. The relative due date is the number of days before or after the defined period end date that the task will be due each period. A due time is also assigned to each task. The due time is set by using the context of your time zone and will be converted to the time zone for each user.

You can assign a task in the template to one or more companies where that task applies. If a different person is assigned to complete that work effort in each company, you might find it helpful to create multiple tasks for the same work effort. Create one task for each company. You can create multiple financial close templates. You can then use the various templates to track the closing processes for different period types, such as month end or year end, or to track companies that use different closing processes. After one template is created, you can copy it to a new template and make the required changes. You can assign only one template to each closing schedule. The closing template contains who does what, when, which company and dependencies. The following screenshot shows the template form. Navigate to **General ledger** | **Period close** | **Financial period close configuration,** then select **Templates**:

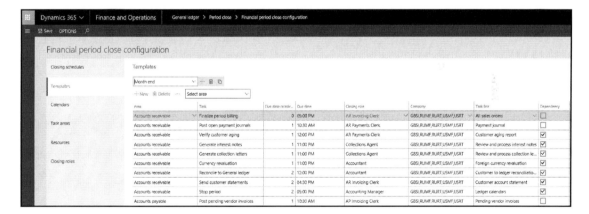

You can define task dependencies in the template. If a task has been set up to depend on one or more tasks, that task can't be marked as completed until all the dependencies have been completed. Set dependencies for **Currency revaluation** of **Accounts receivable** and mark records as shown here:

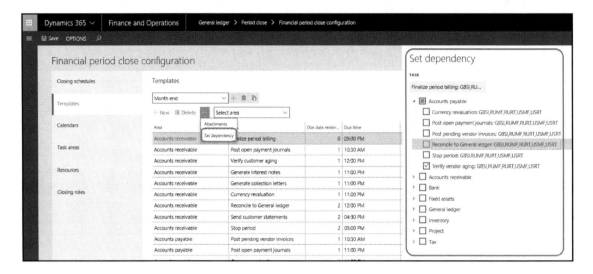

The **Task link** menu item is associated with the task work effort and can be used to go directly to the associated page from the task link in the workspace. For example, a closing task to run the currency revaluation process for accounts payable can be linked to the associated foreign currency revaluation page in Microsoft Dynamics 365 for Finance and Operations. You can also link to an external URL, as shown in the following screenshot:

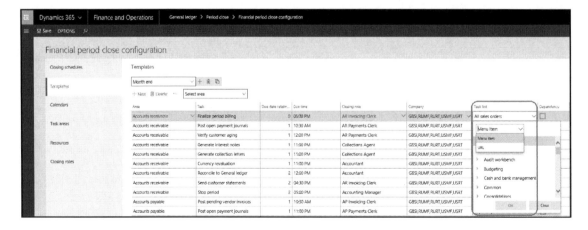

Calendars

Calendars is the place where you will define the working days for closing processes, and will be used for scheduling closing tasks. Create a new calendar, and indicate the working days to be used for task scheduling. It is best to create a calendar for a long period of time, such as a year or multiple years, since it can be edited after creation. After creating the calendar, click the **Edit** button to update the calendar for specific days, such as holidays. Closing tasks will be scheduled on days when the **Control value** is set to **Open**. If closing tasks should not be scheduled on a specific day, that day should have the **Control value** set to **Closed**. The following screenshot shows the calendars setup:

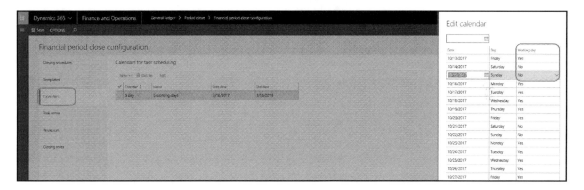

Task areas

You use **Task areas** to group closing tasks into logical areas of ownership within your organization. For example, accounts payable, accounts receivable, or general ledger might be used as task areas. Check the already created task areas, which represent departments:

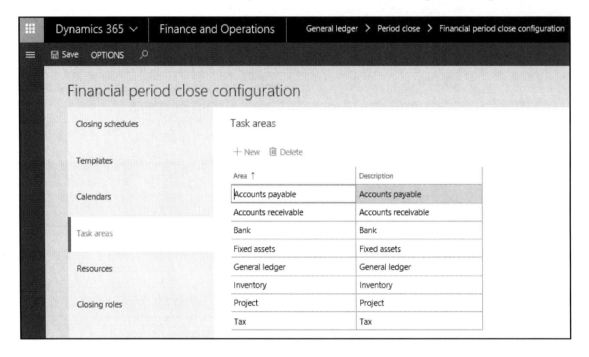

The preceding screenshot illustrates the task area.

Resources

On the **Resources** tab, you define the people who are involved in the closing processes. Any employee who is responsible for a closing task must first be assigned here. You must also specify the employee's view of the workspace. The following options are available:

- **Only assigned tasks**: The user will see only the tasks that are assigned to them
- **All tasks and status**: The user will see all closing tasks and the status of the overall process

Users who have permissions to view only their assigned tasks won't be able to add tasks to the task list, edit tasks, or remove tasks from the task list. The following screenshot shows the resources setup:

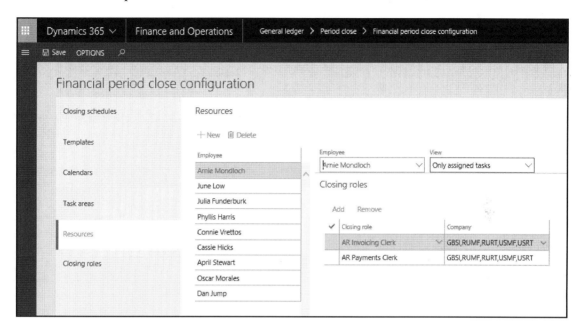

Closing roles

This is the place where you identify the roles participating in the closing process. The following screenshot illustrates the closing roles:

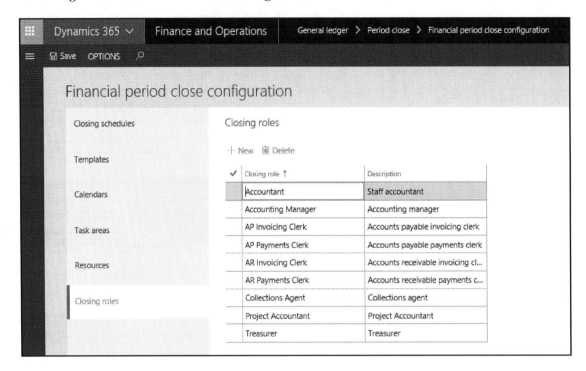

Period management is an administrative task. There are three stages for period status: **Open**, **On hold**, and **Permanently closed**. To access the **Period status** window, navigate to **General ledger** | **Calendars** | **Ledger calendars**, then go to the **Legal entities** fast tab, as shown in the following screenshot:

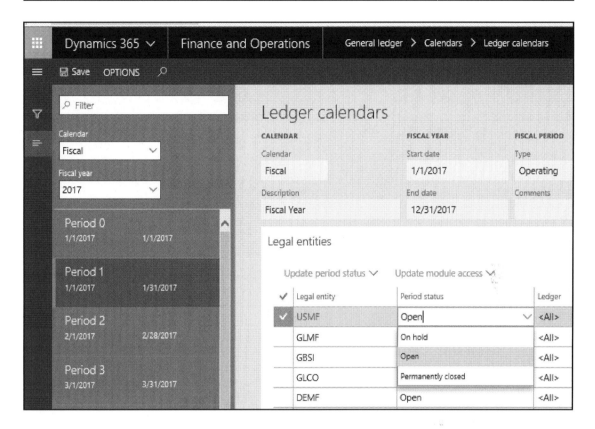

Since the previous version of Microsoft Dynamics 365 for Finance and Operations (that is, AX 2012 R3), the system administrator can manage all legal entities from one form, and can execute a mass update.

All transactions that are executed have the **Open** status in the **Period status** drop-down list.

After ensuring that all departments have entered and posted their transactions (relevant to the current month) as well as the financial post (the month-end adjustment transactions), the financial period status drop-down list is set to **Open** for a specific user group and modules, and this can be managed per module.

After dealing with the details of the financial department, make all the required adjustments for the current month. The financial **Period status** drop-down list is set to **On Hold**, which prevents any entry being posted in that period, but it can be reopened after that.

There is another possible scenario: changing **Period status** to **Permanently closed**. However, this status cannot be reopened again.

Summary

In this chapter, we discussed the practices in the financial implementations of Microsoft Dynamics 365 for Finance and Operations. We focused on the general ledger, covering the types of main accounts, classifications, and control points. We also explained shared financial data. We also learned about opening balance best practices, daily transactions, global general ledger, Microsoft Excel integration. We then moved to the financial period close functionality and the monthly closing procedure.

In the next chapter, we will cover financial dimensions and practice practical reporting in Microsoft Dynamics 365 for Finance and Operations.

3
Exploring Financial Dimensions

One of the major objectives of an ERP implementation is to provide clear business insights that can provide support for the organization's top management in the decision-making process. This requires analyzing the numbers, understanding them clearly, and then being able to examine the same numbers from different perspectives. Hence, a detailed structure is required to decide how an organization wants to analyze their numbers.

In this chapter, we will cover the following topics:

- Understanding the concept of financial dimensions
- Understanding the ledger account segmentation
- Posting types in Microsoft Dynamics 365 for Finance and Operations
- Exploring dimension reporting

Understanding the concept of financial dimensions

The main source of financial reporting is the main accounts. The components of financial reporting include a balance sheet, income statement, trial balance, cash flow, and more. The normal scenario is that the main account's balances do not mean much when it comes to analysis. This is because it is a total of the posted transactions' amounts, and it is required to be able to dig into this total breakdown. In other words, it provides us with information on how this amount is allocated, for example, among business units and departments. This allocation gives the lowest level of analysis to break down the same balance for a main account by more than one dimensional perspective.

The following diagram shows the financial dimension allocation for the **main account**:

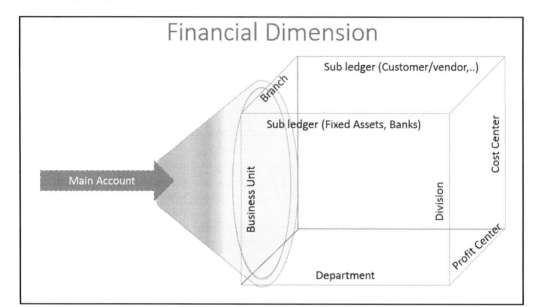

Financial dimensions provide us with a deeper analysis of the transactions posted on the general ledger accounts, where it gives the controller an analytical view of the transactions that occurred on the expenses account. For example, you can analyze the account balance according to the financial dimensions assigned to the main account.

The Microsoft Dynamics 365 for Finance and Operations financial dimension allows an organization to reach the lowest level of breakdown and analysis. There are three main standpoints to consider while discussing the financial dimension:

- The first standpoint is the required breakdown analysis for each main account in the chart of accounts, in order for it to be utilized at the reporting level.
- The second standpoint is the controls and validations while doing the data entry, in order to certify that the keyed-in transactions are allocated to the required dimensions before the transaction is posted. This directly affects the accuracy of reporting.
- The third standpoint is the reconciliation between the sub-ledger and the general ledger, and the ability to break down the balance using the sub-ledger (customers, vendors, items, banks, and more).

These standpoints are shown in the following diagram:

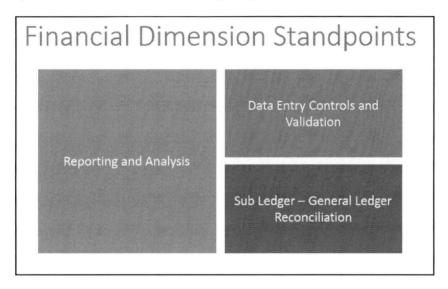

The role of the Microsoft Dynamics 365 for Finance and Operations consultant is to clarify the best usage of financial dimensions to the concerned parties. The key process owners who ascertain the financial dimensions' requirements are the **Chief Financial Officer (CFO)** and the financial controller. The three main standpoints of financial dimension can be summarized as follows:

- **Reporting and analysis**: This is used to identify reporting needs and data entry results
- **Data entry controls and validations**: This is used for data entry filtration
- **Sub-ledger and general ledger reconciliation**: This is used for reconciliation of transactions between the sub-ledger and the general ledger

The implementation team ascertains the financial dimensions' requirements during the analysis phase to understand what the business needs are at the reporting and analysis stages, and then identifies the required number of financial dimensions and how to utilize these dimensions.

 Microsoft Dynamics 365 for Finance and Operations supports an unlimited number of financial dimensions.

According to the business domain, every business needs to build the structure of their chart of accounts and financial dimensions. They also need to identify which sub-ledger should be tracked at the general ledger level. To build the structure of the chart of accounts and financial dimensions, follow these steps:

1. Classify the required dimensions for each main account, verifying whether it is mandatory or optional
2. Categorize the financial dimensions that are interrelated and are dependent on each other to filter dimensions based on the previously selected value
3. Categorize the intra-related dimensions; these are not dependent on the previously selected dimension

Microsoft Dynamics 365 for Finance and Operations supports the use of the existing sub-ledger master data to define financial dimensions. The following diagram illustrates the usage of financial dimensions:

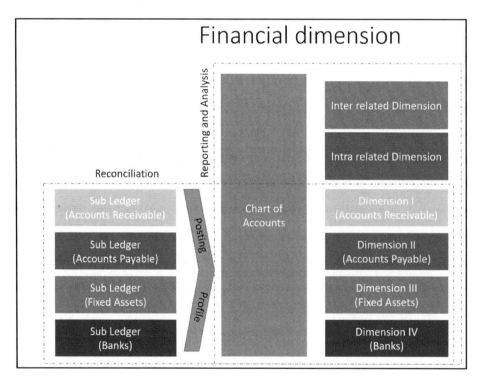

The heart of a financial dimension is the chart of accounts, as shown in the previous diagram. It should be carefully structured and set to the required dimension validation of each main account. It is important to consider this structure of the chart of accounts and dimensions' validation in the opening balance upload, as it will affect reporting and analysis, in addition to an automatic transaction, such as the exchange rate adjustment, and inventory recalculations.

> Changing the financial dimension's structure and validation during operations should be wisely planned, evaluated, and executed, as it may affect some historical transactions and some automatic transactions (for example, exchange rate adjustment, inventory adjustment, and settlement). It is recommended that you apply it at the beginning of a month when all historical transactions, along with the old structure and validation, are closed.

Understanding the ledger account segmentation

The following section covers the segmented ledger account entry in Microsoft Dynamics 365 for Finance and Operations and the financial dimensions' assignment in a one-line voucher entry.

Segmented ledger accounts

Microsoft Dynamics AX 2012 introduced the segmented ledger account where the main account and the financial dimension are combined in a single line. This gives more flexibility and control to the data that is entered than the previous versions.

The data entries are considered as the major sources of information quality. During the analysis phase, the implementation team exploring the reporting requirements as well as the process owners and top management require reliable information, and this information is generated by the data entry. It is required to control the data entry to ensure that the entered data is formatted in the correct way. The application consultant can fulfill these requirements to ensure the quality of data entry by performing the following tasks: default some values from the master data that are automatically populated in the transaction, by changing fields to be mandatory for reporting and identifying the required financial dimensions, to the transaction level.

Microsoft Dynamics 365 for Finance and Operations offers a very powerful entry mechanism that is built on the account structure. The segmented entry control is a function that simplifies the data entry and controls the complex combination of accounts and financial dimensions.

It is a simple cheat sheet window that gives the user hints on which segment should be entered, in addition to the lookup for that segment.

To access the general journal, navigate to **General ledger** | **Journal entries** | **General journals**, then create a new journal then select **Lines**. The following screenshot shows the simple cheat sheet in detail:

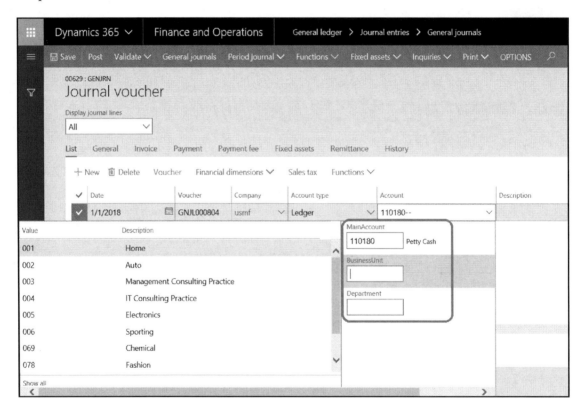

Financial dimensions entry

In this section, we will explore the further enhancement of segmented entries that gives more flexibility to Microsoft Dynamics 365 for Finance and Operations to accommodate the one-line entry to allocate the segments. This was followed in previous versions of Microsoft Dynamics 365 for Finance and Operations, where the default application assigned dimensions to both the sides (debit and credit), enforcing the use of double-line entries to work around this issue.

Microsoft Dynamics 365 for Finance and Operations covers this point completely. If an entry is created in a one-line style, the voucher created is that of a debit (vendor) or credit (bank) and requires the assigning of different segments. Here is a feature where we will be able to assign different financial dimensions for **Account** and **Offset account**. Navigate to **General ledger | Journal entries | General journals**, and then go to **Lines**. In the **General journals** form, click on the **Financial dimensions** button. There are two options here, **Account** and **Offset account**, as shown in the following screenshot:

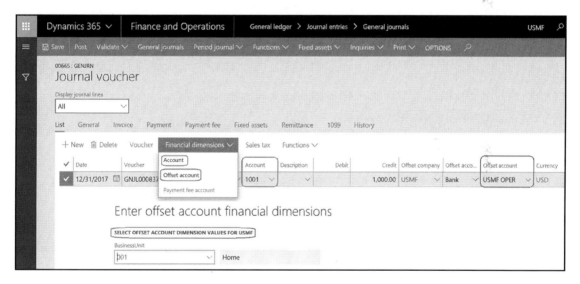

Creating financial dimensions

There was an obstacle facing the implementation team in assigning master data to financial dimensions such as vendors, customers, fixed assets, items, and banks, and the best-case scenario to tackle this is an automatic (online) assignment, in order to keep the integrity. The solution for this requirement is that it will either be maintained manually or by an automatic trigger (customization). Microsoft Dynamics 365 for Finance and Operations has bridged this gap. Microsoft Dynamics 365 for Finance and Operations has two types of financial dimensions, as shown in the following diagram:

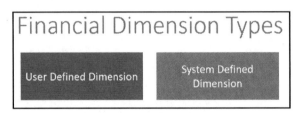

The first type is the user-defined dimension which allows users to add an unlimited number of dimensions (business unit, cost center, purpose, profit center, and more) as per the outcome of the analysis. The second type is the system-defined dimension. It helps in assigning the master data to newly created dimensions such as vendors, customers, fixed assets, and items.

The steps to create a new dimension are as follows:

1. Navigate to **General ledger** | **Chart of accounts** | **Dimensions**:

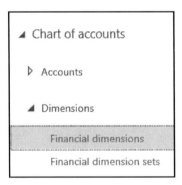

2. Within **Dimensions**, navigate to **Financial dimensions**, as shown in the previous screenshot. You'll be redirected to the **Financial dimensions** page, as shown in the following screenshot:

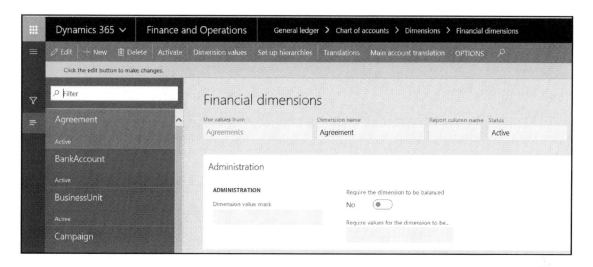

3. Create a new financial dimension by clicking on **New** in the **Financial dimensions** window, as shown in the following screenshot:

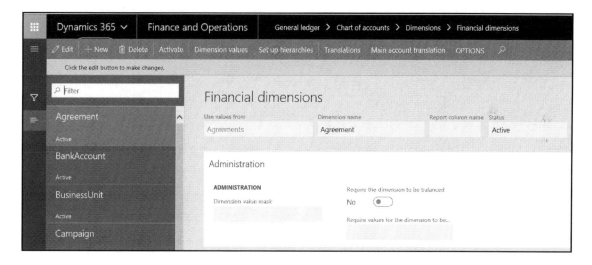

To create a new record, the shortcut is *Alt + N.*

4. Select the dimension type.
5. If you want to add a user-defined dimension, select **<Custom dimension>**, as shown in this screenshot:

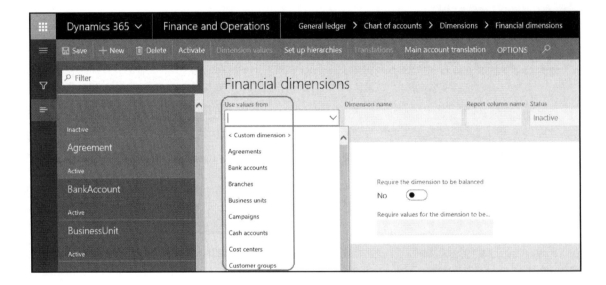

6. Enter the user-defined dimension list and configure the dimension value by its dates of activation and/or suspension by filling the **Active from**, **Active to**, and **Suspended** fields, as shown in the following screenshot:

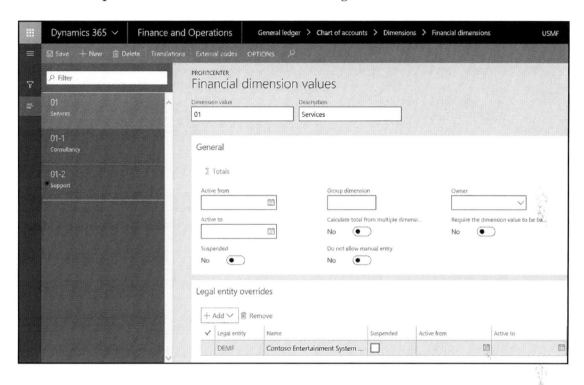

7. Select the sub-ledger values, for example, `Customers`. Then select the financial values called from the customer's master data and configure the dimension value by its dates of activation and/or suspension, as shown:

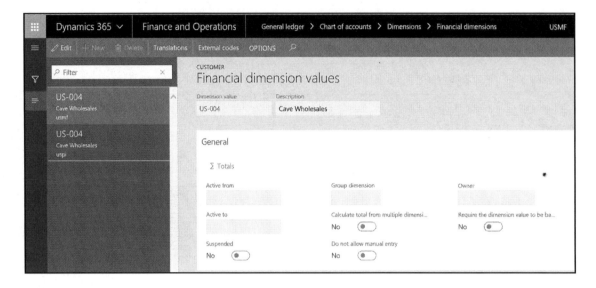

Financial dimensions controls

In the following section, we will discuss the financial dimensions controls. As seen in the following figure, in Microsoft Dynamics 365 for Finance and Operations there are two levels of controls. The first is on the financial dimension level, which consists of financial dimension activation, and requires the dimension value to be balanced. The second is on financial dimension values, which consists of do not allow manual entry, activation dates, suspend financial dimension, identify owner for the dimension, balance control, and legal entity overrides:

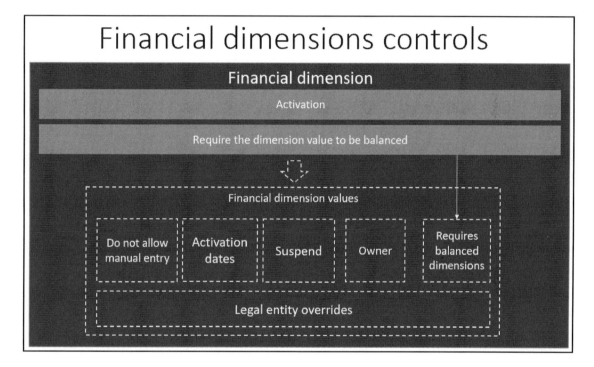

Financial dimension activation

The creation of a financial dimension does not make it available to be used; the financial dimension must be activated first. Whenever a new financial dimension is created in the application, users receive a message indicating that the financial dimension is not ready to be used until dimension activation is run. The following screenshot illustrates the message:

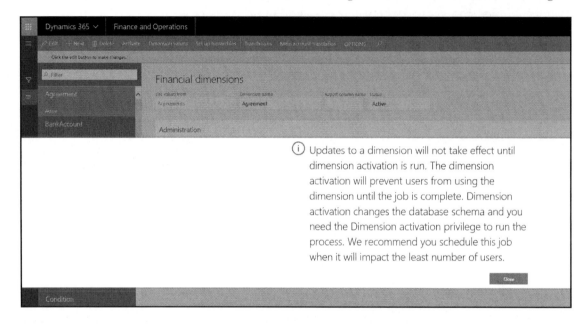

To activate the financial dimension, go to **General ledger | Chart of accounts | Dimensions | Financial dimensions**, then select **Activate**—the following screenshot illustrates the activation message:

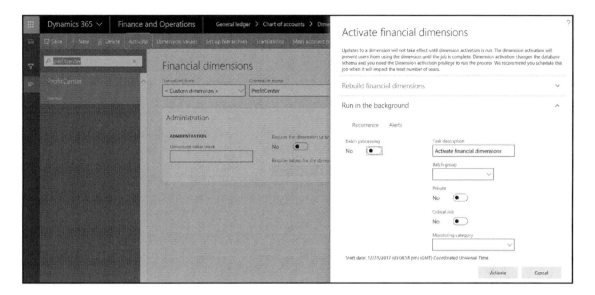

The activation process could be run manually or in a batch job.

Adding a financial dimension to the account structure is covered in a separate section in this chapter.

Require financial dimension to be balanced

The controller may need to ensure the balancing of specific financial dimensions. In Microsoft Dynamics 365 for Finance and Operations, the financial consultant can optionally define a balancing financial dimension. On the **General** fast tab (under **General ledger** | **Chart of accounts** | **Dimensions** | **Financial dimensions**), you can define the financial dimension that should be balanced. Then, whenever transactions are posted to that financial dimension, the system automatically creates and posts entries to make the financial dimension balanced.

Do not allow manual entries

The financial controller may need to restrict posted transactions to the financial dimension to be posted from sub-ledgers, and prevent posting manual entries to it. This is the same concept that we discussed in main accounts controls. The following screenshot shows **Do not allow manual entry** under **General ledger** | **Chart of accounts** | **Dimensions** | **Financial dimensions**:

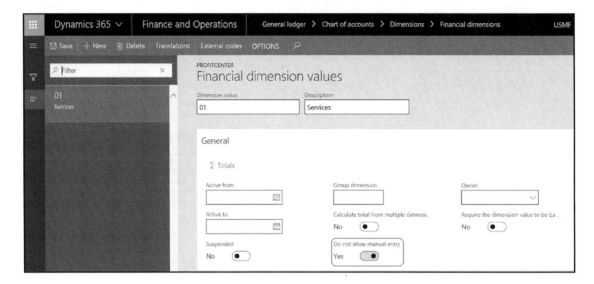

In the course of the transaction, if an end user selects the financial dimension, the system will throw an error message indicating that the selected financial dimension is not allowed for manual entry. The following screenshot shows the general journal entry under **General ledger | Journal entries | General journals** and illustrates the warning message:

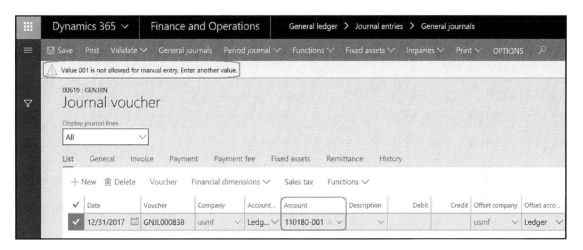

Dates activation

The activation date is commonly used for newly created dimensions (which will be active for operations at a future date) and in another scenario for main accounts (which can be deactivated after a specific period), as shown in the following screenshot:

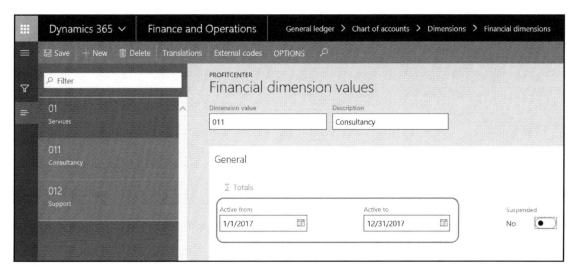

If an accountant wants to work with a main account, but it has not been a day since its activation, a message bar will pop up during the processing of a transaction that will state that dimension ##### is not active, as shown in the following screenshot:

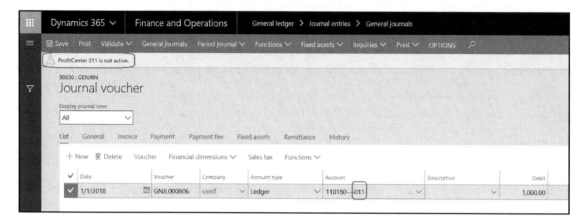

Suspending financial dimensions

The suspending financial dimensions is used in cases where there is a dimension that needs to be stopped from an operation, as it will not be used any more. As shown in the following screenshot, there is a control to suspend a financial dimension from operational posting:

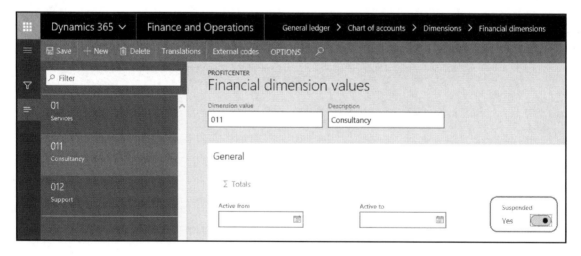

During the processing of a transaction, if an accountant selects a financial dimension that is suspended, a message bar will pop up stating that financial dimension ##### is closed, as shown in the following screenshot:

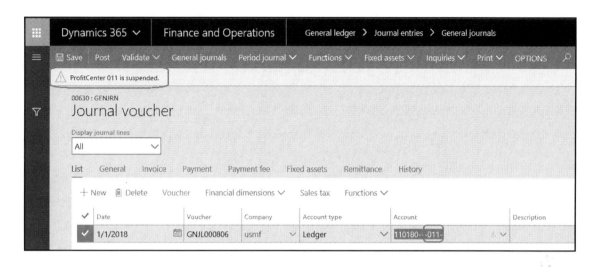

Assigning an owner to a financial dimension

Each financial dimension could be assigned to an owner, and this could be used in the purchase requisitions reviews. The workflow process uses the financial dimension owner to determine whom to route the expenditure to. The following screenshot shows the owner assignment on the financial-dimension level:

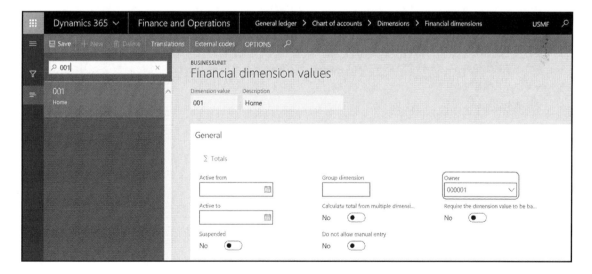

Configuring the account structure

The account structure's configuration identifies the required dimensions for the main account. The account structure is attached to the company's ledger setup (refer to `Chapter 2`, *Understanding the General Ledger*). As you can see in the following diagram, an account structure is a combination of the main account and financial dimensions:

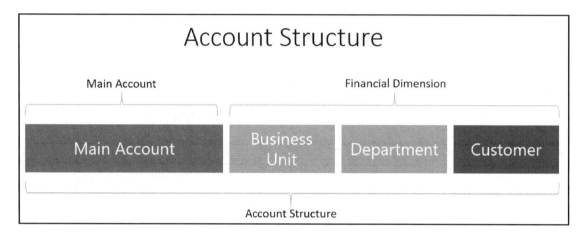

Microsoft Dynamics 365 for Finance and Operations provides flexibility to add the account structure for main accounts, with any combination of financial dimensions. The following section illustrates the account structure configuration.

1. Navigate to **General ledger** | **Chart of accounts** | **Structures** | **Configure account structures** to configure the account structures. As you can see in the following screenshot, **Configure account structures** should be in the edit mode to be edited:

2. Add a segment (financial dimension) to the account structure that is already defined (regardless of whether it has user-defined or system-defined dimensions) by clicking on the **Add segment** option, as shown in the following screenshot:

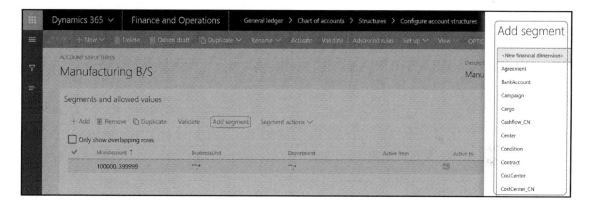

3. Microsoft Dynamics 365 for Finance and Operations provides an option to identify the main account by identifying one specific account and/or a part of the main accounts. This is done by selecting **Allowed value details**, as shown in the following screenshot. In addition to that, accepting a blank (null) value in the dimension is possible. The feature of accepting a value or keeping it blank is introduced prior to Microsoft Dynamics 365 for Finance and Operations, and it allows users to leave the dimension blank; this provides the availability to use the filtration option:

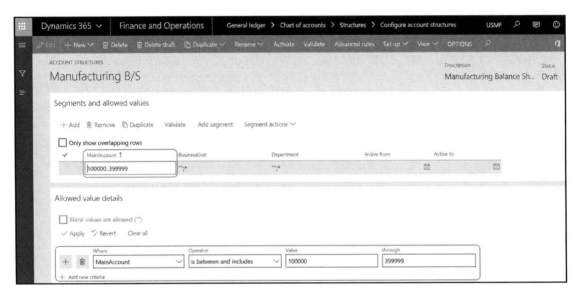

4. As you can see in the following screenshot, it is possible to arrange the order of the dimensions by moving the segments to the left or right, or by clicking to the **Segment actions**:

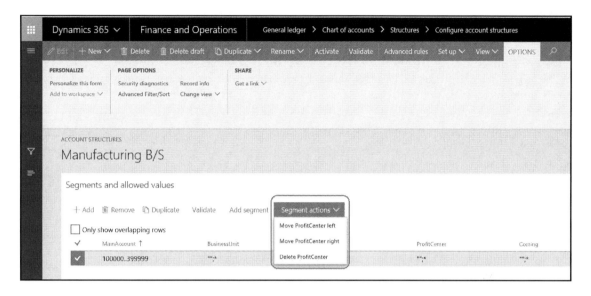

5. To apply the **ACCOUNT STRUCTURES** configuration, it must be activated, as shown in the following screenshot:

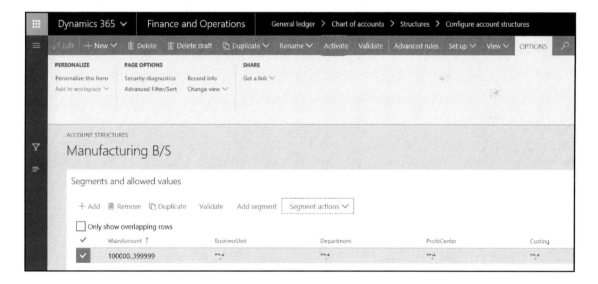

In Microsoft Dynamics 365 for Finance and Operations, there a fact box in the **ACCOUNT STRUCTURES** form that shows the legal entities that use the account structure.

Advanced rules structure

There is a limitation in the account structure—you can have only 10 dimensions, but more dimensions may be required. The **advanced rules structure** can add an unlimited number of dimensions. The concept of the advanced rules structure is to create an advanced rule structure record, add the required segments to it, and activate it. This also involves attaching it to the account structure. The following diagram illustrates the concept of the advanced rules structure:

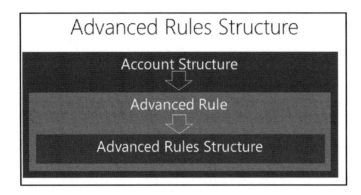

The following section illustrates the advanced rules and advanced account structure configuration.

1. In order to create an advanced rules structure, navigate to **General ledger | Chart of accounts | Structures | Advanced rule structures**, as shown in the following screenshot:

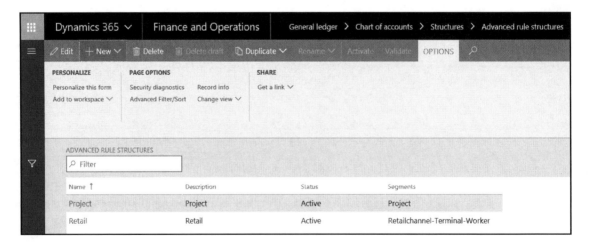

2. Click on a record or the **New** button to create a new record. Now, this action will open a new form, click on **Edit**, then **Add segment** to add dimension segments, and then click on **Activate**:

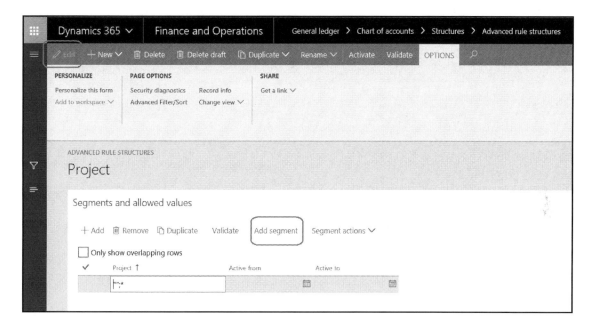

3. In order to attach the advanced rule structure to the account structure, navigate to **General ledger | Setup | Chart of accounts | Structures | Configure account structures**. On the account structure form, ensure that it is in the edit mode, and then click on **Advanced rule** in the ribbon. Create a new record by clicking on the **New** button. After entering the ID and description, move to the **Advanced rule structures** fast tab, click on **Add** and select the **Advanced rule structure** value. Then, make sure you activate the account structure configuration:

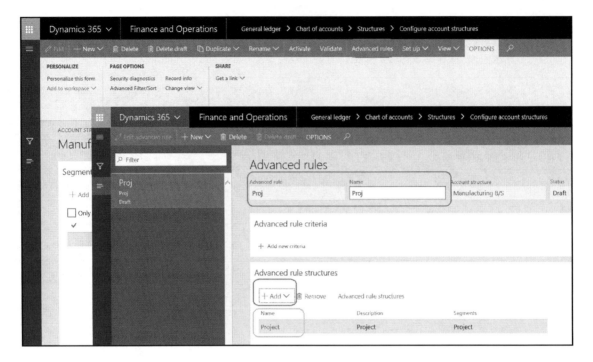

4. This allows the system to add extra dimensions based on the advanced rule structure. If you navigate to **General Ledger** | **Journal entries** | **General journals**, then in the voucher line, you'll see the custom dimensions:

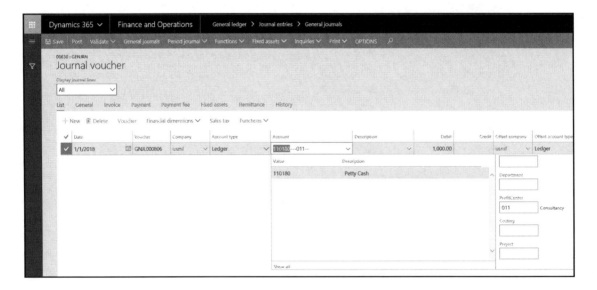

In Microsoft Dynamics 365 for Finance and Operations, there is a fact box in the account structure form that shows the assigned advanced structure rules.

Fixed dimension

In some cases, there is a business requirement to fix a particular dimension on a specific main account. A fixed dimension is at the company level. In order to activate the fixed financial dimension, the account should be specified for a particular company.

In order to set up a financial dimension on the main account, navigate to **General ledger | Chart of accounts | Accounts | Chart of accounts**, and then select the **Chart of accounts**. Then click on **Edit**. This will open the main accounts in the edit mode. As shown in following screenshot, select a specific account, then go to the **Legal entity overrides** fast tab, and then select the company ID in the **Legal entity** field. This will show the **Default financial dimensions** tab.

Here, the dimension could be **Not fixed**, which means the dimension value will be as proposed, or **Fixed value**, which means the dimension value will always be used for this main account. When we select a fixed value, a dialog box will always pop up:

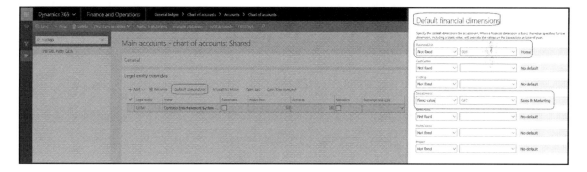

The result of this setup when we create and post the general journal looks like what is shown in the following screenshot. Navigate to **General ledger | Journal entries | General journals** and do not select the **Department** value with the `110180` account. Now post the journal. Under the voucher inquiry, the system fixes the **Department** dimension value on the account as per the main account setup:

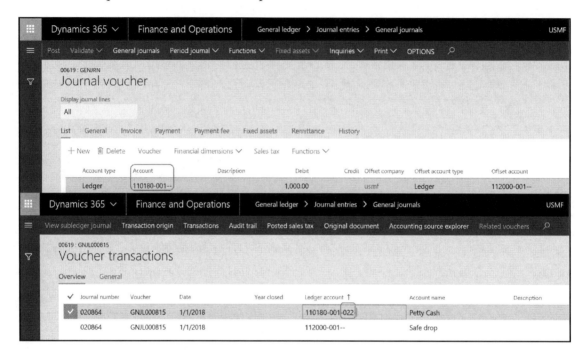

Posting types in Microsoft Dynamics 365 for Finance and Operations

In Microsoft Dynamics 365 for Finance and Operations, there are two ways to post transactions to the main account. The first way is through the posting profile, which represents the integration point between the general ledger and sub-ledger and generates the financial entries automatically, according to the posting profile's setup. The second way is the journal entries, which post directly to the ledger accounts.

The posting profile concept

Posting profiles are the point of integration between the sub-ledger (fixed assets, accounts payable, inventory, banks, accounts receivable, project, and production) and the general ledger. It is a set of main accounts that are used to generate the automatic ledger entry in which a transaction has occurred. It is possible to select different main accounts for each type of sub-ledger transaction. Microsoft Dynamics 365 for Finance and Operations offers flexibility in setting up posting profiles. Posting could be on four different levels, as shown:

- **All**: Any transaction occurring on any sub-ledger such as customers, vendors, items, and/or items will be redirected to the main account, which is assigned to all the customers, vendors, and/or items.
- **Group B**: Any transaction for a particular customer, vendor, and/or item inherits the posting profile of the customer, vendor, and/or item group to which they are assigned.
- **Category**: Any transaction for a particular item category inherits the posting profile of the item category to which they are assigned. This is only available for item and inventory transactions.
- **Table**: Any transaction that occurs for a sub-ledger, vendor, and/or item will be directed to the ledger account, which is assigned to the posting profile.

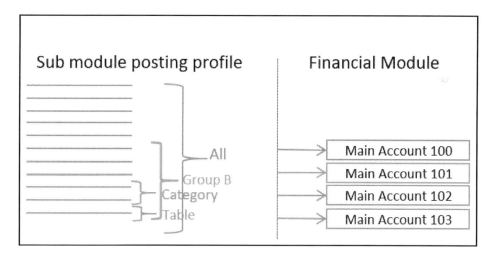

The common question during the design phase is this: which level out of **All**, **Group B**, and **Table** will prevail over the other levels? Customers can be assigned to a specific group, but in some exceptions, such as this one, the customer should be directed to another ledger account. The lowest level of all is **Table**, which specifies the customer ID and will prevail over **Group B** and **All**.

To access the posting profile, navigate to the following paths:

- For the accounts payable posting profiles, navigate to **Accounts payable** | **Setup** | **Vendor posting profiles**
- For the accounts receivable posting profiles, navigate to **Accounts receivable** | **Setup** | **Customer posting profiles**
- For the inventory posting profile, navigate to **Inventory management** | **Setup** | **Posting** | **Posting**

The ledger accounts specified in the posting profile must not allow a manual entry to be created in the general ledger, to preserve the integrity between the general ledger and sub-ledger.

Journal posting

The journal model in Microsoft Dynamics 365 for Finance and Operations is a journal header that contains voucher lines. Here, the default data in the journal name (header), such as currency and sales tax, is copied to the voucher lines. This data can also be changed in the voucher lines. Every sub-ledger has its own journal name based on the transaction type. Navigate to **General ledger** | **Journal setup** | **Journal names** to access the journal names.

The voucher line can be a ledger account, vendor account, customer account, fixed asset, bank, or project. If the selected account is an option other than the ledger account, the sub-ledger posting profile will direct the posting to the ledger account.

Journal posting controls is the only component of journal posting, the rest are its sub-components; let's look at it here.

Journal posting controls: The journal posting controls consist of embedded controls that cannot be changed or avoided. The voucher balance and other controls form the basic setup for each journal name that can be applied at any time. This can be explained as follows:

- **Voucher balance and journal balance**: The basic accounting principle, which is a financial entry, must be balanced so that the debit side is equal to the credit side. Microsoft Dynamics 365 for Finance and Operations prevents posting any transaction if there are any discrepancies between the transactions sides (debit or credit). This validation occurs on the voucher line as well as the journal.
- **Transaction date**: The balance voucher must be posted on the same date. Microsoft Dynamics 365 for Finance and Operations applies the concept of one-line voucher entry and two-line entries. This control is validated if the entry appears on two lines.
- **Offset account**: Fixing an offset account on a specific journal will prevent users from changing or modifying the offset account on the voucher line. It can be a proposal and it may be changed at the transaction level.
- **Blocking the journal name**: During the daily operations on the journal entries in Microsoft Dynamics 365 for Finance and Operations, whether these journals are related to the general ledger, fixed assets, accounts payable, accounts receivable, inventory journals movement, transfer journals, or BOM, it is normal to have more than one journal name under the same journal type. Each journal name serves a specific business transaction based on the business requirements gathered in the analysis phase. Microsoft Dynamics 365 for Finance and Operations gives this control to a private user group in the journal name configuration. This allows the use of that journal only for the appropriate user group.
- **Journal approvals**: Approval controls on the general ledger journals are divided into two levels. The first level is the one-step approval, and the second level is the workflow approval. The workflow approval requires an automatic batch job to run at a specific interval in order to ensure that the approvers receive the documents that require approval. The two levels of approval can be explained as follows:
    - **One-step approval**: This is considered as a simple configuration for the journal's approvals, as it assigns a user group to be the approval group for a specific journal name.
    - **Workflow approval**: This approval needs to configure a workflow approval step. This gives you the flexibility to add a complex approval matrix that will be triggered if the condition occurs on the journal. Thus, the workflow approval offers more control on journal posting.

Financial dimensions' posting mechanism in transaction documents

The posting of financial dimensions in transaction documents (purchase order and sales order) has a specific mechanism that complies with financial posting. Here, at the first posting stage (product receipt/packing slip), the entries are generated from the item posting profile; in other words, from the lines. And at the second posting stage (invoice), the entries are generated from the header that reverses the first stage entry and generates the invoice entry from the header posting profile and the inventory posting profile.

Microsoft Dynamics 365 for Finance and Operations has two options of how financial dimensions are posted: the first option is source document and the second option is accounting distribution. The following diagram illustrates financial dimension posting:

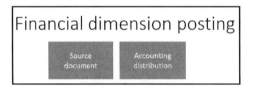

This configuration is located on **General ledger | Ledger setup | General ledger parameters** under the **Accounting rules** fast tab, as shown in this screenshot:

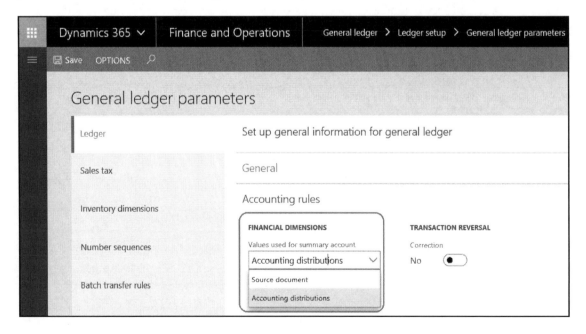

In the **Accounting rules** fast tab, two options will be available:

- **Source document**: Select the **Source document** option to display the financial dimension values from the **Financial dimensions** tab on the header of the source document as the offsetting sub-ledger journal account entries. The following diagram illustrates the logic of dimensions posting when using the **Source document** option:

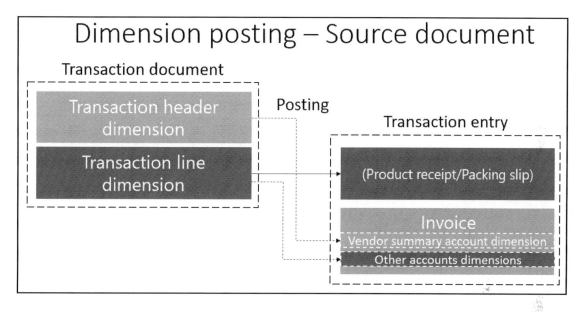

The autogenerated financial transactions of the purchase order are the product receipt and invoice. The financial dimensions are automatically inherited from the purchase order form (purchase order header and purchase order lines). The financial dimension's assignment to voucher entries has a certain mechanism; it should be addressed and communicated with the controllership to make them aware of this treatment. This mechanism is as follows:

- The generated voucher entry, which represents the invoice, inherits the financial dimensions from the purchase order header for vendor summary account. The **purchase order header** contains information on assigning the vendor, their address, payment terms, method of payment, and financial dimension. To access the purchase order header, navigate to **Procurement and sourcing** | **Purchase orders** | **All purchase orders** | **Header** view as shown in the following screenshot:

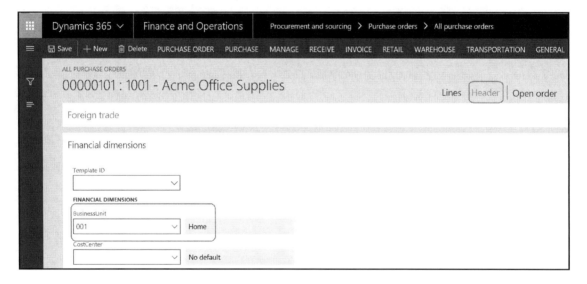

- The generated voucher entry, which represents the product receipt, inherits the financial dimensions from the purchase order lines. The **purchase order lines** contain information on assigning the item, its quantity, price, and financial dimension. To access purchase order lines, navigate to **Procurement and sourcing** | **Purchase orders** | **All purchase orders** | **Lines** view as shown in the following screenshot:

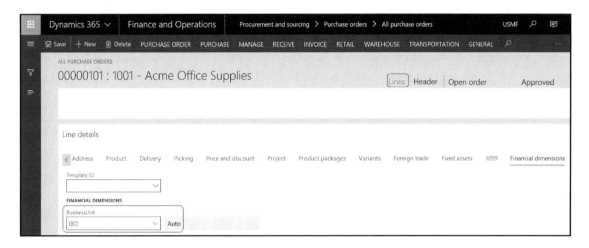

The posted voucher entry of the product receipt is as shown in the following screenshot. To access the product receipt voucher, from the purchase order form go to the **Receive** tab, then go to **Journals** and select **Product receipt**. In the product receipt form, go to **Voucher**:

 The product receipt entry inherits the financial dimensions from the purchase order lines. In this demonstration, the entry assigned dimension 002.

The posted voucher entry of purchase order invoice is as shown in the following screenshot. To access the invoice voucher, from the purchase order form go to the **Invoice** tab, then **Journals** and select **Invoice.** In the product receipt form, go to **Voucher**:

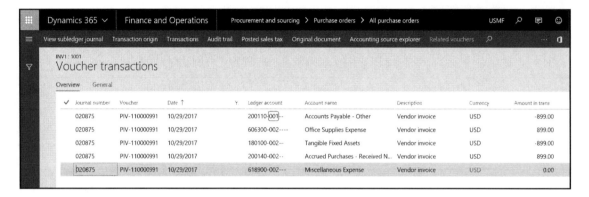

 The invoice entry inherits the financial dimensions from the purchase order header for the vendor summary account. In this demonstration, the vendor summary account entry has assigned dimension 001. The rest of the dimensions are recalled from the purchase lines.

- **Accounting distribution**: Select accounting distribution option to create the offsetting sub-ledger journal account entries, based on the financial dimension values on the accounting distribution. The following diagram illustrates the logic of dimensions posting when using the accounting distribution option:

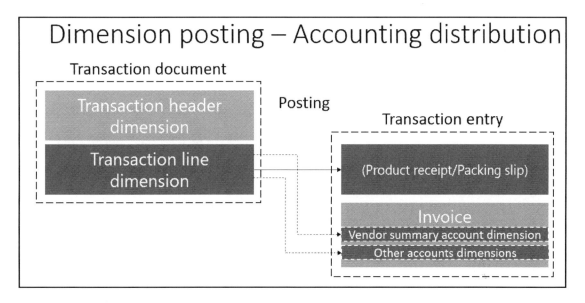

The autogenerated financial transactions of the purchase order are product receipt and invoice. The financial dimensions are automatically inherited from the purchase order form (purchase order header and purchase order lines). The financial dimension's assignment to voucher entries has a certain mechanism; it should be addressed and communicated with the controllership to make them aware of this treatment. This mechanism is as follows:

- The generated voucher entry, which represents the product receipt, inherits the financial dimensions from the purchase order lines
- The generated voucher entry, which represents the invoice, inherits the financial dimensions from the purchase order lines for the vendor summary account

Exploring dimension reporting

Overall, this chapter covers the financial dimension model from business and application angles. The required configuration for the main accounts and the account structure directly affects the accuracy of the data entered, by controlling the dimensions' selection and validation.

The following section will explore financial dimensions' reporting capabilities in a trial balance and dimension statement.

Financial dimension sets

Financial dimension sets are the result of reporting transactions based on financial dimensions. They can be a combination of more than one financial dimension. Financial dimension sets are initially designed, along with the designing of financial dimensions, in the design phase, to accommodate the reporting perspective, and they can be extended during the operations.

As you can see in the following diagram, the financial dimension set is to be used as a focal point in reporting, where it can analyze numbers by one dimension focus or more than one focus:

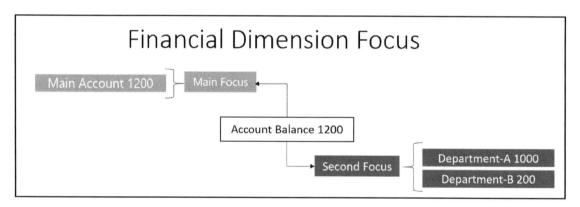

Identify the financial dimension set by selecting one or more dimensions from **AVAILABLE FINANCIAL DIMENSIONS** as an analyzing level, as shown in the following screenshot:

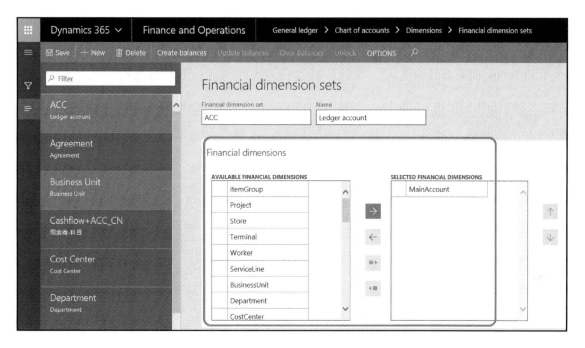

To access the financial dimension sets, navigate to **General ledger | Chart of accounts | Dimensions | Financial dimension sets**.

Trial balance is one of the major financial reports where it will be able to generate a transaction's trial balance for all the main accounts. In Microsoft Dynamics 365 for Finance and Operations, this report is a form.

To access **Trial balance**, navigate to **General ledger | Inquiries and reports | Trial balance**, as shown in the following screenshot.

Identify the reporting date of the trial balance by entering the following dates:

- **From date**: In this field, enter the start date of the report date range
- **To date**: In this field, enter the end date of the report date range

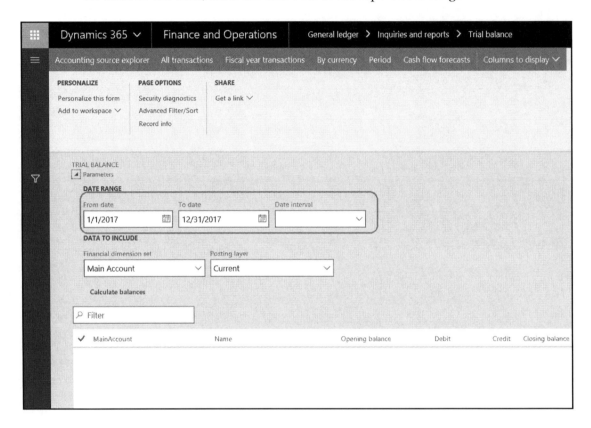

 The date range of **Trial balance** should be within one fiscal year. Thus, a warning message bar should be displayed in the following format: **From date** is in fiscal year 20XX, **To date** is in fiscal year 20XX. Dates must be in the same fiscal year.

For example, **From date** is in fiscal year 2010, **To date** is in fiscal year 2011.

Identify **Financial dimension set** as a focus option, as shown in this screenshot:

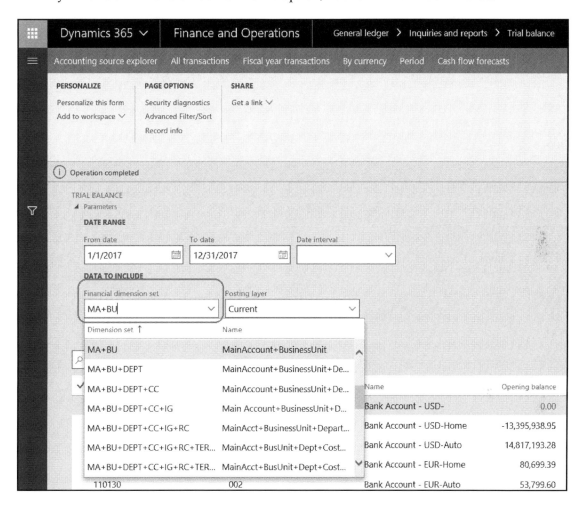

Trial balance is broken down by the selected **Financial dimension set**, as shown in the following screenshot:

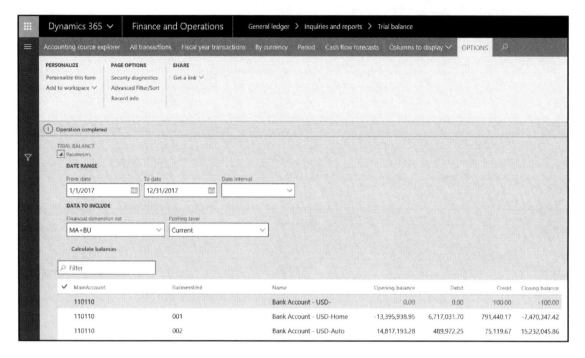

Trial balance contains the following information:

- **Ledger account**: This shows the main account or the account structure dimension
- **Opening balance**: This shows the opening balance amount after closing the fiscal year
- **Debit**: This shows the transaction of the amount debited on that account (monthly movement)
- **Credit**: This shows the transaction of the amount credited on that account (monthly movement)
- **Closing balance**: This shows the closing balance for that account at the end; the date range is calculated as the sum of the net difference and the opening balance

To retrieve data in trial balance form, the user should click on **Calculate balance**.

The **Dimension** statement is the most commonly generated report by the controller to examine the main account balance, along with the dimensions' allocation. Navigate to **General ledger** | **Inquiries and reports** | **Ledger reports** | **Dimension statement** to access the dimension statement.

The financial dimensions' report filtration identifies the following parameters:

Parameter	Description
Primary financial dimension set	This is used to select the primary financial dimension set for the report.
Secondary financial dimension set	This is used to select the secondary financial dimension set for the report.
Date interval	This is used to select the current date interval for the report.
From date	This is used to enter or select the start of the date range to print transactions for.
To date	This is used to enter or select the end of the date range to print transactions for.
New page	Select this checkbox to insert a page break between each account.

Parameter	Description
Posting layer	This is used to select how the posting layer or combination of posting layers should be included for the selected column such as the following: • **Current**: This column will contain transactions that are included in the current posting layer • **Operations**: This column will contain transactions that are included in the current posting layer or the operations posting layer • **Tax**: This column will contain transactions that are included in the Microsoft Dynamics 365 for Finance and Operations posting layer • **Operations minus tax**: This column will contain the net transactions from the operations posting layer minus the tax posting layer • **Only operations**: This column will contain transactions that are included in the operations posting layer • **Only tax**: This column will contain transactions that are included in the tax posting layer • **Operations plus tax**: This column will contain transactions that are included in the operations posting layer or the tax posting layer • **Total**: This column will contain transactions that are included in the current posting layer, operations posting layer, or tax posting layer
Include the opening transaction amounts in detail	Select this checkbox to include the opening transactions from the line of the report that lists the opening balance. Opening transactions are displayed in the report details.
Closing transactions	Select this checkbox to display the closing transactions as transactions. Clear this checkbox to display the closing transactions in the closing balance in the summary form.

The following screenshot shows the **Statement by dimensions** report query:

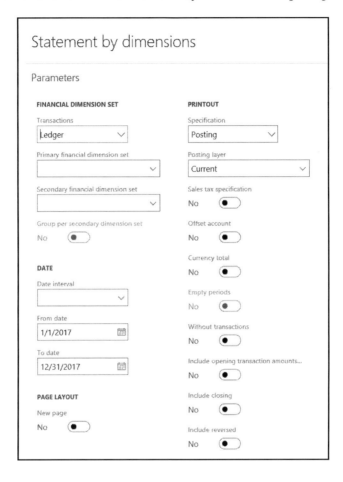

As you can see in the next screenshot, the dimension statement breaks down the account balance by business unit:

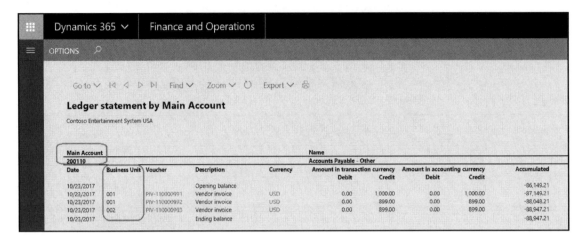

Summary

In this chapter, we covered the business concept of financial dimensions, and explored the practical usage of financial dimensions as a control and analysis tool. Then we moved to the segmentation of ledger accounts and the way it works. We also covered Microsoft Dynamics 365 for Finance and Operations posting profile types, journal posting, and its controls, then discussed the financial dimensions' posting mechanism in transaction documents, and finally covered financial dimensions' reporting.

In the next chapter, we will explore sales tax and its integration with other modules, sales tax calculation, and the full cycle of the sales tax process, in addition to the withholding tax concept.

4
Understanding Sales Tax

The sales tax module is the place where a company's sales tax and withholding tax are configured and listed. In this module, a company can calculate the sales tax on each transaction as per the legal requirements, and process the tax payments to tax authorities. The financial controller and chief financial officer will be able to assess sales tax and withholding accuracy. This chapter covers the following topics:

- Exploring sales tax high-level cycles and entries
- Understanding sales tax integration with other modules
- Understanding sales tax setup and configuration
- Exploring the sales tax mechanism, calculations, and entries
- Exploring conditional sales tax
- Understanding withholding tax

Exploring sales tax high-level cycles and entries

In this section, we will explore the sales tax business process, and the generated financial entries in tax payable and tax receivables.

Sales tax business process

Sales tax is a tax paid to the government for the trading of some goods and services. As shown in the following diagram, the sales tax receivable is generated from vendor transactions, whether from a purchase order invoice or service invoice. The sales tax payable is generated from customer transactions, whether from a sales order invoice or a service invoice. Then, the net of the tax receivable and tax payable is settled to be paid to the sales tax authority:

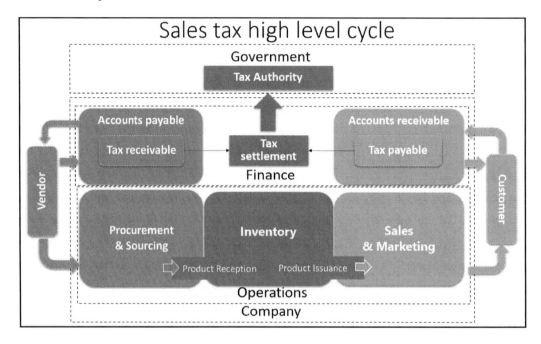

The generated financial entries in the sales tax cycle are as follows:

- **Tax receivable—accounts payable**: The financial entries generated in the course of posting the vendor invoice transaction are debiting expenses, sales tax, and crediting accounts payable.

- **Tax payable—accounts receivable**: The financial entries generated in the course of posting the customer invoice are debiting accounts receivable, crediting revenue, and sales tax.

- **Tax settlement**: The financial entries generated in the course of posting sales tax settlements are creating transactions for tax payable and tax receivable, as follows:
    - Debiting the sales tax amount that was generated in sales tax receivable
    - Crediting the sales tax amount that was generated in sales tax payable

    Then, the tax authority liability is recorded on the credit side during tax settlement and, optionally, the credit side could be posted to a vendor submodule or to a ledger account, as follows:

    - The tax authority liability could be posted to a vendor account that is integrated with accounts payable and execute the payment as a vendor payment transaction from the accounts payable module.
    - The tax authority liability could be a sales tax settlement ledger account that represents the credit side and the payment is posted against the sales tax settlement account.

The following diagram illustrates the financial entries that are generated during vendor invoice, customer invoice, and sales tax settlement:

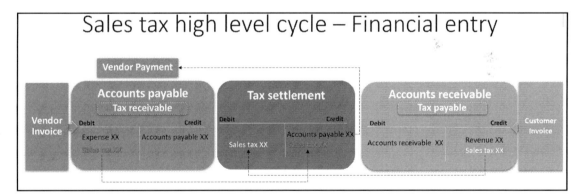

Understanding sales tax integration with other modules

In this section, we will explore the integration between the sales tax submodule and general ledger, accounts payable, accounts receivable, and inventory management modules. We will also illustrate the integration elements of each module at a high level.

Sales tax integration points

In Microsoft Dynamics 365 for Finance and Operations, sales tax is a separate module. Sales tax is integrated with general ledger, accounts payable, accounts receivables, and inventory management:

- The **tax module** is the place to set up sales tax calculations, tax authorities, and settlement periods. The general ledger is the place to set up sales tax controls and mechanisms that configure tax deduction options.
- The **accounts payable module** is the place to set up sales tax options and execute vendor transactions (invoices and payments).
- The **accounts receivable module** is the place to set up sales tax options and execute customer transactions (invoices and payments).
- The **inventory management module** is the place to set up items that are subject to sales tax.

The following diagram illustrates sales tax integration with other modules:

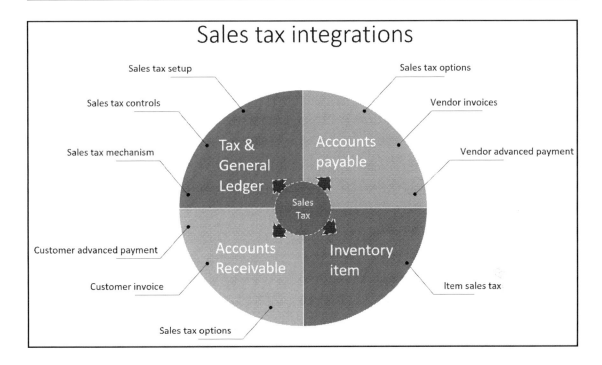

Sales tax setup and configuration

In this section, we will be discussing the sales tax setup elements and the sales tax mechanism in Microsoft Dynamics 365 for Finance and Operations, in addition to different configuration options that affect sales tax calculation and posting.

Sales tax setup elements

At the heart of sales tax is sales tax code. It carries settlement periods, ledger posting groups, and tax calculations. The settlement periods contain settlement period intervals, terms of payment, and optionally, the vendor ID, which represents the sales tax authority. Then, there are two main groups where the tax code is attached. The first is the sales tax group, which is assigned to vendors, customers, or ledger accounts. The second group is the item sales tax group, which is assigned to items or ledger accounts.

The following diagram illustrates the sales tax elements:

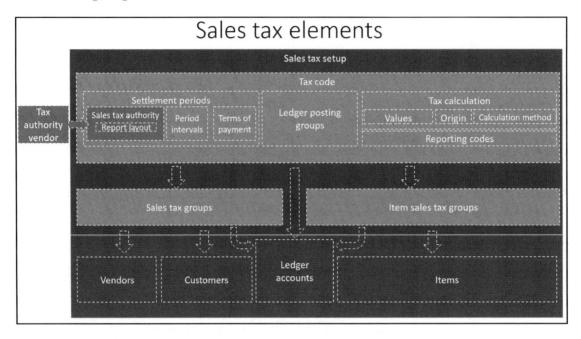

To create a sales tax authority, go to **Tax** | **Indirect taxes** | **Sales tax** | **Sales tax authorities**. The **Sales tax authorities** form contains a vendor account ID, which the sales tax is posted to. Identify the **Report layout** and the **Rounding form**, either by selecting **Downward**, **Rounding-up**, or **Own advantage**. Also set the **Round-off** requirements. All this information is captured during the analysis phase, and should be verified by the customer's financial controller during the design and testing phases. The following screenshot shows the **Sales tax authorities** form and rounding options:

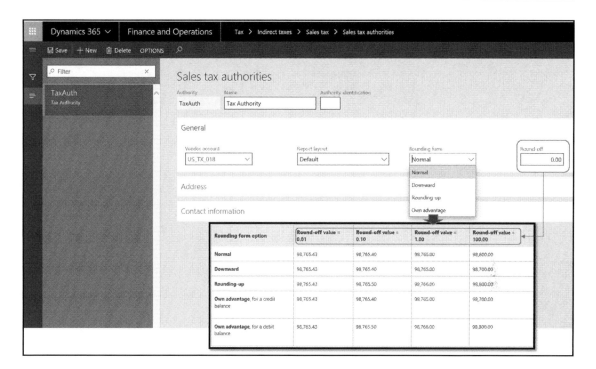

 The preceding rounding table shows how an amount of **98,765.43** is rounded by using each rounding method.

The sales tax settlement period form contains the authority code that we identified earlier (terms of payment can be assigned optionally), and the period interval unit in days, months, or years.

 Sales tax settlement can also be run using batch processing.

As shown in the following screenshot, the sales tax settlement periods form can be accessed from **Tax | Indirect taxes | Sales tax | Sales tax settlement periods**:

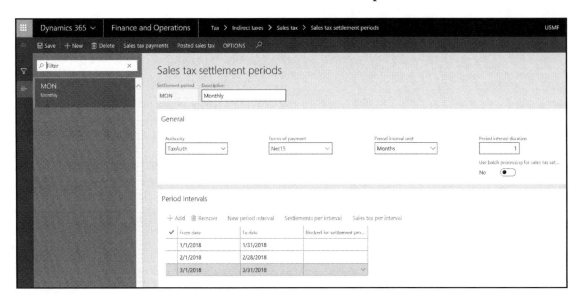

Ledger posting groups are the integration point between the tax and general ledger, where we identify which accounts will be used for tax posting during the vendor invoice, customer invoice, and sales tax settlement. To access **Ledger posting groups**, go to **Tax | Setup | Sales tax | Ledger posting groups**, as shown in the following screenshot:

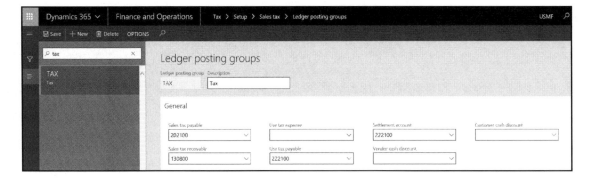

The sales tax mechanism in Microsoft Dynamics 365 for Finance and Operations

Sales tax is registered on both the vendor/customer level and the item level, to cope with international suppliers that show different tax rates for the same item. The system must recognize the same tax rate in the vendor/customer and item levels to process the transaction. The calculated sales tax on the finance module is shown in the following figure:

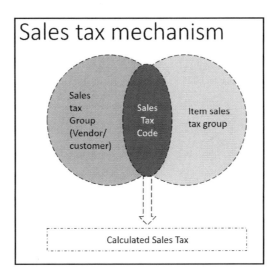

In order to create the sales tax code, navigate to **Tax** | **Indirect taxes** | **Sales tax** | **Sales tax codes**. In the **General** fast tab, assign the **Settlement period** and **Ledger posting group**. In the **Calculation** fast tab, assign the following parameters:

- **Origin**: This is the field that represents the origin from which the sales tax is calculated
- **Marginal base**: This represents the base of tax limits
- **Calculation method**: This represents whether the sales tax is calculated for the entire amount or for just part of it

These parameters are shown in the following screenshot:

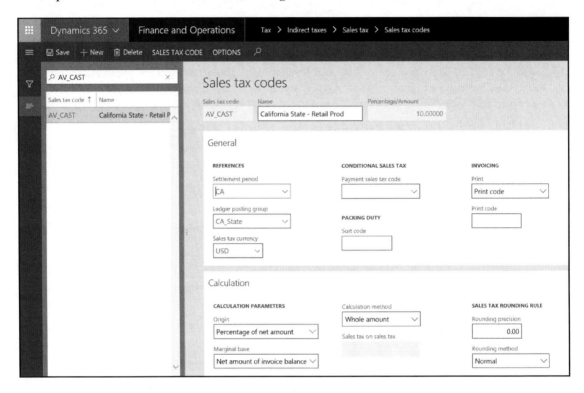

To identify the sales tax percentage, go to **SALES TAX CODE** | **Values**. Enter a value in the **Value** field, as shown in the following screenshot:

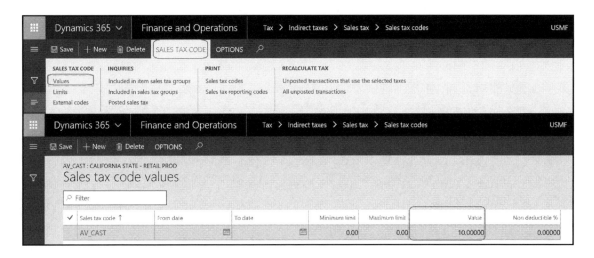

Sales tax can be changed based on government regulations. To apply the changes in sales tax based on government regulations, add a new line and enter the starting date to apply the new tax rate.

In order to create a sales tax group, navigate to **Tax** | **Indirect taxes** | **Sales tax** | **Sales tax groups**. Under the **Setup** fast tab, add the **Sales tax code** value, as shown in the following screenshot:

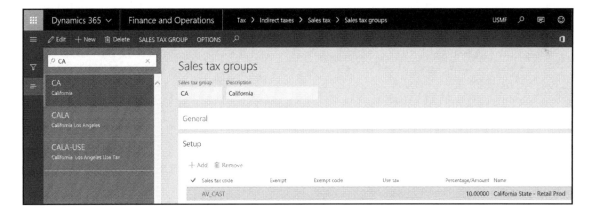

In order to create an item sales tax group, navigate to **Tax** | **Indirect taxes** | **Sales tax** | **Item sales tax groups**. Under the **Setup** fast tab, click on **Add** and enter the **Sales tax code** value, as shown in the following screenshot:

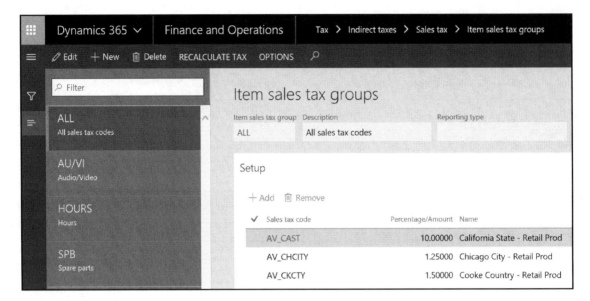

In order to apply the sales tax in a general ledger transaction, navigate to **General ledger** | **Journal entries** | **General journals**. Create a new journal, and then move to voucher lines.

In the voucher line, select the **Account type** value as **Vendor**, select the vendor ID, enter 1,000 as the **Credit** amount, and select the **Offset account** value. Then, select the **Sales tax group** and **Item sales tax group** fields; the system will calculate the sales tax amount, as shown in the following screenshot:

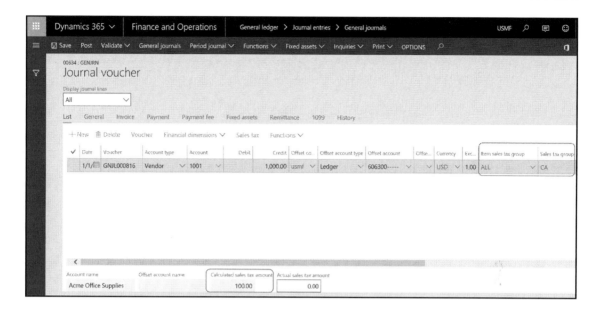

Sales tax calculation and posting configurations

There is an effect on the price based on the sales tax rule. Whether the price includes or excludes the sales tax can be defined as follows:

- **Price includes sales tax**: For a 10% sales tax and a 1,000 USD price, the system will allocate 1,000 USD to the vendor or customer summary account and 90.91 USD to the sales tax account. The following diagram illustrates the calculation and posting entries for tax receivable and tax payable:

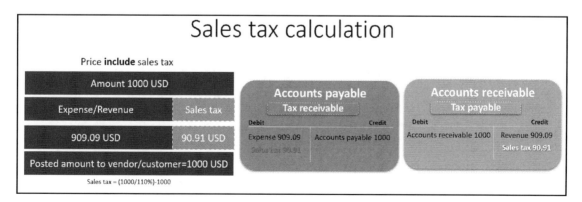

- **Price excludes sales tax**: For a 10% sales tax and a 1,000 USD price, the system will allocate 1,100 USD to the vendor/customer summary account and 100 USD to the sales tax account. The following diagram illustrates the calculation and posting entries for tax receivable and tax payable:

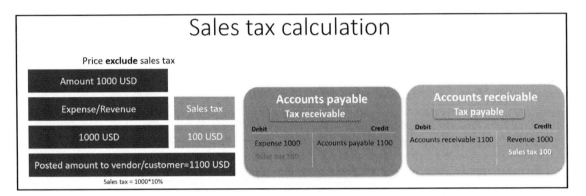

Please note that the price including the sales tax rule is configured from the following paths:

- Navigate to **General ledger** | **Ledger setup** | **General ledger parameters**, and then go to the **Sales tax** tab. Check the **Amounts include sales tax** checkbox.
- The vendor master data form can be accessed by navigating to the **Accounts payable** | **Vendors** | **All vendors** | **Invoice and delivery** fast tab. Check the **Price included sales tax** checkbox.
- The customer master data form can be accessed by navigating to the **Accounts receivable** | **Customers** | **All customers** | **Invoice and deliver** fast tab. Check the **Price included sales tax** checkbox.
- On transaction journals for example **General ledger** | **Journal entries** | **General journal**, then move under the **Setup** tab and check the **Price included sales tax** checkbox.
- On the sales order and purchase order headers, in the **Setup** fast tab, check the **Price included sales tax** checkbox.

There is a parameter that controls the sales tax posting for vendor invoices, allowing you to either add the tax amount to the expense account or to post the sales tax to a separate ledger account. This is under **Apply sales tax taxation rules**; you can find it under **Tax | Setup | Parameters | General ledger parameters | Sales tax**, as shown in the following screenshot:

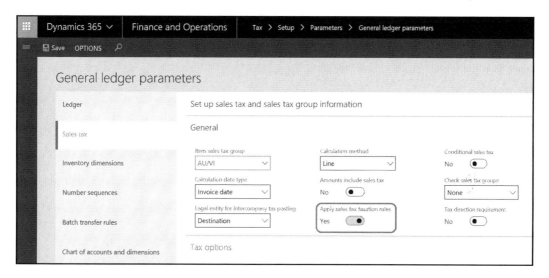

In the following section, we will walk you through the two different options of **Apply sales tax taxation rules**:

- **Apply sales tax taxation rules (Yes)**: If the controller requires you to add a sales tax amount to an expense account, this means there is no posting to a sales tax receivable account. It is disabled from the ledger posting groups form; this is illustrated in the **Ledger posting groups** form under **Tax | Setup | Sales tax | Ledger posting groups**, as shown in the following screenshot:

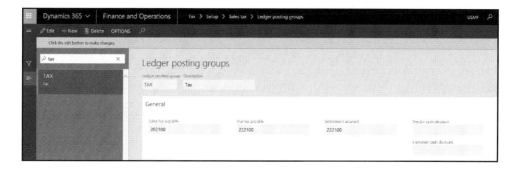

The following diagram illustrates that the financial entries in case of **Apply sales tax taxation rules** is set to **Yes**. The effect is on the tax receivable side, where the sales tax amount is added to the expense account. On the other hand, there is no effect on the tax payable side:

- **Apply sales tax taxation rules (No)**: If the controller requires the sales tax amount to be posted to a separate account for tax receivable transactions, this means that the tax receivable will be available in **Ledger posting groups**. This is illustrated in the **Ledger posting groups** form under **Tax | Setup | Sales tax | Ledger posting groups**, as shown in the following screenshot:

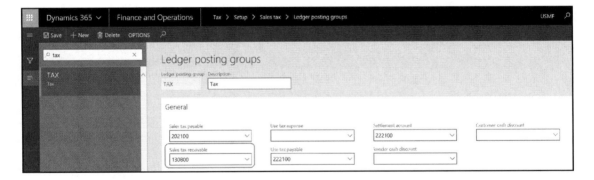

The following diagram illustrates the financial entries if **Apply sales tax taxation rules** is set to **No**. The effect is on the tax receivable side, where the sales tax amount is posted to the sales tax account. On the other hand, there is no effect on the tax payable side:

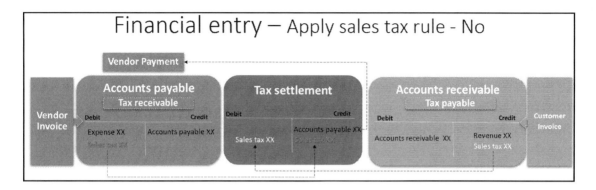

Sales tax calculations may be affected if there is a cash discount involved in the transaction. Microsoft Dynamics 365 for Finance and Operations has parameters to control sales tax calculations when it comes to a cash discount, whether sales tax is calculated before or after the cash discount. To access **Tax options**, go to **Tax** | **Setup** | **Parameters** | **General ledger parameters** and go to **Sales tax**. Then, go to the **Tax options** fast tab, as shown in the following screenshot:

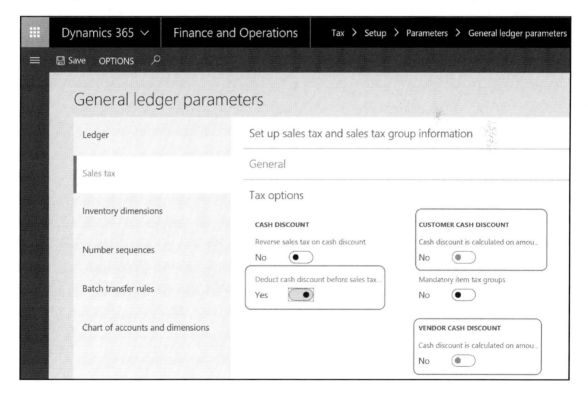

Cash discount is calculated on the amount, including the sales tax options for vendor and customer cash discount. These are set to **No** and grayed out if **Deduct cash discount before sales tax...** is set to **Yes**.

Exploring conditional sales tax

Conditional sales tax is paid to the tax authority when the payment is posted. In the following section, we will explore conditional sales tax setup, configurations, and entries.

Conditional tax business process

The conditional sales tax is captured in the course of payment execution and, during the invoice transaction, the sales tax amount is posted to the conditional tax main account. It will then be reversed after posting the payment, and it will post the sales tax amount. The following diagram illustrates the high-level cycle of conditional tax from the perspective of both tax receivable and tax payable:

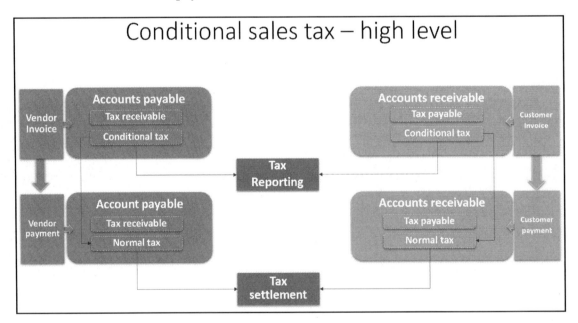

Conditional tax setup and configuration

The conditional tax should be activated first, then the conditional sales tax code should be identified and attached to the conditional sales tax code in the sales tax group and item sales tax. The invoice document will inherit the sales tax group and item sales tax group, where the conditional tax will be posted. In the course of payment transactions, the conditional tax entry is reversed, and the post to the tax account will be settled at the end of the period. The following diagram illustrates the conditional sales tax setup:

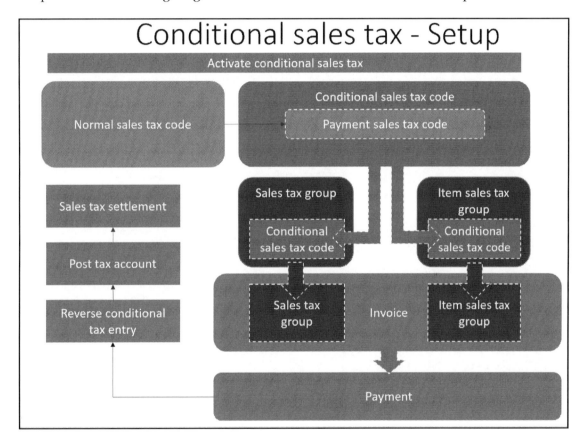

You need to create separate ledger posting groups and settlement periods for conditional sales tax codes.

In the conditional ledger posting group, make sure to create separate accounts for tax payable and tax receivable.

In order to activate conditional tax, go to **Tax** | **Setup** | **Parameters** | **General ledger parameters**, then select **Sales tax**, and move to the **General** fast tab, as shown in the following screenshot:

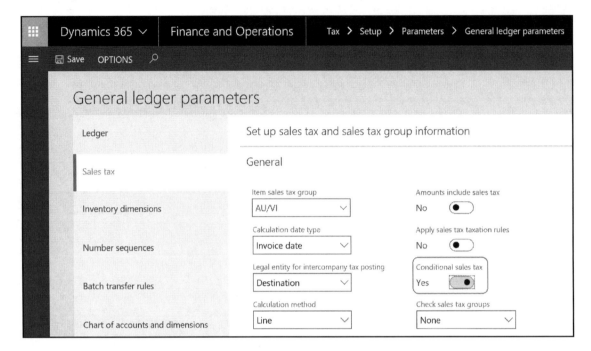

In order to create a conditional sales tax code, go to **Tax** | **Indirect taxes** | **Sales tax** | **Sales tax codes**, then move to the **General** fast tab to assign a sales tax code that will be used during payment, as shown in the following screenshot:

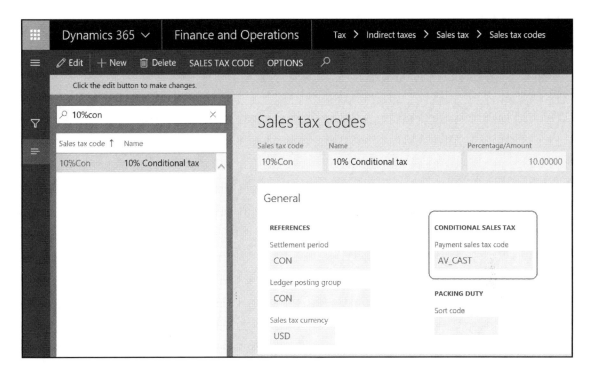

To add a conditional sales tax code to a sales tax group, go to **Tax | Indirect taxes | Sales tax | Sales tax groups**.

To add a conditional sales tax code to an item sales tax group, go to **Tax | Indirect taxes | Sales tax | Item sales tax groups**.

In the course of invoice transaction, select **Conditional sales tax group**, and **Conditional item sales tax group**. The system will generate the conditional tax entry and, during payment, the system will reverse the conditional tax transaction and post it to the sales tax account. The following diagram illustrates the entries:

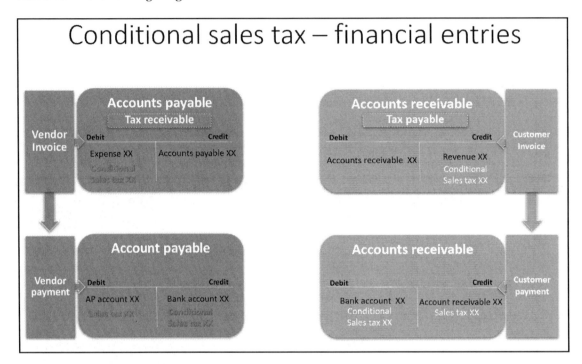

Understanding withholding tax

Withholding tax is calculated and executed at the vendor payment process. The calculated reflection of the withholding tax on the finance module will be as follows:

- **Price includes sales tax**: For a 1% withholding tax, 10% sales tax, and a 1,000 USD price including tax, 909.09 USD excludes tax, and this amount is the base of the withholding tax (909.09 * 1%). The system will allocate 9.09 USD to the withholding tax payable account, and 990.91 USD will be allocated to the payable account. The following diagram shows the calculation:

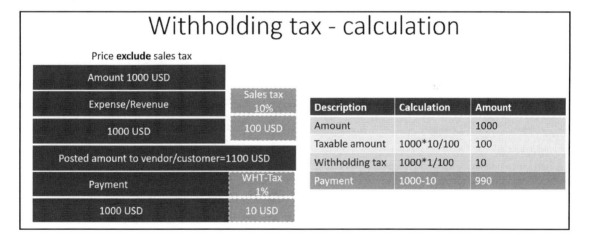

Withholding tax - calculation

Price **include** sales tax

Amount 1000 USD

| Expense/Revenue | Sales tax 10% |
| 909.09 USD | 90.91 USD |

Posted amount to vendor/customer=1000 USD

| Payment | WHT-Tax 1% |
| 1000 USD | -9.09 USD |

Description	Calculation	Amount
Amount		1000
Taxable amount	1000/110*100	909.09
Withholding tax	909.09*1/100	9.09
Payment	1000-9.09	990.91

- **Price excludes sales tax**: For a 1% withholding tax, 10% sales tax, and a 1,000 USD price excluding sales tax, this will be the base of the withholding tax calculation (1,000 * 1%), and the amount including sales tax is 1,100 USD. The system will allocate $10 to the withholding tax payable account and 990 USD will be allocated to the payable account. The following diagram shows the calculation:

Withholding tax - calculation

Price **exclude** sales tax

Amount 1000 USD

| Expense/Revenue | Sales tax 10% |
| 1000 USD | 100 USD |

Posted amount to vendor/customer=1100 USD

| Payment | WHT-Tax 1% |
| 1000 USD | 10 USD |

Description	Calculation	Amount
Amount		1000
Taxable amount	1000*10/100	100
Withholding tax	1000*1/100	10
Payment	1000-10	990

The **Withholding tax** checkbox on the vendor master data form must be checked in order to let the system calculate the withholding tax during the payment process. In the vendor master data form, navigate to **Accounts payable | Vendors | All vendors | Invoice and delivery** fast tab and set **Calculate withholding tax** to **Yes**.

The setup of withholding tax is initiated by creating a withholding tax code; assign it to the withholding tax group. Attach the withholding tax group to the vendor master data, and activate the withholding tax on the vendor level. The withholding tax calculation and posting will take place during the course of vendor payment. The following diagram illustrates setup elements:

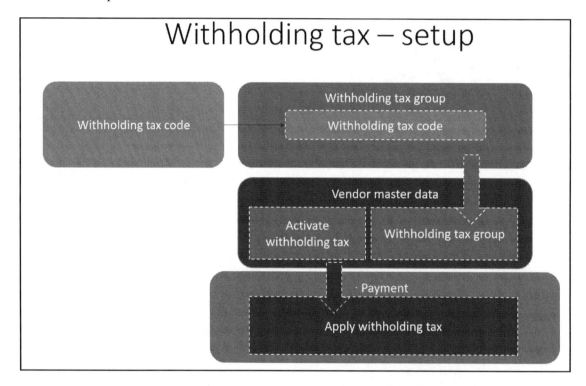

In order to set up withholding tax, go to **Tax** | **Indirect taxes** | **Withholding tax** | **Withholding tax codes**, as shown in the following screenshot:

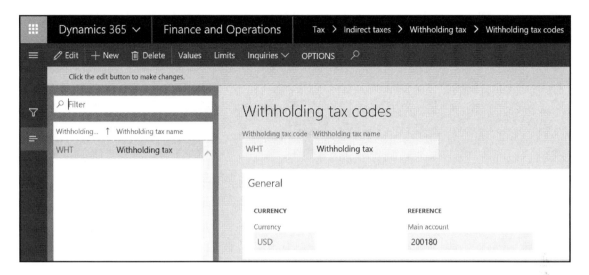

To assign a withholding tax code to the withholding tax group, go to **Tax | Indirect taxes | Withholding tax | Withholding tax groups**, as shown in the following screenshot:

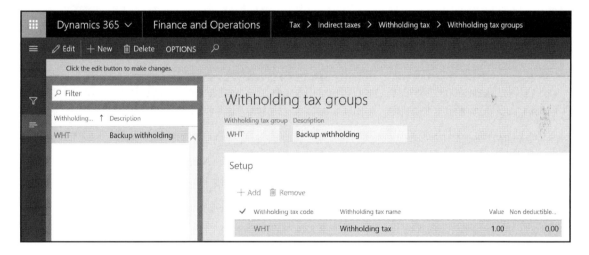

To assign withholding tax groups to vendor master data, go to **Accounts payable** | **Vendors** | **All vendors**, then move to the **Invoice and delivery** fast tab. Set **Calculate withholding tax** to **Yes**, and select withholding tax group code, as shown in the following screenshot:

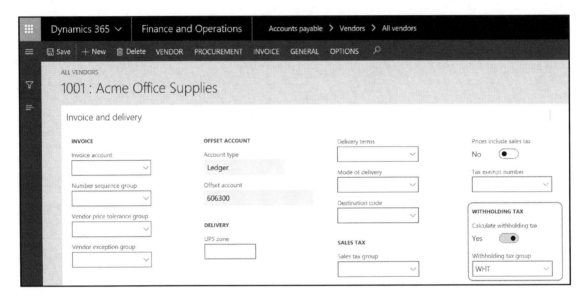

To execute a vendor payment, go to **Accounts payable** | **Payments** | **Payment journal**, then go to **Lines**, and select **Settle transactions**. The system will indicate that there is a withholding tax calculated on this payment, as shown in the following screenshot:

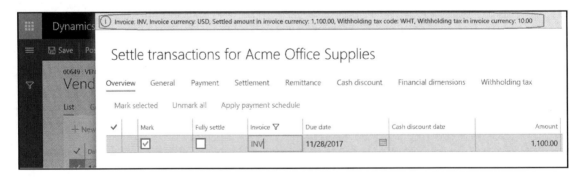

The final step in the sales tax cycle is to declare sales taxes to the tax authority so that it can be paid accordingly. In order to declare sales tax to the tax authority, go to **Tax | Declarations | Sales tax | Settle and post sales tax**. Select the **Settlement period** (from-to dates), as shown in the following screenshot:

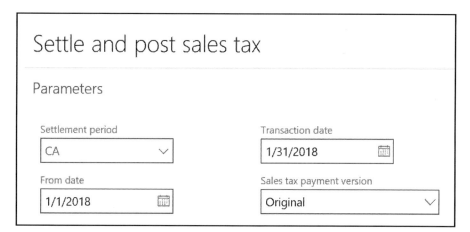

Summary

In this chapter, we discussed the sales tax business process with generated financial entries in Microsoft Dynamics 365 for Finance and Operations. Then, we moved on to illustrate the integration between the sales tax submodule and other modules. In addition to this, we covered the sales tax configurations, setup, transactions, and financial entries. We also explored conditional sales tax setup and transactions, and at the end of the chapter, covered the withholding tax setup and sales tax declaration.

In the next chapter, we will cover multi-currency applicabilities in Microsoft Dynamics 365 for Finance and Operations. We will then move to multi-currencies in action and revaluation mechanism.

5
Working with Currencies

With the current business requirements in the new economy, organizations need to deal with vendors and customers in foreign currency, and posted transactions in foreign currency need to be translated into the local currency. In addition to that, the company may operate in several countries and needs to have currency translation for its operations. In this chapter, we will cover:

- Understanding multi-currency in Microsoft Dynamics 365 for Finance and Operations
- Exploring basic setups for currencies
- Exploring multi-currency transactions in action
- Working with currency revaluation mechanisms

Understanding multi-currency in Microsoft Dynamics 365 for Finance and Operations

Currency is any kind of money that circulates in an economy. Organizations must have one accounting currency, also known as the company currency or home currency. The accounting currency is identified based on how the company wants to represent its financial reports. On the other hand, companies report their transactions in a specific currency, known as **reporting currency**. It is normal to post transactions in a different currency, and this amount of money is translated to the home currency, using the current exchange rate. This is a business need in enterprises that operate in a multinational environment.

Each subsidiary has its local reporting currency and at the same time, there should be a specific secondary reporting currency. All the transactions are translated into the reporting currency, using the exchange rate.

Currency elements are defined in the **General ledger** module. It is important to gather the currency business requirements in the early stages of the analysis phase. It is mainly used to identify the accounting currency, reporting currency, exchange rates that will be used, and how it will be maintained, either manually or through automated jobs. Additionally, the main accounts have three options for currency revaluation; the first option is if the main account is subjected to be reevaluated, the second option is, the exchange rate type, and the third option is the financial reporting exchange rate type. The following diagram illustrates the basic elements of currency in Microsoft Dynamics 365 for Finance and Operations:

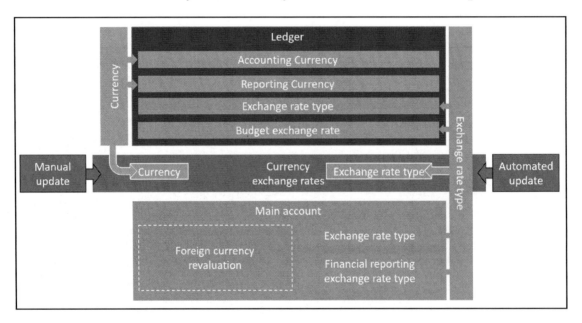

Currency code is the heart of the **Currencies** setup. Microsoft Dynamics 365 for Finance and Operations is shipped with world currency codes and uses the standard three-digit designation used by banks. The following screenshot illustrates the currency setup: to access the **Currencies** form, navigate to **General ledger** | **Currencies** | **Currencies**:

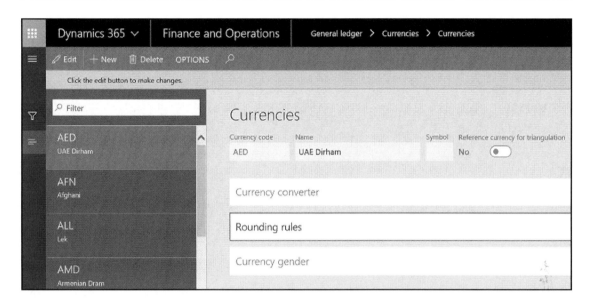

Exchange rate types represent different exchange rates that could be used within one company. Companies may use different exchange rates for budgeting, and this decision is taken during the analysis and design phases of the implementation. To access exchange rate types, navigate to **General ledger** | **Currencies** | **Exchange rate types**, as shown in the following screenshot:

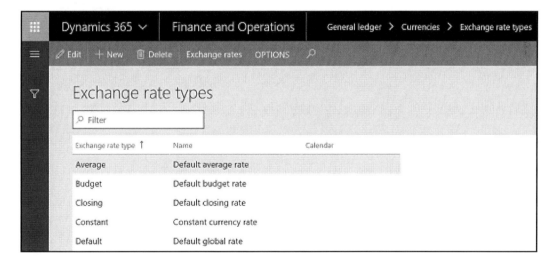

Currency and exchange rate types are assigned in the **Ledger** form, or the main account form. The form, as shown in the following screenshot, is where you define the accounting currency, the reporting currency, the exchange rate type, and the budget exchange rate. To access the **Ledger** form, navigate to **General ledger | Ledger setup | Ledger**:

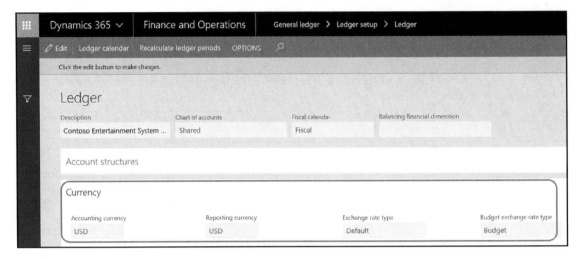

Now move on to the exchange rates where the company assigns the exchange rate for a pair of currencies. To access the currency exchange rate, navigate to **General ledger | Currencies | Currency exchange rates**. The exchange rate type is identified in this form automatically, and it contains the exchange rate of any pair of currencies on a specific date. The following screenshot represents the **Currency exchange rates** form:

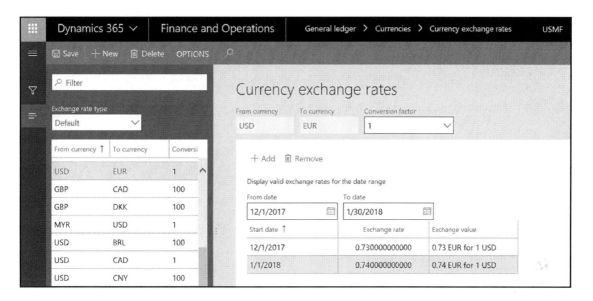

Based on the preference of the company's CFO and controller, **From**, **To**, and **Conversion factor** are configured. As shown in the preceding screenshot, 1.00 USD is equal to 0.7400 EUR for January 2018. In the course of the transaction with the EUR currency, the system fetches the exchange rates from the exchange rate table, based on the transaction date. The following screenshot shows the exchange rate on different dates in the **General journals** entry; to navigate to the **General journals** form go to **General ledger** | **Journal entries** | **General journals**:

The exchange rate on December 2017 is equal to 1.3698630136 (1/0.73).

The exchange rate on January 2018 is equal to 1.351351351351 (1/0.74).

The posted voucher represents the transaction currency, the accounting currency, and the reporting currency in three different columns, as shown in the following screenshot:

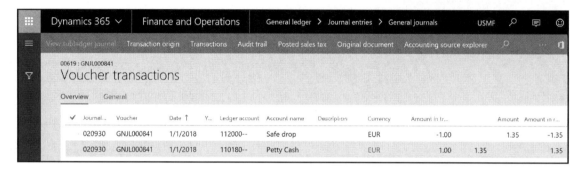

If the company is operating in a country that is transitioning economically to the EURO zone, this is identified on the **Currency** form by marking **Reference currency for triangulation**. If a country is converting its local currency to EUR during a specific period of time based on a fixed rate, this is known as a denomination currency. Transactions using the denomination currency will be translated to EUR then converted to USD, and this is known as triangulation. To access the denomination currency, go to **General ledger | Currencies | Denomination currencies,** as shown in the following screenshot:

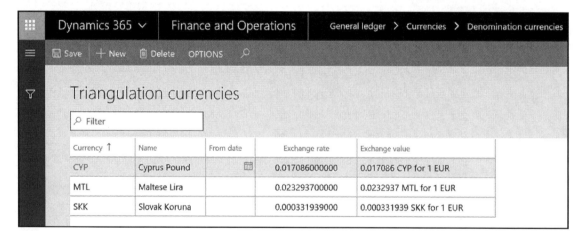

As an example, if an accountant is posting a transaction in Cyprus Pounds, which is the denomination currency, and assuming the transaction amount is 1 CYP, the system fetches the defined exchange rate on the denomination currency from CYP to EUR, as shown in the following screenshot of the **General journals** form. To access the **General journals** form, navigate to **General ledger** | **Journal entities** | **General journals**:

In the generated voucher for the preceding entry, the transaction currency is CYP and equals 1, and the amount in the accounting currency is 79.09 USD. The calculation is done as illustrated in the following diagram:

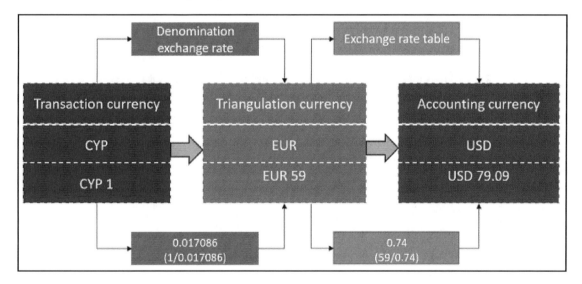

The exchange rate update frequency is based on the company requirements or country regulations. In Microsoft Dynamics 365 for Finance and Operations, exchange rates can be updated manually or automatically. A manual update is done by the accountant keying in the exchange rates for a specific date in the currency exchange rate form. The automatic update is done by feeding the exchange rates from an external provider, automatically. In order to configure exchange rate providers, navigate to **General ledger | Currencies | Configure exchange rate providers** and create a new record by pressing *Alt + N*. Microsoft Dynamics 365 for Finance and Operations is shipped with three providers, as shown in the following screenshot:

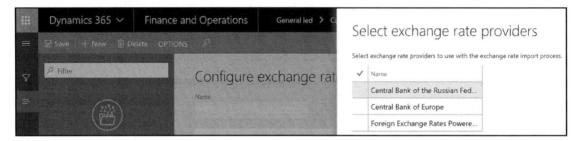

 If the customer needs to use different exchange rate providers other than the out-of-the-box providers, this can be customized through development with the partner or the customer.

To import the exchange rate, navigate to **General ledger | Currencies | Import currency exchange rates**; the accountant will need to identify the **Exchange rate type**, **Exchange rate provider**, and **Import as of**, as shown in the following screenshot:

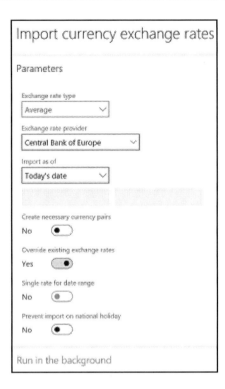

 After completion of the process, a message will pop up in the message center indicating that the process is finished.

Moving to the main account configuration for multi-currency, we have three options on the main account form related to currencies:

- **Foreign currency revaluation**: This indicates whether the account is subject to be considered in the general ledger foreign currency revaluation process or not. If this option is cleared (set as **No**), this means that this particular account will be excluded from the general ledger foreign currency revaluation process.
- **Exchange rate type**: This indicates the exchange rate type that will be used when running the general ledger exchange rate revaluation process.
- **Financial reporting exchange rate type**: This indicates the exchange rate that will be used when generating financial reporting, and then identifies if the translation type is weight average, average, current, or transactions date.

To navigate to the main account form, go to **General ledger** | **Chart of accounts** | **Accounts** | **Main accounts**, as shown in the following screenshot:

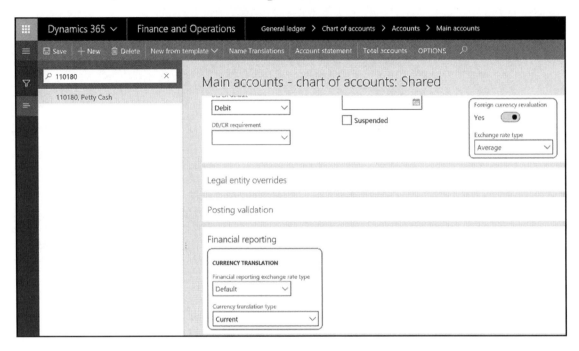

Exploring multi-currency in action

Daily operations may need to execute transactions in foreign currency, whether in general ledger transactions, vendor transactions, or customer transactions. Due to economy fluctuations in exchange rates, the company should reevaluate foreign currency transactions to reflect the current economic value for each currency, and this should be assigned to different ledger accounts for financial reporting. Microsoft Dynamics 365 for Finance and Operations differentiates between an exchange rate being realized or unrealized, and whether it is a gain or loss.

In order to set up accounts that are used in exchange rates, navigate to **General ledger |
Ledger setup | Ledger**; in the form go to the **Accounts for currency revaluation** fast tab
and identify the required accounts, as shown in the following screenshot:

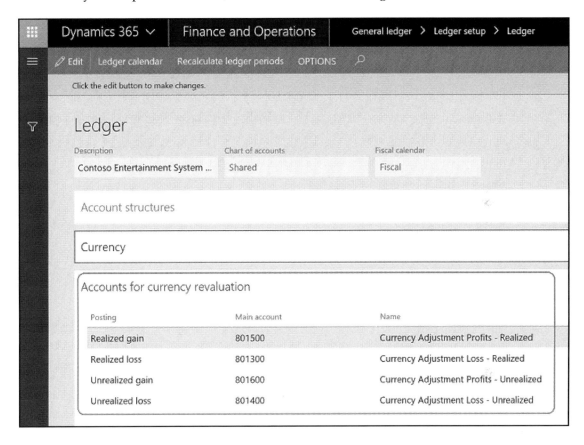

The revaluation accounts shown in the preceding screenshot are used across all currencies. Microsoft Dynamics 365 for Finance and Operations has an option to identify different currency revaluation accounts per currency code. To use a separate account for each currency, navigate to **General ledger** | **Currencies** | **Currency revaluation accounts** setup and select the currency code and the legal entity, and then identify the accounts, as shown in the following screenshot:

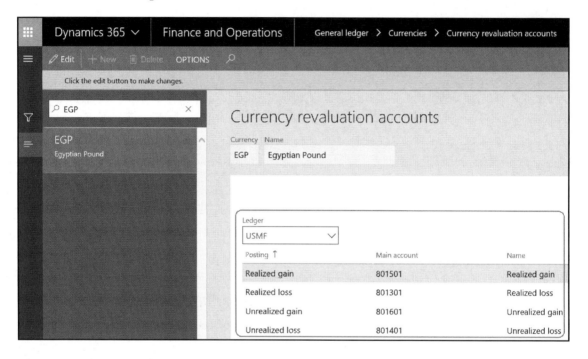

The posting accounts for currency revaluation are as follows:

- **Realized gain**: The ledger account that is used for posting a realized gain in the current currency. This is calculated when settlement occurs.
- **Realized loss**: The ledger account that is used for posting a realized loss in the current currency. This is calculated when settlement occurs.
- **Unrealized gain**: The ledger account that is used for posting an unrealized gain in the current currency for open transactions.
- **Unrealized loss**: The ledger account that is used for posting an unrealized loss in the current currency for open transactions.

In this section, we will explore the foreign currency revaluation process on the general ledger, and accounts payable and receivable. Currency revaluation is a part of the monthly closing procedure, and it runs on the submodules first, then is executed on the general ledger; this is discussed in `Chapter 2`, *Understanding the General Ledger*. When running currency revaluation, the system generates the unrealized gain/loss transaction for transactions that are posted in a foreign currency. The unrealized gain/loss has different logic between the submodules and the general ledger:

- **Unrealized gain/loss in submodules (accounts payable and accounts receivable)**: The previously posted revaluation is completely reversed, and a new revaluation transaction is posted as an unrealized gain/loss.
- **Unrealized gain/loss in general ledger**: The previous revaluation is not reversed, and a transaction is created for the delta between the balance of the main account, including any previous revaluation amounts.

Assume a vendor invoice transaction is posted on January 1, 2018 in the EUR currency, the exchange rate is 1.18 USD, equal to 1.00 EUR:

- Transaction amount is 1,000 EUR
- Transaction in accounting currency is 1,180 USD

To navigate to the vendor invoice, go to **Accounts payable | Invoices | Invoice journal,** as shown in the following screenshot:

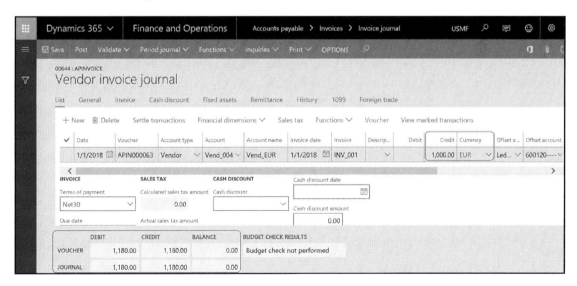

In order to run the foreign currency revaluation for accounts payable, navigate to **Accounts payable | Periodic tasks | Foreign currency revaluation**. As shown in the following screenshot, there is an option to run a simulation before posting: this important step enables the accountant to simulate the process before posting:

The **Simulation** dialog opens, as shown in the following screenshot:

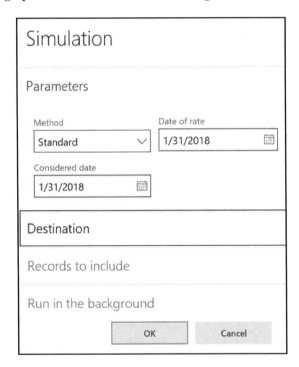

The simulation dialog parameters have the following options:

Method: The applied method of foreign currency revaluation, whether it is standard or minimum:

- **Standard**: Post foreign currency revaluation based on the exchange rate used on the date specified on the date of rate; the currency revaluation will be posted whether the results are profit or loss

- **Minimum**: Post foreign currency revaluation only if the result is loss

Considered date: Identifies all transactions that are open on that date and executes foreign currency revaluation, if necessary

Date of rate: The date representing the exchange rate that is used in the foreign currency revaluation

Assume the exchange rate on January 31, 2017 is 1.20 USD for 1 EUR, and the accountant runs the simulation while closing the month. The simulation report will be as shown in the following screenshot:

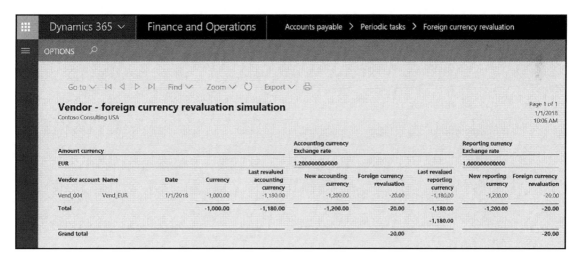

The normal step after running the submodule simulation for foreign currency is to post it to the submodule and general ledger accordingly. To run the foreign currency revaluation, navigate to **Accounts payable** | **Periodic tasks** | **Foreign currency revaluation,** as shown in the following screenshot:

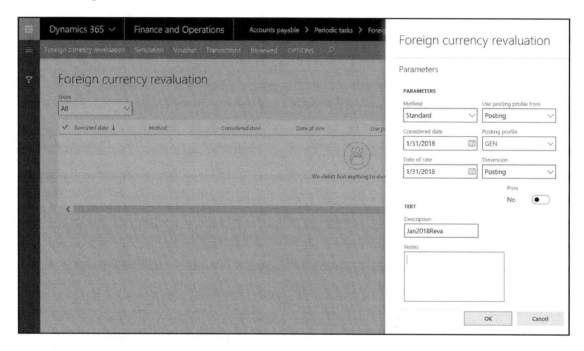

The foreign currency revaluation dialog parameters have the following options:

- **Use posting profile from**: The posting profile that will be used during foreign currency revaluation:
    - **Posting**: The posting profile that is assigned to the vendor/customer transaction will be used
    - **Select**: Manually select a posting profile in this posting profile field
- **Financial dimensions**: The financial dimensions that are posted on the foreign currency revaluation entries:
    - **None**: No financial dimensions are posted during the foreign currency revaluation process
    - **Table**: The financial dimensions defined on the customer or vendor are posted during the foreign currency revaluation process
    - **Posting**: The financial dimensions of posted transactions will be used during foreign currency revaluation

The generated unrealized transaction is as shown in the following screenshot:

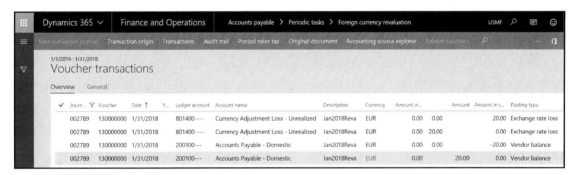

Assume the payment is posted on February 28, 2018 and the rate at this date is 1.50 USD for 1 EUR, the payment is posted from the vendor payment transaction. Go to **Accounts payable** | **Payments** | **Payment journal**, then go to **Posted voucher** then **Related vouchers**, the **Voucher transactions**; form opens, as shown in the following screenshot:

Moving to the general ledger revaluation process, enhancements were introduced in Microsoft Dynamics 365 for Finance and Operations; navigate to **General ledger** | **Currencies** | **Foreign currency revaluation**, select **Foreign currency revaluation** and a dialog window will open, as shown in the following screenshot:

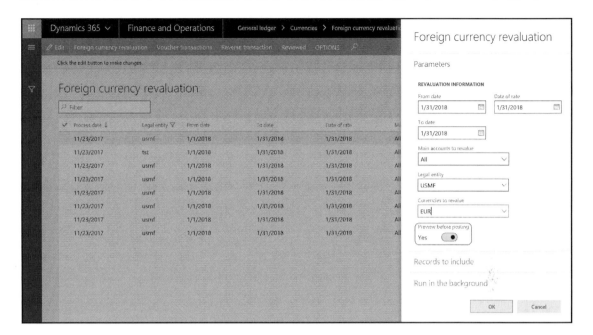

As presented in the preceding screenshot, an option, **Preview before posting**, simulates the revaluation process. In addition to that, the accountant has the option to run the revaluation for multiple legal entities without switching the legal entity. The currency revaluation preview opens, as shown in the following screenshot:

As presented in the preceding screenshot, there are options: **Post**, **Select legal entity to post**, **Export to Microsoft Excel**, or **Cancel**. The unrealized voucher is generated after posting the revaluation transaction, as shown in the following screenshot:

Summary

This chapter discussed multi-currency setups and configurations in Microsoft Dynamics 365 for Finance and Operations, then moved on to triangulation currency handling, and the automatic importing of the currency exchange rate. Finally, we covered multi-currency transactions in action in the submodules and the general ledger.

In the next chapter, we will cover accounts payable integration with another module, vendors' master data, and its controls.

6
Understanding Accounts Payable Basics and Controls

Accounts payable cycles are vendor invoicing and payment. These business processes manage and control the execution of vendor expenditure processes. These processes are based on procurement, purchasing, and product reception cycles in the procurement and sourcing processes. This cycle is known as the procure-to-pay cycle. This chapter covers the following topics:

- Understanding accounts payable integration with other modules
- Exploring vendor master data characteristics
- Exploring accounts payable controls

Understanding accounts payable integration with other modules

The accounts payable module manages and controls vendor transactions from the accounting point of view, where it records vendor master information and the basic transactions related to vendor invoicing, payment, and settlement. The accounts payable function is integrated with other business functions.

The first integration point with procurement and sourcing business functions is procuring goods and services for the company, the second integration is invoicing the purchase order based on received goods in the warehousing, and the third integration, with cash and bank management business functions, is performing vendor payment and settlement against invoices. The full cycle of procure-to-pay is shown in the following diagram:

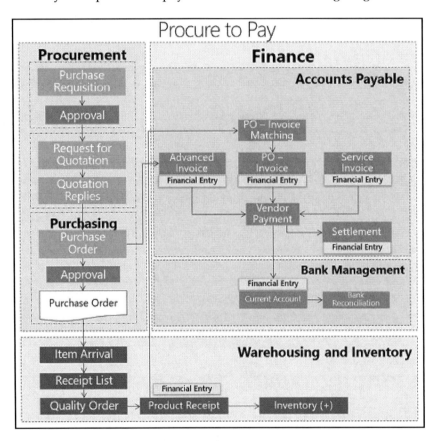

The normal practice for enterprise organizations is that no purchase orders are created directly. This can lead to creating purchase orders that are not needed and exposing the company to uncontrolled expenditures. This business process must be controlled, as it is the source of company expenditure. On the other hand, it can significantly impact the inventory cost, which will be reflected in the cost of production for a manufacturing environment, along with the cost of sales, and this affects the company's profitability accordingly.

The purchasing process for items, typically, goes through specific internal procedures to replenish items known as **finished goods** for a distribution environment and raw materials for a manufacturing environment, from the procurement department. The procurement process begins with either an automatic planned order from operations for specific items based on sales consumption against an on-hand inventory, or by entering the purchase requisition manually.

The purchase requisition goes through a workflow approval cycle that gives the necessary control to operations management to examine the requested quantities and might require top management approval, according to the organization's internal policies. In some projects or business scenarios, the purchase requisition cycle is not utilized; in such cases, a sole vendor supplies specific materials and the workflow can be utilized on the purchase order itself, through the change management functionality.

The approved purchase requisition is passed to the procurement agent (buyer) to execute the request for the quotation process, where it records the vendors who will potentially supply the required items. A request for a quotation is then sent to them. When the vendor sends back its replies, the procurement agent (buyer) records them and identifies the awarded vendor who will supply the required items. The approved purchase requisition can then be transformed into a purchase order if the item is supplied from a sole vendor, which is defined in the workflow configuration. The purchase order can then go through the approval workflow cycle and be confirmed.

The following are the purchase order types:

- **Purchase order**: This is a commitment document sent to a vendor to supply the required goods/services.
- **Journal**: This is a draft/template document that does not accept any further transactions, nor does it affect inventory or finance.
- **Returned order**: This is a credit note document used to reverse a purchase order invoice.
- **Purchase agreement**: This is a commitment document that is sent to a vendor to supply goods/services over specific time periods and prices. This is a new function introduced in AX 2012, and it replaces the blanket order in AX 2009.

The following are the purchase order statuses:

- **Open order**: This indicates that the purchase order has either been newly created, not totally received, or not totally invoiced
- **Received**: This indicates that the purchase order is fully received
- **Invoiced**: This indicates that the purchase order is fully invoiced
- **Canceled**: This indicates that the ordered quantities in the purchase order have been totally canceled

The following are the purchase order approval statuses:

- **Draft**: This indicates that the purchase order is a draft that has not been submitted for approval in the purchase order workflow
- **In review**: This indicates that the purchase order was submitted for approval in the purchase order workflow and the approval is pending
- **Rejected**: This indicates that the purchase order was rejected during the approval process
- **Approved**: This indicates that the purchase order is approved
- **Confirmed**: This indicates that the purchase order is confirmed; a purchase order cannot be confirmed until it has been approved
- **Finalized**: This indicates that the purchase order is made final; it is financially closed and can no longer be changed

The following are the purchase order document statuses:

- **None**: This indicates that the purchase order is created and no further documents have been posted
- **Purchase order**: This indicates that the purchase order has been confirmed
- **Receipt list**: This indicates that the receipt list document has been posted on the purchase order
- **Product receipt**: This indicates that the product receipt document has been posted on the purchase order
- **Invoice**: This indicates that the purchase order invoice has been posted

The product reception process occurred in two steps. The preliminary reception (receipt list) assigns inventory dimensions such as a serial number and batch number, in addition to the quality inspection, if required. The product receipt increases the physical quantities in the inventory and reduces the quantity remaining in the purchase order.

Product receipt transactions do not reflect any transactions on the vendor.

The vendor invoice is the document that represents the company's liability to vendors who deliver goods or services to the company. Afterwards, the payment process is executed based on the vendor invoices. The normal practice in enterprise organizations is that vendor payments will have two different scenarios: payment after receiving the goods/service invoice or an advance payment before rendering any reception process. The advanced payment can be assigned to a specific purchase order. Each payment transaction is settled against a vendor invoice. This affects company liabilities and the projection of future vendor payments. The payment transactions are executed by several payment methods; the most commonly used method is from bank accounts. The following diagram shows the document integration between invoices, payment, and settlement:

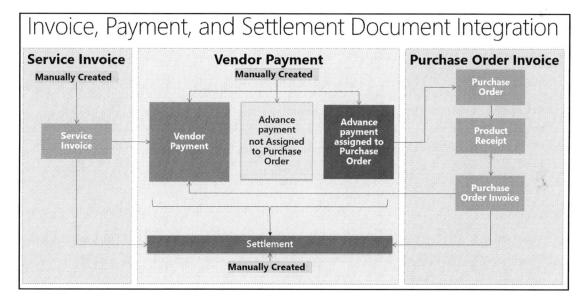

There are service and purchase order invoices, the payments transaction, which can be an advance payment that is assigned to a particular purchase order or not related to a purchase order, and the settlement transactions, which settle the payments against invoices.

Each transaction is represented in a document type in Microsoft Dynamics 365 for Finance and Operations, with the document that contains the details of the transaction. The transaction data, irrespective of whether it is inherited from the master data, entered manually, and/or automatically inherited from another transaction, is linked to a specific reference. The integration between invoice and payment transaction documents gives visibility to trace the original purchase order and the reception document, which is related to the invoice, together with who approves the invoice and payment.

Exploring vendor master data characteristics

The vendor record has essential information that directly affects accounts payable transactions. In this section, we will cover the basic information that should be considered when creating a new vendor record.

In order to create a new vendor record, the user should navigate to **Accounts Payable |** **Vendors | All vendors**, as shown in the following screenshot:

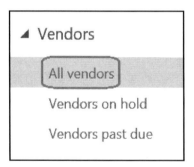

 On the vendor list page, press *Alt + N* to create a new vendor record, or click on **New vendor** in the ribbon.

The General fast tab

As shown in the following screenshot, when the vendor form is opened, under the **General** fast tab, the mandatory fields are **Vendor account** and **Group**:

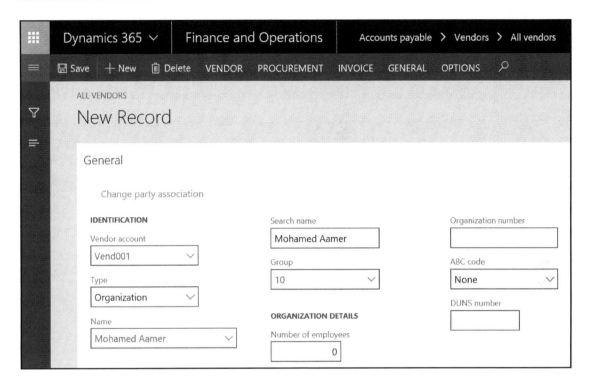

Vendor account can be assigned manually or automatically through the number sequence.

Group is a mandatory field that represents the vendor group that this particular vendor belongs to, and this is considered as the integration point between accounts payable and general ledger through the posting profile; however, the posting profile can be on the level of the vendor code. The vendor grouping is a joint effort between the procurement department and the financial department, as the procurement perspective groups the vendor from the operational and reporting points of view. On the other hand, the financial grouping, as per the relevant account, will get the financial posting when the operational action occurs.

The Purchasing demographics fast tab

In the **Purchasing demographics** fast tab, shown in the following screenshot, the **Currency** field is mandatory. This represents the default currency for this particular vendor transaction; however, it can be changed at the transaction level, as per the business case:

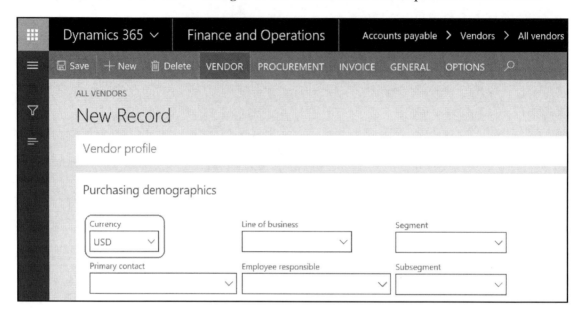

Invoice and delivery fast tab

Switching to the **Invoice and delivery** fast tab in this section, we will cover three field groups: **INVOICE**, **SALES TAX**, and **WITHHOLDING TAX,** as shown:

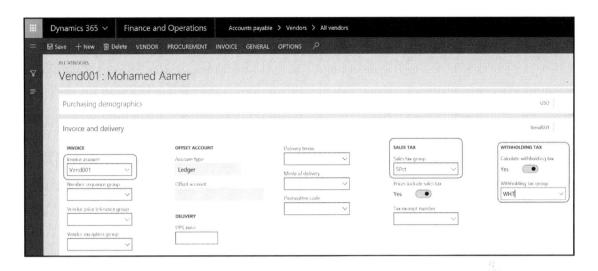

The INVOICE field group

In the **INVOICE** field group, the **Invoice account** field represents the account used in the invoicing process (the default invoice account is the vendor code), but Microsoft Dynamics 365 for Finance and Operations gives the flexibility to point invoice posting to another vendor. Assuming that there are two different vendors supplying goods, the invoice will be issued to one of the two vendors.

The relationship between the vendor code and the invoice account, where the vendor invoice can be linked to one vendor code or multiple vendor codes, is shown in the following diagram:

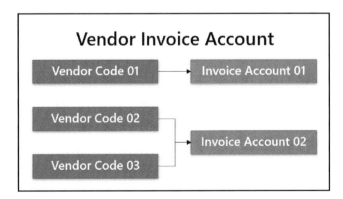

The SALES TAX field group

The **SALES TAX** field group represents the tax treatment that will be applied to this vendor. It can be the sales tax, prices including or excluding sales tax, and the tax exempt number, if there is any. An explanation of each field in the **SALES TAX** field group is as follows:

- **Sales tax group**: This field represents the sales tax group assigned to this particular vendor, and this record will be the default value for all transactions that will be inherited from the vendor master data
- **Price include sales tax**: This field indicates that the invoice amounts should include or exclude sales tax
- **Tax exempt number**: This field is used for reporting and statistical extractions

    Sales tax group can be set as the default at the vendor group level; just navigate to **Accounts Payable | Vendors | Vendor groups**. Also, it can be overridden by the user on the vendor form.

Setting sales tax at the vendor group level will cascade down to newly created vendors in this group. This ensures that the sales tax will be filled in automatically. On the other hand, it can be overridden on the vendor form or at the transaction level for exceptional cases. It is recommended not to leave the overwrite permission with the end users, to avoid issues in the posted sales tax.

The WITHHOLDING TAX field group

The **WITHHOLDING TAX** field is activated at the vendor level by marking the **Calculate withholding tax** field, and this will activate the **Withholding tax code** field to assign the withholding tax code that will be applied during the payment process.

The Purchase order defaults fast tab

Let's switch to the **Purchase order defaults** fast tab. In this section, we will explore the **DISCOUNT** field group, which contains **Price group**, **Line discount group**, **Multiline discount group** and **Total discount group**.

The DISCOUNT field group

The **DISCOUNT** field group represents the discount and pricing options that can be applied on this particular vendor. As shown in the following screenshot, the **DISCOUNT** field group consists of discount and pricing groups that this vendor belongs to:

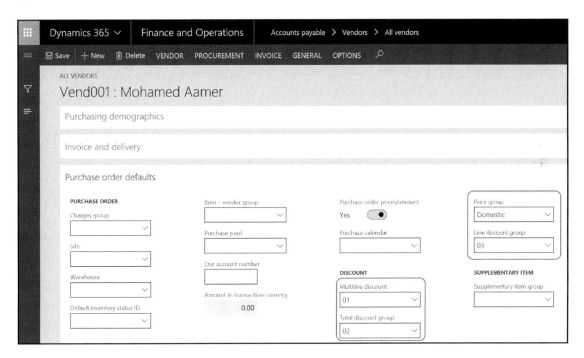

Vendor price/discount groups

Vendor price/discount groups consist of the four pricing groups shown in the following diagram:

From the preceding diagram, we can see:

- **Price group**: This represents the vendor's price group used for price proposal upon purchase; this price group is attached to the vendor master
- **Line discount group**: This represents the purchase line discount used for purchase; this is attached to the vendor master
- **Multiline discount group**: This represents the multiline discount group used to control discounts across several purchase lines; this is attached to the vendor master
- **Total discount group**: This represents the total discount that attaches the vendor master data to a total discount group

In order to create vendor price/discount groups, you need to navigate to **Inventory management** | **Setup** | **Price/discount** | **Vendor price/discount groups**; this is shown in the following screenshot:

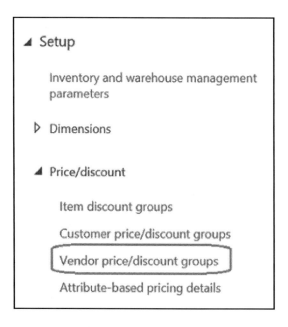

The **Vendor price/discount groups** form shows the **Price/discount** options and helps create groups for each **Price/discount** option, as shown in the following screenshot:

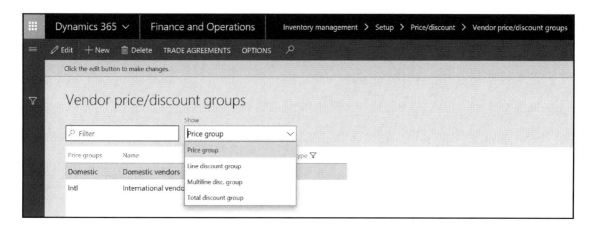

The **Price/discount** option must be activated by navigating to **Procurement and sourcing** | **Setup** | **Prices and discounts** | **Activate price/discount**.

In the **Domestic** value created for the price group, navigate to **TRADE AGREEMENTS** | **Create trade agreements**, as shown in the following screenshot:

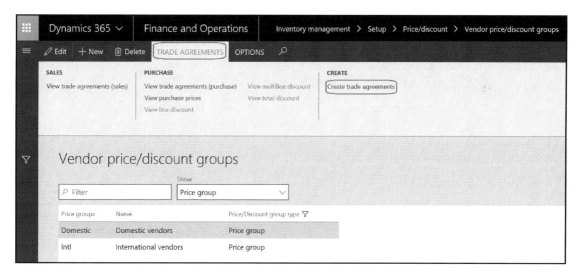

The trade agreement journal will pop up; create a new journal by pressing *Alt + N*, select the journal name, and then click on **Lines**. The prices defined in the trade agreement represent a combination of the vendor and item; this combination provides flexibility with the following options:

- **All**: Any transaction occurring for any vendor will inherit the price that is assigned to all vendors
- **Group**: Any transaction for a particular vendor price group inherits the price that is assigned to the price group
- **Table**: Any transaction that occurs for a vendor will inherit the price that is assigned to this particular vendor

As shown in the following screenshot, select **Price (purch.)**. Now, select **Account code** as **Table** to make this price correspond to a particular vendor; in **Item code**, select **Table** to make this price correspond to a particular item when it is purchased from the mentioned vendor and from a specific warehouse. The trade agreement journal line should be posted:

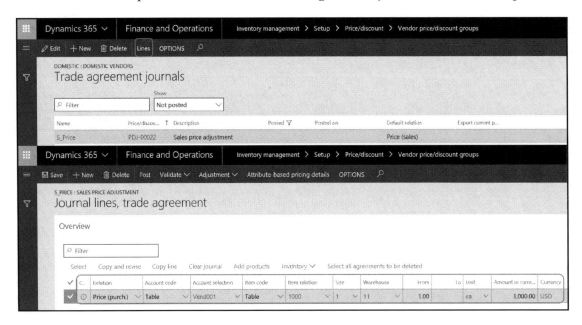

As shown in the following purchase order screenshot, navigate to **Accounts payable** | **Purchase orders** | **All purchase orders**; this setup recalls the purchase price on the purchase line automatically from the posted trade agreements journal:

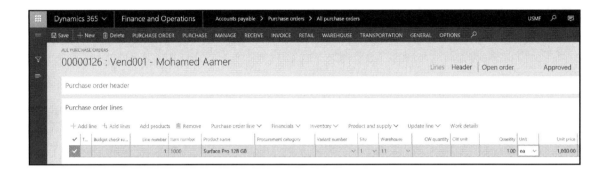

The Payment fast tab

In the **Payment** fast tab, under the **PAYMENT** field group, the information needed for vendor payment arrangements is shown (see the following screenshot). The available fields are **Terms of payment**, **Method of payment**, **Payment type**, **Payment specification**, and **Cash discount**.

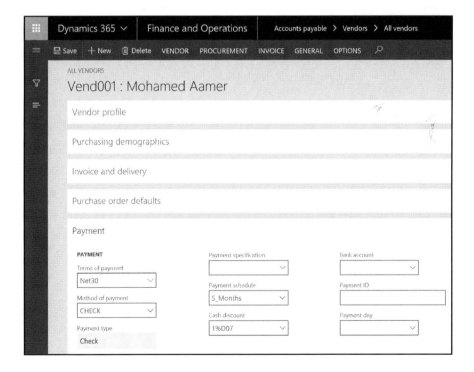

Terms of payment

The **Terms of payment** field represents the calculated due date to pay the vendor. The **Terms of payment** creation form is shown in the following screenshot. In order to access this form, navigate to **Accounts payable** | **Payment setup** | **Terms of payment**:

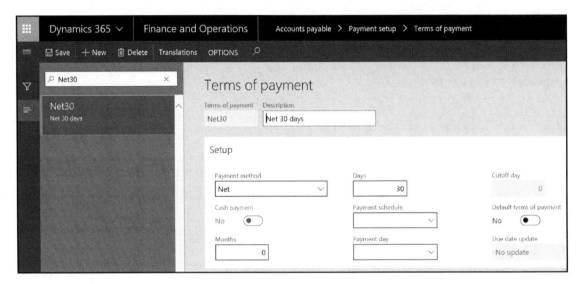

Identify the due date base in the **Payment method** combo-box, which contains six options. Assume that the vendor invoice is posted on January 1, 2018 and the number of days is 20; the due date will be changed based on the selected payment method option, as shown in the following diagram:

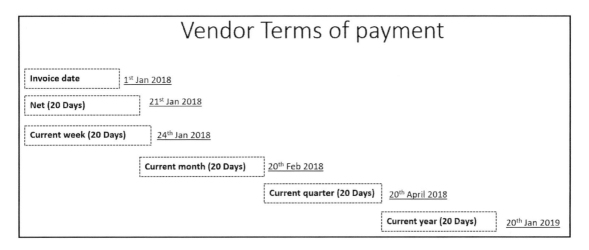

From the preceding diagram, we can see:

- **Net**: The due date will be calculated from the invoice posting (1ˢᵗ Jan + 20 days), which is **21ˢᵗ Jan 2018**
- **Current week**: The due date will be calculated from the end of the week that the invoice was posted in (4ᵗʰ Jan + 20 days), that is, **24ᵗʰ Jan 2018**
- **Current month**: The due date will be calculated from the end of the month that the invoice was posted in (31ˢᵗ Jan + 20 days), in this case **20ᵗʰ Feb 2018**
- **Current quarter**: The due date will be calculated from the end of the quarter that the invoice was posted in (31ˢᵗ March + 20 days), which in this case is **20ᵗʰ April 2018**
- **Current year**: The due date will be calculated from the end of the year that the invoice was posted in (31ˢᵗ December + 20 days); here it will be **20ᵗʰ Jan 2019**
- **Cash on delivery (COD)**: This represents the cash payment upon delivery; with this option, a ledger account must be specified that will be used while posting a purchase order invoice

Method of payment

The payment method refers to the way the vendor is paid, whether by check, bank transfer, or cash. In order to access the **Methods of payment** form, navigate to **Accounts payable** | **Payment setup** | **Methods of payment**, as shown in the following screenshot. Setting the required controls will be applied on the transaction if it is using this particular method of payment, in addition to the file formats of checks printout:

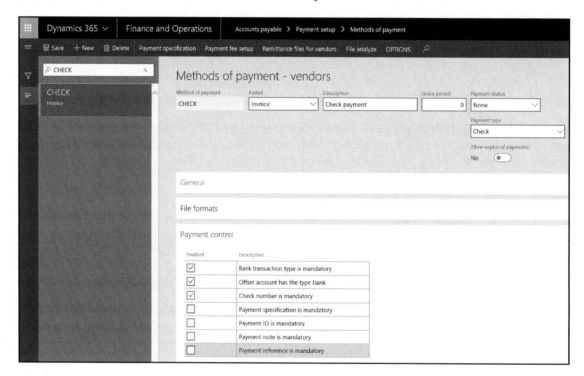

The PAYMENT SCHEDULE field group

The **PAYMENT SCHEDULE** field represents the installment type that will be used after invoicing. In order to access the payment schedule form, navigate to **Accounts payable** | **Payment setup** | **Payment schedules**. This is shown in the following screenshot; our main aim is to identify the type of installment, that is, whether it is over a fixed number of months or has a fixed amount:

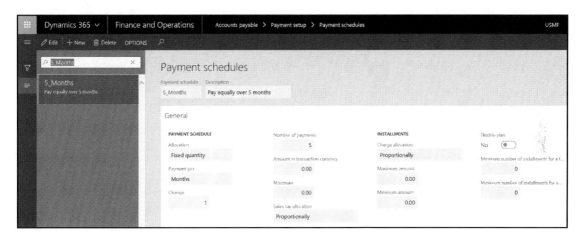

Assume that the purchase order invoice is posted on January 1, 2018, its amount is 5,000 USD, and it is assigned a payment schedule of five months, with the terms of payment set as net 30 days. Navigate to **Accounts payable** | **Purchase orders** | **All purchase orders**; then, on the purchase order form, navigate to **Header view** | **Price and discount** and assign a payment schedule.

In order to check payment installment dates, in the ribbon, navigate to **INVOICE** | **BILL** | **Payment schedule**. The payment schedule form will pop up. Then, go to the **Payment lines** tab; the following screenshot shows the payment schedules where the payment is divided into five installments for five months:

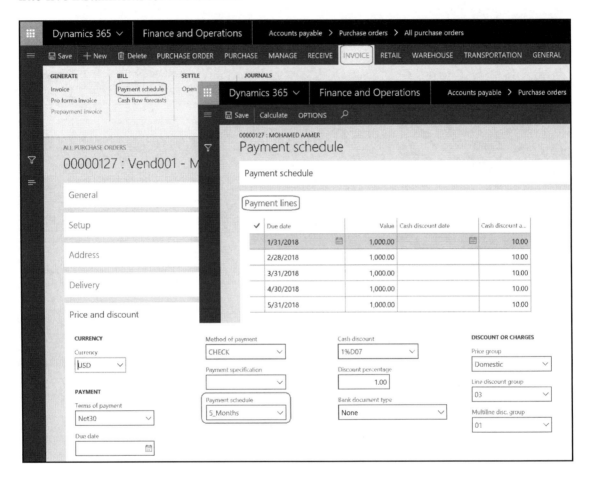

Cash discount

The **Cash discount** field represents the discount that will be applied during the vendor payment if it is paid before the due date; it has the flexibility to assign the next cash discount. In order to create the cash discount record, navigate to **Accounts payable | Payment setup | Cash discounts**, as shown in the following screenshot. The **Setup** fast tab identifies the discount percentage, number of months, and number of days. It is important to assign the main account for the vendor discount, in order to apply the discounted amount to a particular main account:

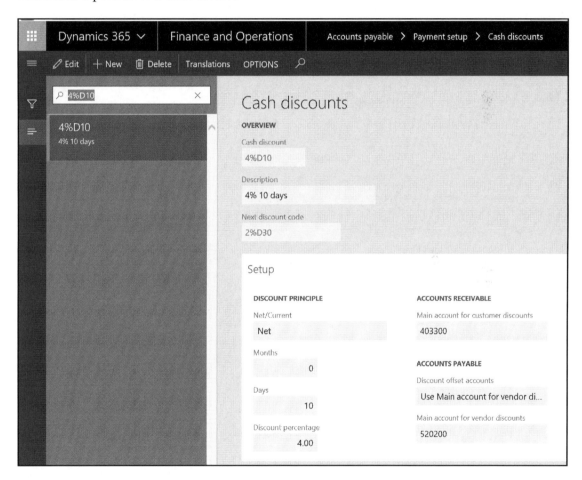

Assuming that an invoice has been posted on January 1, the cash discount is **4%** if the invoice is paid within **10** days and the terms of payment is net 20 days.

To navigate to the vendor invoice, go to **Accounts payable | Invoices | Invoice journal**, as shown in the following screenshot; the cash discount date is January 11 and its amount is −40.00:

When we go on to create a payment transaction and settle it against the posted invoice on January 10, as shown in the following screenshot, the payment amount is 960 (1,000 − 40 = 960). To access the payment amount, navigate to **Accounts payable | Payments | Payment journal | Lines | Settle transactions**:

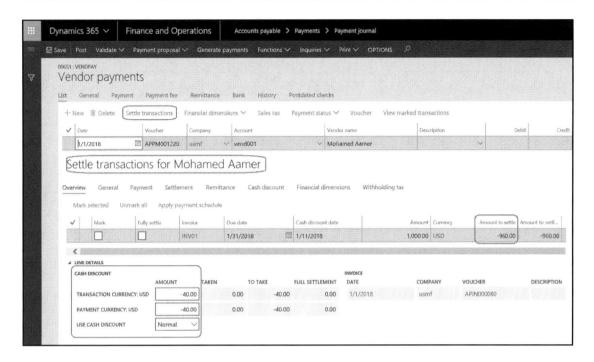

In order to apply the cash discount, the user should choose **Always** or **Normal** under **USE CASH DISCOUNT**:

- **Normal**: The cash discount is used only if the invoice is settled by the date that is defined for the cash discount.
- **Always**: The last available cash discount is used if the invoice is settled after the cash discount date. If the invoice is settled by the date that is defined for the cash discount, the cash discount amount is the same as if you select **Normal**.
- **Never**: No cash discount is applied even if the invoice is settled on or before the discount date.

In the following screenshot, we changed the payment day to January 19 and the cash discount goes to the next cash discount code, that is, 2% for 30 days:

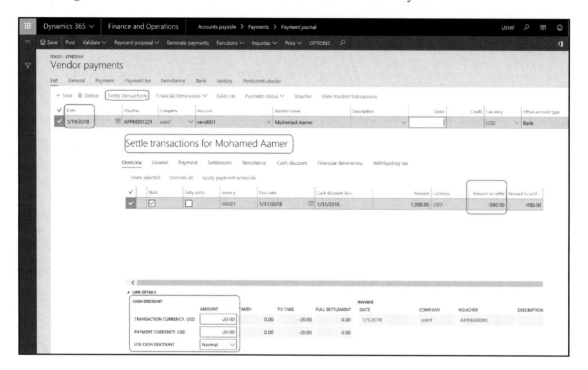

In this section, we explored vendor master data, purchasing demographics, and vendor sales tax treatment, in addition to withholding tax. Then, we explored price and discount options, in addition to alternatives for payments, terms of payment, and methods of payment.

Exploring accounts payable controls

Accounts payable controls are an essential task to be discussed during the analysis and design phases, and assessed in the operation phase for enhancements. Microsoft Dynamics 365 for Finance and Operations addresses the required procedures for accounts payable controls. It is important for a business to control the execution of accounts payable processes, as this directly affects the company's liabilities; this is why it should be controlled and monitored. In the upcoming sections, we will explore vendor hold activities, invoicing controls, and posting profiles.

Vendor hold activities

In daily business operations in accounts payable, the accounting manager might need to stop transactions on a specific vendor; the **On hold** function for vendors in Microsoft Dynamics 365 for Finance and Operations is located at the vendor level. To access this function, navigate to **Accounts payable** | **Vendors** | **All vendors** | **Maintain**. In the ribbon, click on **On hold**.

As shown in the following screenshot, the **On hold** function has several options based on the vendor transaction type, that is, **Invoice**, **Payment**, **Requisition**, **Never**, **All**, and **No**, which is the default value. These options can be used to control vendors by preventing them from executing particular transactions, or by stopping a vendor altogether:

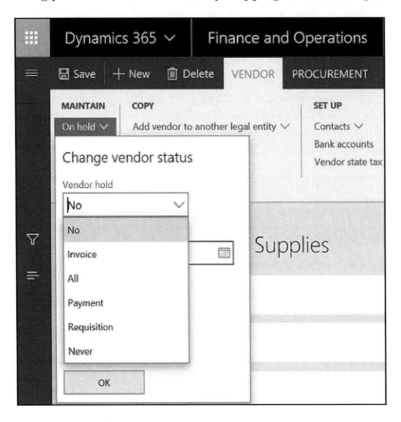

The **On hold** options for the vendor transaction types are as follows:

- **No**: This represents that the vendor is allowed for all transaction types, but if the vendor is inactive, it will be set on hold automatically when running the vendor inactivity job
- **Invoice**: This represents that the vendor is prevented from executing invoice transactions only
- **All**: This represents that the vendor is prevented from executing any transaction

- **Payment**: This represents that the vendor is prevented from executing payment transactions only
- **Requisition**: This represents that the vendor is prevented from executing purchase requisition transactions only
- **Never**: This represents that the vendor is allowed for all transaction types, but the vendor will be excluded when running the vendor inactivity job and will not be set on hold automatically

 To automatically put a vendor on hold who was recently inactive, the **On hold** function automatically runs the **Vendor inactivation** job by navigating to **Procurement and sourcing | Periodic | Vendors | Vendor inactivation**.

As shown in the following screenshot, when we set the **On hold** value as **All** for example, the system shows a message bar to indicate that the vendor has been set on hold:

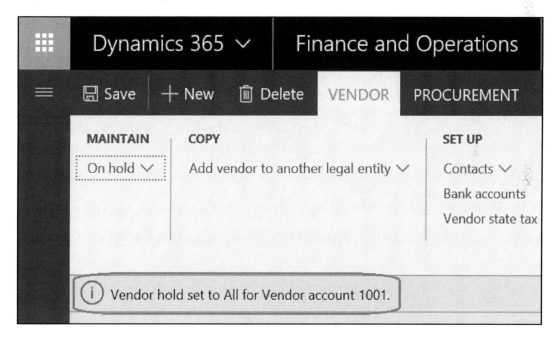

If an end user tries to select a vendor with the **On hold** status as **All,** the system will prevent them from creating any transaction if the vendor status is on hold, as shown in the following screenshot, where the user tried to create a purchase order:

There are other options for **On hold**, where the accounting manager can plan the future release date of the vendor from the **On hold** status for a particular transaction. In the **On hold** selection, set the **Vendor hold release date** field; this will be considered as the last day for putting the vendor on hold.

As shown in the following screenshot, we will set the vendor on hold for a particular transaction and set the release date; here, the release date is March 31, 2018:

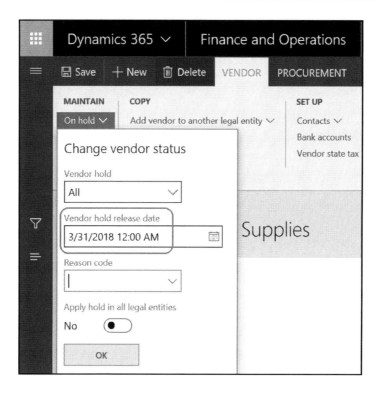

If a user tries to create a transaction for this vendor on March 29, the system will prevent the transaction from being created, and as shown in the following screenshot, an error message will pop up:

The vendor hold release date is based on the computer (machine) date.

Invoice matching controls

There are several options for invoice matching controls in Microsoft Dynamics 365 for Finance and Operations; in the following section, we will explore the invoicing matching policies and options. The following diagram illustrates the invoice matching options:

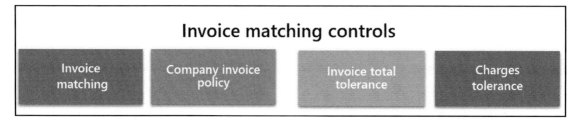

Invoice matching

The vendor invoice matching process is a control point that is concerned with the invoices received from the vendors before recording the invoice as a liability on the company. There are two types of invoice matching, and they are as follows:

- **Three-way matching**: This is normally used with inventory items, where three documents are compared: the vendor invoice against the purchase order document and the product receipt document.
- **Two-way matching**: This is normally used with service items, where two documents are compared: the vendor invoice against the purchase order. This requires manual approval to pass these transactions.

The following diagram illustrates vendor invoice matching:

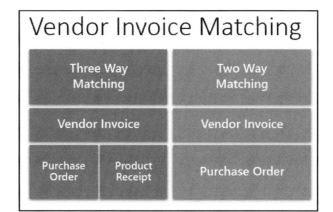

The basic document in three-way matching is the **vendor invoice**, where the price and quantities in the vendor invoice document are compared against the price in the purchase order, which was already agreed upon, and the actual received quantities in the reception process. This is important for processing payments only to vendors at the agreed prices and based on the actual delivered quantities in the warehouses.

The following diagram illustrates the three-way matching concept:

The basic document in two-way matching is also the **vendor invoice**, where the price of the vendor invoice is compared against the price in the purchase order; as this is for inventory items, there is no need to compare quantities. This is a control feature delivered in Microsoft Dynamics 365 for Finance and Operations where we differentiate the matching process for inventory and non-inventory items. The following diagram illustrates the two-way matching concept:

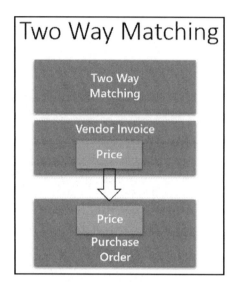

Numerous layers of vendor invoice matching in Microsoft Dynamics 365 for Finance and Operations give you the flexibility to apply matching controls, all of which are required in real-life business. The invoice matching control must be activated on the legal entity level:

- The first layer is the company layer where we identify a matching policy (whether it is two-way, three-way, or not required); this policy will be cascaded down to all vendors and items on this particular legal entity. The acceptable price tolerance is the base of comparison between the vendor invoice and the purchase order price. The price tolerances can be for all vendors and items, or for a specific vendor or item, and finally for a specific combination of vendors and items. On this layer, we configure the matching policy for total invoice tolerance and charge tolerance.

- The second layer matches the policy level, where we identify exceptions from the company-wide configuration; this exception can be applied on the matching policy for a specific vendor, an item, or a combination of vendors and items, where we can modify the default company-wide parameters. If the company's matching policy is three-way matching for all vendors, and the controller decided to exclude the service vendors from this policy and apply two-way matching on these services vendors, then the controller could completely exclude trusted vendors from the matching policy. The exception could be done on the invoice total level, or miscellaneous charge code level.
- The third layer is vendor invoice policies where configuring a precise combination on a purchase order header or purchase order line has to be approved before posting. This can be applied for risky purchases where the purchase amount exceeds a certain amount.

The following diagram illustrates vendor invoice matching layers in Microsoft Dynamics 365 for Finance and Operations:

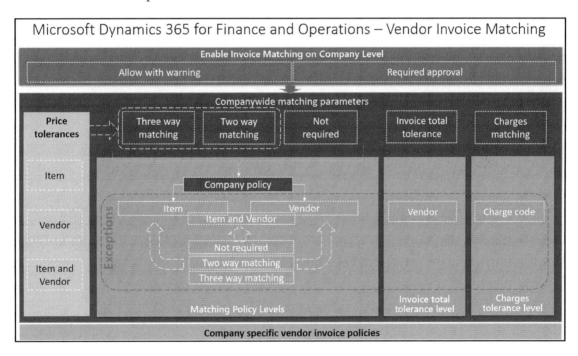

In order to activate invoice matching validation on Microsoft Dynamics 365 for Finance and Operations, navigate to **Accounts Payable | Setup | Accounts payable parameters | Invoice validation**.

As shown in the following screenshot of the **Accounts payable parameters**, mark the **Enable invoice matching validation** checkbox and set the procedure that will be applied if there are matching discrepancies, that is, whether it should be **Allow with warning** or **Require approval**. The first option allows posting a transaction with a matching discrepancy, and the second option prevents posting an invoice transaction with a matching discrepancy:

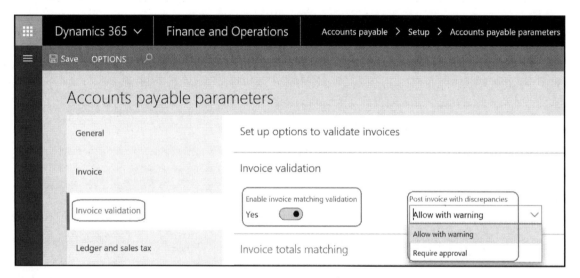

In the **Price and quantity matching** field group, set whether or not the company-wide matching policy is required, and if it is whether it is two-way matching or three-way matching. Identify the matching policy override, that is, whether it is **Higher than company policy** or **Lower than company policy**. Set the **Display unit price match icon** field as **If greater than tolerance** or **If greater than or less than company policy**. Set the **Match price totals** field as **None**, **Percentage**, **Amount**, or **Percentage and price**.

This is a company-wide configuration on a legal-entity level. This can be overridden by the matching policy.

The following screenshot shows the **Price and quantity matching** field group:

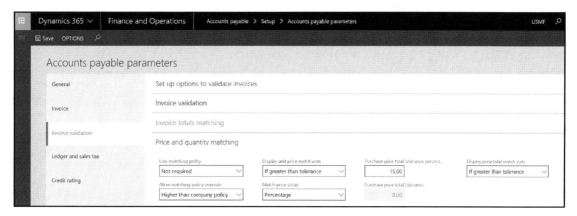

Price tolerance

The path to access the price tolerance is shown in the following screenshot; go to **Accounts payable** | **Invoice matching setup** | **Price tolerances**:

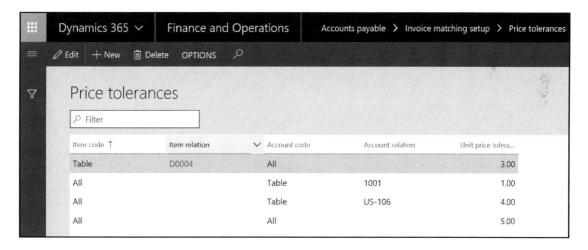

In the **Price tolerances** form, set the acceptable unit price tolerance percentage; this indicates the relationship between the vendor and supplied items. It is flexible because we can set a different price tolerance for each vendor or each item. Otherwise, it can be set to a combination of vendors and items. Remember that **Group** dominates over **All**, and **Table** dominates over **Group** and **All**.

In order to configure the exceptions on the matching-policy level, that is, whether it is on vendors, items, or a combination of a vendor and an item, navigate to **Accounts payable |
Invoice matching setup | Matching policy**. As shown in the following
screenshot, **Matching policy** illustrates the company-wide configuration of the line
matching policy. In the **Matching policy level** combo-box, select **Vendor**, **Item**, or **Item and
vendor**. Assign the line matching policy for each vendor, item, or item and vendor, where
we will be able to keep the default company-wide parameters as **Company policy**.
Otherwise, assign a different matching policy according to organizational needs (whether it
should be two-way matching, three-way matching, or not required at all):

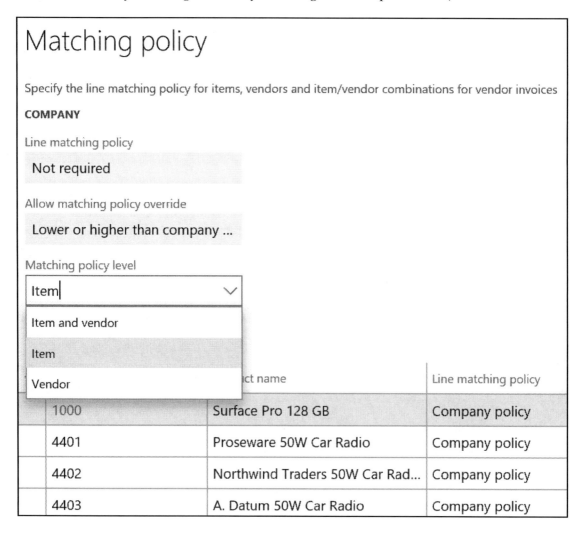

The following screenshot displays the execution of a purchase order invoice with a difference in price and quantity with three-way matching and with a line matching policy assigned.

There is a prerequisite for this scenario; create a purchase order by navigating to **Accounts payable** | **Purchase orders** | **All purchase orders**. Now, create a new order and select a vendor ID.

Create a purchase line and then add the required fields: item ID, site, warehouse, quantity 1, and price, which in this case is 1,000 USD. Then, post the product receipt by navigating to **Receive** | **Product Receipt**; enter the product receipt number and click on **OK**. As shown in the following screenshot, which shows the purchase order's **Line** fast tab, expand **Line details** | **Setup** | **Matching policy**:

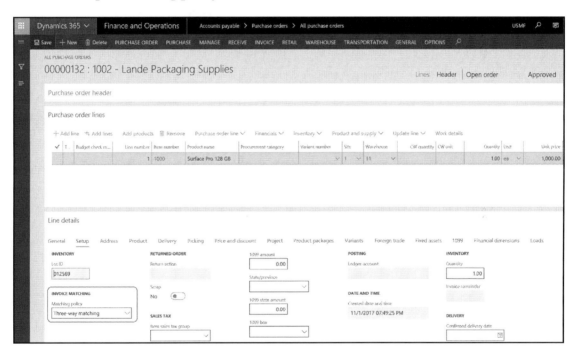

Go to the **INVOICE** ribbon and enter the invoice number, assuming that the invoice has a difference in price, which is 1,050.01 USD; the price tolerance is 5%, which means 1,050.00 USD, so the invoice price is greater than the acceptable tolerance by 0.01 USD. Also, the quantity difference from the product receipt is two pieces. The following screenshot shows the purchase order invoice with matching variance with quantity and price. In order to check the details of variance, go to the **REVIEW** ribbon and select **Matching details**:

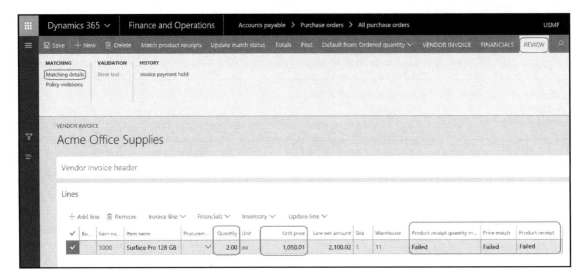

The preceding screenshot depicts the invoice matching details form. The line has three fields indicating that the matching failed in **product receipt quantity**, **price match**, and **price total match**.

In the details level, the comparison between the purchase order and invoice prices is shown in the following screenshot:

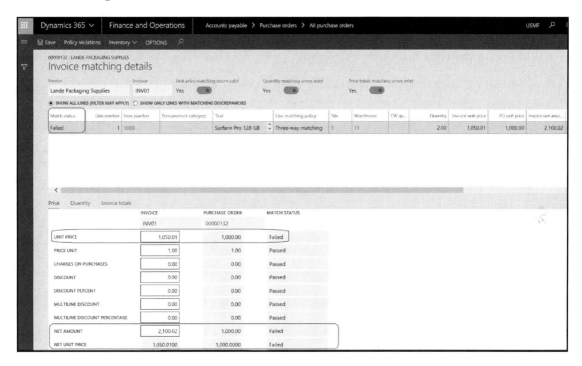

This is in addition to the comparison between the product receipt quantity and vendor invoice quantity:

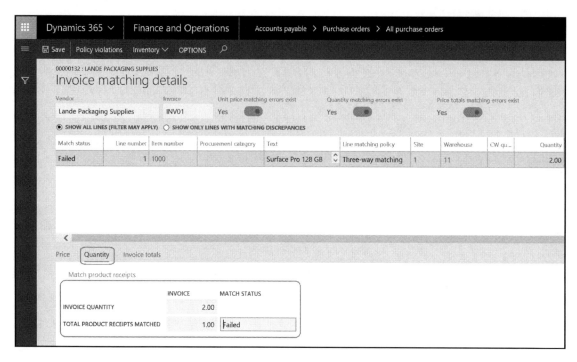

The invoice control can be extended to check the total purchase order amount, in addition to the total invoice amount.

In the following example, the total purchase order amount of a purchase order has two-way matching, where we compare the purchase order invoice price against the purchase order price. The purchase order price is 1,000 USD and the purchase order invoice price is also 1,000 USD. During the matching process, the user adds an additional piece of data (for example, the quantity is changed to 2) and the purchase price is within the acceptable tolerance, so the purchase order total amount is 2,000 USD. The configured acceptable tolerance for the purchase price total is 15%, which means 1,150 USD.

The invoice matching form indicates **UNMATCHED PURCHASE ORDER TOTAL**, as shown in the following screenshot:

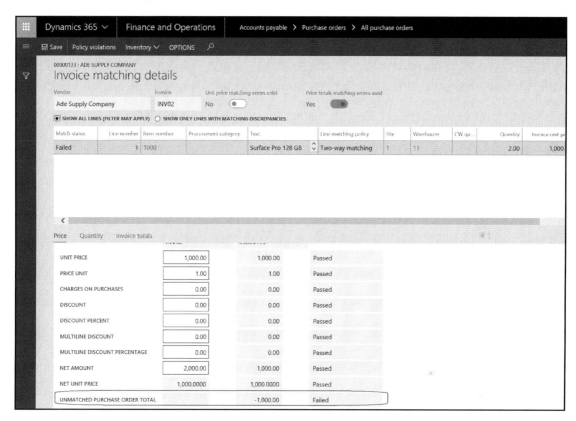

In the preceding example, assume that the invoice quantities are equal to the purchase order quantity, but we're adding additional service items on the vendor invoice by 100.01 USD. The invoice matching form indicates the **INVOICE AMOUNT** discrepancy, as shown in the following screenshot:

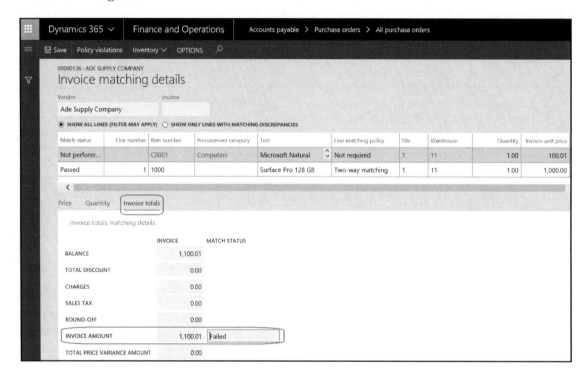

In the following screenshot, the **Invoice totals matching details** tab is illustrated, showing the invoice total tolerance percentage, actual invoice total, expected invoice totals, and variance percentage:

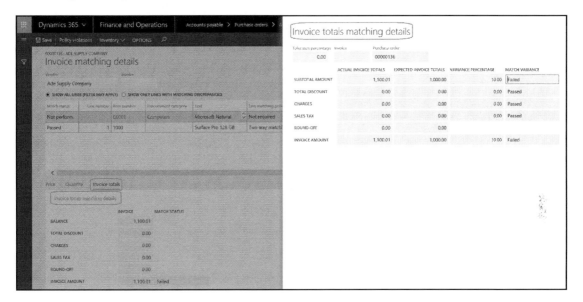

In the preceding example, assume that the purchase order line has assigned charges with 100 USD, and the invoice quantities are equal to the purchase order quantity, but the purchase order invoice lines charges have been modified to 125.01 USD and the acceptable charges tolerance is 25%.

The selected charges should be added to the vendor invoice, which only has **Customer/Vendor** on the credit side. In order to create a charges code, navigate to **Accounts payable | Charges setup | Charges code**. As shown in the following screenshot, the charges form illustrates the setup for the charges, and it is important to let Microsoft Dynamics 365 for Finance and Operations consider the charges during the invoice-matching process; for this, the **Compare purchase order and invoice...** value checkbox must be checked:

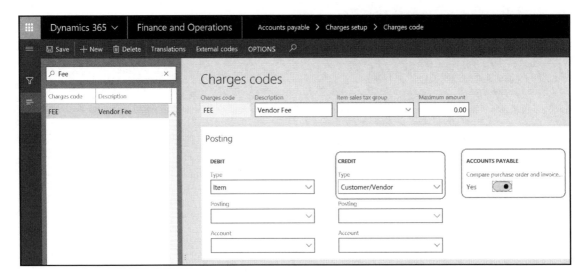

In the preceding screenshot:

- **DEBIT**: This represents the debit side, which will be affected by the added charges
- **CREDIT**: This represents the credit side, which will be affected by the added charges
- **Type**: This represents the different types, which are **Item**, **Ledger**, and/or **Customer/Vendor**. They are explained as follows:
    - **Item**: This represents the charges that will be posted on the item; this is only applicable for the debit side
    - **Ledger**: This represents the charges that will be posted on a particular ledger account and must have a posting type and account number
    - **Customer/Vendor**: This represents the charges that will be posted on the customer/vendor on the purchase order or sales order

As shown in the following screenshot, the invoice matching form indicates a discrepancy in the compared charge:

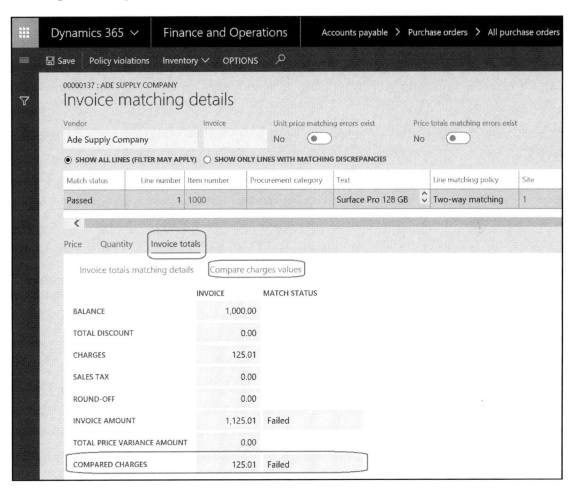

In the following screenshot, we illustrate the compare charges values, and show the actual total calculated amount, expected calculated amount, variance amount, variance percentage, and tolerance percentage:

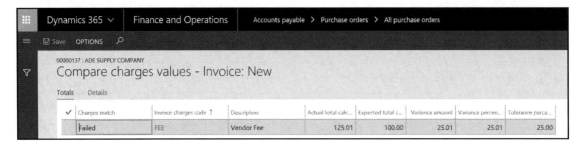

The invoice number

The invoice document represents vendor invoice recording in company accounts (liability). The invoice has a reference number (invoice number) based on the vendor serial number and the accounts payable accountant records the invoice number, which can be used in the reconciliation process with the vendor; it is used in the payment process as well. In Microsoft Dynamics 365 for Finance and Operations, the invoice number is a mandatory field and can be controlled to be a unique value. This uniqueness is considered per vendor and can be within the fiscal year. In order to access the invoice number control, navigate to **Accounts payable** | **Setup** | **Accounts payable parameters** | **Invoice** and go to the **Check the invoice number used** section.

The following screenshot illustrates the available options for the invoice number control:

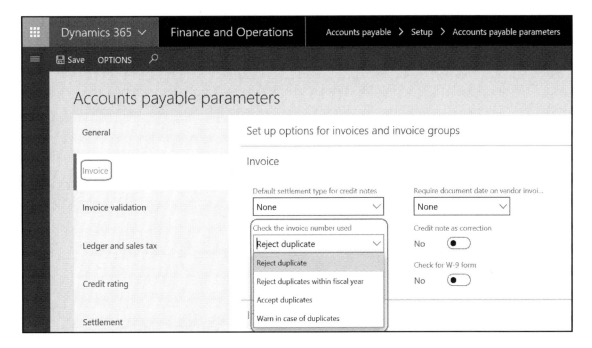

The **Check the invoice number used** field has the following options:

- **Reject duplicate**: This option will block using the same invoice number from the same vendor. For example, if vendor A has the invoice number INV-001, this value cannot be used with the same vendor, but can be used with vendor B.

- **Reject duplicates within fiscal year**: This is the same as the previous option, in addition to the validation that will be executed during the fiscal year.

- **Accept duplicates**: This option accepts duplicates.

- **Warn in case of duplicates**: This option gives a warning message if the value has been used before.

The Posting profile

The **Posting profile** represents the integration point between the general ledger and subledger, and it generates financial entries automatically, according to the posting profile's setup. Accounts payable posting profiles are assigned to the module parameters; navigate to **Accounts payable** | **Setup** | **Accounts payable parameters** | **Ledger and sales tax**, and go through the following process:

- In the **Posting** fast tab, assign the posting profile for general accounts payable transactions; in other words, this represents the accounts payable account
- In the **Payment** fast tab, assign the posting profile for advance payment transactions; in other words, this represents the advances from the vendor account
- In the **Prepayment invoice** fast tab, assign the posting profile for prepayment invoices

These options can be seen in the following screenshot:

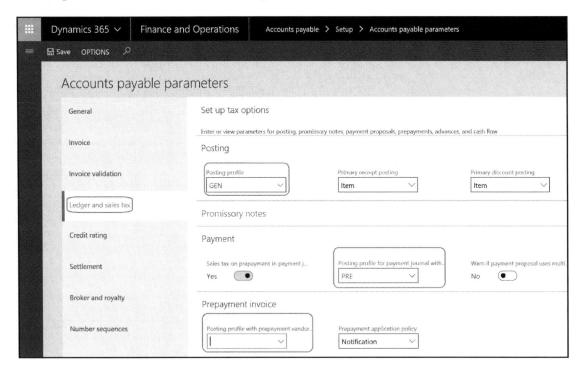

Summary

This chapter covered the accounts payable module in Microsoft Dynamics 365 for Finance and Operations, its integration with other modules, procurement, and inventory, and then explored vendor master data and characteristics that affect vendor transactions. We also learned about controls for invoice matching, three-way matching for products and two-way matching for services, putting vendors on hold, and invoice numbering.

In the next chapter, we will discuss accounts payable transactions invoicing, payment, prepayment, and settlement.

7
Exploring Accounts Payable Transactions

The accounts payable transactions includes vendor invoicing that relates to purchase orders, service invoices, and non-purchase order invoices, in addition to vendor payments, prepayments, and settlement transactions. This chapter covers the following topics:

- Exploring accounts payable transactions
- Exploring vendor invoicing
- Exploring vendor payments and settlements

Exploring accounts payable transactions

This section will explore the transactions of the accounts payable module; transactions are divided into two main categories, invoicing and payment:

- **Invoicing**: This is divided into purchase-order-related invoices and non-purchase-order-related invoices:
  - **The purchase-order-related invoices**: These invoices represent the invoices that are normally attached to a purchase order(s). Invoices related to a purchase order can be the final invoice of the purchase order, which is received after delivering the goods, or the prepayment invoice, which is recorded before delivering the goods. The attached prepayment invoice to a particular purchase order is a new functionality released prior to Microsoft Dynamics 365 for Finance and Operations.

- **The non-purchase-order-related invoices**: These invoices represent the vendor liabilities for services rendered to the company; there are two ways of recording service invoices. The first is non-inventory invoices, which are related to non-stockable items and are commonly used by the company departments to record their expenses. The other type is the invoice journal for services, which is posted directly to the expense account; it is commonly used by accountants.

- **Payment**: The second category is the vendor payment. There are two types. The first is a prepayment transaction, which is considered as vendor advances. This can be assigned to a particular purchase order, or need not be assigned to a purchase order. The second type is the vendor payment, which is settled against the vendor invoice.

The categories are summed up in the following diagram:

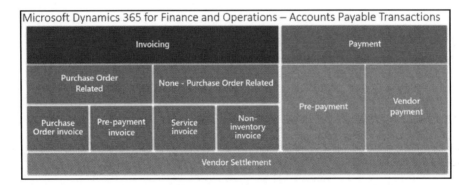

The purchase order invoice

The purchase order invoice document can be posted from two different forms; the first form is the purchase order form, and the second form is the vendor open invoices.

Open the vendor invoices form, this is a function introduced prior to Microsoft Dynamics 365 for Finance and Operations. This form is used also for non-purchase order invoices.

To post a purchase order invoice from the purchase order form, navigate to **Accounts Payable** | **Purchase orders** | **All purchase orders**, after choosing the required purchase order, then go to the **INVOICE** ribbon and navigate to **GENERATE** | **Invoice**. The following screenshot illustrates the **Purchase order invoice path from Purchase order lines form**:

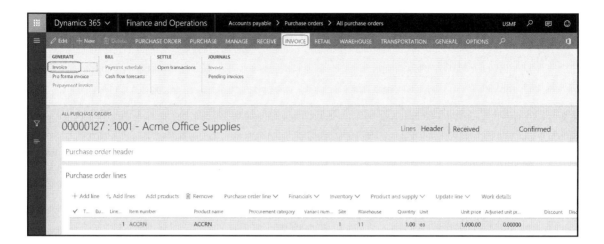

In the vendor invoice form, the purchase order and product receipts are retrieved automatically; then, enter the invoice number and description. Click on **Post** to generate the invoice transaction. The following screenshot shows the vendor invoice form:

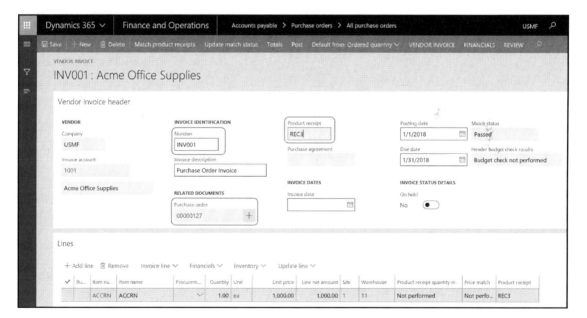

The **Update match status** should be clicked before proceeding to posting the invoice.

The vendor invoice form is the non-purchase order invoice when accessed from **Accounts payable** | **Invoices** | **Open vendor invoices**. Also, it is a shared form.

The relationship between the vendor invoice, product receipt, and purchase order is that the purchase order has more than one product receipt and the invoice can cover one purchase order with more than one product receipt. In some business cases, the vendor invoices cover receipts that occur on more than one purchase order.

The following diagram illustrates the relationship between the purchase order, product receipt, and invoice:

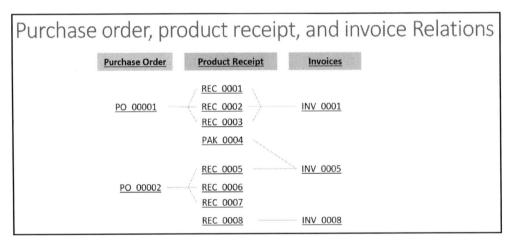

This business scenario can be managed on Microsoft Dynamics 365 for Finance and Operations in several ways. The following section illustrates the most common functionalities to post an invoice that covers more than one product receipt or purchase order.

Navigate to **Account payable** | **Invoices** | **Pending vendor invoices** on the vendor invoice form under the **VENDOR INVOICE** ribbon; there are two options there, whether to retrieve the product receipts or the purchase order, as shown in the following screenshot:

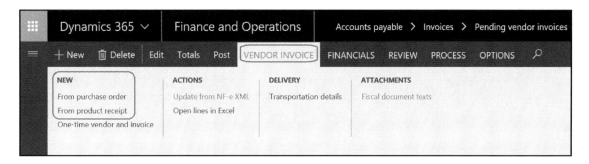

The first option, **From purchase order**, opens the filtration query, as shown in the following screenshot. The user can retrieve information based on the values in the query; this can be a product receipt, vendor ID, and so on:

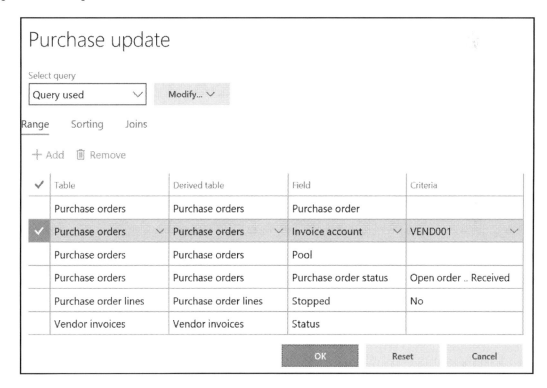

As shown in the following screenshot, two lines have been retrieved according to the entered query, that is, two purchase orders with two different product receipts. This represents two different invoices for each line:

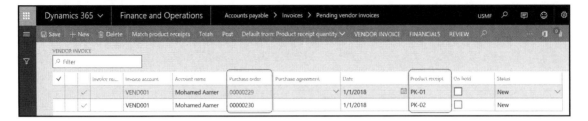

To consolidate the two invoices into one invoice document, go to the **MAINTAIN** ribbon and select **Consolidate invoices**. The following screenshot illustrates the **Consolidate** option:

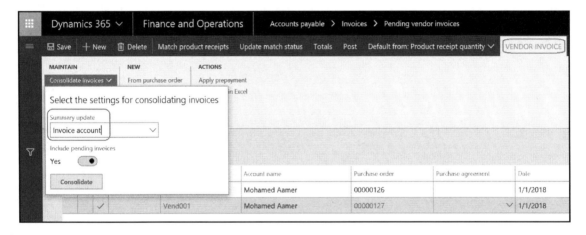

The **Summary update** drop-down has four options, as follows:

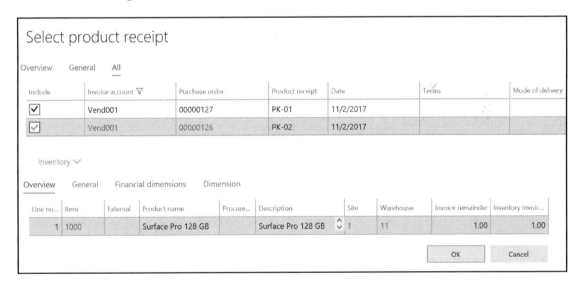

- **None**: There are no summary updates.
- **Invoice account**: Summary update all selected orders according to the criteria set in the **Accounts payable parameters** or **Summary update parameters** form.
- **Order**: Summary update a selected range of orders into, for example, one invoice. The orders will be summary updated according to the criteria set in the **Accounts payable parameters** or **Summary update parameters** form.
- **Automatic summary**: Summary update all selected orders automatically according to the criteria set in the **Accounts payable parameters** or **Summary update parameters** form.

The second option, **From product receipt**, lists all product receipts and their lines. As represented in the following screenshot, the marked product receipts will be included in the vendor invoice. To go to the **Product receipt** form, navigate to **Accounts payable | Invoices | Pending vendor invoices | New | From product receipt**:

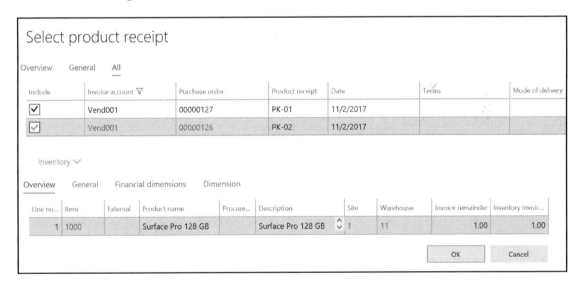

Select product receipt

Overview   General   All

Include	Invoice account ▽	Purchase order	Product receipt	Date	Terms	Mode of delivery
☑	Vend001	00000127	PK-01	11/2/2017		
☑	Vend001	00000126	PK-02	11/2/2017		

Inventory ∨

Overview   General   Financial dimensions   Dimension

Line nu...	Item	External	Product name	Procure...	Description	Site	Warehouse	Invoice remainder	Inventory invoic...
1	1000		Surface Pro 128 GB		Surface Pro 128 GB	1	11	1.00	1.00

OK   Cancel

There is another functionality that can be used to post one vendor invoice for multiple purchase orders or product receipts. Navigate to **Accounts payable** | **Invoices** | **Open vendor invoices**, create a new record, and enter the invoice number and description. Then, go to the **RELATED DOCUMENTS** filed group and select the plus icon under the **Vendor invoice header** fast tab, as shown in the following screenshot:

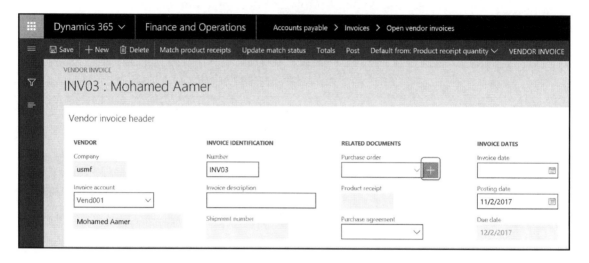

As shown in the following screenshot, a list of purchase orders with their product receipts is shown in this form. The user can mark which product receipts will be included in the invoice:

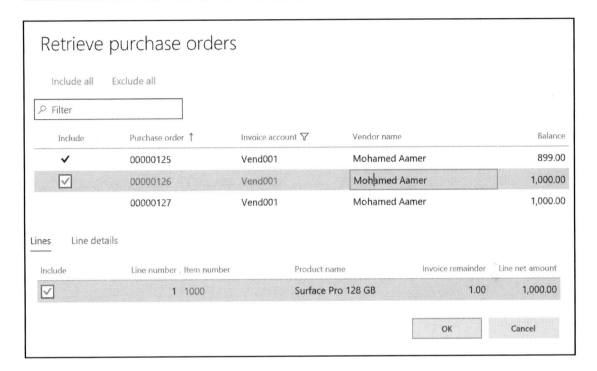

Retrieve purchase orders

Include all   Exclude all

🔍 Filter

Include	Purchase order ↑	Invoice account ▽	Vendor name	Balance
✓	00000125	Vend001	Mohamed Aamer	899.00
☑	00000126	Vend001	Mohamed Aamer	1,000.00
	00000127	Vend001	Mohamed Aamer	1,000.00

Lines   Line details

Include	Line number . Item number	Product name	Invoice remainder	Line net amount
☑	1 1000	Surface Pro 128 GB	1.00	1,000.00

OK   Cancel

This invoice is already consolidated into one invoice.

The following screenshot shows that the invoice-related documents are multiple and are on the lines of the relationship between the purchase order and product receipt:

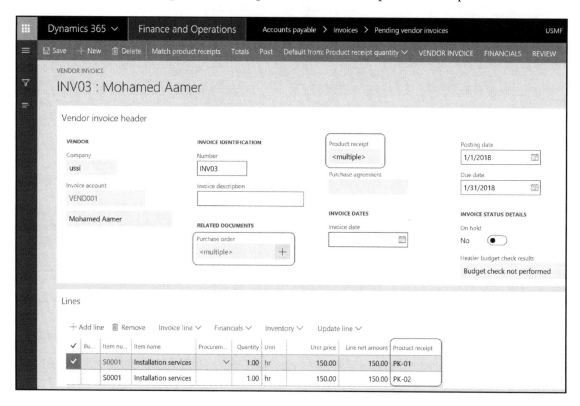

To inquire about the vendor balance, navigate to **Accounts payable** | **Vendors** | **All Vendors** and click on the **Balance** ribbon. As shown in the following screenshot:

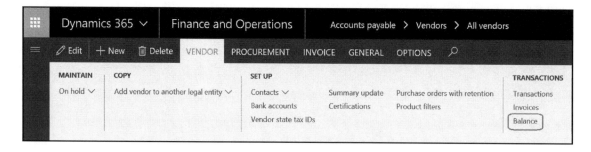

As illustrated in the following screenshot, the balance form shows the current vendor balance:

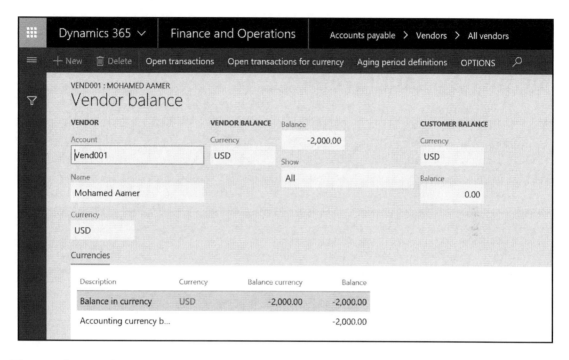

The purchase order invoice automatically generates the liability financial entry, based on the vendor posting and inventory posting profiles. The inventory posting profile must be carefully structured during the design phase, where the controller should understand the mechanism of invoice posting well.

The generated invoice entry is divided into four lines; two entries represent the product receipt entry reversal, and the other two entries represent the vendor liability entry:

- The financial entry of a product receipt in Microsoft Dynamics 365 for Finance and Operations is two-liner entry, as follows:
    - Dr. Product receipt account
    - Cr. Vendor accrual account
- The other two entries represent the vendor liability, as follows:
    - Dr. Vendor accrual account
    - Cr. Product receipt account
    - Dr. Purchase inventory receipt
    - Cr. Vendor balance

The inventory posting profile access path is **Inventory management** | **Setup** | **Posting** | **Posting** | **Purchase order**.

The prepayment invoice

The vendor prepayment function gives a company's controller the ability to minimize the risk by applying the segregation of duties between company departments and control the prepayment process, where accounts payable does not perform the prepayment transaction without assigning the prepayment linked to the purchase order and harmonizing the business process between procurement and accounts payable. Assume that the company has agreed with a vendor to supply goods to the company and the vendor has a condition to receive a prepayment before executing the goods delivery, and this is a normal practice in the daily business.

The vendor prepayment cycle is executed among the procurement agent, accounts payable, and bank accountants. The following diagram illustrates the business process of the prepayment:

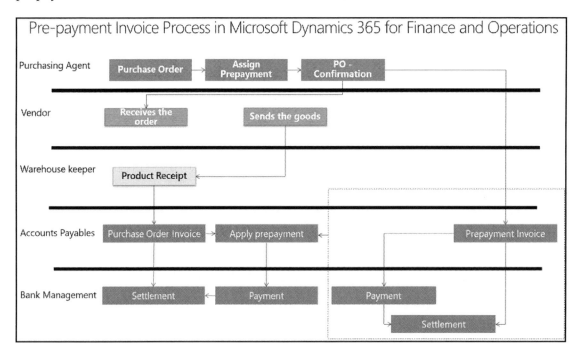

From the preceding diagram, we can see that:

- The procurement agent creates a purchase order.
- The procurement agent assigns the prepayment to a purchase order as per the agreement. with the vendor; here, the prepayment is a fixed amount or a percentage from the total purchases of the PO.
- The procurement agent confirms the purchase order.
- The vendor issues a prepayment invoice.
- The accounts payable accountant posts the prepayment invoice, and the prepayment invoice amount is inherited from the previous prepayment assignment.
- Bank accountants have open invoices that need to be paid and settled against the payment.
- After the warehouse keeper receives the goods in the warehouse, the vendor sends the final invoice.
- The accounts payable accountant applies the prepayment to the final invoice and posts the PO invoice. If the AP accountant does not apply the prepayment invoice to the PO invoice, they can apply it later on.
- The bank accountant opens the invoice with a vendor residual balance that needs to be paid and settled against the payment.

To assign a prepayment invoice on a created purchase order, navigate to **Accounts payable** | **Purchase orders** | **All purchase orders**. Navigate to **PURCHASE** | **Prepayment**, as shown in the following screenshot:

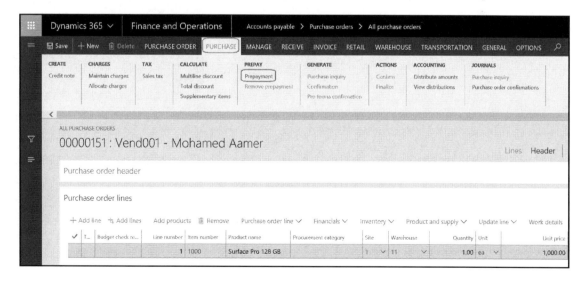

The prepayment dialogue will pop up as shown in the following screenshot; enter the prepayment description, select whether the prepayment will be **Fixed** or **Percent** from the purchase cost, and select the procurement category:

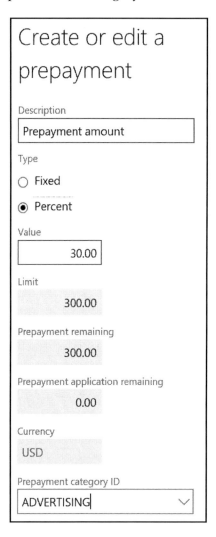

 The purchase order must be confirmed to generate the prepayment.

As shown in the following screenshot, navigate to **INVOICE** and select **Prepayment invoice** in the purchase order form:

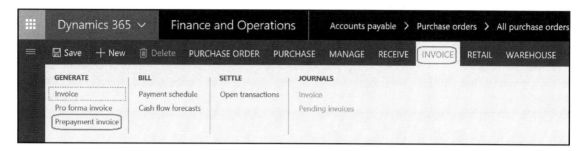

 The prepayment account must be selected in the inventory posting profile under the **Purchase order** tab.

Navigate to **Inventory management | Setup | Posting | Posting | Purchase order**.

Then, post the prepayment invoice from the vendor invoice form, as shown in the following screenshot, and enter the invoice number and description:

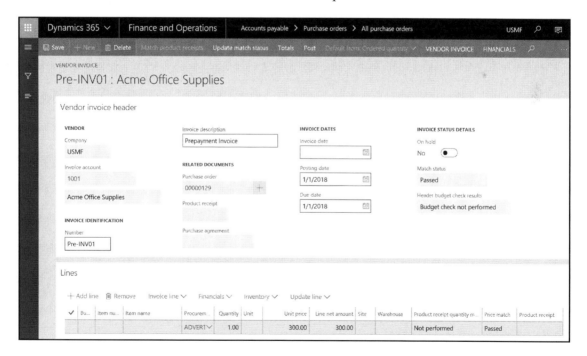

The financial entry is automatically generated based on the inventory posting profile as follows:

- Dr. Prepayment
- Cr. Vendor balance

At this point, there is a liability on this particular vendor with the prepayment amount, and this liability appears in the open transactions, which are not settled yet. This form is **Settle transactions**; in order to access this form, navigate to **Accounts payable** | **Vendors** | **All vendors**, select a particular vendor, then go to the **INVOICE** ribbon and select **Settle transactions**, as shown in the following screenshot:

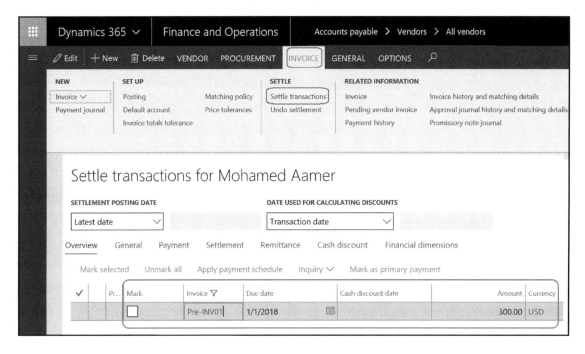

The prepayment invoice is ready to be paid; to perform a vendor payment transaction, navigate to **Accounts payable** | **Payments** | **Payment journal**, create a new journal number, and then go to **Lines**. Select the vendor code and then go to **Functions** | **Settlement**. The following screenshot illustrates the journal and its line along with the settlement access path:

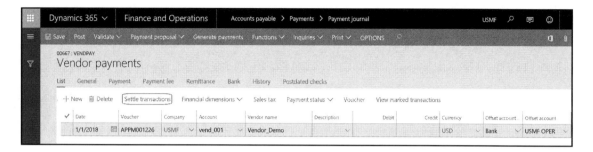

As shown in the following screenshot, in the **Settle transactions** form, mark the invoice that will be paid and close the form:

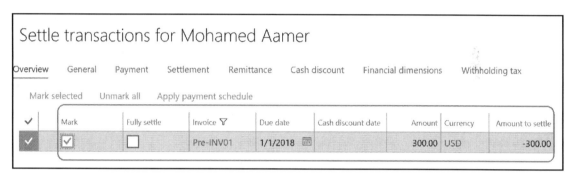

The amount will be automatically populated in the voucher line on the debit side; validate and post the payment transactions. In this transaction, the vendor invoice has been settled against payment transactions and moved to closed transactions, as shown in the following screenshot:

The financial entry is automatically generated as follows:

- Dr. Vendor balance
- Cr. Bank account

To access closed transactions, navigate to **Accounts payable** | **Vendors** | **All vendors**; select a particular vendor and then navigate to **INVOICE** | **Undo settlement**. The following screenshot shows the payment and the settled invoice against it:

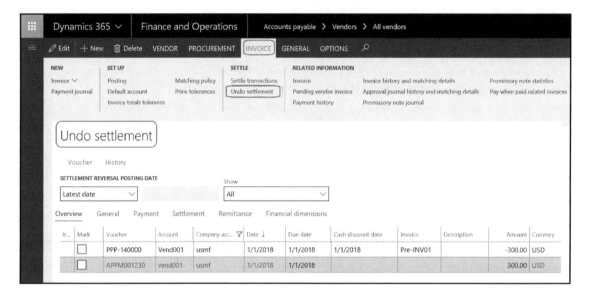

 The settled transactions can be reversed from the **Undo settlement** form.

Then, post the purchase order invoice and consider the prepayment amount by applying the prepayment on the final vendor invoice to get the realistic vendor liability; there are two scenarios here: apply the prepayment before a post-purchase order invoice or after posting the vendor invoice.

 The prepayment has a transaction type as payment during prepayment posting.
The prepayment has a transaction type as **Prepayment application** during apply prepayment transaction.

The following screenshot illustrates the prepayment application process before posting the purchase order invoice; navigate to **Accounts payable** | **Purchase orders** | **All purchase orders**, select the purchase order that needs to be invoiced, go to the **INVOICE** ribbon, and select **Invoice**:

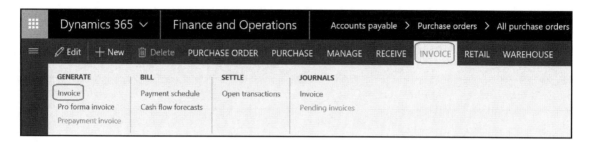

The vendor invoice form will open up, enter the invoice number and invoice description. Then go to **Apply prepayment**. The **Apply prepayment** form with open up, select the **Prepayments to apply,** as shown in the following screenshot:

If you are posting a vendor invoice and it has a prepayment invoice, a message bar will appear indicating that one or more pending invoices have unapplied paid prepayment invoices available to apply. Use the **Apply prepayment** form to apply prepayment values to the selected invoice.

The applied prepayment amount appears in the invoice line with a negative sign; this will lead to the net invoice amount (*total invoice amount—prepayment amount*). As shown in the following screenshot, the total invoice (1,000) minus the prepayment amount (300) equals 700, so the net invoice amount is 700:

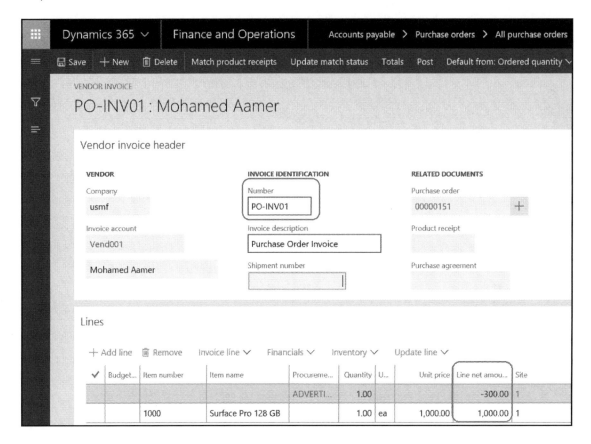

The invoice financial entry for a purchase order invoice that has a prepayment applied is generated; the entry consists of four lines; two lines for the prepayment application and the other two lines for the liability entry, as follows:

- Dr. Vendor balance (the prepayment amount)
- Cr. Prepayment (the prepayment amount)
- Dr. Purchase inventory receipt (the total purchase order amount)
- Cr. Vendor balance (the total purchase order amount)

Vendor invoice register, invoice approval, and invoice pool

We covered the vendor invoice posting from the purchase order document. In some scenarios, the handling of posting vendor invoices varies from company to company, depending on the company size and structure. Microsoft Dynamics 365 for Finance and Operations supports several methods of handling vendor invoices. The following diagram illustrates the invoice register process, followed by invoice approval journal or invoice pool, which then moves to invoice matching and posting the purchase order invoice:

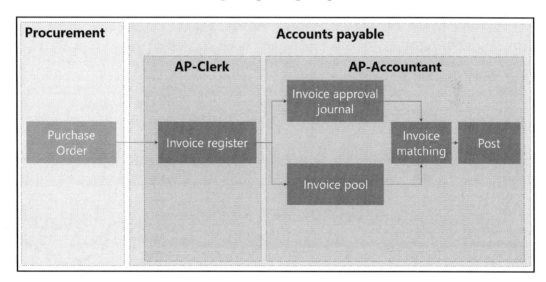

The invoice register process assumes that all vendor invoices are received by the accounts payable clerk, this step is considered a pre-registration of vendor invoice, and needs to be approved by the accounts payable accountant. Optionally, the accounts payable clerk can assign a registered invoice to a purchase order. To access the **Invoice register** journal, navigate to **Accounts payable | Invoices | Invoice register**, then create a new **Journal** and go to **Lines,** then the **Vendor invoice register** line form will open, as shown in the following screenshot:

The generated financial entry is as the following:

- Dr. Accounts payable—Offset invoice pending approval
- Cr. Invoice pending approval

> The accounts are called from the vendor posting profile under **Accounts payable | Setup | Vendor posting profiles**, then assign accounts in **Arrival**, and **Offset account**.
>
> The entry is not posted to vendor transactions.

The pre-registered invoice is ready for approval by the accounts payable accountant, to access **Invoice approval** navigate to **Accounts payable | Invoices | Invoice approval**, create a new **Journal** and go to **Lines**, then select **Find vouchers** to fetch the pre-registered invoice, as shown in the following screenshot:

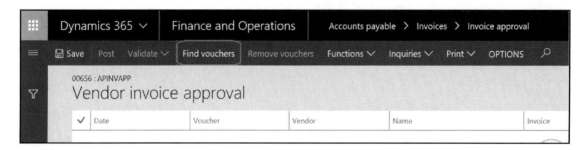

The **Find vouchers** form shows the pre-registered invoice, as shown in the following screenshot:

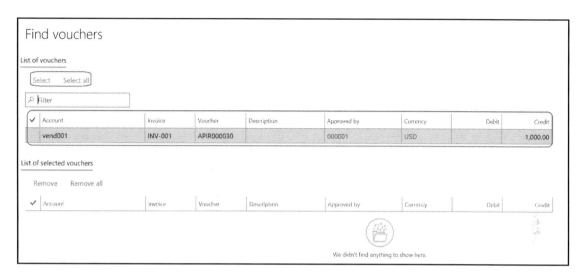

Select the invoice line and click **Select**, the invoice line will be moved to the **List of selected vouchers**, as shown in the following screenshot:

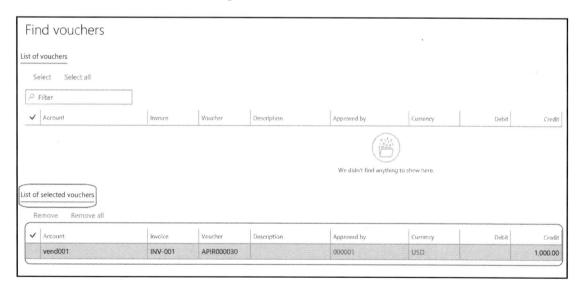

In the **Vendor invoice approval** journal form, the system retrieves the vendor summary account, and accounts that reverse the invoice register entry, and the accountant should locate the expense account, as shown in the following screenshot:

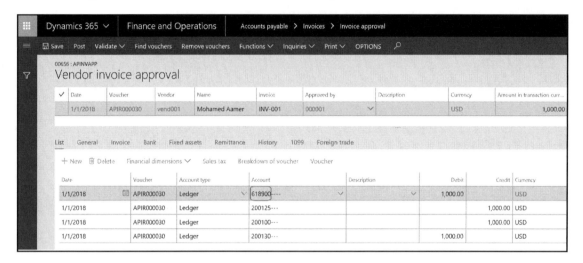

Then, the accountant moves to the vendor invoice matching step, go to **Functions** and then select **Purchase order**. As shown in the following screenshot, select **Update match status**, then **Post**:

The generated financial entry contains the reversal of the invoice register entry, and vendor liability entry as the following:

- Invoice register reversal:
  - Dr. Vendor pending invoice
  - Cr. Accounts payable—offset invoice pending approval

- Vendor liability:
    - Dr. Cost of purchased materials
    - Cr. Vendor invoice

Assume after posting the vendor invoice register, the process requires the user to go to the **Invoice pool**; to access **Invoice pool**, navigate to **Accounts payable | Invoices | Invoice pool**, the form shows the invoices that have been already registered, then move to the invoice matching process to post the invoice, as shown in the following screenshot:

The non-purchase order invoices can be service invoices recorded by the accounting team recording the invoice through **Invoice journal**, or the invoices recorded by the concerned departments, where each department will record their expenses invoices through the new vendor invoice form that has been newly introduced prior Microsoft Dynamics 365 for Finance and Operations.

The **Invoice journal** is accessed by navigating to ;**Accounts payable | Invoices | Invoice journal**, as shown in the following screenshot. We can see the invoice journal lines; select the vendor ID and enter the invoice number, the amount in the credit side, and the ledger offset account. The posted **Invoice journal** generates a vendor liability and ledger entry, as well:

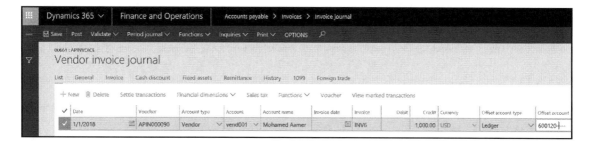

Non-inventory vendor invoices

The non-inventory invoices are mainly used with non-stocked items, where each service item is represented as a specific expense type. This concept is more familiar for departments rather than selecting ledger accounts, as the concerned department that entered the expense invoice does not have experience in accounting, and descriptive expense service items are more familiar with data entry.

To access the **Open vendor invoices** form, navigate to **Accounts payable** | **Invoices** | **Open vendor invoices**. To create a new invoice record, navigate to the **INVOICE** ribbon and select **Vendor invoice**, as shown in the following screenshot:

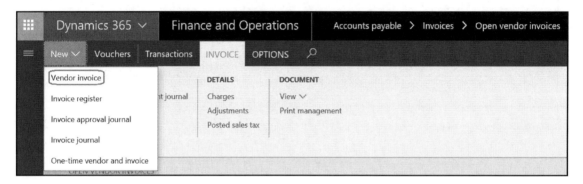

In the vendor invoice form, select the vendor ID and enter the invoice number, description, item number, and then the amount.

Global vendor invoice journal

The global invoice journal is a newly introduced feature in Microsoft Dynamics 365 for Finance and Operations; it gives the ability to move between legal entities in the vendor invoice journal without switching the legal entity. It increases the productivity of AP accountants who are working across all legal entities. To access **Global invoice journal,** go to **Accounts payable** | **Invoices** | **Global invoice journal**, as shown in the following screenshot, the user logged in USMF and can see other companies journals:

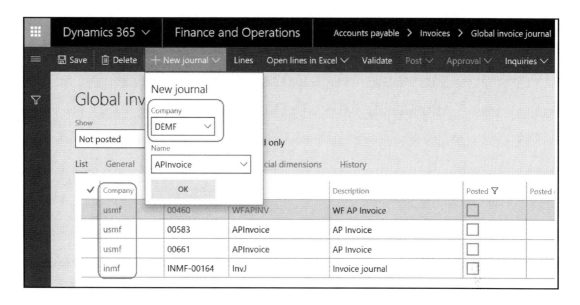

Vendor payment proposal

The vendor payment transactions represent the settlement of vendor invoices; the payment process could be executed individually per vendor or run payment proposal process, to collect multiple payments. To access the vendor payment proposal, navigate to **Accounts payable** | **Payments** | **Payment journal**, create a new **Journal**, then go to **Lines**, in the lines form select **Payment proposal** then **Create payment proposal**, as shown in the following screenshot:

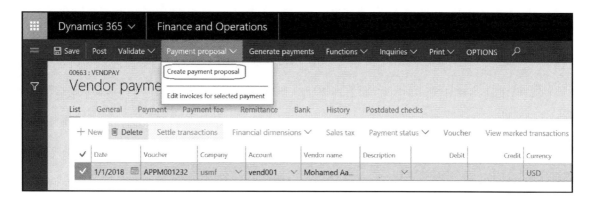

In the vendor payment proposal dialogue, the accountant can select payment parameters to collect all payment transactions that meet the selected criteria, as shown in the following screenshot:

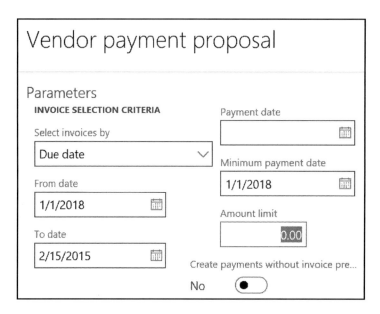

Vendor payment proposal retrieves payments that meet the selection criteria, the accountant still has the option to remove payments from the list, or change search criteria, then select **Create payments**:

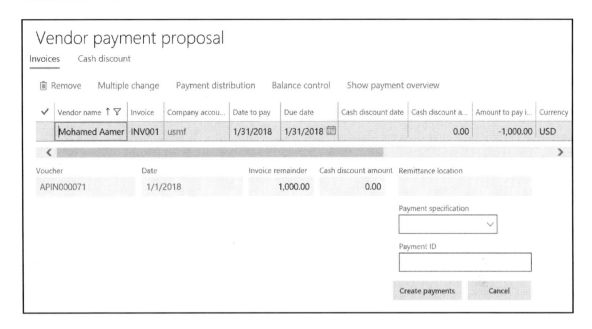

Payment lines are retrieved in the payment journal lines, and ready to be posted:

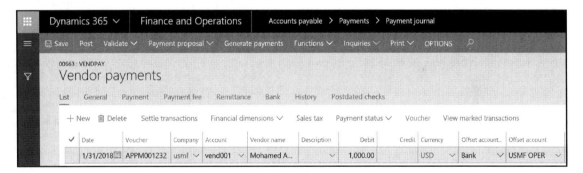

Vendor advanced payment

An advance payment is a regular business scenario where vendors are required to pay some amount of money as a down payment, regardless of whether there is a purchase order; this could occur with a partner with whom they have regular business. To perform an advance payment transaction in Microsoft Dynamics 365 for Finance and Operations, navigate to **Accounts payable** | **Payments** | **Payment journal** and create a new journal; then move to **Lines**, enter the vendor ID, and enter the amount, then switch to the **Payment** tab and check the **Prepayment journal voucher** checkbox.

After this, the default posting profile value to the prepayment posting profile will be changed, as shown in the following screenshot:

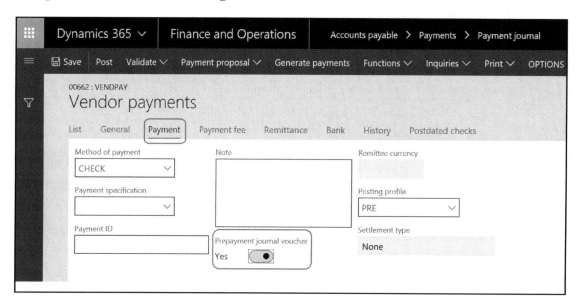

The journal contains prepayment transactions and must therefore include sales tax.

The prepayment posting profile is created under the **Accounts payable posting profile**. Under **Accounts payable parameters** | **Ledger and sales tax**, assign the prepayment posting profile.

Vendor settlement

A settlement is an accounting transaction that occurs on accounts payable, accounts receivables, and the general ledger. This transaction is used mainly to settle vendor invoices against vendor payments or advance payments:

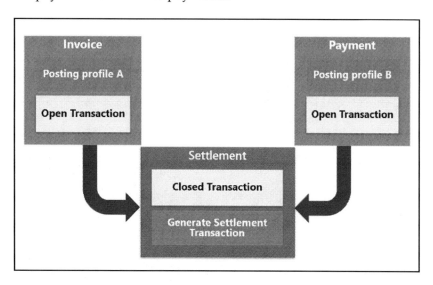

It is necessary to classify posting profiles of the vendor and customer in the opening balance, as it will affect the settlement process.

The settlement transaction affects vendor and customer balances, and it is reported in the vendor or customer statement report that identifies the following:

- The vendor
- The open (unsettled) invoice and payments
- The closed (settled) invoice and payments
- The vendor balance

A settlement transaction can occur during a payment or collection transaction, if the accountant marks the invoice that will be paid or collected. On the other hand, the settlement can be performed at the vendor or customer level, and these transactions can be unsettled.

The settlement transaction should take into consideration the currency, as it can be performed in the company's home currency by an equivalent amount, which is calculated based on the currency exchange rate, or it can be settled in the same currency of the invoice by identifying the currency in the payment process.

The vendor settlement mechanism in Microsoft Dynamics 365 for Finance and Operations

A vendor settlement in Microsoft Dynamics 365 for Finance and Operations is a transaction that occurs to settle vendor advance payments against vendor invoices, on a monthly basis.

Vendor settlements have the following effects:

- The first one is at the vendor level, which occurs when the vendor transaction closes
- The second is the financial entry, which occurs only if the posting profile of the advance payment and invoice are different

Here, I will illustrate the mechanism of vendor advance payment, invoices, and vendor settlement financial entries—the vendor advance payment posting profile is advanced, and the financial entry will be:

- Dr. Advances to vendor 1,200 USD
- Cr. Bank 1,200 USD

- Open transactions: 1,200 USD advance payment. The vendor invoice posting profile is **General**, and the financial entry is:
    - Dr. Expense 1,000 USD
    - Cr. Payable 1,000 USD
    - Open transactions: 1,200 USD advance payment and 1,000 USD vendor invoice
- The vendor settlement is as follows:
    - Dr. Payable 1,000 USD
    - Cr. Advances to vendor 1,000 USD
    - Open transactions: 200 USD advance payment
    - Closed transactions: 1,000 USD advance payment and 1,000 USD vendor invoice

- If the posting profiles of the advance payment and invoicing are different, a settlement financial entry will be created.

Summary

This chapter covered the accounts payable module in Microsoft Dynamics 365 for Finance and Operations transactions. We also learned the accounts payable transactions vendor invoice, invoice register, invoice approval journal, and vendor invoice pool. We then moved to global vendor invoice across legal entities, vendor payment proposal, the prepayment invoice and its processing, and finally covered advance payments, and the settlement mechanism.

In the next chapter, we will discuss accounts receivable master data, control, and transactions.

8
Understanding Accounts Receivable

The accounts receivable module is the module that represents a customer's data and their transactions. The accounts receivable cycles are customer invoicing, customer payment, and settlement. These business processes manage and control the execution of customer sales processes. These processes are based on sales activities and product delivery cycles in the sales and marketing processes, which manage and control the execution of the order to cash business processes. In this chapter, we will cover the following topics:

- Understanding the accounts receivable module's integration with other modules
- Exploring customer master data characteristics
- Exploring accounts receivable controls
- Exploring accounts receivable transactions

Understanding the accounts receivable module's integration with other modules

The accounts receivable module manages and controls customer transactions from the accounting point of view, where recording customer master information and the basic transactions related to customer invoicing, payment, and settlement happen. The accounts receivable function is integrated with other business functions.

The integration points with accounts receivable are as follows:

- **Sales and marketing module**: This is where goods and services are quoted to the customer, and then the sales order is created
- **Inventory and warehousing module**: This is where goods are delivered to customers, and invoicing is based on delivered goods from the warehousing module
- **Cash and bank management**: This is where customer payment and settlement against invoices are done

The full life cycle of the Order to Cash is shown in the following diagram:

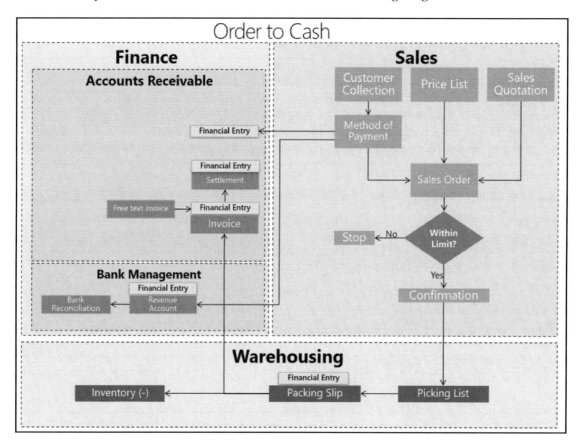

The normal practice with enterprise organizations is that no sales orders are created directly. This can lead to creating unnecessary sales orders and exposing the company to uncontrolled open orders. This business process must be controlled since it is the source of company revenues. On the other hand, unnecessary sales order can significantly impact the cost of goods sold and customer balances, in addition to the company's profitability.

The selling process typically goes through specific internal procedures to deliver items or services from the sales department. The sales process begins either by automatic orders of sales based on a sales quotation for a specific customer, or by entering the sales order manually.

The **sales quotation** is a document representing the company's offer to the customer, and indicates the item or service, price, receipt date, and other information. The quotation is sent to the customer to evaluate the company's offer. The customer then replies to the sales agent by either confirmation or rejection. A confirmed sales quotation is a document that is ready to be converted to a sales order document.

The following are **sales quotation** statuses:

- **Created**: The sales quotation has been created, but has not been sent to the customer. The sales quotation can be modified if its status is **Created**.
- **Sent**: The sales quotation status is updated once the sales quotation document is sent to the customer.
- **Confirmed**: This status shows when the sales quotation has been confirmed by the customer.
- **Lost**: This status will be displayed once the sales quotation has been refused by the customer.
- **Canceled**: This status will be displayed once the sales quotation and all sales quotation lines have been canceled.

There are several types of sales orders in Microsoft Dynamics 365 for Finance and Operations. They are listed as follows:

- **Sales order**: This is a commitment document sent to a customer to deliver the required goods or services to them.
- **Journal**: This is a draft document that does not accept any further transactions, nor does it affect the inventory or finance.
- **Subscription**: This is a recurring sales order to supply the same item, quantity, and price. The system recreates the sales order after invoicing.
- **Returned order**: This document represents the **returned material authorization (RMA)** and handles quantity returns and customer credit notes.
- **Item requirements**: This is a type of sales order that relates the sales order to project requirements.
- **Sales agreement**: A sales agreement is a document that is sent to a customer to deliver goods or services over a specific time period and includes prices.

The following are types of sales order status:

- **Open order**: This indicates that the sales order is at one of the following stages: newly created, not totally received, or not totally invoiced
- **Delivered**: This indicates that the sales order is fully delivered
- **Invoiced**: This indicates that the sales order is fully invoiced
- **Canceled**: This indicates that the ordered quantities in the sales order have been canceled

The following are types of sales order document status:

- **None**: This indicates that the sales order is created and no further documents have been posted
- **Confirmation**: This indicates that the sales order has been confirmed
- **Picking list**: This indicates that the picking list document has been posted on the sales order
- **Packing slip**: This indicates that the packing slip document has been posted on the sales order
- **Invoice**: This indicates that the sales order invoice has been posted

The delivery of goods from the company warehouse occurs via the following two steps:

- The preliminary step is the picking list that assigns inventory dimensions such as serial number and batch number, in addition to the quality inspection, if required. The preliminary step in the picking list does not affect the on-hand inventory. The packing slip transaction decreases the physical quantities in the on-hand inventory.
- The final step in a sales order is posting the invoice that represents the revenue recognition of the sales order, or in other words, the **cost of goods sold** (**COGS**).

 The packing slip document does not reflect any transactions in the customer balance.

The customer payment is the document that shows that the company is receiving an amount of money from the customer who receives goods or services from the company. The customer payment process is executed based on customer invoices. The normal practice in enterprise organizations is that the customer collection will have two different scenarios: collection after issuing the sales order invoice, or advanced collection before creating a sales order.

The advanced collection can be assigned to a specific sales order. Each collection transaction is settled against a customer invoice. This affects the company's cash position and cash projection for the future customer collection. The customer pays the amount of money after issuing the sales invoice. Then the accounts receivable accountant records the collection transactions and settles them against an invoice. The invoice could be settled automatically, if the advanced collection is linked to a sales order.

The bank accountant executes the check collection process and bank reconciliation accordingly, as shown in the following diagram, which illustrates the customer collection, invoice, and settlement document integration:

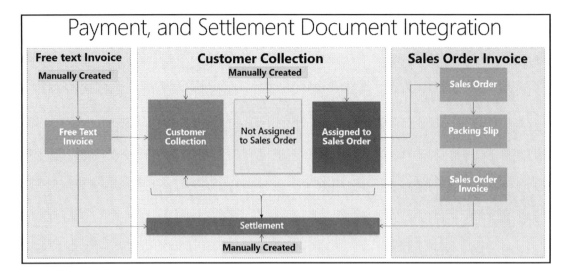

Each transaction is represented in a document type in Microsoft Dynamics 365 for Finance and Operations, with the document containing the details of the transaction. The transactions data, whether inherited from the master data, entered manually, and/or automatically inherited from another transaction, is linked with a specific reference. The integration between the collection and other customer transaction documents gives us the visibility to trace what the original sales order and packing slip that are related to the invoice are, together with who confirmed the sales order.

Exploring customer master data characteristics

The customer record has essential information that directly affects accounts receivable transactions. In the following section, we will cover the basic information that should be considered when creating a new customer record.

In order to create a new customer record, you should navigate to **Accounts receivable | Customers | All customers**.

On the customer list page, press *Alt + N* to create a new customer record. As shown in the following screenshot, the mandatory fields are **Customer account**, **Name**, **Customer group**, and **Country/region**. You can either save the entered information and complete it afterwards or go to the transaction form, whether **Sales quotation**, **Project quotation**, and/or **Sales order**:

We can see the following in the preceding screenshot:

- The **Customer account**, whether assigned manually or automatically through the number sequence.
- **Group** is a mandatory field that represents the customer group that the particular customer belongs to, and this is considered the integration point between accounts receivable and the general ledger, through the posting profile. However, the posting profile could be on the level of the customer code.
- **Address** represents the country and address information that this customer belongs to.

- The **Currency** field is mandatory, and it represents the default currency for the particular customer transaction. However, it can be changed on the transaction level, as per the business case.

Click on **Save and open**, and then select **Customer**. This will open the customer master data form.

The Sales order defaults fast tab

In the customer creation form, go to the **Sales order defaults** fast tab. In this section, we will explore the **DISCOUNT** field group.

The DISCOUNT field group

The **DISCOUNT** field group represents the discount and pricing options that could be applied on the particular customer. The **DISCOUNT** field group consists of the discount and pricing groups to which the customer belongs, as shown in the following screenshot:

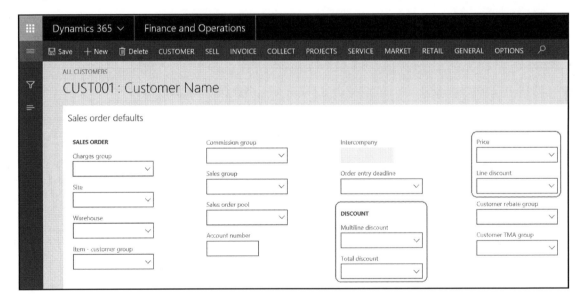

Customer price or discount groups

Customer price and discount groups consist of four pricing groups, as shown in the following diagram:

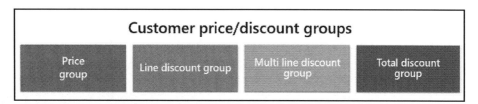

In order to create the customer price or discount groups, the user navigates to **Inventory management** | **Setup** | **Price/discount** | **Customer price/discount groups**. The **Customer price/discount groups** form shows the **Price/discount** options, and we should be able to create groups for each **Price/discount** options. The following screenshot shows the definition of the price/discount group options:

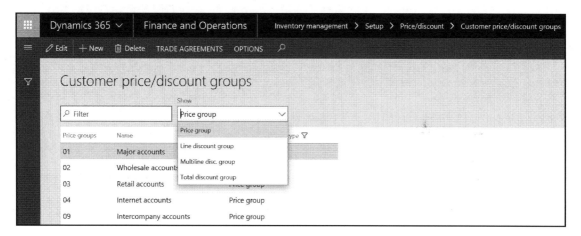

The price or discount must be activated by navigating to **Sales and marketing** | **Setup** | **Price/discount** | **Activate price/discount**.

Customer price/discount groups contains the following options:

- **Price group**: This represents the customer's price group used for price proposals upon sales, and this price group is attached to the customer master data.
- **Line discount group**: This represents the sales line discount used for sales, which is attached to the customer master data.
- **Multiline discount group**: This represents the multiline discount group used to control discounts across several sales lines. It is attached to the customer master data.
- **Total discount group**: This represents that the total discount group is attached to the customer master data in a field called total discount group.

In the created **Major accounts** value for **Price group**, navigate to **TRADE AGREEMENTS** | **Create trade agreements**, as shown in the following screenshot:

The **Trade agreement journals** screen will pop up. Create a new journal by pressing *Alt + N*, selecting a journal name, and then clicking on **Lines**. As shown in the following screenshot, we will create a journal line (or lines) by selecting, under **Relation**, the **Price (sales)** value. Then we select the **Account code** field as **Table**. To make this price related to a particular customer, in **Item relation**, select **Table** to make this price correspond to a particular item when sold to a specific customer from a specific warehouse:

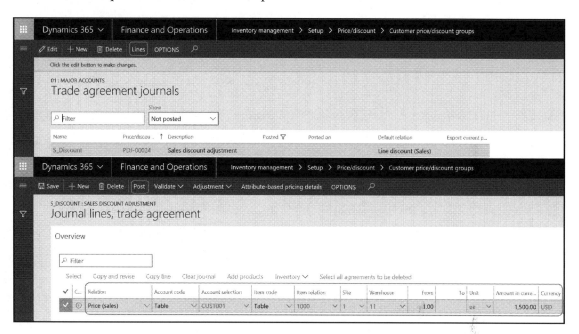

 The trade agreement should be posted to the customer price list.

As shown in the next screenshot, the purpose of this setup is to recall the sales price on the sales line automatically from the posted trade agreements journal. To access the sales order form, navigate to **Accounts receivable** | **Orders** | **All sales orders**:

The PAYMENT fast tab

In an opened customer form, move to the **PAYMENT** fast tab: under the **PAYMENT** field group, there is some required information for customer payment arrangements. The available options are as follows:

- **Terms of payment**
- **Method of payment**
- **Payment specification**
- **Payment schedule**
- **Payment day**
- **Cash discount**

The preceding options are displayed like this:

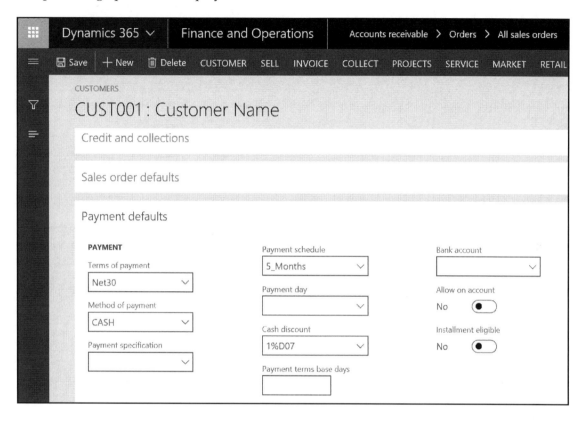

Terms of payment

The **Terms of payment** field represents the calculated due date to pay for the customer. In order to access the **Terms of payment** creation form, go to **Accounts receivable** | **Payments setup** | **Terms of payment**, as shown in the following screenshot:

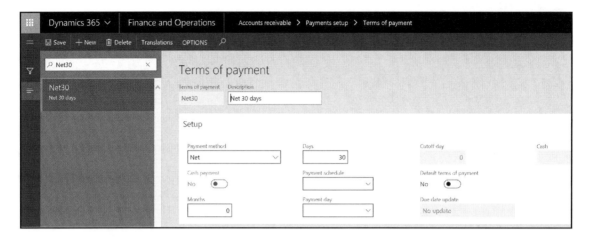

Identify the due date based in the **Payment method** combobox, which contains six options. Assuming that the customer invoice is posted on January 1, 2018, and the number of days is **20**, the due date will be changed based on the selected payment method option, as shown in the following diagram:

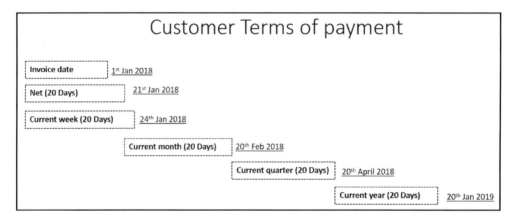

We can see the following in the preceding diagram:

- **Net**: The due date will be calculated from the invoice posting (January 1 + 20 days = **21ˢᵗ Jan**).
- **Current week**: The due date will be calculated from the end of the week in which the invoice was posted (January 4 + 20 days = **24ᵗʰ Jan**).
- **Current month**: The due date will be calculated from the end of the month in which the invoice was posted (January 31 + 20 days = **24ᵗʰ Feb**).

- **Current quarter**: The due date will be calculated from the end of the quarter in which the invoice was posted (March 31 + 20 days = **20th April**).
- **Current year**: The due date will be calculated from the end of the year in which the invoice was posted (December 31 + 20 days = **20th Jan**).
- **Cash on delivery**: This represents the cash payment upon delivery. With this option, a ledger account must be specified; it will be used when posting the sales order invoice.

Method of payment

The method of payment represents the way of receiving payment from the customer by check, bank transfer, credit card, or cash. In order to access the **Methods of payment** form, navigate to **Accounts receivable | Payment setup | Methods of payment**. As shown in the following screenshot of the **Methods of payment** form, the required controls will be applied on the transaction. In this case, the **CASH** method of payment is used:

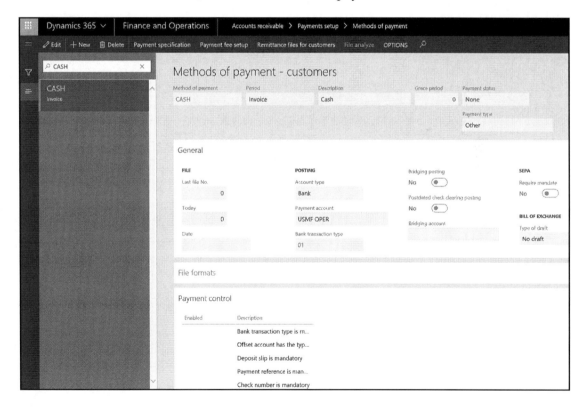

Payment specification

The payment specification represents codes, according to the agreement with the bank that is specified for the selected method of payment. The payment specification is tied to the method of payment.

Payment schedule

The payment schedule represents the installment that will be used after invoicing. To access the **Payment schedule** form, navigate to **Accounts receivable** | **Payments setup** | **Payment schedules**. We can identify an installment with a fixed number of months or a fixed amount, as shown in this screenshot:

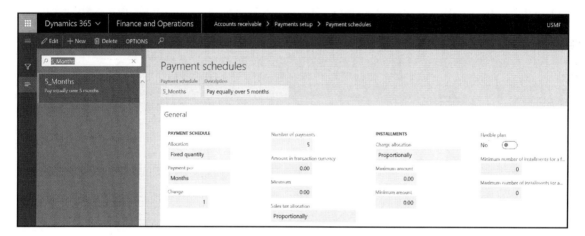

Assume that the sales order invoice is posted on January 1, 2018, its amount is 5,000 USD, and it is assigned a payment schedule for five months, with the terms of payment as net 30 days. Navigate to **Accounts receivable** | **Orders** | **All sales orders**. Then open a sales order by navigating to **Header view**, and under the **Price discount** fast tab assign a payment schedule.

It can be automatically inherited from the customer master data and can be modified on the sales order header, as shown in the following screenshot:

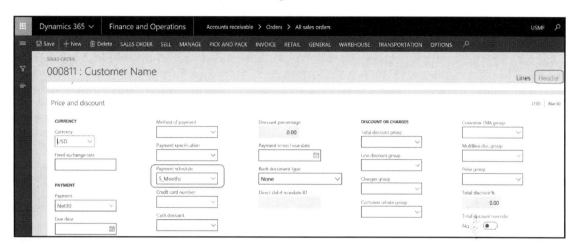

In order to check the payment installment dates, from the ribbon navigate to **INVOICE | BILL | Payment schedule**. The **Payment schedule** form will pop up. Then go to the **Payment lines** tab. The following screenshot shows the payment schedules, divided into five installments for five months:

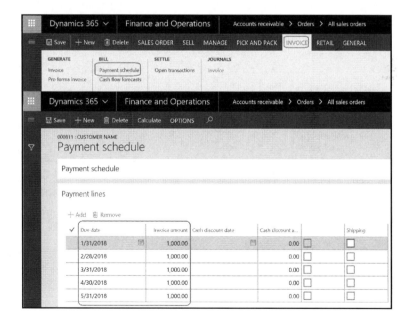

Cash discount

Cash discount represents the discount that will be applied to the customer payment, if the payment is made before the due date. This encourages the customer to pay before the due date. Cash discount has the flexibility to assign the next cash discount, which could be a deal with the customer. In order to create the cash discount record, navigate to **Accounts receivable** | **Payments setup** | **Cash discounts**.

As shown in the following screenshot, which represents the **Cash discounts** form, the **Setup** fast tab identifies the discount percentage, number of months, and number of days. It is important to assign the main account for customer discounts:

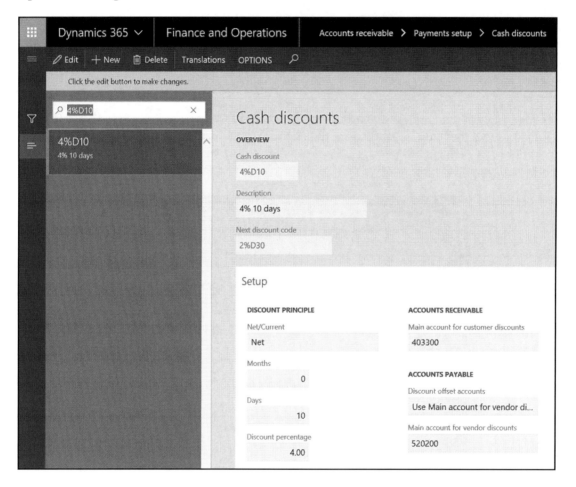

Assume that an invoice has been posted on January 1, the cash discount is 4% if the invoice is paid within 10 days, and the terms of payment are net 20 days. The invoice amount is 1,000 USD. The sales tax is 6%, which becomes equal to 60 USD (*invoice amount * sales tax*) (*1000 * 6%*).

The total invoice amount is 1,060 USD (*invoice amount + sales tax*) (*1000 + 60*).

The cash discount is 4% of the invoice amount "before sales tax", 40 USD is the discount amount, which is calculated based on the invoice amount which is 1,000 USD, and note that the invoice amount excludes the sales tax (*invoice amount * cash discount*) (*1000 * 4%*).

The invoice amount after the cash discount is 960 USD (*invoice amount – cash discount amount*) (*1,000 – 40*).

The total invoice amount to be paid is 1,020 USD (*invoice amount after cash discount + sales tax amount*) (*960 + 60*).

The cash discount date of the customer free text invoice is January 11, and its amount is –40.

We then go to the **Customer payments** form by navigating to **Accounts receivable | Payments | Payment journal** and create journal, then move to its lines, select customer ID in account field and settle it against the posted invoice on January 1. As shown in this screenshot, the payment amount is **1,020.00**:

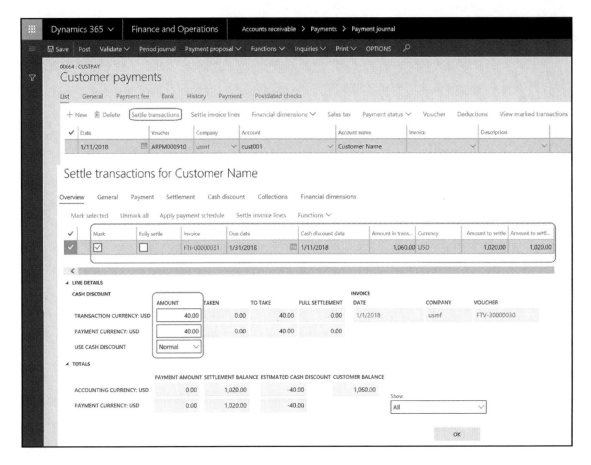

In order to apply the cash discount, the user should choose **Always** or **Normal** under the **USE CASH DISCOUNT** field.

In the following screenshot, the changed payment date, January 19, is visible and the cash discount goes to the next cash discount code. It is 2% within 30 days:

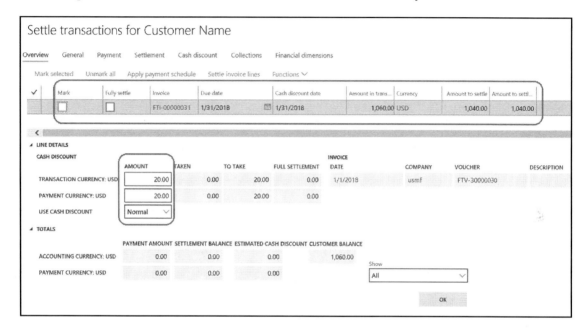

The Invoice and delivery fast tab

In this section, we will cover the **Invoice and delivery** and **SALES TAX** field groups, as shown in this screenshot:

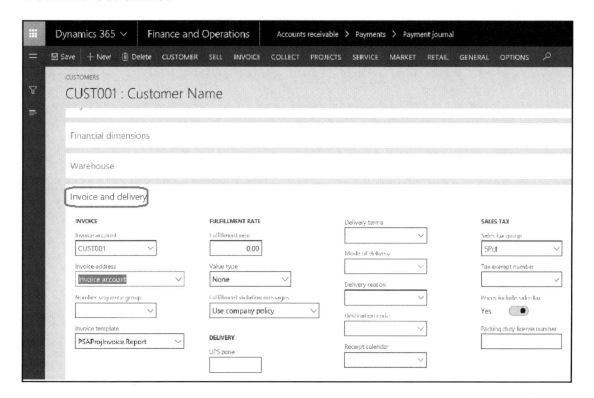

The INVOICE field group

In the **INVOICE** field group, the **Invoice account** field represents the account used in the invoicing process. The default invoice account is the customer code, but Microsoft Dynamics 365 for Finance and Operations gives flexibility to point invoice posting to another customer. Assume that the company sends goods to two different customers, then the invoice will be issued to one particular customer out of the two.

The relationship between the customer code and the invoice account, where the customer invoice could be linked to one customer code or multiple customer codes, is shown in the following diagram:

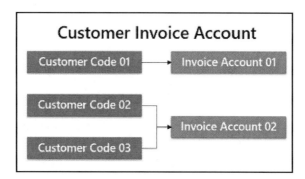

The SALES TAX field group

The **SALES TAX** field group represents the tax treatment that will be applied on the customer, which includes the sales tax, prices including sales tax or excluding, and the tax exempt number if any. Each field can be explained as follows:

- **Sales tax group**: The **Sales tax group** section represents the sales tax group assigned to a particular customer. This record will be a default value on all transactions that will be inherited from the customer master data.
- **Prices include sales tax**: The **Prices include sales tax** field indicates whether the invoice amount includes sales tax or excludes it.
- **Tax exempt number**: The **Tax exempt number** field is used for reporting and statistical extractions.

The **Sales tax group** can be set as the default at the customer group level. Simply navigate to **Accounts receivable** | **Setup** | **Customer groups**. It can also be overridden by a user in the customer form.

Exploring the accounts receivable module's controls

The accounts receivable module's controls are an essential task to be discussed during the analysis and design phases, in addition to being assessed in the operation phase for enhancements. Microsoft Dynamics 365 for Finance and Operations addresses the required basic business procedures for this module's controls. It is significant to the business to control the execution of accounts receivable processes, since it directly affects company revenues. Therefore, it should be controlled and monitored. In the following section, we will explore:

- Customer hold activities
- Customer credit limit management

Customer hold activities

In daily business operations in accounts receivable, the accounting manager may need to stop transactions on a specific customer. The on-hold function for customers in Microsoft Dynamics 365 for Finance and Operations is located at the customer level. To access this function, navigate to **Accounts receivable** | **Customers** | **All customers**, select a customer, and go to the **Credit and collections** fast tab.

As shown in the following screenshot, the on hold function has several options based on customer transaction type, whether it is **Invoice**, **All**, **Payment**, **Requisition**, **Never**, or **No** (**No** is the default value). These options are used to prevent customers from executing particular transactions or to stop customers entirely:

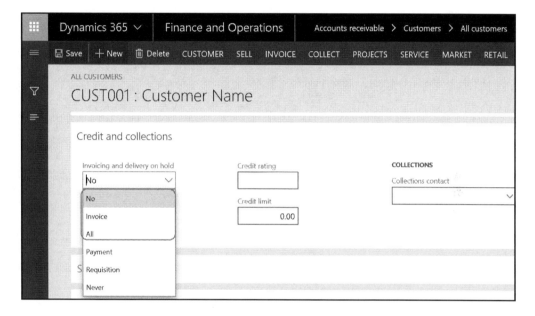

The customer on hold stats has the following options for customer transactions:

- **No**: This option means that the customer is allowed to execute all transaction types
- **Invoice**: This option means that the customer is prevented from executing invoices transactions only
- **All**: This means that the customer is prevented from executing any transaction

The other options, **Payment**, **Requisition**, and **Never**, are related to the accounts payable module.

If an end user tries to select a customer with an on hold status, the system will prevent the transaction from proceeding to the creation step. This is shown in the following screenshot, where a user tried to create a sales order:

Customer credit limit management

There is a common practice in some business domains where the sales are only on a cash basis. The customer pays an amount of money up front, and this payment creates a balance in the customer account. This account is allowed to receive only those goods that are covered by this amount of money, then the settled sales invoices are calculated against advanced collections.

Microsoft Dynamics 365 for Finance and Operations manages the customer credit limit on the customer level, and there are two ways that affect customer balance additions, partly where there is an increase in the customer balance, which consists of a cash transaction (customer advanced collection) and a non-cash transaction credit limit. The second way is a transaction that deducts the customer balance. Here is a diagram that illustrates customer balance elements:

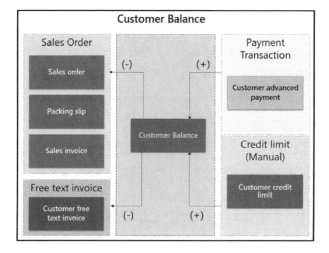

In order to activate and configure the credit limit, navigate to **Accounts receivable** | **Setup** | **Accounts receivable parameters** | **Credit rating**. The following screenshot shows credit rating options:

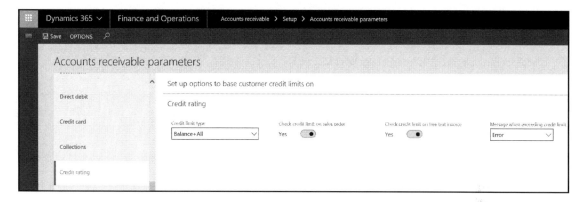

In the **Credit rating** section, identify whether the message to be displayed when the credit limit is exceeded is just a warning message or an error message. The difference in both of them is as follows:

- The warning message will not stop the transaction
- The error message will prevent the transaction from being executed

The **Credit limit type** field has four different options that represent the base of credit limit calculation; the options are listed as follows:

- **None**: The credit limit check is not activated on the module level, and can be overridden on the customer level
- **Balance**: The credit limit is checked against the customer balance
- **Balance + packing slip or product receipt**: The credit limit is checked against the customer balance and deliveries
- **Balance + All**: The credit limit is checked, considering open orders and delivered orders in it

On the customer master information, navigate to **Accounts receivable** | **Customers** | **All customers** | **Credit and collections**, as shown in the following screenshot:

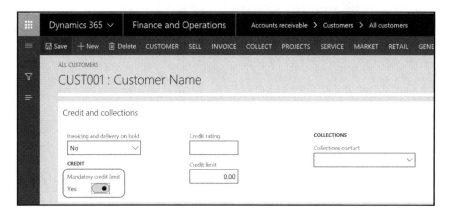

The **CREDIT** field group has the activation checkbox and the **Credit limit** amount on the customer level. These are explained as follows:

- **Mandatory credit limit**: If this is checked, the credit limit control will be applied on the customer. Otherwise, it will not be applied.
- **Credit limit**: This specifies the credit limit amount, and the customer cannot exceed this amount. If the amount is zero, the customer should deposit the amount through payment transactions.

The sales order amount created during the sales order transaction by navigating to **Accounts receivable** | **Orders** | **All sales orders** is 1,000 USD for the **CUST001** customer ID. Then navigate to **MANAGE** | **Check credit limit**. Microsoft Dynamics 365 for Finance and Operations displays the message bar to indicate that the credit limit has been exceeded. A credit limit can be an automatic action, as well:

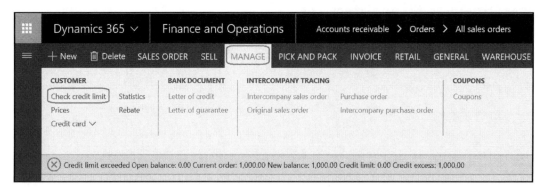

Now we can see the following information:

- **Open balance: 0.00**: This shows the current customer balance from customer advanced collections and open sales orders
- **Current order: 1,000.00**: This is the current sales order amount
- **New balance: 1,000.00**: This is the customer balance
- **Credit limit: 0.00**: This is the non-cash credit limit that is assigned to the customer
- **Credit excess: 1,000.00**: This is the amount that exceeds the customer balance

The following are credit limit equations:

- *Open balance = - customer advanced collection + open sales order amount*

- *New balance = Open balance + current order*

- *Credit excess = New balance - credit limit*

Then post a prepayment transaction with 250 USD, which affects the customer balance by 250 USD. Check the same sales order balance; it will give the upcoming results.

In order to post the prepayment transaction, navigate to **Accounts receivable | Payments | Payment journal**. Create a new journal by pressing *Alt + N*. Then go to the lines. Select the customer and enter 250 in the credit side, as shown in this screenshot:

Then move to the **Payment** tab and select the **Prepayment journal voucher** checkbox. The **Posting profile** will be automatically updated to be the **PRE** posting profile, as shown in the following screenshot:

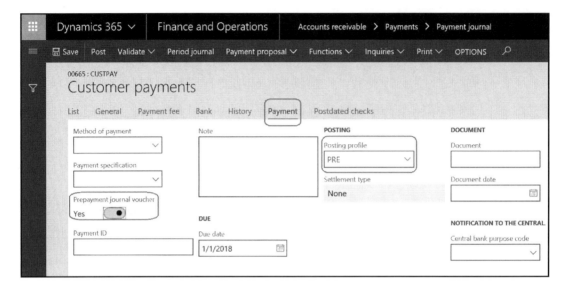

Go to the sales order in order to check the credit limit by navigating to **Accounts receivable | Orders | All sales orders**, and then go to the **MANAGE** ribbon and select the **Check credit limit** option, as shown in the following screenshot:

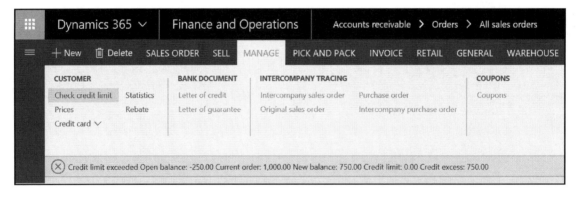

We can see the following results:

- **Open balance: -250.00**: This is the current customer balance from the customer advanced collections and open sales orders

- **Current order: 1,000.00**: This is the current sales order amount
- **New balance: 750.00**: This is the customer balance
- **Credit limit: 0.00**: This is the non-cash credit limit that is assigned to the customer
- **Credit excess: 750.00**: This is the amount that has exceeded the customer balance

Assume that a credit limit of 150 USD has been added to a customer, the current balance is 400 USD, and the remaining is 600 USD.

 If the credit limit is added to the customer master data, it will be recalculated automatically.

As shown in the following screenshot, navigate to **Accounts receivable** | **Customers** | **All customers**. Then navigate to **CUSTOMER** | **Balance** from the ribbon:

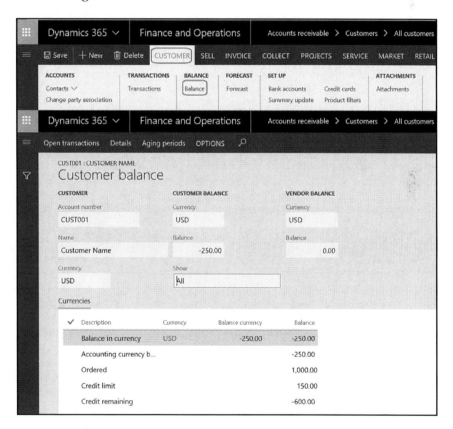

While checking the sales order credit limit, we get a message bar, like this:

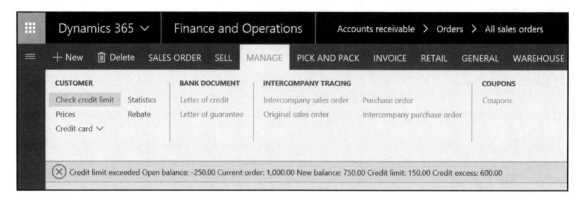

We can see the following results:

- **Open balance: -250**: This is the current customer balance from the customer advanced collections and open sales orders
- **Current order: 1,000.00**: This is the current sales order amount
- **New balance: 750.00**: This is the customer balance
- **Credit limit: 150.00**: This is the non-cash credit limit that is assigned to the customer
- **Credit excess: 600.00**: This is the amount that has exceeded the customer balance

Assume that another sales order of 1,000 USD has been created, and then check the sales order credit limit, as shown in the following screenshot:

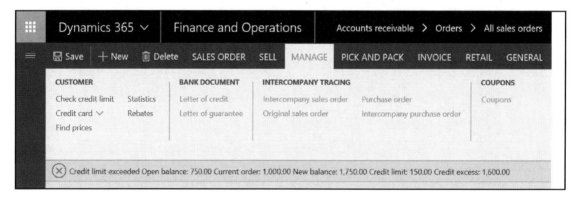

We can see the following results:

- **Open balance: 750.00**: This is the current customer balance from the customer advanced collections and open sales orders
- **Current order: 1,000.00**: This is the current sales order amount
- **New balance: 1750.00**: This is the customer balance
- **Credit limit: 150.00**: This is the non-cash credit limit that is assigned to the customer
- **Credit excess: 1600.00**: This is the amount that has exceeded the customer balance posting profile

Posting represents the integration point between the general ledger and subledger, and it automatically generates financial entries according to the posting profile's setup. Accounts receivable posting profiles are assigned in the module parameters. Navigate to **Accounts receivable | Setup | Accounts receivable parameters | Ledger and sales tax**. Then perform the following steps:

1. In the **General** fast tab, select a **Posting profile** value for general accounts receivable transactions. In other words, this represents the accounts receivable ledger account.
2. In the **Prepayment journal voucher** field group, select a **Posting profile with prepayment journal voucher** value. In other words, this represents advances from the customer ledger account.

The accounts receivable module posting profile is assigned in the accounts receivable parameters, as shown in the following screenshot:

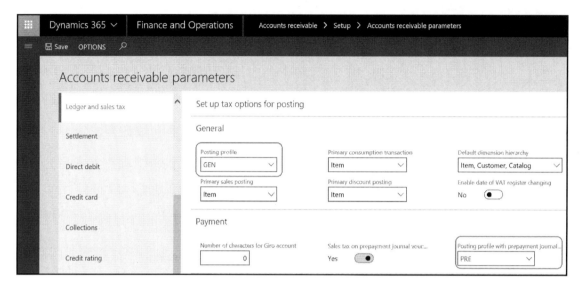

Exploring accounts receivable transactions

The following section will explore the types of transactions of the accounts receivable module. The transactions are divided into the following main categories:

- **Invoicing**: This is divided into sales order-related and free text invoices. The **Sales Order Invoice** represents the invoices that are normally attached to a sales order (or sales orders). The **Sales Order Invoice** could be the final invoice of the sales order. In that case, it is issued after delivering the goods. The **Free Text Invoice-Correction** function is a newly introduced feature prior to Microsoft Dynamics 365 for Finance and Operations.
- **Payment**: The second category is **Payment**. This category consist of two types. The first type is prepayment transactions are considered as customer advances from clients and could be assigned to sales orders. The second type is customer payment, which is settled against a customer invoice.

The following diagram will make things clearer:

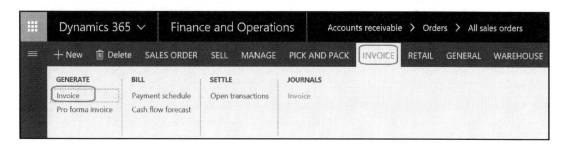

Sales order invoice

The sales order invoice document represents revenue recognition. This document is posted from the sales order form. It could be related to one sales order or multiple sales orders.

In order to post a sales order invoice from the sales order form, navigate to **Accounts receivable | Orders | All sales orders**. After choosing a particular sales order, go to the **INVOICE** ribbon and then navigate to **GENERATE | Invoice**. The following screenshot illustrates the sales order invoice menu:

On the customer invoice form, the sales order and packing are retrieved automatically. Click on **OK** to generate the invoice transaction. Here is a screenshot showing the customer invoice form:

The preceding screenshot depicts the relationship between the customer invoice, packing slip, and sales order. The sales order has more than one packing slip, and the invoice may cover one sales order with more than one packing slip. In some business cases, customer invoices cover packing slips occurring on more than one sales order. The following diagram illustrates the relationship between the sales order, packing slip, and invoice:

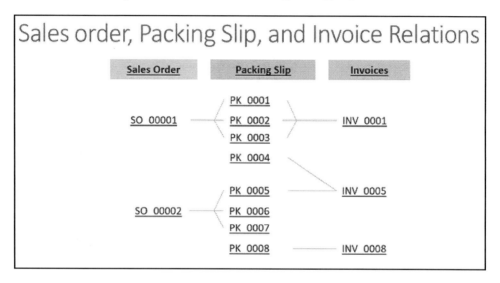

This business scenario shows which invoice covers more than the packing slip and sales order. This can be managed on Microsoft Dynamics 365 for Finance and Operations by navigating to **Accounts receivable** | **Invoices** | **Batch invoicing** | **Invoice**.

This opens the filtration query, as shown in the following screenshot. The user can retrieve information based on values in the query (this could be a packing slip, customer ID, and so on). Assume that a company invoices its customers on a weekly basis for delivered goods, and this requires identifying delivered packing slips within the specific period to be invoiced:

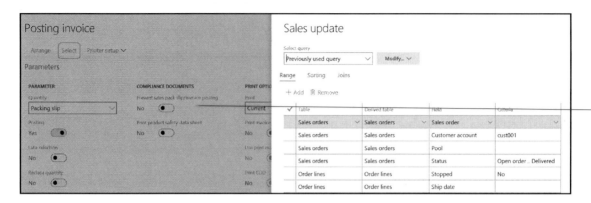

As shown in the next screenshot, there are two lines that have been retrieved according to the entered query—two sales orders with two different packing slips. The following posting invoice form represents two different invoices for each line:

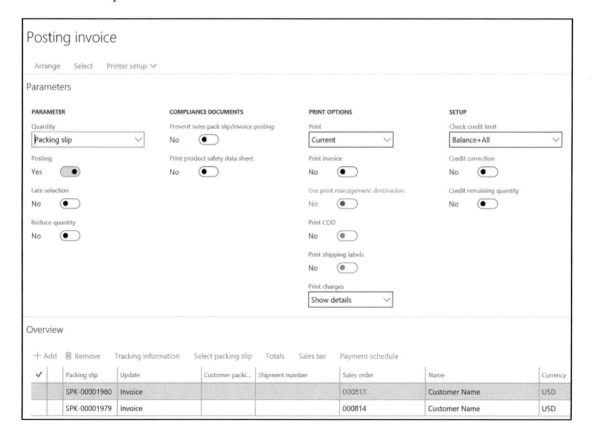

In order to consolidate multiple invoices in one invoice document, go to **Arrange**. The following screenshot illustrates the consolidate option:

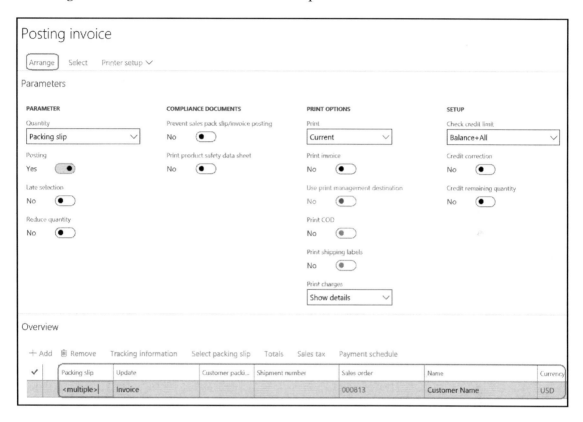

In order to activate the **Arrange** function, the **Summary update** should be identified by navigating to **Accounts receivable** | **Setup** | **Accounts receivable parameters** | **Summary update**. The **Default values for summary update** field can have **None**, **Invoice account**, **Order**, or **Automatic summary** values, as shown in this screenshot:

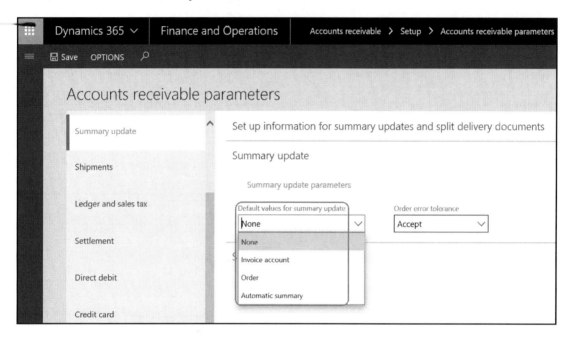

Alternatively, you can go to the **Other** tab on the posting invoice form, select **Summary update for**, and select one option from **None**, **Invoice account**, **Order**, and **Automatic summary**.

The generated sales order invoice mainly consists of the following entries: the reversal of packing slip entry, cost of goods sold entry, and revenue entry. The financial entry for the packing slip is as follows:

- **Dr. Accounts receivable – not invoiced**
- **Cr. Customer accrued account**

The next two entries represent the customer revenue:

- **Dr. Customer accrued account**
- **Cr. Accounts receivable – not invoiced**
- **Dr. Customer balance**

- **Cr. Sales revenue**
- **Dr. Cost of goods sold (COGS)**
- **Cr. Inventory**

 To access the inventory posting profile, navigate to **Inventory management** | **Setup** | **Posting** | **Posting**. Then go to the **Sales order** tab.

Free text invoice

The free text invoice represents service invoices that are issued to the customer and are not related to inventory items or sales orders. The free text invoice is not attached to a sales order. It consists of a header and lines for the ledger main account. The free text invoice document could be used for services, such as training fees.

In order to access the free text invoice, navigate to **Accounts receivable | Invoices | All free text invoices,** as shown in the following screenshot. In the free text invoice form, we will select a **Customer account**. In the invoice lines, we will select the offset main account, sales tax, and amount. The line view is the default view. To switch to the header view, click on **Header view** in the ribbon. The header view shows information about the customer, such as terms of payment, method of payment, and posting profile:

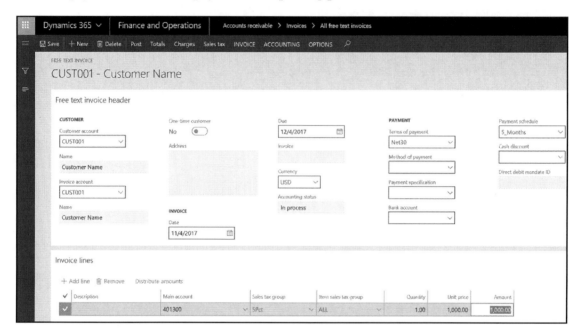

Free text correction

Free text invoice correction represents a business process used to correct posted free text invoices, assuming that, after issuing a training service invoice, the customer has realized that there is an error in the issued invoice and it needs to be corrected.

As shown in the following screenshot, to access free text invoice correction navigate to
Accounts receivable | Invoices | Open customer invoices, select **Invoice record**, and then
go to **INVOICE**. In the **CANCEL** ribbon, then move to **Correct invoice** and select the
Reason code value and enter a value in the **Canceling invoice date** field:

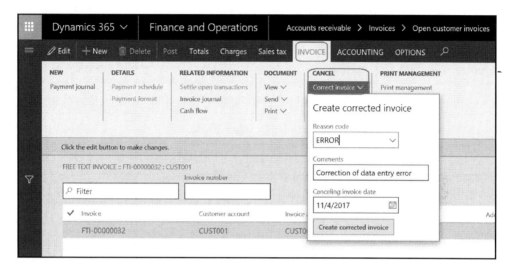

As shown in the next screenshot, the **FREE TEXT INVOICE** correction form will pop up.
There is an indication that this invoice form is for correction (**You are correcting a free text
invoice**). Edit the amount and post the entry:

In order to post the free text invoice correction, go to the ribbon and click on **Post**. Behind the scenes, Microsoft Dynamics 365 for Finance and Operations posts both the canceled transaction and the corrected transaction. The following screenshot shows the message dialogue with the posted transactions:

In the next screenshot, we can see the free text invoice. Navigate to **Accounts receivable | Invoices | All free text invoices**:

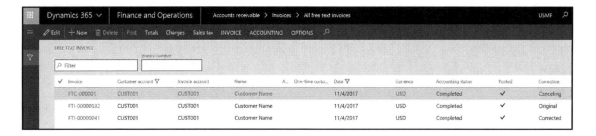

This screenshot shows the following transactions:

- **Original**: This represents the original transaction
- **Canceling**: This represents the reversal of the original transaction
- **Corrected**: This represents the corrected invoice after editing the amount

Collection management

Companies need to follow up on customers who have delayed payment, and the controller may need to add extra fees if the customer has delayed. It is important to record these follow-ups on Microsoft Dynamics 365 for Finance and Operations, and the system will generate the interest entries, if they exist. In the following section, we will explore the collection letter and interest note.

Collection letter

When a customer does not pay an invoice, depending on company policy it usually sends a collection letter to that customer. In addition to that, the company has the ability to add fees to be charged on each generated collection letter, in addition to that, the customer could be blocked from invoice transactions. The following diagram illustrates the main building blocks for the collection letter:

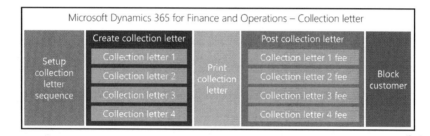

To set up the collection letter sequence, navigate to **Credit and collections** | **Collection letter** | **Set up collection letter sequence**; the **Collection letters** form contains a collection letter sequence ID, collection letter code, main account (optional), fee in currency (optional), days, and block check box, as shown in the following screenshot:

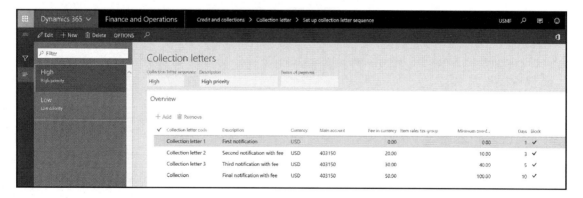

The collection letter sequence should be attached to accounts receivable posting profiles: **Accounts receivable** | **Setup** | **Customer posting profiles**.

Assume that a customer has a past due invoice on January 2, with the amount at 1,000 USD; the accounts receivable accountant will run the collection letter process, and the system will create the first collection letter for this customer. To create a collection letter, navigate to **Credit and collections** | **Collection letter** | **Create collection letters**; a dialog will pop up, as shown in the following screenshot:

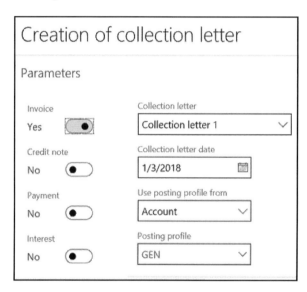

Then, move to **REVIEW AND PROCESS COLLECTION LETTERS**; this form allows the Accounts receivable accountant to print, send, and post collection letters. Navigate to **Credit and collections** | **Collection letter** | **Review and process collection letters**, as shown in the following screenshot:

Collection letter 1 was recorded with a **Created** status.

Then, print and post the collection letter, as shown in the following screenshot:

 Collection letter 1 was updated with a **Posted** status.

Assume that the customer payment is due on January 5 and the accounts receivable accountant runs the second collection letter and posts it; at this stage the system posts a fee to the customer's open transactions. Navigate to **Accounts receivable | Customers | All customers,** select the customer record and move to the **COLLECT** ribbon, and select **Settle transactions**; a dialog form will pop up as shown in the following screenshot:

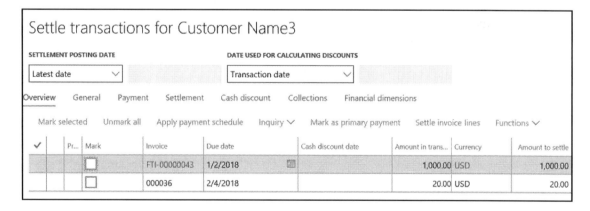

As per the collection letter sequence, the customer is set on hold for invoices; navigate to **Accounts receivable | Customers | All customers**, select the customer record and move to the **Credit and collections** fast tab.

Interest note

If collection letters are sent out and the customer still does not pay, the company may want to charge interest on the late payments. For each interest calculation, a fee can be charged and is added to a customer. To create an interest code, navigate to **Credit and collections | Interest | Set up interest codes**, as shown in the following screenshot:

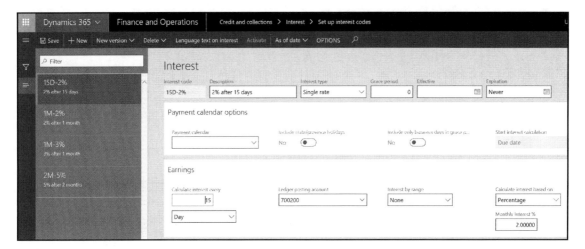

Assume that a customer has a past due invoice on January 3 and the accounts receivable accountant runs the interest notes process: navigate to **Credit and collections | Interest | Create interest notes**.

An interest calculation dialog will pop up, as shown in the following screenshot:

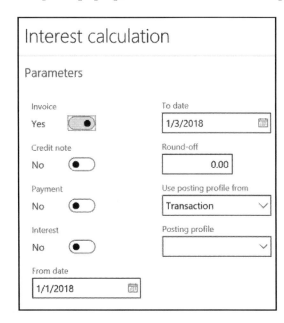

The accounts receivable accountant can review and process the interest note by navigating to **Credit and collections | Interest | Review and process interest notes**. Here, the accountant can print and post the interest note, as shown in the following screenshot:

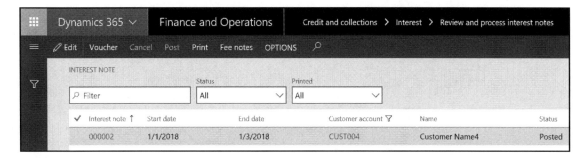

The system posts an interest fee and adds it to customer transactions. Navigate to **Credit and collections** | **Customers** | **All customers**, then move to the **CUSTOMER** ribbon and select **Transactions**, as shown in the following screenshot:

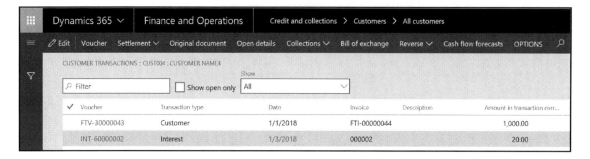

Customer settlement

Settlement is an accounting transaction that occurs in accounts payable, accounts receivable, and the general ledger. This transaction is mainly used to settle customer invoices against customer payments or advanced payments. As shown in the following diagram, if the invoice has a different posting profile from the payment, the settlement will generate a transaction:

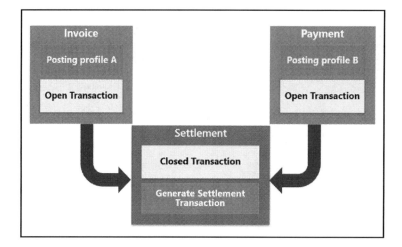

It is necessary to classify the posting profiles of the customer in the opening balance, as it will affect the settlement process.

The settlement transaction affects customer balances, and it is reported in the customer statement report, which identifies the following:

- Customer
- The open (unsettled) invoice and collections
- The closed (settled) invoice and collections
- Customer balance

A settlement transaction could occur during a payment or collection transaction, if the accountant marks the invoice that will be paid or collected. On the other hand, the settlement could be performed at the vendor or customer level, and these transactions could be unsettled.

The settlement transaction should take into consideration the currency, because it could be performed in the company's home currency by an equivalent amount that is calculated based on the currency exchange rate, or it could be settled in the same currency as that of the invoice, by identifying the currency in the payment process.

Customer settlement mechanism – Dynamics 365 for Finance and Operations

In Microsoft Dynamics 365 for Finance and Operations, customer settlement is a transaction used to settle customer advanced collections or collections against customer invoices, and this function is done on a monthly basis.

Customer settlement has the following effects:

- The first effect is at the customer level. It closes the customer transaction.
- The second effect is on the financial entry, and occurs if the posting profiles of the advanced collection and invoice are different.

Next, I will illustrate the mechanism of the customer advanced collection, invoices, and customer settlement financial entries, as follows:

- The customer advanced collection posting profile is **Prepayments**, and the financial entry will be as follows:
    - **Dr. Banks**: 1,200 USD
    - **Cr. Customer deposits**: 1,200 USD
    - **Open transactions**: 1,200 USD advanced collection

- The customer invoice posting profile is **General**, and the financial entry is this:
    - **Dr. Receivables**: 1,000 USD
    - **Cr. Sales revenue**: 1,000 USD
    - **Open transactions**: 1,200 USD advanced collection, and a 1,000 USD sales invoice
- The customer settlement's entry is as follows:
    - **Dr. Customer deposits**: 1,000 USD
    - **Cr. Receivables**: 1,000 USD
    - **Open transactions**: 200 USD Advanced collection
    - **Closed transactions**: 1,000 USD advanced collection, and 1,000 USD sales invoice

If the posting profiles for advanced payment and invoicing are different, a settlement financial entry will be created.

Summary

This chapter covered the accounts receivable module in Microsoft Dynamics 365 for Finance and Operations and its integration with other modules. We then explored the customer master data, the controls for customer credit limits, and the on hold function. We looked at accounts receivable transactions, the customer invoice, free text invoice, collection letters, interest notes and the settlement mechanism.

In the next chapter, we will cover bank management basic configurations, controls, and integrations with other modules (general ledger, accounts payable, and accounts receivable), and we will also perform a bank reconciliation.

9
Understanding Cash and Bank Management

The cash and bank module is the place where a company's bank accounts—current and deposit accounts—are listed. In this module, a company can monitor and control its bank transactions. The financial controller and chief financial officer will be able to assess the cash position and bank reconciliation accuracy. This chapter covers the following topics:

- Understanding cash and bank integration
- Controlling cash and bank management
- Exploring cash and bank management in action
- Bank account reconciliation
- Bank facility – letter of guarantee
- Working with vendors checks

Understanding cash and bank integration

The modules' transactions represent the customer's deposits in the company's bank accounts, either by cash or by check, and also payments to vendors through cash or check. Bank reconciliation is an important procedure performed weekly or monthly (according to the number of transactions and the customers' business needs). This process should be performed once a month, before the closing period, to ensure that bank transactions (bank statements) are matched with book transactions, which are recorded in Microsoft Dynamics 365 for Finance and Operations. The following diagram shows the integration of cash and bank management:

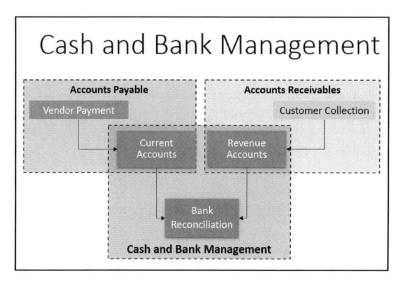

The **Cash and Bank Management** module is a shared module between the **Accounts payable** module and the **Accounts receivable** module (as seen in the preceding diagram), where vendor payments are executed by a check or cash that can be printed through Microsoft Dynamics 365 for Finance and Operations. The customers' collections are deposited into the bank's account. The key factor here is the method of payment, which is assigned to a transaction level that may recall a specific bank account ID, require a check number, fire payment steps for the check process, and so on.

Controlling cash and bank management

Microsoft Dynamics 365 for Finance and Operations offers five main controls over bank and cash management. It is one of the key objectives of ERP that it controls in order to make the most of having an ERP application in place. These control functionalities should be highlighted to the process owners to be utilized efficiently.

Microsoft Dynamics 365 for Finance and Operations emphasizes control, as well as new business functionalities. Some of these controls were introduced prior Microsoft Dynamics 365 for Finance and Operations. Some Microsoft Dynamics 365 for Finance and Operations cash and bank controls are shown in the following diagram:

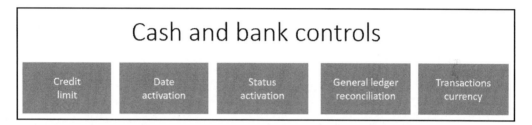

The controls shown in the preceding diagram are defined as follows:

- **Credit limit**: This allows for credit limit control on the bank account
- **Date activation**: This detects activation dates control
- **Status activation**: This detects the activation status on bank transactions
- **General ledger reconciliation**: This assigns one ledger account to more than one bank account
- **Transaction currency**: This allows multiple currency transactions to be executed on the bank account

Credit limit

The credit limit control stops posting transactions if it exceeds the credit limit that the bank can propose. To access the cash and bank credit limit tolerance window, navigate to **Cash and bank management** | **Setup** | **Cash and bank management parameters** | **General**. The following screenshot shows the **CREDIT LIMIT TOLERANCE** control:

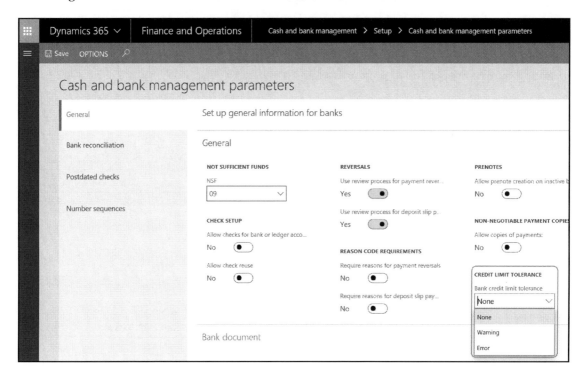

The **CREDIT LIMIT TOLERANCE** field must be activated, so it gives a warning or an error, or it is deactivated. The credit limit amount is defined for every bank account under **General** information. The amount must be negative; if it is not, you will receive this message: **Credit limit must be in negative**, as you can see in the following screenshot. For cash and bank credit limit tolerance, navigate to **Cash and bank management | Bank accounts | Bank accounts**. Click on **Edit** or double-click to open the bank form under the **General** fast tab:

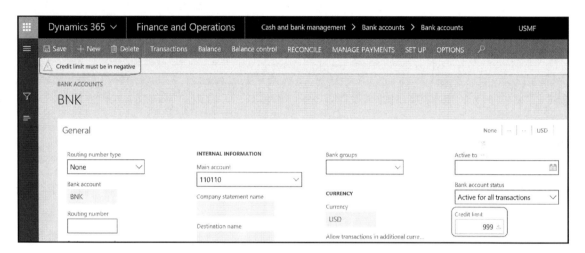

Over the course of transaction processing, if an accountant validates or posts a credited amount that surpasses the bank's credit limit, a message bar will open showing a message that says: **You cannot post the journal because the bank's credit limit has been exceeded**, as shown in the following screenshot:

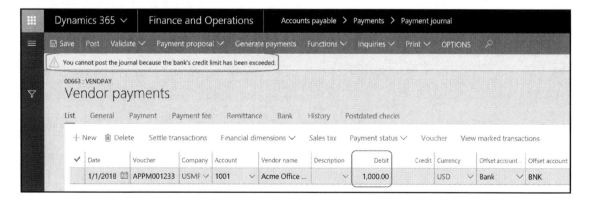

Date activation

Date activation for the bank account recognizes the activation range for every bank account. To access the cash and bank date activation window, navigate to **Cash and bank management** | **Bank accounts** | **Bank accounts**. Click on **Edit** or double-click to open the bank form under the **General** fast tab, as shown in the following screenshot:

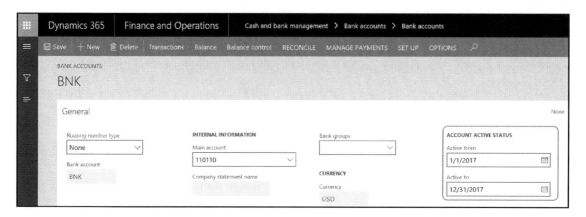

Over the course of transaction processing, if an accountant posts or validates a transaction date that is not in the active date range, a message bar will open showing this message: **You cannot use the company bank account '######' for this transaction because that bank account is not active**, as shown in the following screenshot:

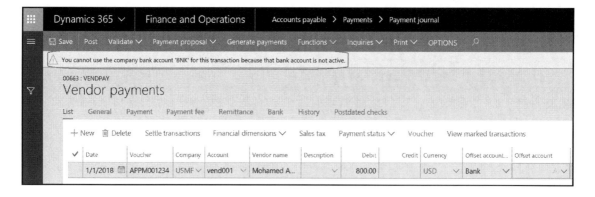

Status activation

As you can see in the following screenshot, status activation has three options: **Active for all transactions**, **Inactive for new transactions**, and **Inactive for all transactions**. To access the cash and bank status activation window, navigate to **Cash and bank management | Bank accounts | Bank accounts**. Click on **Edit** or double-click to open the bank form under the **General** fast tab:

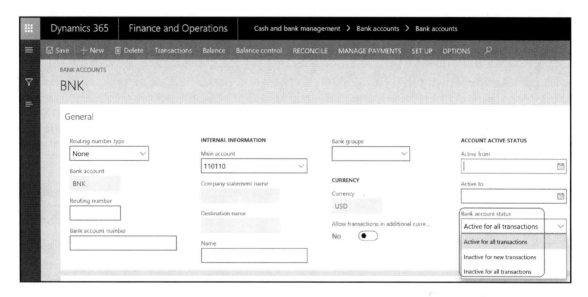

The three options for status activation are explained in detail as follows:

- **Active for all transactions:** This means that a bank account is active and available for all transactions.

- **Inactive for new transactions**: This means that no new transactions can be posted for a bank account. The existing transactions that have not been finalized yet, such as pending payments, will still take place as they were originally posted.
- **Inactive for all transactions**: This means no transactions, either new or existing, can be processed for a bank account.

General ledger reconciliation

The creation process of a new bank account must be assigned to a main account. Microsoft Dynamics 365 for Finance and Operations gives a warning message to say that this account is already assigned to another bank's main account, and this should be considered during the reconciliation process with the general ledger's main accounts. As seen in the following screenshot, the warning message that appears is: **Main account ##### is already used by bank account #####. If you associate multiple bank accounts with a main account, the General Ledger Bank Reconciliation report will contain information from multiple bank accounts**:

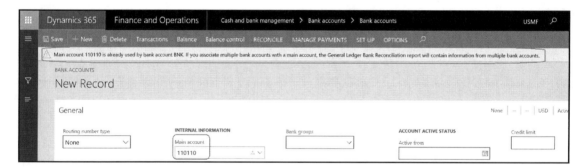

Transaction currency

Transaction currency for bank accounts could be one currency or multiple currencies; it is suggested you assign a single currency for every bank account. You have to navigate to **Cash and bank management** | **Bank accounts** | **Bank accounts** then move to the **General** fast tab, as shown in the following screenshot:

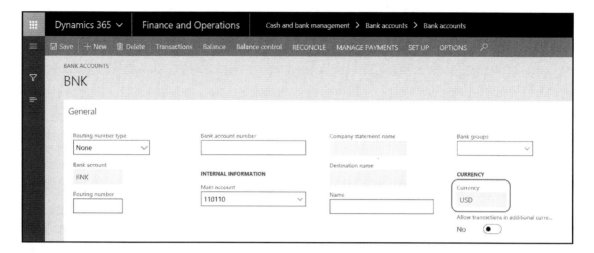

If, over the course of transaction processing, an accountant tries to post an entry in a bank account that does not permit multiple currencies, a message bar will open showing this message: **Currency EUR not allowed for account BNK**, as shown in the following screenshot:

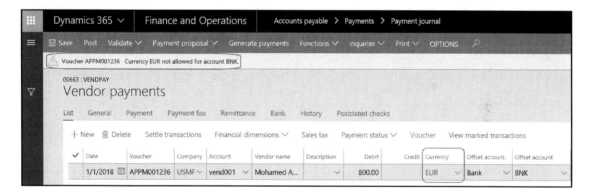

Exploring cash and bank management in action

The following section will explore cash and bank management in daily transactions. It will focus on bank account reconciliation, which is a key process to ensure that all recorded transactions match the bank statement, and the bank facility will focus on the letter of guarantee.

Bank account reconciliation

Bank account reconciliation is a validation process of the bank's account statement and recorded transactions in the cash and bank management module, through customer deposits and vendor payments.

There are two reconciliation mechanisms that you can apply for each bank account: the first one is the manual reconciliation mechanism, and the second one is the automatic import of bank statements. You have to navigate to **Cash and bank management | Bank accounts | Bank accounts | Select bank account**. In the **RECONCILE** ribbon, click on **Account reconciliation**, as shown in the following screenshot:

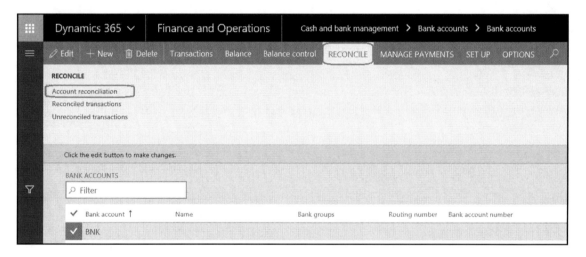

The procedure begins when the company receives the bank account statement from the bank. Under **Cash and bank management | Bank accounts | Bank accounts**, select the **Bank account | Bank account** ribbon then **Account reconciliation**. In the **Account reconciliation** form, enter the reconciliation date, statement number, and statement ending balance, as shown in the following screenshot:

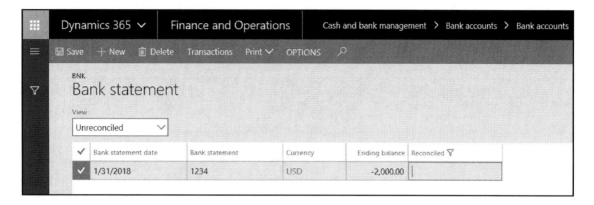

Under reconciliation transactions, only transactions booked through Microsoft Dynamics 365 for Finance and Operations modules are listed. If it matches the bank statement, mark it as **Cleared**, as you can see in the following screenshot:

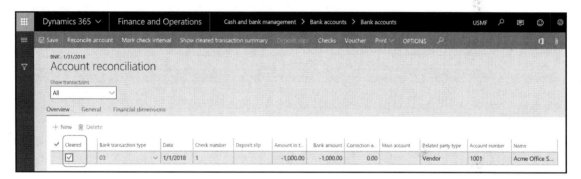

After marking all transactions, click on **Reconcile account** to confirm the reconciliation process. If the reconciliation is successful, a message bar will open displaying this message: **Account has been reconciled**. This is shown in the following screenshot:

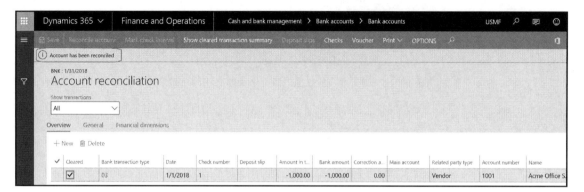

Automatic bank reconciliation requires to be set up on three areas: the resources on Visual Studio, data management, and the cash and bank management module, as shown in the following diagram:

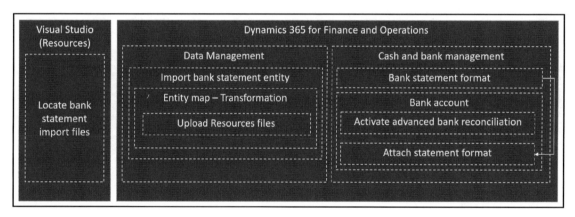

Open Visual Studio, move to **Application Explorer**, and filter on `bankstmtimport` as shown in the following screenshot:

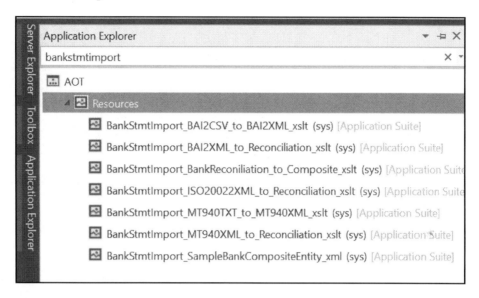

Then create a folder under the C drive and copy the following exported files as shown in the following screenshot:

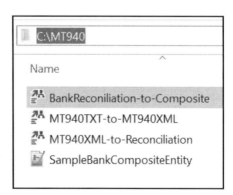

Then, move to Microsoft Dynamics 365 for Finance and Operations and go to the **Data management** workspace, select **Import** and **XML-Element** for **Source data format** and **Bank statements** in **Entity name**, then select **SampleBankConsiteEntity** in the file upload, as shown in the following screenshot:

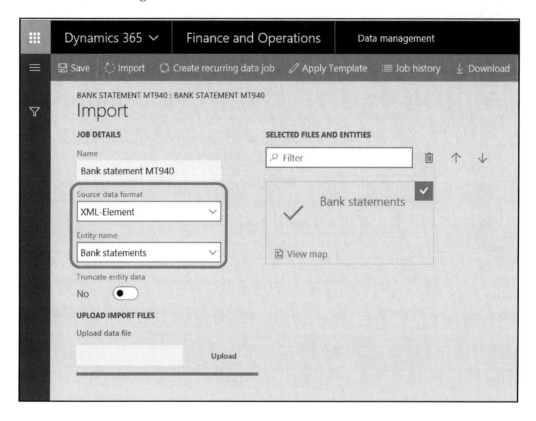

Select **View map** and the **Composite** entities form will open, and then select **View map,** as shown in the following screenshot:

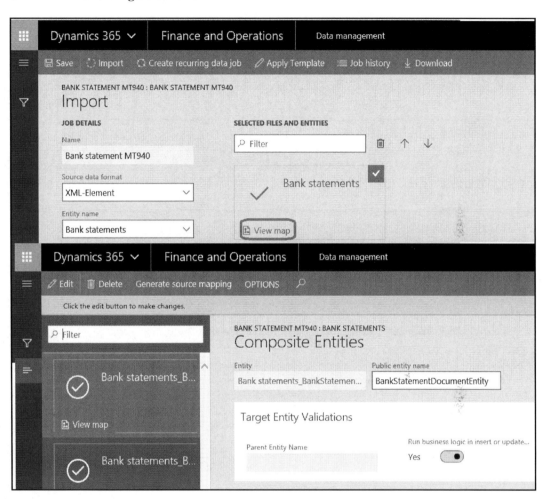

The **Map source to staging** form will open, then move to **Transformations,** create new lines, and upload files from the C:MT940 folder, as shown in the following screenshot:

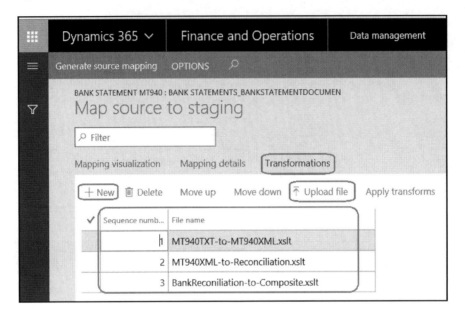

The order should be as shown in the preceding screenshot.

The **Execution summary** will show **Succeeded**, as shown in the following screenshot:

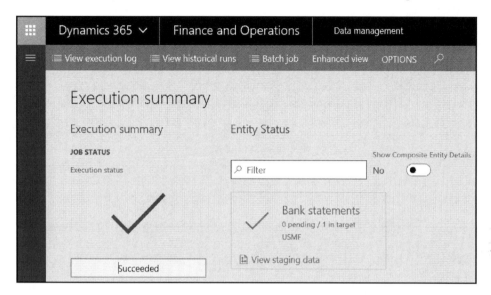

Then move to **Cash and bank management** I **Setup** I **Advanced bank reconciliation setup** I **Bank statement format**, create a new line, and link it to the created processing group:

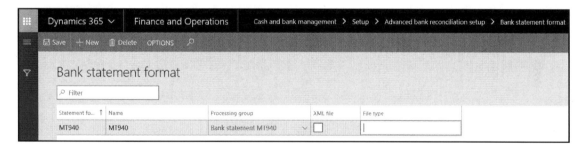

To automatically import bank statements, you must activate the **Advanced bank reconciliation** option. In order to activate the **Advanced bank reconciliation** option, navigate to **Cash and bank management** | **Bank accounts** | **Bank accounts** | **Edit** | **Reconciliation**. The following screenshot displays the **Advanced bank reconciliation** option under the **Reconciliation** fast tab:

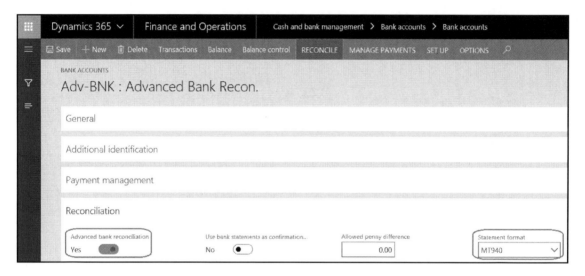

As you can see in the following screenshot, the **Advanced bank reconciliation** option cannot be turned off after activation:

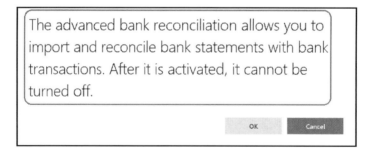

The process of importing bank statements starts by selecting **RECONCILE** and then by clicking on **Bank statements**, as you can see in the following screenshot. In order to go to the **Bank statements** section, navigate to **Cash and bank management | Bank accounts | Bank accounts**. Select a bank account, and then go to the **RECONCILE** ribbon and select **Bank statements**:

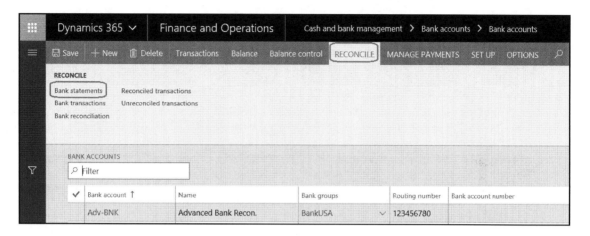

In the **Bank statement** screen, a journal line has been created with a status of **Open**. To import the bank statement, click on **Import statement**. To go to the **Bank statement** section, navigate to **Cash and bank management | Bank accounts | Bank statement**. A dialog box will pop up to select the file to be imported. Choose a bank account, locate the file path, and then click on **OK**. In order to go to the **Import bank statements** section, you have to navigate to **Cash and bank management | Bank statement reconciliation | Bank statement**. In the **Bank statement** ribbon, select **Import statement**.

The **Import bank statements** window is shown in the following screenshot:

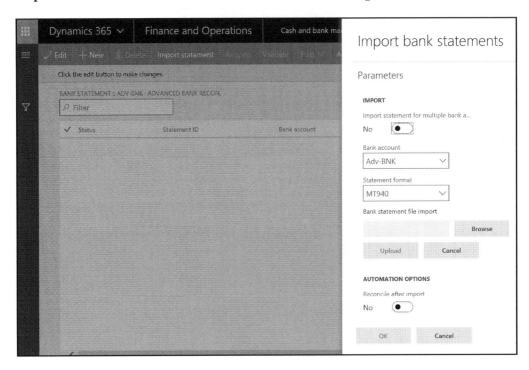

The bank statement is imported with the **Open** status as shown in the following screenshot:

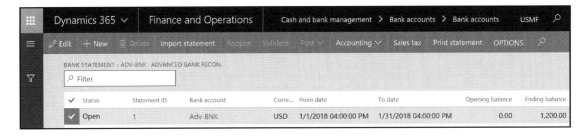

The **Bank statement** form contains the transaction lines of the imported bank transactions, in addition to the opening balance, ending balance, and net amount details. Click on **Validate** to validate the imported bank statement. If there is an error with the opening or ending balance, the validation process will stop. In order to edit the bank statement, you have to navigate to **Cash and bank management | Bank accounts**, then move to the **RECONCILE** ribbon, and select **Bank statements**. Select the **Bank statement record** as shown in the following screenshot:

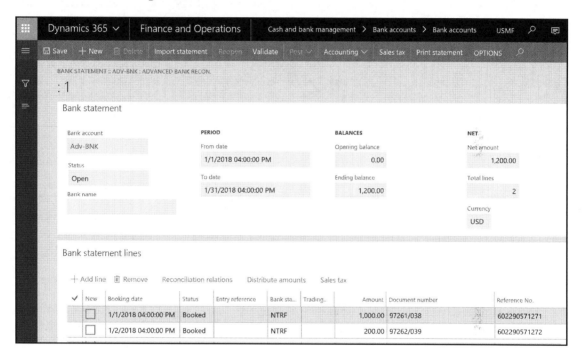

As you can see in the following screenshot, the **Message details** window will open to confirm that the statement passes the validation process:

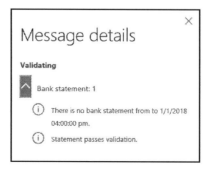

In order to match the bank transactions with the bank statement, go to the **Bank reconciliation** journal by navigating to **Cash and bank management** | **Bank statement reconciliation** | **Bank reconciliation**, create a new record, and select bank account ID; the filed information will be populated automatically. Then select **Worksheet**, as shown in the following screenshot:

The bank reconciliation worksheet contains the following fields:

- **Open statement lines**: This represents the imported transactions of the bank statement
- **Open bank documents**: This represents the bank transactions posted on Microsoft Dynamics 365 for Finance and Operations
- **Matched statement lines**: This represents the matched line in the statement with posted transactions
- **Matched bank documents**: This represents the matched bank document in the statement with posted transactions

While checking a bank statement line with a posted transaction, click on **Match**. As you can see in the following screenshot, the matched lines on **Unmatched transactions** fast tab:

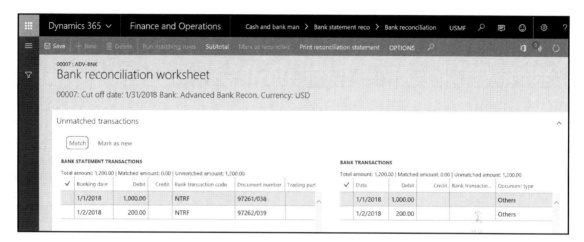

After matching all transactions against the bank statement, click on **Mark as reconciled** as shown in the following screenshot:

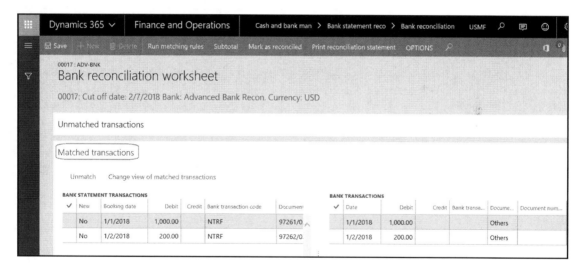

message bar will open indicating that the reconciliation process is finished.

Bank facility – the letter of guarantee

A letter of guarantee is an agreement by a bank (the guarantor) to pay a set amount of money to another person (the beneficiary), if the bank's customer (the principal) defaults on a payment or an obligation to the beneficiary. Letters of guarantee are not transferable, and apply only to the beneficiary named in the guarantee agreement. The principal can request an increase or decrease in the value of a letter of guarantee, subject to the terms of the agreement.

The following diagram illustrates the required configuration and setups in order to utilize the letter of guarantee function. The **Letter of Guarantee – LG** function configuration should be activated, in addition to the basic setups, including **Bank documents posting profile**, **Bank facility agreements**, and **Bank facility**.

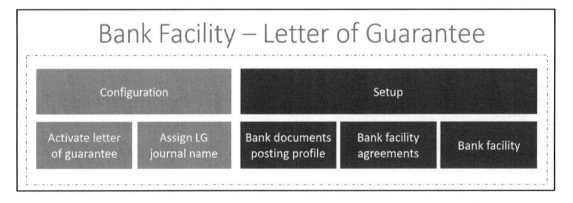

The first step in the configuration is to activate the letter of guarantee checkbox in **Cash and bank management parameters**, and assign the journal name that will be used to post the issuance commission and margin transaction. In order to perform this function, navigate to the **Cash and bank management** | **Setup** | **Cash and bank management parameters** | **General** | **Bank document** fast tab.

The activation screen is shown in the following screenshot:

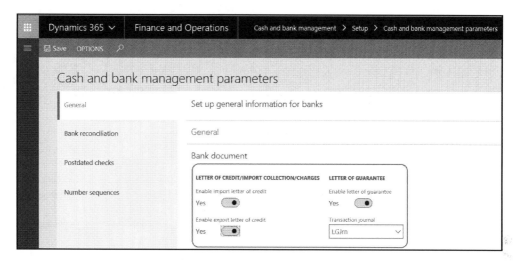

 The journal name type is daily.

Create the bank facilities records by navigating to **Cash and bank management | Setup | Bank facilities**. As shown in the following screenshot, go to the **Facility groups** fast tab and create a new record by clicking on **New** or by pressing *Alt + N*. Enter the **Facility group** code and the **Description** value:

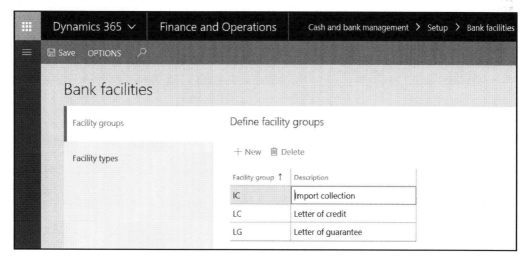

Then move to the **Facility types** fast tab, and create a new record by clicking on **New** or by pressing *Alt + N*. Enter the **Facility type** code and the **Description** value, and select **Facility group** and **Facility nature** (whether it is **Letter of credit**, **Import collection**, or **Letter of guarantee**). The **Facility types** fast tab is shown in the following screenshot:

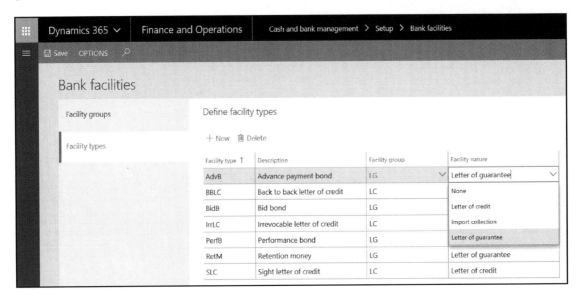

Create the bank facility agreements by navigating to **Cash and bank management** | **Letters of guarantee** | **Bank facility agreements** in the **General** fast tab. Identify the start and end date of the facility agreement, in addition to the amount of facility limit and used amount. In the **Letter of guarantee** fast tab, identify the **Cash margin**, **Issuance commission**, **Extension commission**, **Increase value commission**, and **Decrease value commission**.

The facility agreements are shown in the following screenshot:

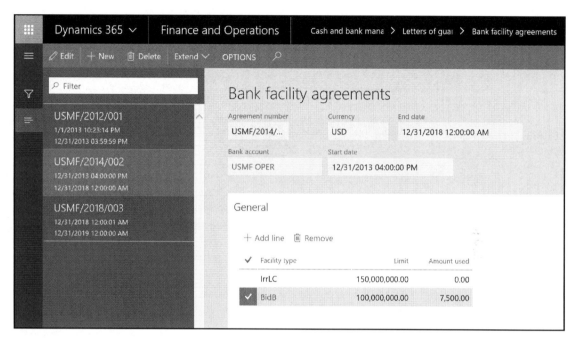

Create the bank documents posting profile by navigating to **Cash and bank management | Setup | Bank documents posting profile** where you can identify the accounts: **Settle account**, **Charges account**, **Margin account**, and **Liquidation account**. The posting profile can be distinguished by the bank facility type, facility group, and so on. The **Bank documents posting profile** window is shown in the following screenshot:

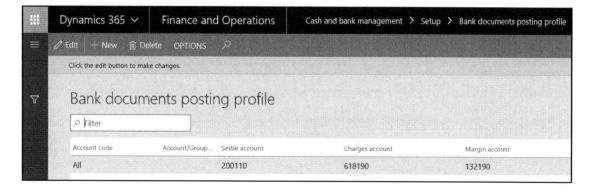

A letter of guarantee is used in sales activities where the customer provides the guarantee to deliver goods or services. In the following section, we will explore a sales order transaction with a letter of guarantee. Navigate to **Sales and marketing** | **Sales orders** | **All sales orders**. The sales order menu is shown in the following screenshot:

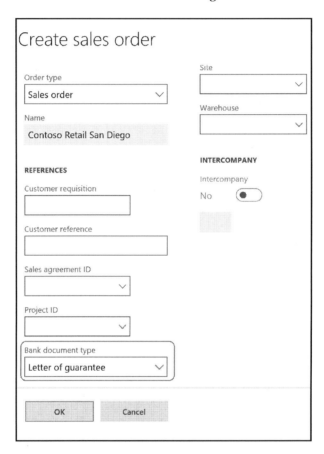

Create a new record by pressing *Alt* + *N*, select a customer account, and then move to the **General** fast tab. In the **Bank document type** field, select **Letter of guarantee**. The sales order creation window is shown in the preceding screenshot.

In the sales order form, select the item ID (such as sold, quantity, price, site, and warehouse) of the product. Then move to the **MANAGE** ribbon, and then select **Letter of guarantee**. The sales order form line is shown in the following screenshot:

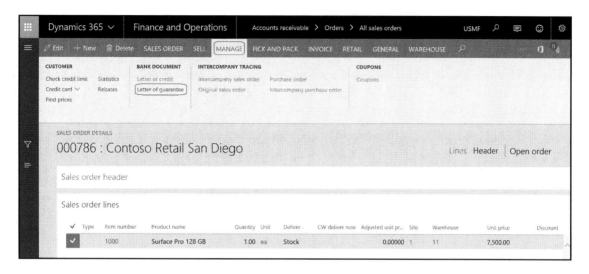

In the letter of guarantee form, click on **Request** to create a letter of guarantee request and select values for the **Type, Value,** and **Expiration date** fields. The letter of guarantee request is shown in the following screenshot:

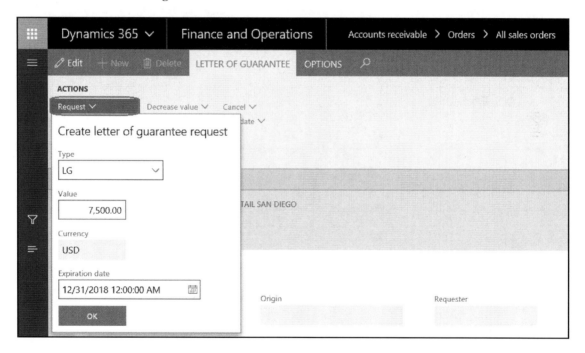

Then, move to the letter of guarantee process. This process is executed from the cash and bank management module by navigating to **Cash and bank management | Letters of guarantee | Letters of guarantee**. The first step in the letter of guarantee process is submitting the letter of guarantee to the bank. The current **Status** value is **Request**, and the **Facility status** value is **Requested**. The letter of guarantee, status, and other related information is shown in the following screenshot:

Click on **Submit to bank**, select the **Bank account** and **Facility type** values, and then click on **OK**. The **Submit to bank** process is shown in the following screenshot:

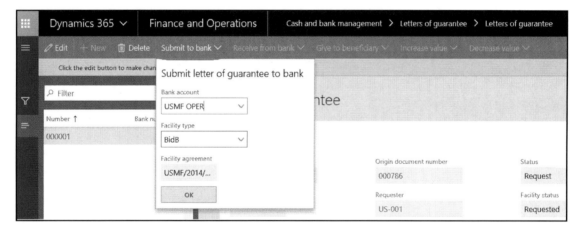

The **Status** field is updated to **Submitted to bank**, and the **Facility status** field still shows **Requested**. The financial details are updated with the bank submission information. Status updates and updated submission information are shown in the following screenshot:

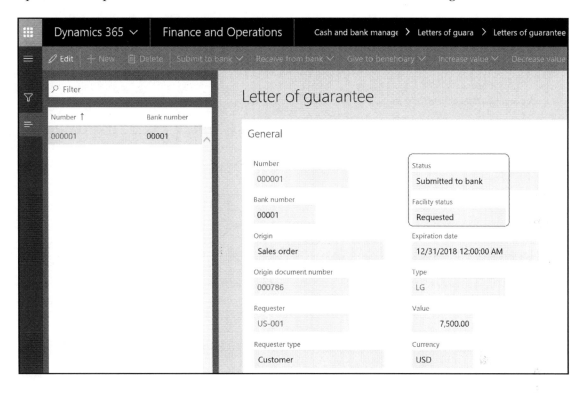

The company receives confirmation from the bank and the system automatically calculates the **Margin** and **Expense** values. A confirmation received from the bank function is shown in the following screenshot:

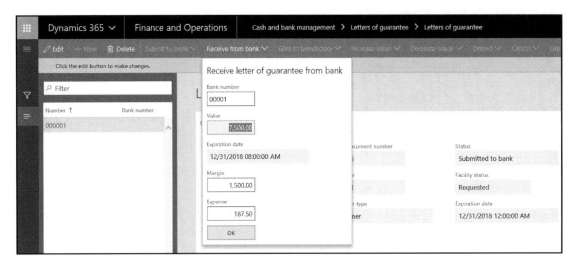

The system generates and posts a general journal transaction; the message bar will open, displaying a message indicating that the journal has been posted, as shown in following screenshot:

In order to check the posted transaction, you have to navigate to **General Ledger** | **Journal entries** | **General journals** | **Posted** and filter on the letter of guarantee journal name. Posted journals are shown in the following screenshot:

The letter of guarantee document's **Status** field is updated to **Received from bank** and the **Facility status** field is updated to **Open**. The letter of guarantee status update is shown in the following screenshot:

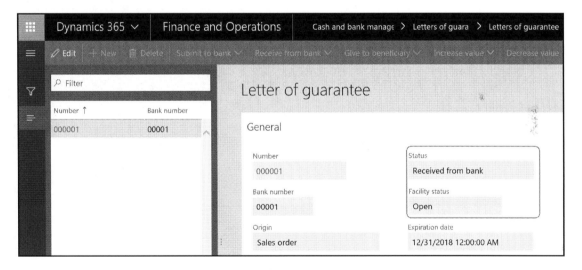

Then you should navigate back to **Sales and marketing** | **Sales orders** | **All sales orders** and filter to the previously created sales order. On the ribbon move to **Manage** and select **Letter of guarantee** in order to request the letter of guarantee to the customer. The request to give the letter of guarantee to the beneficiary is shown in the following screenshot:

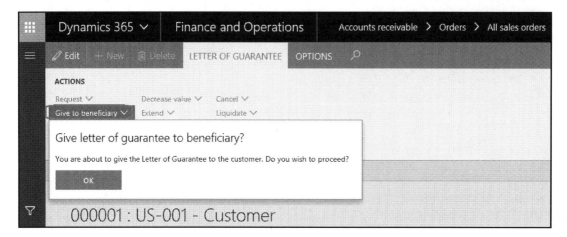

The **Status** field is updated to **Request give to beneficiary** and the bank **Facility status** field still shows **Open**. The status update is shown in the following screenshot:

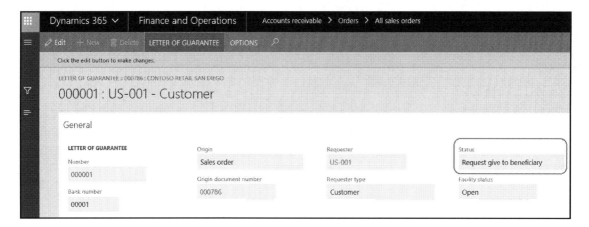

Then, navigate to **Cash and bank management | Letters of guarantee | Letters of guarantee** to give the letter of guarantee to the beneficiary. The following screenshot shows the action of giving the letter of guarantee to the beneficiary:

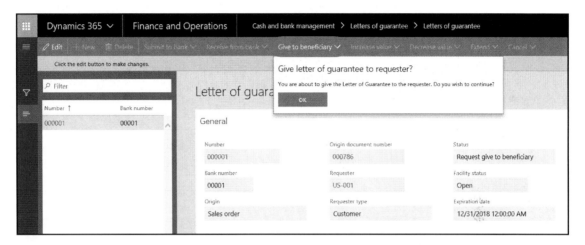

The **Status** field is updated to **Given to beneficiary** and the **Facility status** field still shows **Open**. The letter of guarantee is shown in the following screenshot:

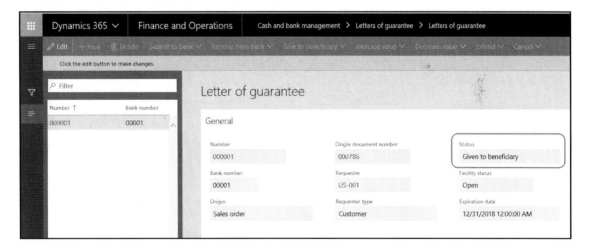

There are other options that could be performed after this stage:

- Increase or decrease the letter of guarantee
- Cancel or extend it
- Liquidate the letter of guarantee

Working with vendor checks

Checks are payment instruments that are used to pay vendors. Microsoft Dynamics 365 for Finance and Operations provides check design and generation. The checks are assigned to bank accounts and then used in the vendor payment journal. The following diagram illustrates the check elements:

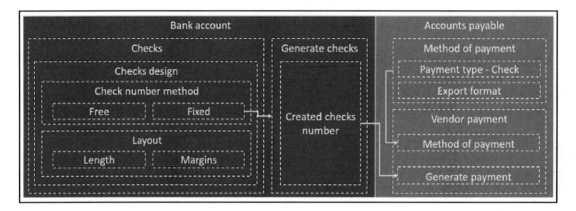

In order to create and design checks, navigate to **Cash and bank management | Bank accounts | Bank accounts** and then move to the **Setup** tab and **Layout.** In the **Check layout** form, identify the following:

- **Check number method (fixed or free)**: The fixed check number represents predefined check numbers that are created then get used in vendor payment. The free check number represents the manual entry of check numbers in the vendor payment.
- **Layout**: This represents the design of the printed check, and helps identify the paper length and margins.

The following screenshot illustrates the **Check layout** form:

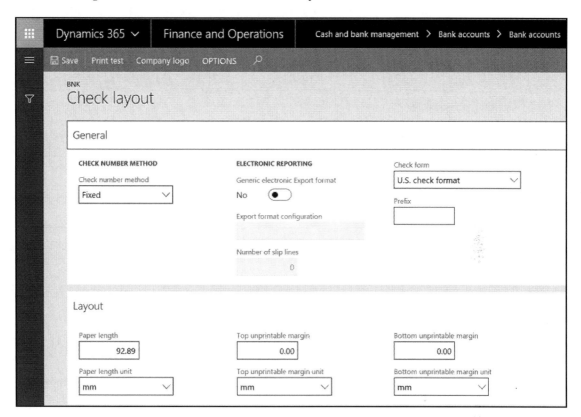

Printable paper length must be set to at least 92.89 mm for checks.

In the vendor method of payment, identify the payment type and export file format as **Check**. Navigate to **Accounts payable | Payment setup | Methods of payment**, as shown in the following screenshot:

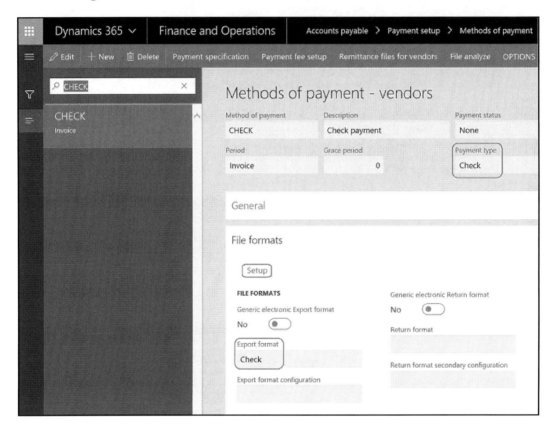

Move to **Setup** to select **Check** under **File format** for methods of payment, as shown in the following screenshot:

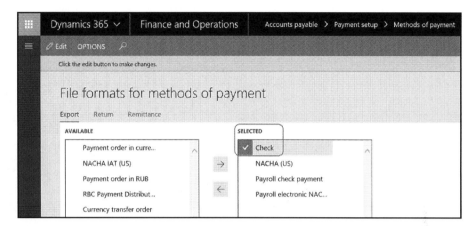

To execute the vendor payment transaction, navigate to **Accounts payable | Payments | Payment journal**, select a vendor account, and enter the amount in the debit side, and the method of payment as **CHECK**, as shown in the following screenshot:

Then, generate the payment from the bank account, as shown in the following screenshot:

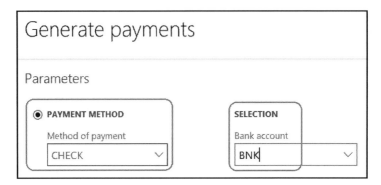

Assigning a check number will be done automatically in the **Payment by check** dialog, as shown in the following screenshot:

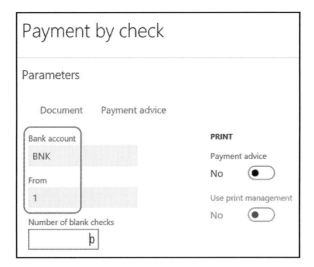

After posting the vendor payment, go to **Cash and bank management | Bank accounts | Bank accounts** to check the bank transactions as shown the following screenshot:

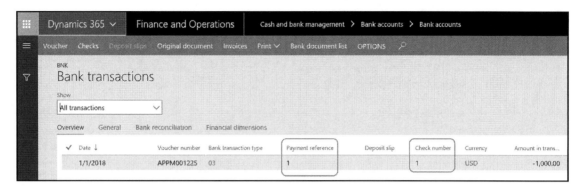

Summary

This chapter covered the integration of the cash and bank module with accounts payable, accounts receivable, and the general ledger. We discussed the controls offered by Microsoft Dynamics 365 for Finance and Operations. We also explored bank reconciliation transactions executed at the end of each month. We then explored the letter of guarantee as the bank facility option, and finally discussed vendor payment by check.

In the next chapter, we will discuss the cash flow management integration concept, basic configurations, and transactions.

10
Functioning of Cash Flow Management

Cash flow management is a tool that predicts a company's future cash requirements. Cash flow management mainly covers the cash out and cash in events. Cash out is generated from the company's expenditure against the goods or services purchased, whereas cash in is generated from the company's revenue against the sale of goods or services. It gives the company's management a vision of the cash position in order to efficiently manage vendor payments in a specific period, and also the customer collections during the same period to protect the company's cash situation. In this chapter, we will cover the following topics:

- Understanding cash flow integration with other modules
- Exploring cash flow forecast configuration
- Working with cash flow transactions

Understanding cash flow integration with other modules

The integrated modules of cash flow management are **accounts payable**, **accounts receivable**, and **general ledger**. The accounts payable module manages the vendor payments process, the accounts receivable module manages the customer collections process, and the general ledger module identifies the cash and cash-equivalent accounts.

The following diagram shows the integration of the cash flow modules:

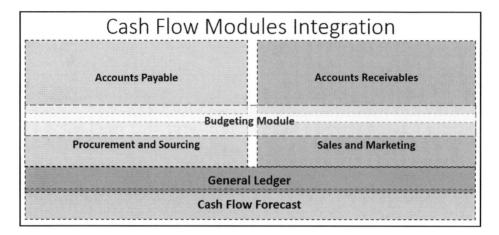

Cash flow forecast management consists of the following elements:

- **Accounts payable**: This identifies the vendors' terms of payment, settlement periods, vendors' posting profiles, accounts used for vendor settlement, and vendor invoice transaction execution
- **Procurement and sourcing**: This identifies the transactional execution of vendor purchase orders and receptions—customer collections management has the following components:
- **Accounts receivable**: This identifies the customers' terms of payment, settlement periods, customers' posting profiles, accounts used for customer settlement, and customer invoice transaction execution
- **Sales and marketing**: This identifies the transactional execution of customer sales orders, issuances, and invoicing
- **Budgeting**: This identifies the budget distributions based on specific time intervals (years, months, and days)
- **General ledger**: This identifies the cash and cash-equivalent accounts that represent the liquidity account
- **Cash flow forecast**: This represents the cash flow position for purchase and sales order transactions

With the Microsoft Dynamics 365 for Finance and Operations consultant, the implementation of cash flow forecast management is a mutual effort between the controller, accounting manager, treasury, budgeting, procurement, and sales.

Cash flow forecast configuration

The cash flow forecast configuration and setups are combined with the integrated modules of cash flow management. The following diagram explains the cash flow forecast configuration in detail:

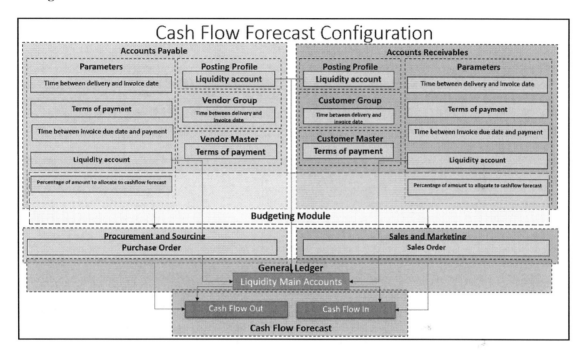

The main configuration and setup of cash flow forecast in Microsoft Dynamics 365 for Finance and Operations is performed in cash and bank management, which covers the following modules:

- Accounts payable
- Accounts receivable
- Budget
- General ledger

Accounts payable

The accounts payable module is further subdivided as follows:

- **Parameters**: This identifies the company-wide parameters for accounts payable. For the parameters of accounts payable, navigate to **Cash and bank management | Cash flow forecasting | Cash flow forecast setup**. Now, go to **Accounts payable** and click on **Purchasing forecast defaults**, as shown in the following screenshot:

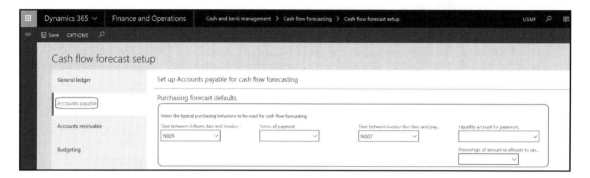

 Also, you can navigate to **Accounts payable | Setup | Accounts payable parameters | Ledger and sales tax** then move to the **Cash flow forecast** fast tab.

- **Time between delivery and invoice date**: This identifies the period between the product's receipt and invoice.
- **Terms of payment**: This identifies the period between the vendor invoice posting and the due date.
- **Liquidity account for payments**: This represents the liquidity account.
- **Percentage of amount to allocate to cash flow forecast**: This represents the allocation key used for budget reduction, with regard to purchase level.

- **Time between invoice due date and payment date**: This identifies the period between the vendor payment due date and the date of payment execution. The terms of payment values are commonly used in the accounts payable's cash flow forecast, where we can set the number of days or months that identify the payment due date. To see the accounts payable's terms of payment, navigate to **Accounts payable** | **Payment setup** | **Terms of payment**, as shown in the following screenshot:

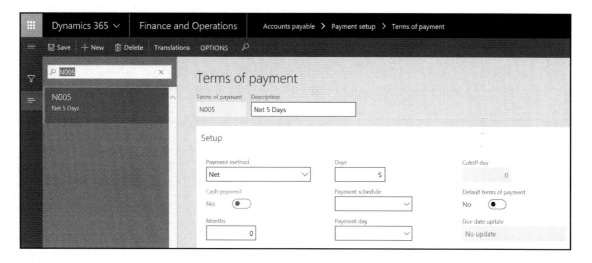

- **Vendor posting profiles**: This is an integration point between the accounts payable sub ledger and general ledger, where identifying a particular ledger account will be used while posting a transaction for a specific vendor. The **Settle account** column in the following screenshot represents the liquidity accounts that are used for vendor payments. For the accounts payable posting profiles, navigate to **Cash and bank management** | **Cash flow forecasting** | **Cash flow forecast setup**. Then move to the **Vendor posting profiles** fast tab. The following screenshot displays the **Vendor posting profiles** page in detail:

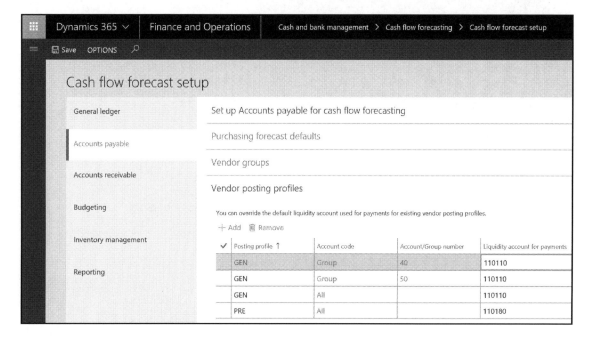

The **Liquidity account for payments** column in the **Vendor posting profile** overrides the **Liquidity account** column under **Module parameters**.

- **Vendor groups**: This represents the vendor's classification and the posting profile assigned to a specific vendor group in order to identify the **Time between invoice due date and payment date** column that is used in cash flow management logic. To see the accounts payable vendor groups profile, navigate to **Cash and bank management | Cash flow forecasting | Cash flow forecast setup**. The following screenshot shows the **Vendor groups** screen as an example:

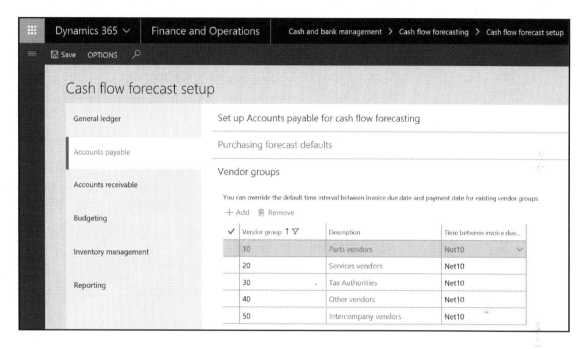

 The **Settle period time between invoice due date and payment date** column in **Vendor groups** overrides the **Time between invoice due date and payment date settle period** column under **Module parameters**.

- **Vendor master**: In the **Vendor master** data information, which is captured and recorded during the creation of vendors and has an effect on the vendor's aging and the cash flow forecast as well, the terms of payment under the payment section is considered as a default value. It is proposed when the vendor is selected in transaction, and can be changed on a transactional level, without modifying the master data record. For the accounts payable vendor master data, navigate to **Accounts payable | Vendors | All vendors**, then click **Edit** on a particular vendor and go to the **PAYMENT** fast tab:

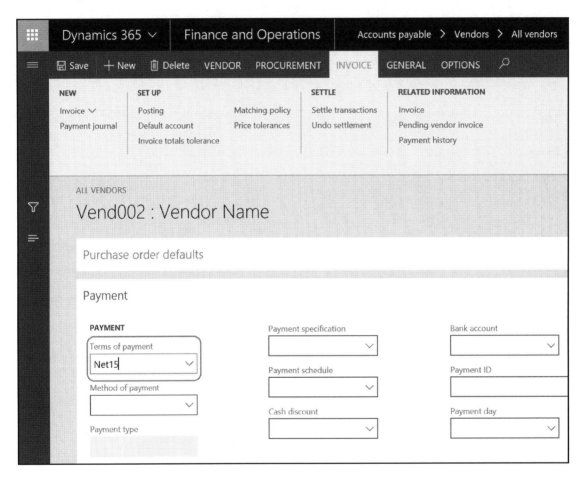

Accounts receivable

The accounts receivable module is subdivided as follows:

- **Parameters**: This identifies the company-wide parameters for accounts receivable. For accounts receivable parameters, navigate to **Cash and bank management** | **Cash flow forecasting** | **Cash flow forecast setup**, then go to **Accounts receivable**, and click on **Sales forecast defaults**, as shown in the following screenshot:

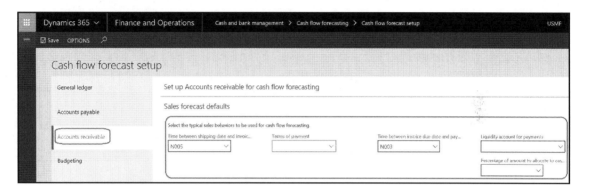

- **Time between shipping date and invoice date**: This identifies the period between the product's issuance and invoicing.
- **Terms of payment**: This identifies the period between the customer invoice posting and due date.
- **Liquidity account for payments**: This represents the liquidity account for settling payments.
- **Percentage of amount to allocate to cash flow cast**: This represents the allocation key used for budget reduction, with regard to the volume of orders.

- **Time between invoice due date and payment date**: This identifies the period between the customer payment due date and payment execution. The terms of payment values are commonly used in the accounts receivable module's cash flow forecast, where we can set the number of days or months that identify the payment due date. To see the terms of payment, navigate to **Accounts receivable | Setup | Payment | Terms of payment**, as shown in the following screenshot:

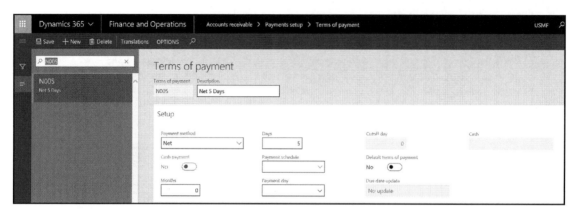

- **Customer posting profiles**: This is an integration point between accounts receivable and general ledger, where identifying the ledger account will be used when posting a transaction on a customer attached to a particular posting profile. The **Liquidity account for payments** column in the following screenshot represents the liquidity accounts that are used for customer payments. To see the posting profiles, navigate to **Cash and bank management | Cash flow forecasting | Cash flow forecast setup**, then go to **Accounts receivable**, and click on **Customer posting profiles**, as shown in the following screenshot:

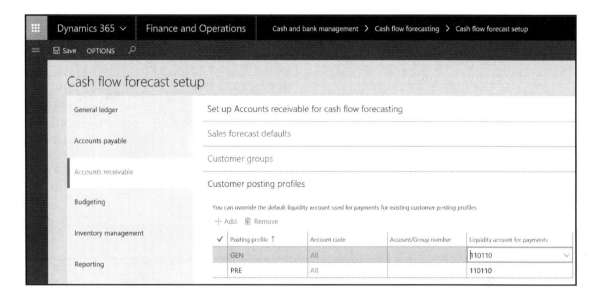

The **Liquidity account for payments** column in **Customer posting profiles** dominates the **Liquidity account for payments** column under **Module parameters**.

Customer groups: This represents the customer classification and the posting profile assigned to a specific customer group. You can also see the **Time between invoice due date and payment date** column in the following screenshot. It is used in the cash flow management logic.

To see the customer groups, navigate to **Cash and bank management** | **Cash flow forecasting** | **Cash flow forecast setup**, then go to **Accounts receivable**, and click on **Customer groups**:

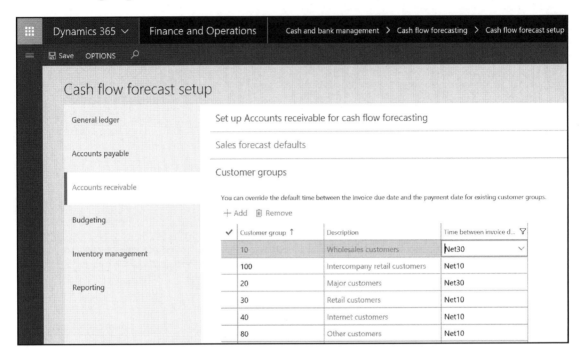

- **Customer master**: In the customer master's data information, which is captured and recorded during the creation of a customer and has an effect on customer aging and the cash flow forecast as well, the **Terms of payment** under the **PAYMENT** section in the customer master data is considered as a default value proposed when the customer is selected in a transaction—the value can be changed on a transactional level without modifying the master data record. For this, navigate to **Accounts receivable** | **Customers** | **All customers**, select a particular customer, and click **Edit**, then move to the **Payment** default fast tab:

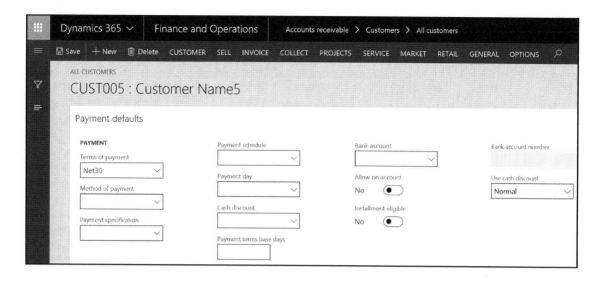

Budget

The core concept in the budget module is the allocation key. This distributes the budgets for a specific period by a weight of allocation percentage, which could be days, months, and/or years. To access the budget allocation key window, navigate to **General ledger | Ledger setup | Period allocation categories**. Click on **Lines** to enter an allocation percentage for each period:

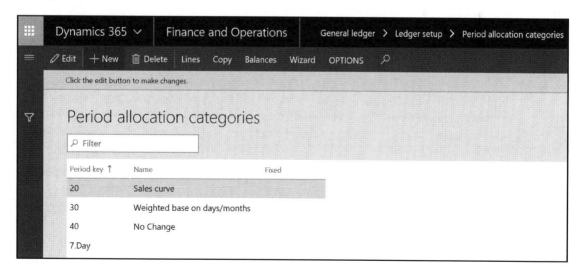

General ledger

The general ledger is subdivided as follows:

- **Main accounts**: Setup cash flow forecasts on the main account will be discussed in the following section. It represents the dependency of other accounts that will affect the company's cash flow, for example, the sales tax payment. To see the main account's cash flow, navigate to **General ledger | Chart of accounts | Accounts**, and select **Main accounts**, then go to **Legal entity overrides** and **Add** the legal entity ID, and the **Cash flow forecast** button will be activated, as shown in the following screenshot:

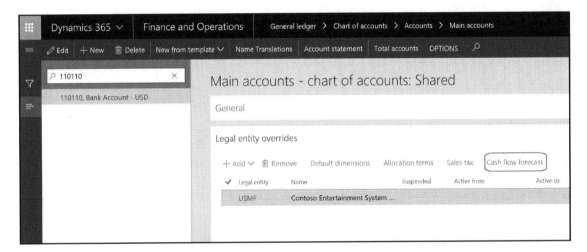

Set the **Main accounts** field to the primary main account where transactions are expected to initially occur. Set the **Dependent account** field to the account that will be affected by the initial transaction against the primary main account. Set appropriate values for the other fields on the line. You can change the value in the **Percent** field to reflect the effect of the primary main account on the dependent main account. For a sales or purchase forecast, select a **Terms of payment** value that is typical for most customers or vendors. Set the **Posting type** field to the expected posting type that is related to the **Cash flow forecast**, as shown in the following screenshot:

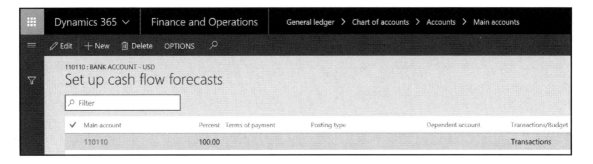

- **Liquidity accounts**: This lists the cash and cash-equivalent accounts that are used to calculate the **Cash flow forecast**. To access the following screenshot, which illustrates the liquidity accounts form, navigate to **Cash and bank management | Cash flow forecasting | Cash flow forecast setup**, then select **General ledger**, and select the **Liquidity accounts** fast tab:

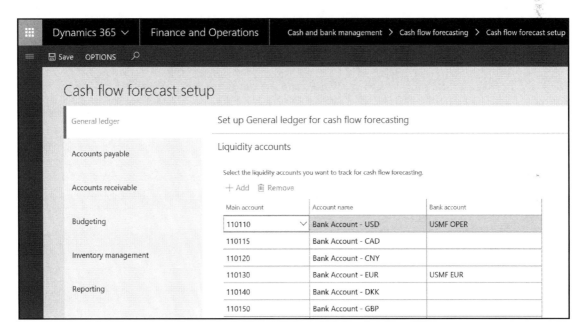

Cash flow transactions

The transactions that affect the cash flow forecast are purchase and sales orders. The cash flow transactions are also dependent on the configuration of the company-wide parameters and the master data setup.

Purchase order cash flow forecast

This section illustrates the cash flow forecast transaction for a **purchase order (PO)**. The order's data is as follows:

- Configuration of the accounts payable module's parameters:
    - **Time between delivery date and invoice date**: 5 days
    - **Time between invoice due date and payment date**: 7 days
    - Vendor master data:
        - **Terms of payment**: 15 days
    - Purchase order data:
        - **Purchase order date**: January 1
        - **Purchase order quantity**: 1 Piece
        - **Default currency**: USD
        - **Purchase price**: 1,000 USD

The purchase order was created on January 1. Based on the setup of the period between delivery and invoice, which is 5 days, the date will be January 6 (by adding 5 days to the PO line date). Then, based on the setup of the terms of payment, which is 15 days, the date will be January 28 (PO line date plus 5 days plus 7 days plus 15 days). Finally, based on the setup of the settle period, which is 3 days, the date will be January 31 (PO line date plus 5 days plus 7 days plus 15 days plus 3 days).

The following diagram represents the cash flow forecast transaction in detail:

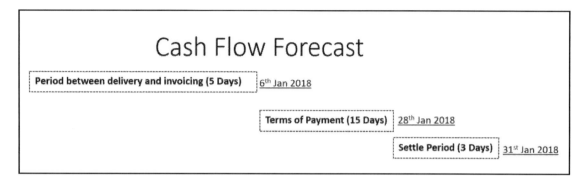

The **Cash flow forecasts** tab can be viewed under **Purchase order**. In the ribbon, navigate to the **Invoice** section, go to the **Bill** group, and select **Cash flow forecasts**. The following screenshot represents the **Cash flow forecasts** form from a purchase order:

The invoice entry date is calculated based on the **Time between delivery date and invoice date** (5 days). Then the invoice entry date will be January 6. The payment entry date is calculated based on the number of days in **Terms of payment**, **Time between invoice due date and payment date**, and **Invoice date** (13 days plus 15 days plus 3 days). Thus, the payment entry date will be January 31.

Summary

In this chapter, we covered the basics of cash flow forecast configurations and setups in Microsoft Dynamics 365 for Finance and Operations, and the integration points between cash flow forecast and accounts payable, accounts receivable, budget, and general ledger to facilitate cash flow functions. We also showed a practical example of a cash flow transaction and inquiries from a purchase order.

In the next chapter, we will discuss budgeting planning and control capabilities on Microsoft Dynamics 365 for Finance and Operations.

11
Exploring Budgeting

Budgeting management is the tool used to predict the results of operations, and it can also be used to compare actual results against a predicted budget. In Microsoft Dynamics 365 for Finance and Operations, the budgeting module is used in two different stages: budget planning and budget control. This chapter covers the following topics:

- Understanding budgeting capabilities in Dynamics 365 for Finance and Operations
- Exploring budget planning
- Exploring budget control
- Exploring budget on transactions

Understanding budgeting capabilities in Dynamics 365 for Finance and Operations

The budgeting module has been improved upon over previous releases of the application. It mainly focuses on the business budgeting process, starting with the budget planning process, which requires organizational efforts from the operations and finance departments. The planning stages consist of all the required steps and workflow approvals, and cover different scenarios of planning approaches to give the needed flexibility in the module's implementation. Then, the approved budget plan is converted to a registered budget that will be the control point during the execution of transactions. The final stage is the reporting, which monitors the operation's performance by comparing actual versus budget. The budgeting process will vary from company to company, based on organization size and its own internal control procedures. There are different types of budgeting methodologies, including zero-based budgeting, historical budgeting, as well as top-down budget planning and bottom-up budget planning.

The elements of the budgeting module in Microsoft Dynamics 365 for Finance and Operations consist of four features:

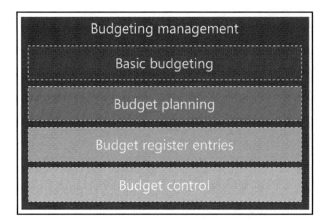

As shown in the proceeding diagram, the elements of the budgeting management module consist of:

- **Basic budgeting**: This feature represents the basic setup and configurations of the budget module, budget models, budget codes, dimensions for budgeting, and budget allocation terms.
- **Budget planning**: This feature represents the setup and configurations of the budget planning process, scenarios, stages, budget planning security options, and budget planning workflow and its stages, in addition to Excel/Word templates.
- **Budget register entries**: This feature represents the approved budgeted amounts for each main account and dimension; it will be used in reporting as well.
- **Budget control**: This feature represents the setup and configurations of budget control on which source documents, and exceptions to exceed the budgets.

Basic budgeting

Basic budgeting is the essential setup for the budgeting module, and it consists of budget models, budget codes, dimensions for budgeting, and budget allocation terms. There are some things that should be considered from the start of the implementation if the company is going to utilize budgeting functions.

The following main points should be discussed during the analysis and design phases with the company's CFO and controller:

- Profit and loss accounts—the budget control feature works with profit and loss (P&L) accounts only.
- Account structure for P&L accounts—the budget control has only one attached account structure, so it is recommended to have one account structure for the P&L account if the company going to use budget control.
- Currency exchange rates that will be used for the budget.

In the following section, we will discuss the budget models, budget codes, dimensions for budgeting, and budget allocation terms.

Budget models

The system requires budget models to post budget register entries; the budget model could consist of submodels. To create a budget model, navigate to **Budgeting** | **Setup** | **Basic budgeting** | **Budget models**, as shown in the following screenshot:

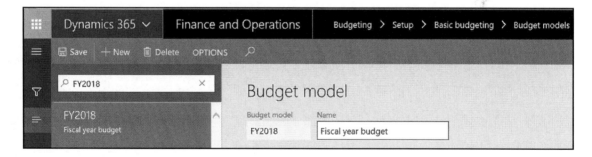

Budget codes

The budget code is the second component that is required to post the budget register entry. The budget codes consists of budget type, and could have a workflow attached to each budget code if it required specific management approvals. To create budget codes, navigate to **Budgeting** | **Setup** | **Basic budgeting** | **Budget codes**, as shown in the following screenshot:

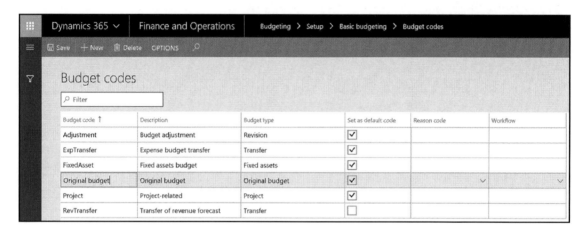

Dimensions for budgeting

You'll need to configure budgeting dimensions for the main account, at the very least. To identify the financial dimensions for budgeting, navigate to **Budgeting** | **Setup** | **Basic budgeting** | **Dimensions for budgeting**, as shown in the following screenshot:

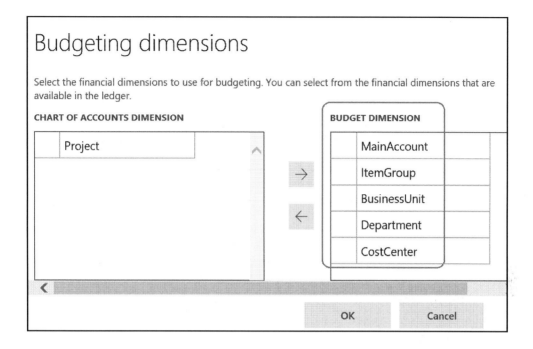

Budget allocation terms

There is more than one method for budget allocation. The allocation concept could be defined as a percentage on the financial dimensions.. The second method for allocation is based on predefined periods. The budget allocation is used in budget planning and budget register entries.

Dimensions allocation terms

The dimensions allocation terms are to identify the predefined distribution of the budget between financial dimensions, for example, the travel expense is distributed between departments (Sales & Marketing 40%, IT 20%, Client Services 10%, and Operations 30%). To create the dimensions' allocation terms, navigate to **Budgeting** | **Setup** | **Basic budgeting** | **Budget allocation terms**, as shown in the following screenshot:

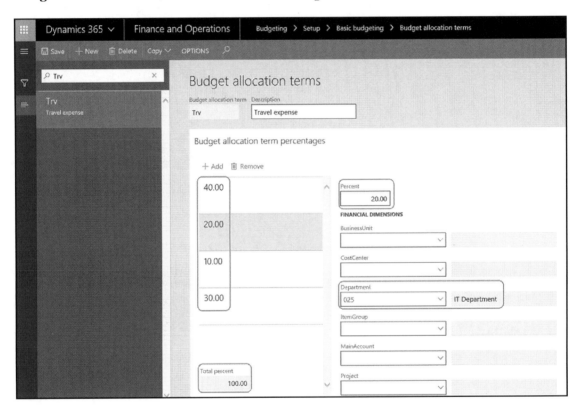

Over the course of budget register entry preparation, the user could distribute the travel expense amount using **Allocate to dimensions**, navigate to **Budgeting** | **Budget register entries**, create a new record, and select **Budget model** and **Budget code**. Then, move to **Budget account entries**, select the P&L account structure, main account, and enter the amount. Click on **Allocate to dimensions**, as shown in the following screenshot:

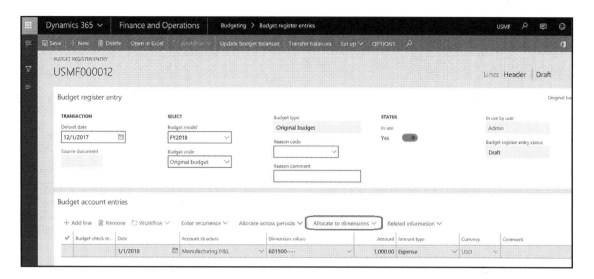

The system will distribute the amount based on dimensions allocation terms. The system will then generate the distributed lines and a negative line with the full amount, as shown in the following screenshot:

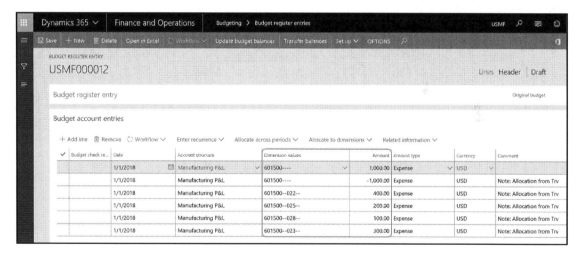

The two lines that represent the original amount and its reversal should be manually deleted.

Period allocation terms

The period allocation terms is to identify the predefined distribution of the budget between periods, for example, the travel expense is distributed over the course of a year. To create period allocation terms, navigate to **General ledger** | **Ledger setup** | **Period allocation categories**, as shown in the following screenshot:

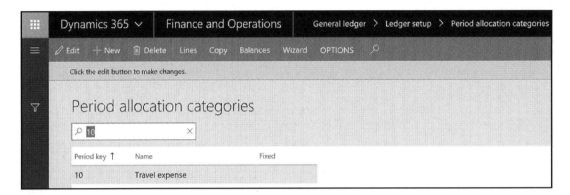

Then move to **Lines**, and enter the allocation percentage for three months, as shown in the following screenshot:

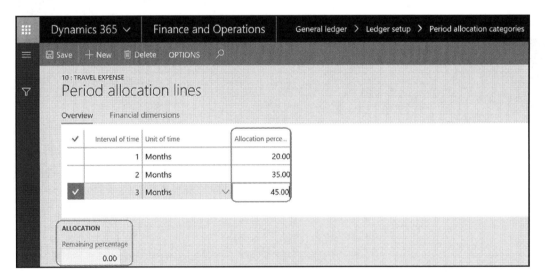

Over the course of the budget register entry preparation, the user could distribute the travel expense amount using period allocation, navigate to **Budgeting** | **Budget register entries**, create a new record, and select **Budget model** and **Budget code**. Then, move to **Budget account entries**, select the P&L account structure, main account, and enter the amount. Click on **Allocate across periods**, as shown in the following screenshot:

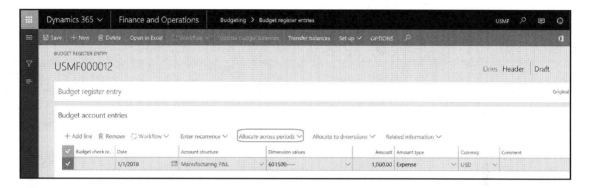

The system will distribute the amount based on period allocation terms. The system will then generate the distributed lines and a negative line with the full amount, as shown in the following screenshot:

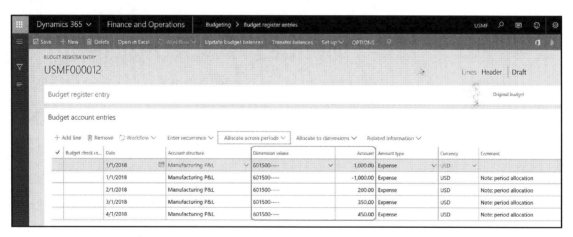

> The two lines that represent the original amount and its reversal should be manually deleted.

Budget planning

As defined in the *Oxford Dictionary of Accounting,* the budget is "*a financial or quantitative statement, prepared prior to a specific accounting period containing the plans and policies to be pursued during that period. It is used as the basis for budgetary control. Generally, a functional budget is drawn up for each functional area within an organization.*"

The budget planning function has been developed since previous versions of Microsoft Dynamics 365 for Finance and Operations. It covers the planning activities, including scenarios, stages, budget planning security options, and budget planning workflow and its stages in addition to Excel/Word templates. The following diagram illustrates the budget planning elements that will be covered in this section:

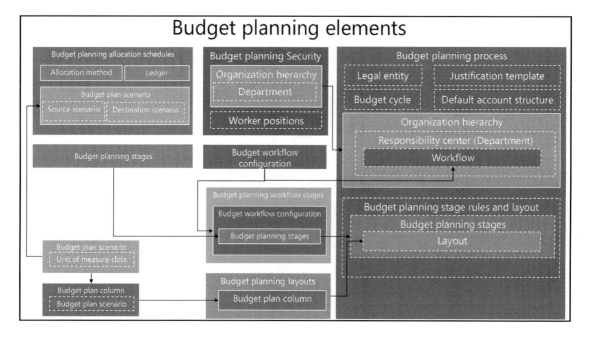

Budget plan scenarios represent the the different scenarios of budget planning and identify the units of measure for each record. The commonly used units of measure for budget planning are Monetary and Quantity. To create a budget plan scenario, navigate to **Budgeting | Setup | Budget planning | Budget planning configurations** and move to the **Scenarios** tab, as shown in the following screenshot:

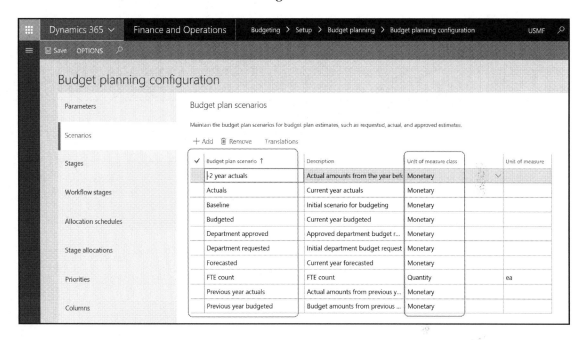

The budget plan scenarios could be attached to budget allocation schedules. The allocation schedules enable allocations to be performed automatically as part of a budget planning workflow. On the allocation schedules, the allocation method and legal entity are identified. To create allocation schedules, navigate to **Budgeting** | **Setup** | **Budget planning** | **Budget planning configurations** and move to the **Allocation schedules** tab, as shown in the following screenshot:

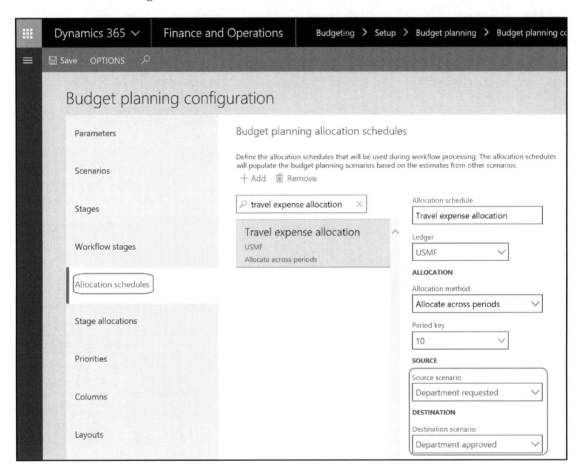

The budget plan scenario is attached to the budget plan column, which represents the layout columns. To create budget plan columns, navigate to **Budgeting | Setup | Budget planning | Budget planning configurations** and move to the **Columns** tab, as shown in the following screenshot:

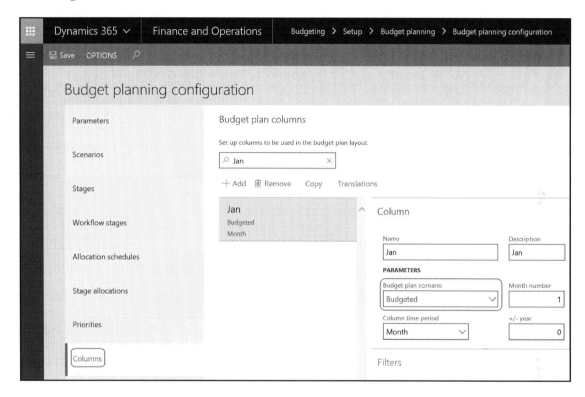

The created columns are attached to the budget planning layout, which is used in the budget plan document. Navigate to **Budgeting** | **Setup** | **Budget planning** | **Budget planning configurations** and move to the **Layouts** tab, as shown in the following screenshot:

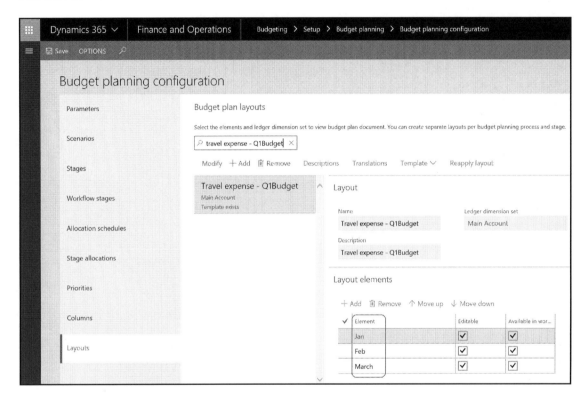

The budget plan has specific workflow configurations that are used in workflow stages and budget planning process. To create a budget workflow, navigate to **Budgeting** | **Setup** | **Budget planning** | **Budgeting workflow**, the budget plan and budget register entry have documents has out of the box workflow configurations.

Budget planning stages represents the different stages of budget planning, and it will be attached to the budget planning workflow. To create budget planning stages, navigate to **Budgeting** | **Setup** | **Budget planning** | **Budget planning configurations** and move to the **Stages** tab, as shown in the following screenshot:

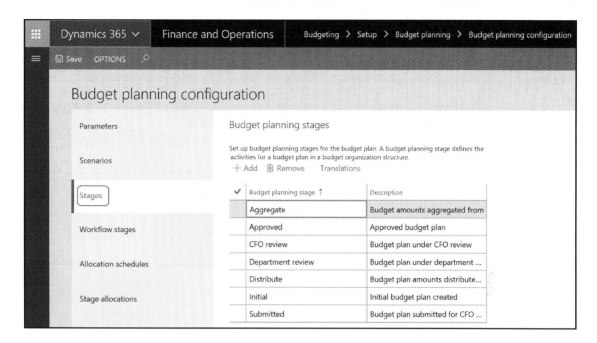

Then navigate to **Budgeting | Setup | Budget planning | Budget planning configurations** and move to the **Workflow stages** tab, as shown in the following screenshot, to assign workflow IDs and select planning stages:

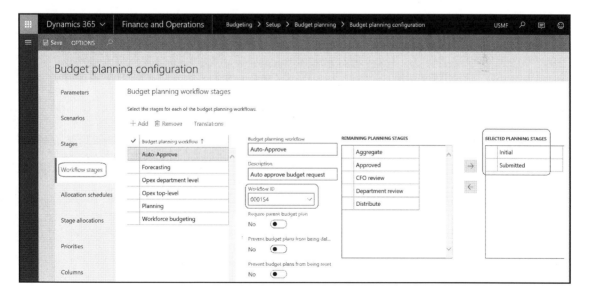

The budget planning security has two directions. The first is based on organization hierarchy, and the second is based on worker position. To configure an organization hierarchy for budgeting, navigate to **Organization administration** | **Organizations** | **Organization hierarchies**, as shown in the following screenshot:

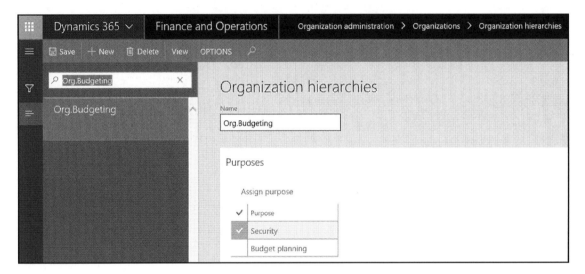

Budget planning and **Security** should be added to the organization hierarchy from **Assign purpose**. **Security** is based on the position assigned to the worker and on the role assigned to the user. To assign roles to users, navigate to **System administration** | **Users** | **Users** then move to **User's roles**, and assign the user to a specific organization.

The security model, whether based on the organization's hierarchy or the worker's position, is configured on a budget planning configuration parameter. To set it up navigate to **Budgeting** | **Setup** | **Budget planning** | **Budget planning configurations** and move to **Parameters** tab, as shown in the following screenshot:

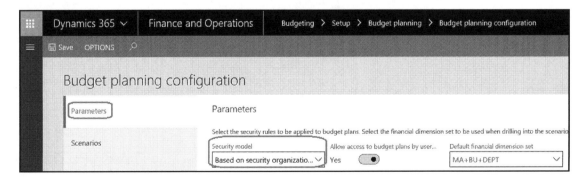

The budget cycle time spans is mandatory for the budget planning process. On the budget cycle form, the user is able to identify starting and end periods. To create budget cycles, navigate to **Budgeting** | **Setup** | **Budget planning** | **Budget cycles**, as shown in the following screenshot:

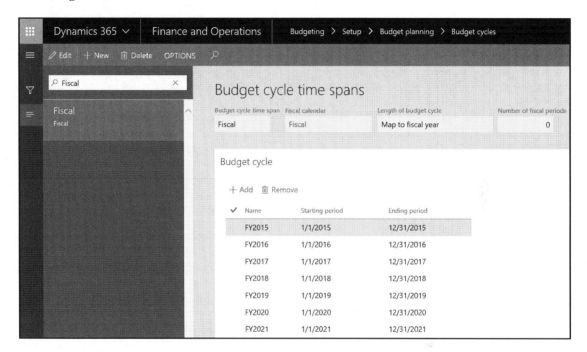

The budget planning process is the form where gathering budget planning configuration elements then get it activated. To access the budget planning process, navigate to **Budgeting** | **Setup** | **Budget planning** | **Budget planning process**, as shown in the following screenshot. Before activating the budget planning process, identify the budget cycle, the ledger (which represents the legal entity), the default account structure, and the justification document template.

Then move to assigning the organization hierarchy and responsibility center, as well as the workflow ID:

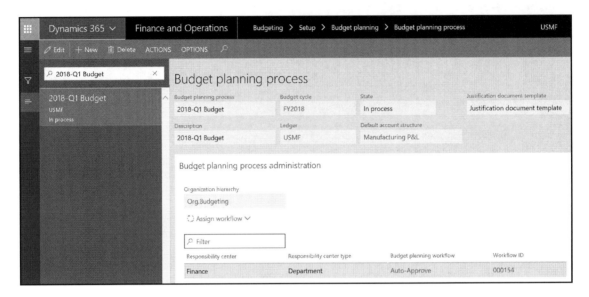

In the budget planning process, assign the budget planning stage, the layouts on the **Budget planning** stage, and the layouts fast tab as well.

To activate the budget planning process, go to **Actions | Activate**. **State** will change from **Draft** to **In process**.

Budget control

As defined in the *Oxford Dictionary of Accounting*, budget control is "*the process by which financial control is exercised within an organization using budgets for income and expenditure for each function of the organization in advance of an accounting period. These budgets are compared with actual performance to establish any variances. Individual function managers are made responsible for the controllable activities within their budgets, and are expected to take remedial action if the adverse variances are regarded as excessive.*"

The budget control function in Microsoft Dynamics 365 for Finance and Operations provides the required configurations of budget control elements. The budget control should be turned on and activated, should identify the account structure and budget control dimensions, should also assign an exception user group, which dictates who can exceed the budget, and should identify which document will be subject to budget control, and calculate the budget's funds.

To configure budget control, navigate to **Budgeting** | **Setup** | **Budget control** | **Budget control configuration**, as shown in the following screenshot:

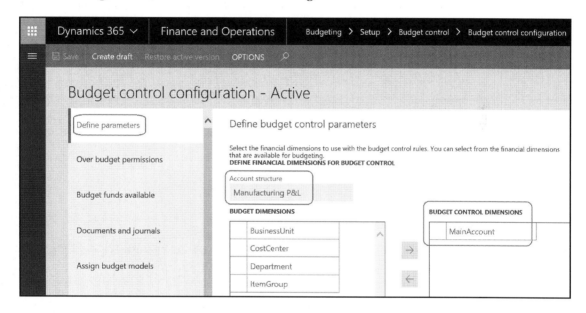

The preceding screenshot represents the account structure and budget control dimensions. The budget control configuration should be in **Draft** mode so you can update it.

It is important to identify available budget funds. This should be reviewed by the CFO and controller to identify amounts to sum and amounts to subtract, as shown in the following screenshot:

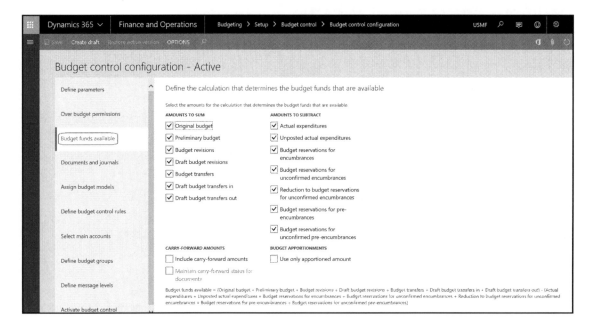

The defined calculations are presented in the form. The preceding calculation is as the following:

Budget funds available = (Original budget + Preliminary budget + Budget revisions + Draft budget revisions + Budget transfers + Draft budget transfers in + Draft budget transfers out) - (Actual expenditures + Unposted actual expenditures + Budget reservations for encumbrances + Budget reservations for unconfirmed encumbrances + Reduction to budget reservations for unconfirmed encumbrances + Budget reservations for pre-encumbrances + Budget reservations for unconfirmed pre-encumbrances)

The documents and journals that are subject to budget control functionality are identified, whether including transaction lines or only document and journal headers. The following screenshot illustrates the documents and journals:

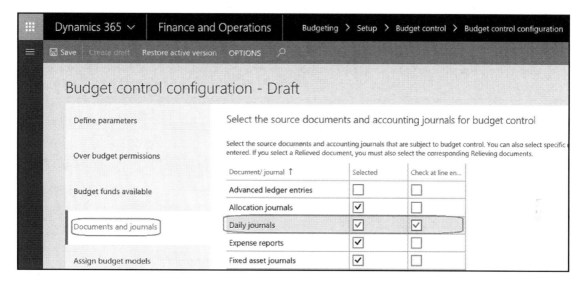

Let's move on to identifying the budget cycle span, budget cycle, and budget model, as shown in the following screenshot:

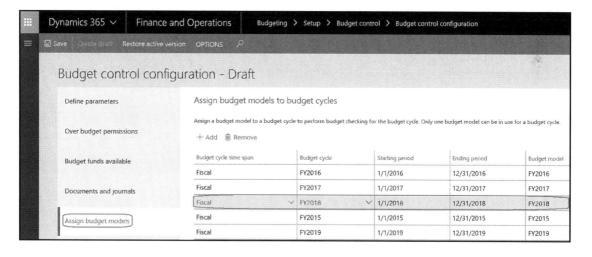

At least one record should be defined on budget control rules. Define the financial dimension combinations for budget control. When budget control is turned on, the financial dimension combinations specified in the range criteria are monitored. If no criteria are specified, then the rule applies to all dimension values. This is represented in the following screenshot:

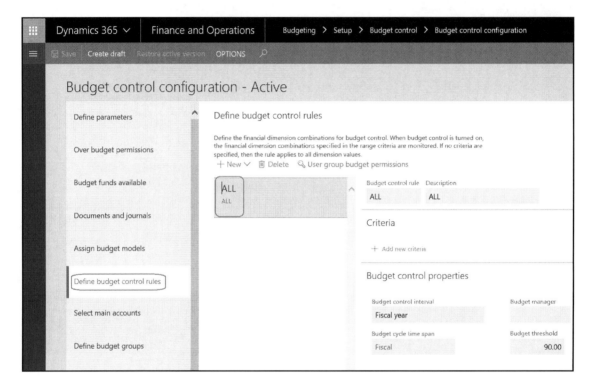

The final step is to activate and and turn on the budget control, as shown in the following screenshot:

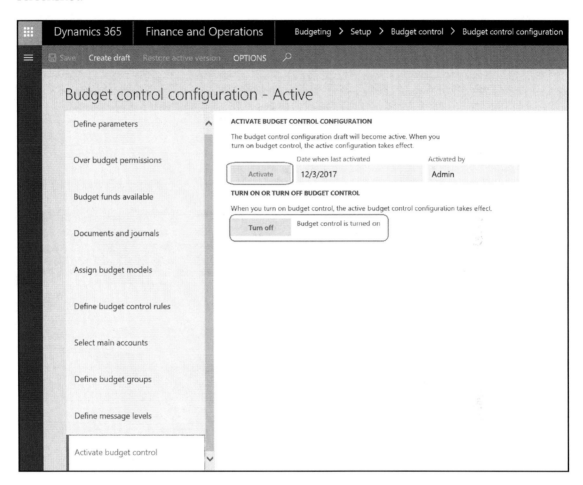

Budget in action

The budget plan could be created manually, or built based on actual transactions. The budget register entries could be created based on a budget plan or created manually. The application recalls the configurations of budget control and executes it over transactions. The following diagram illustrates **Budget management in action**:

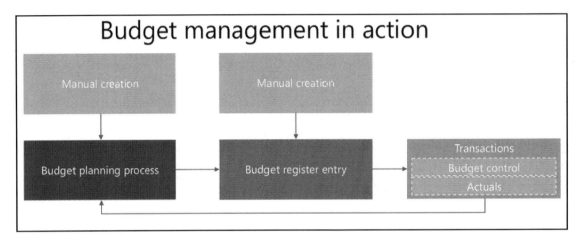

Over the course of the budget planning process for the Q1 expense projection, you'll need to manually create a budget plan. Go to **Budgeting | Budget plans** and create a new record by pressing *Alt + N*, as shown in the following screenshot:

Budget plan lines are recalled from the budget plan layout configuration. This shows the flexibility of designing the budget plan for different customer requirements and scenarios. The following screenshot illustrates the budget plan lines for an expense account for Q1:

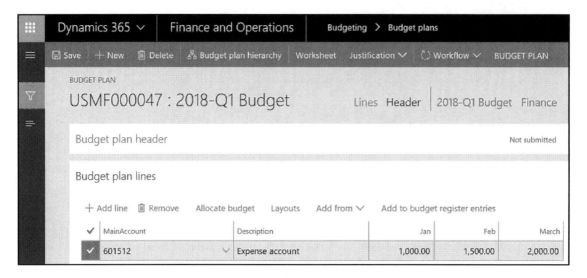

Budget plans should be submitted to the workflow. Their status will be **In review** until they have received the required approvals. The status will be changed to **Approved** once the approvals are received.

Add a budget plan to the budget register entry by selecting ;**Add to budget register entries**:

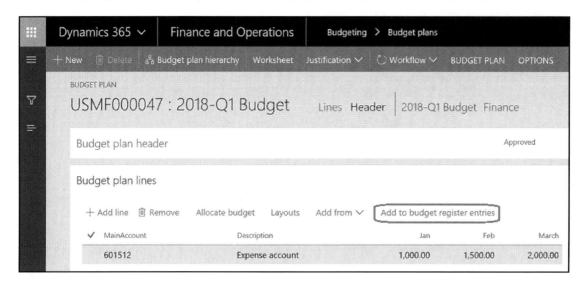

A dialog form will open to generate budget register entries, as shown in the following screenshot:

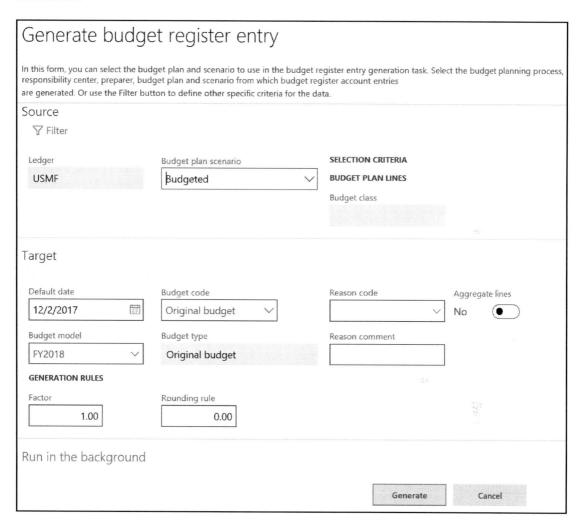

Generate budget register entry

In this form, you can select the budget plan and scenario to use in the budget register entry generation task. Select the budget planning process, responsibility center, preparer, budget plan and scenario from which budget register account entries
are generated. Or use the Filter button to define other specific criteria for the data.

Source

▽ Filter

Ledger	Budget plan scenario	**SELECTION CRITERIA**
USMF	Budgeted ⌄	**BUDGET PLAN LINES**
		Budget class

Target

Default date	Budget code	Reason code	Aggregate lines
12/2/2017 📅	Original budget ⌄	⌄	No ⬤

Budget model	Budget type	Reason comment
FY2018 ⌄	Original budget	

GENERATION RULES

Factor	Rounding rule
1.00	0.00

Run in the background

Generate   Cancel

A message will appear in the message center to indicate the creation of the budget register entries.

Move to the budget register entry form by navigating to **Budgeting** | **Budget register entries**. The budget register entries are created automatically based on budget planning records, as shown in the following screenshot:

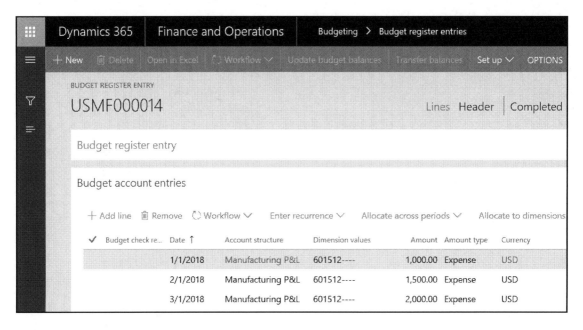

Create general journal transaction by navigating to **General ledger** | **Journal entries** | **General journals** and select the expense account. Assuming that the accountant entered 4500.01, which is greater than the budgeted amount 4500.00, the system will perform the budget check and will indicate that it failed, as shown in the following screenshot:

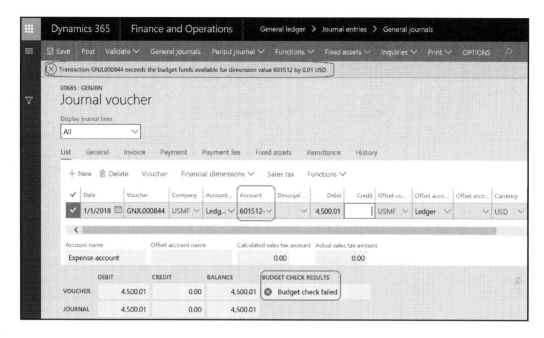

If the accountant adjusted the entered amount to `500.00`, the budget check results will indicate that the check passed, as shown in the following screenshot:

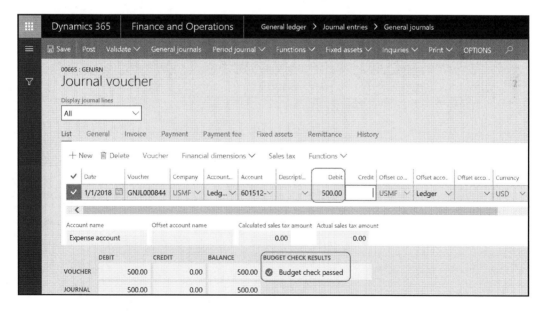

Summary

In this chapter, we discussed the budget management capabilities of Microsoft Dynamics 365 for Finance and Operations. We explored the basic budgeting configuration of budget models, budget codes, dimensions for budgeting, and budget allocation terms. Then we moved on to the budget planning process, and covered scenarios, stages, budget planning security options, budget planning workflow and its stages, and budget control configuration. Finally, we explored budget management in action by creating a budget plan, where we moved it to the budget register entry and presented the budget control in the general ledger.

In the next chapter, we will cover the intercompany basic setups and transactions.

12
Working with Intercompany Accounting

Organizations that operate in multi companies need to execute transactions among the subsidiary units of the same entity. While these intercompany transactions can occur for a variety of reasons, they often occur as a result of business relationships that exist between parent and subsidiary units. This chapter covers the following topics in Microsoft Dynamics 365 for Finance and Operations:

- Exploring intercompany accounting
- Understanding the setup and configuration of intercompany accounting
- Exploring intercompany from an operational perspective and transactions

Exploring intercompany accounting

Intercompany accounting represents the relationship among companies that are within the same group, normally enterprises having a holding company, and subsidiaries. The intercompany transactions are captured in the financial records of the subsidiaries that are involved in the intercompany.

There are several formats of intercompany transactions among the subsidiaries, and the following diagram illustrates these intercompany transactions formats:

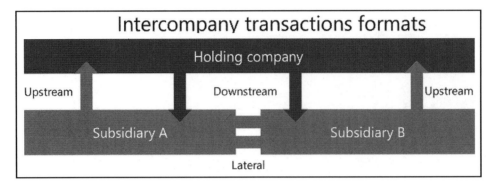

As shown in the preceding diagram, there are three types, which can be explained as follows:

- **Upstream**: An intercompany transaction flowing from the subsidiary to the parent
- **Downstream**: An intercompany transaction flowing from the parent to the subsidiary
- **Lateral**: An intercompany transaction flowing from one subsidiary to another subsidiary

In Microsoft Dynamics 365 for Finance and Operations, transactions posted in one legal entity lead to a related transaction to be posted automatically in the other company. Let's say that we have two subsidiaries, UMSF and USRT. The two companies have finalized an advertising campaign, and need to pay for the expenses. USMF will execute the payment transaction, but need to identify in the records that USRT should hold 30% of this expense. If the advertising expense is equal to $1,000 USD, then $700 USD will be posted as USMF's expenses, and $300 USD as USRT's expenses.

The financial entry will be as the following:

- Posted entry on USMF
    - Dr. Advertising expense $700 USD
    - Dr. Due from USRT $300 USD
    - Cr. Bank $1,000 USD

- Posted entry on USRT
    - Dr. Advertising expense $300 USD
    - Cr. Due to USMF $300 USD

Understanding the setup and configuration of intercompany accounting

The intercompany elements in Microsoft Dynamics 365 for Finance and Operations include defining main accounts to be used for intercompany entries. It is recommended to use different accounts for each subsidiary in order to streamline the reconciliation of intercompany entries. Then, each subsidiary should have separate journal names for intercompany transactions, and should also use different vouchers for intercompany transactions for easy tracking. Finally, moving on to intercompany accounting configuration, assign the created due to and due from main accounts for the originating company and the destination company, in addition to a journal name. The following diagram illustrates the intecompany elements:

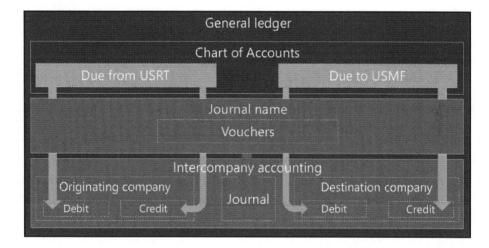

To configure intercompany accounting, navigate to **General ledger | Posting setup | Intercompany accounting**, as shown in the following screenshot:

To execute intercompany transactions, Microsoft Dynamics 365 for Finance and Operations has an option to select the company name in the transaction, and it will recall the chart of accounts that is assigned to the selected legal entity. Navigate to the general journal from workspaces; it was newly introduced in Microsoft Dynamics 365 for Finance and Operations. It gives more usability to the form; as such, the accountant can create a new general journal, view transactions that were posted today, view transactions that were not posted, and more tiles. To do this, perform the following steps:

1. Go to **Workspaces | General journal processing**, as shown in the following screenshot:

2. Create a new journal, then select the **Intercompany Journal**'s name, as shown in the following screenshot:

3. After moving to lines, select the company ID **USRT**. This will recall the chart of accounts for this company. This will be posted directly to the **USRT** company, as shown in the following screenshot:

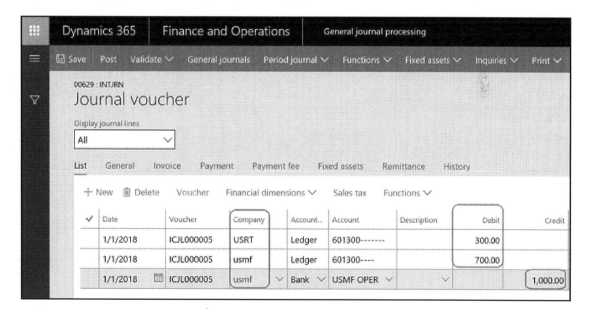

4. Inquire the posted voucher on the USMF company; **Due from USRT** is debited by the advertising expense amount:

5. Then, move to USRT company, and explore the posted transactions from **General ledger** | **Inquiries and reports** | **Audit trial** and view the posted voucher. Since USMF's account is credited, this entry is generated automatically:

Summary

This chapter covered the intercompany accounting concept, configuration, and setup in Microsoft Dynamics 365 for Finance and Operations. We then covered the execution of intercompany general journal entries, and explored transactions in originating and destination companies.

In the next chapter, we will cover consolidation and elimination in Microsoft Dynamics 365 for Finance and Operations.

13
Working with Consolidation and Elimination

Consolidation is the process of combining financial information from individual subsidiaries to the parent holding company, in one consolidated financial statement. If the subsidiaries have inter-company transactions, then these should be eliminated in consolidated reports. In this chapter, we cover the following topics:

- Exploring consolidation and its approaches
- Exploring consolidation and eliminations in action

Exploring consolidation and its approaches

Consolidation and elimination are two different processes but they are connected. Consolidation is gathering transactions from several company accounts into a single entity to print consolidated financial reports. Elimination is excluding inter-company transactions between subsidiaries and it is performed prior to the consolidation process; the elimination process could be executed separately or within the consolidation process.

Microsoft Dynamics 365 for Finance and Operations has four consolidation approaches; the company's CFO and controller should decide which approach will be followed and of course this will be driven by business needs.

The following diagram illustrates the different consolidation approaches in Microsoft Dynamics 365 for Finance and Operations:

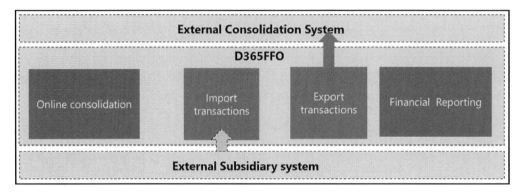

As shown in the preceding diagram, the consolidation approaches are:

- **Online consolidation**: It represents the process of consolidation that will be executed within Microsoft Dynamics 365 for Finance and Operations. This approach requires consolidation and elimination company to be in place.
- **Import transactions**: Assuming that there are subsidiaries within the holding group that are operating in separate instances of Dynamics 365 for Finance and Operations, or maybe in an complete external system, this needs to be part of the consolidation; this is the option used to import transactions from an external system into the Dynamics 365 for Finance and Operations consolidation company.
- **Export transactions**: Assuming that the holding company is using different instances or systems for consolidation, this is the option used to export transactions from Dynamics 365 for Finance and Operations.
- **Financial reporting**: Using the capabilities of Financial reporting to design consolidation and elimination reports, this does not require a separate consolidation and elimination company. The reports are called from subsidiary transactions directly.

Assuming an enterprise consists of three different company levels, the lowest level is the group subsidiaries that are used to record the daily operational transactions, and maybe these subsidiaries have inter-company transactions. Then, each group of subsidiaries has a parent company consolidating the transactions. At this level, elimination is required if inter-company transactions are posted between subsidiaries. If inter-company transactions are not eliminated, it will give incorrect consolidation results.

The highest level is the holding company where consolidating the parent company's financial reporting in a consolidated financial report. The following diagram illustrates the hierarchy of **Contoso Group**:

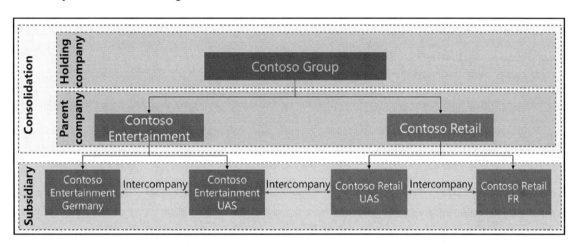

The following section covers the basic elements of consolidation and elimination in Microsoft Dynamics 365 for Finance and Operations. The consolidation and elimination characteristics are listed in the following points; these points should be considered during consolidation implementation workshops. The application consultant should discuss these features with the company's CFO and controller:

- Consolidation and elimination companies are separate legal entities in Microsoft Dynamics 365 for Finance and Operations
- A consolidation legal entity could carry out the elimination process
- Elimination could be performed in a separate legal entity
- Consolidation and elimination companies are not used for posting daily transactions
- Consolidation and elimination can be performed at any time and can be reversed
- Consolidation and elimination can be performed within the Microsoft Dynamics 365 for Finance and Operations instance, and this is called online consolidation
- Consolidation and elimination can be performed by importing financial data from an external system to Microsoft Dynamics 365 for Finance and Operations
- Consolidation and elimination can be performed on reporting level of financial reporting
- There are no restrictions on the number of consolidation levels in Microsoft Dynamics 365 for Finance and Operations

- The consolidation hierarchy can be changed at any time and run retroactively
- Configuring a separate exchange rate type for consolidation to accommodate multinational enterprises requirements where subsidiaries operating in their own local currency, and consolidation need to be translated to single currency

There are two levels of consolidation configuration; the first level is on consolidation and elimination entity, and the second level is on subsidiary entity. The required setup needed in a subsidiary company depends on how closely the chart of accounts and dimensions for the consolidated company and the subsidiary are aligned. If the subsidiary chart of accounts has the same chart of accounts as the consolidated company, there is no need to manually map the subsidiary main accounts to consolidate the company accounts. The consolidation and elimination configuration is like any other legal entity in Microsoft Dynamics 365 for Finance and Operations. The following diagram illustrates the configuration elements for consolidation and elimination:

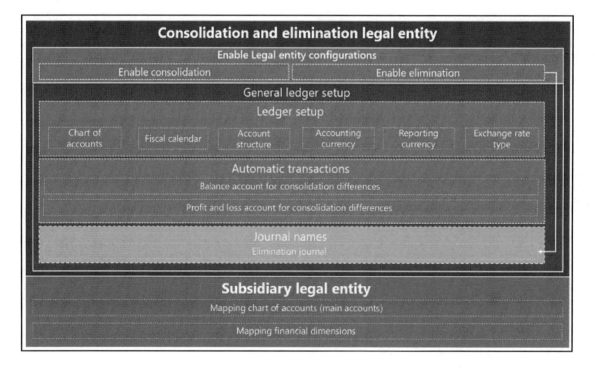

The special option for consolidation and elimination is on legal entity options; there are two separate options that determine if the legal entity is for consolidation, or for elimination, or for both. To access legal entity configurations, navigate to **Organization administration** | **Organizations** | **Legal entities** and move to the **General** tab, as shown in the following screenshot:

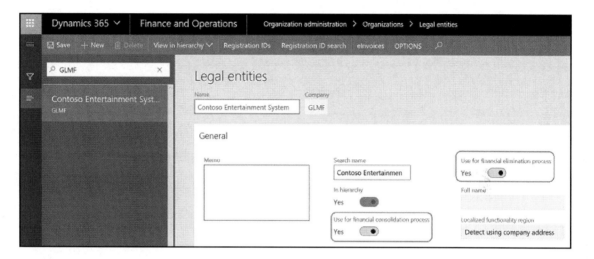

The consolidation legal entity does not accept any kind of posting daily transactions. The system throws an error message indicating that **It is not possible to post to the consolidated company accounts #####**.

The subsidiary entity that has posted the transaction could not be configured as the consolidation and elimination company. The system throws an error message indicating that **Ledger records exist for the consolidation company. You cannot change the consolidation company option**.

The ledger setup is under **General ledger** | **Ledger setup** | **Ledger** and the elements of the **Ledger** form are the as same as any other legal entity. In some business scenarios, local government requires that the consolidation organization submit a statutory chart of accounts for reporting purposes. In order to map a statutory chart of accounts in Microsoft Dynamics 365 for Finance and Operations, you should create consolidation account groups and configure consolidation accounts.

To create consolidation account groups, go to **Consolidations | Setup | Consolidation account groups**, as shown in the following screenshot:

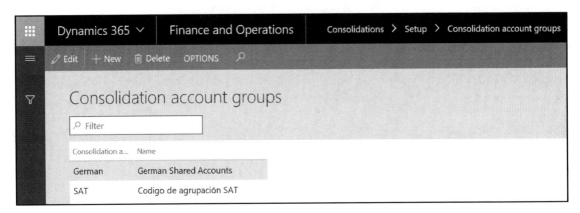

Chart of accounts mapping is performed on the additional consolidation accounts form; navigate to **Consolidations | Setup | Additional consolidation accounts**, select **Chart of accounts**, identify the main account from the **Chart of accounts**, then select the consolidation account group and account name, which could be translated into a different language. The following screenshot illustrates the **Additional consolidation accounts** form:

Because of the changes in the economy, the currency transaction should be considered during the consolidation process. There are two accounts that should be added to the automatic transactions form under **General ledger** | **Posting setup** | **Accounts for automatic transactions**. The posting types of the two accounts are as follows:

- **Balance account for consolidation differences**: Used when consolidating an integrated foreign subsidiary
- **Profit and loss account for consolidation differences**: Used when consolidating a self-sustaining subsidiary

The elimination process has two required setups on the consolidation and elimination entity. The first is the elimination journal name, which is used in the elimination posting. Navigate to **General ledger** | **Journal setup** | **Journal names** and create a journal name with the **Elimination** journal type. The second is setting the elimination rule, to identify source and destination accounts. To set up the ledger elimination rule, navigate to **Consolidation** | **Setup** | **Elimination rule** then move to lines.

The consolidation configuration on the subsidiary level is located on the main accounts, and dimensions. The main task here is to map the subsidiary main accounts and dimensions, if the consolidation company and subsidiary company have a different chart of accounts or dimensions. Navigate to the subsidiary legal entity, **General ledger** | **Chart of accounts** | **Accounts** | **Main accounts**. The **Default consolidation account** is under the **General** fast tab; this field represents the mapped consolidation main account corresponding to the selected main account in the subsidiary company, as shown in the following screenshot:

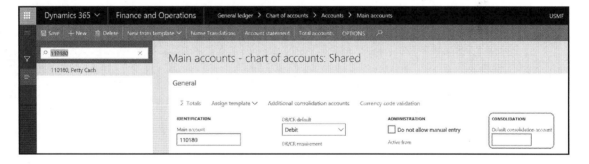

With the same concept, subsidiary financial dimensions could be mapped to **Group dimension** for consolidation. On the subsidiary legal entity, navigate to **General ledger** | **Chart of accounts** | **Dimensions** | **Financial dimensions**, then move the financial dimensions values; the **Group dimension** field represents the consolidation dimensions mapped to the selected dimension on the subsidiary company, as shown in the following screenshot:

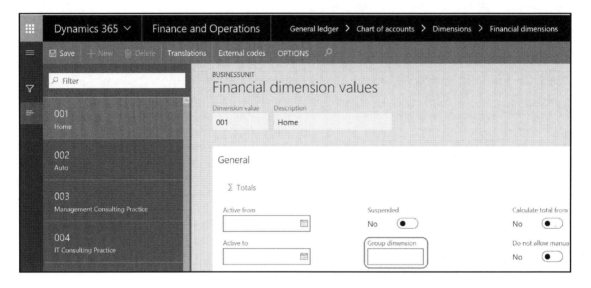

Exploring consolidation and elimination in action

In the course of normal business operations, daily transactions are executed on the subsidiary level, then you run the elimination and consolidation process. Assuming that subsidiaries have inter-company transactions covering marketing expense, the USMF company pays the expense from its accounts and identifies the expense part for the DEMF company. The following diagram illustrates the subsidiary inter-company transaction, in addition to elimination and consolidation process on the parent company level:

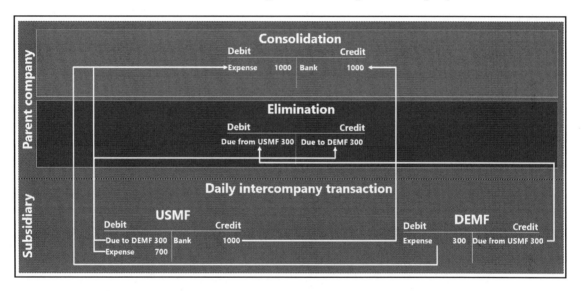

To execute the consolidation and elimination process, navigate to **Consolidation | Consolidate online**; the parameter dialog will open up to identify the consolidation and elimination criteria, as shown in the following screenshot. Enter the description, identify the consolidation period, and include the actual amounts:

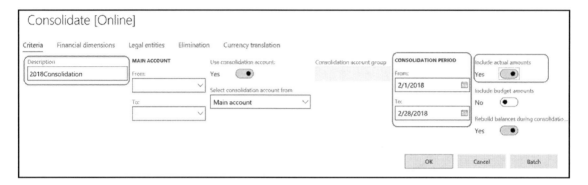

Then, move to **Financial dimensions** to identify which dimensions will be carried on the consolidation process and what the segment order is for each dimension, as shown in the following screenshot:

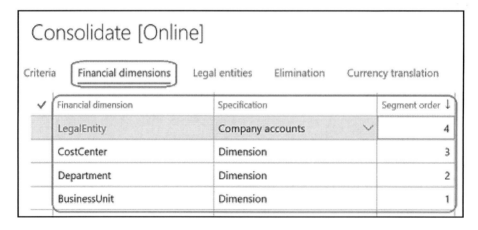

Move to the **Legal entities** tab, to determine which legal entities are included in the consolidation and elimination process, identify the share percentage, and account type of conversion differences, as shown in the following screenshot:

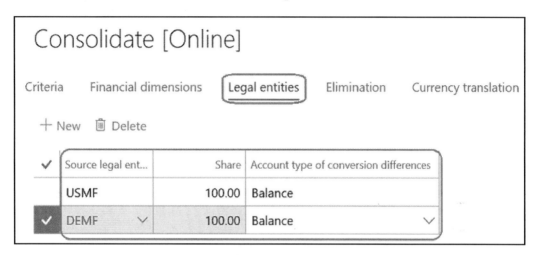

Then, determine the elimination process by identifying the elimination rule in the **Elimination** tab, the GL posting date, and proposal options, as shown in the following screenshot:

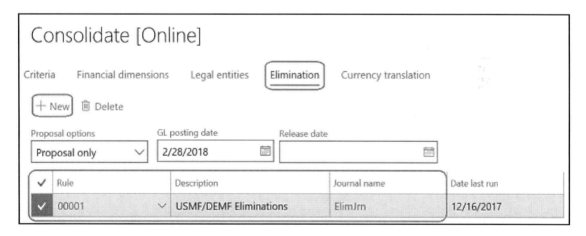

Finally, define the **Currency translation** for companies that have a different accounting currency from the consolidation company, identify the exchange rate type, and designate the applied exchange rate, as shown in the following screenshot:

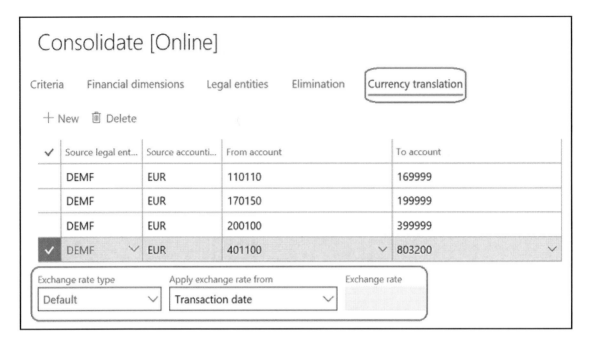

After the process is finished, the elimination journal is created; it eliminates the due to (**133332**) against the due from (**231367**). The due to line is posted in EUR and it is equivalent to the USD amount of due from, as shown in the following screenshot:

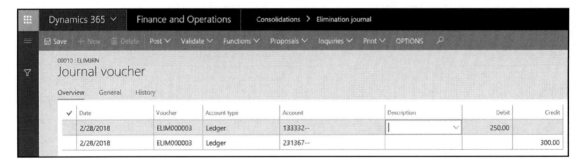

 The used exchange rate from EUR to USD is 1.20.

Then, move to **Consolidations**, where the system gathers transactions from the subsidiary level, as shown in the following screenshot:

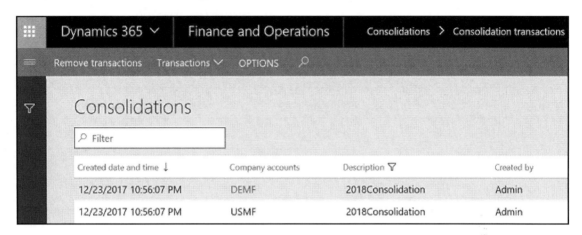

The consolidated trial balance of the parent company represents the total of the expense account 1,000 USD (300 DEMF + 700 USMF); the due to and the due from have been eliminated, and the petty cash account has a credit balance of 1,000 USD. To access the trial balance, go to **General ledger** | **Inquiries and reports** | **Trial balance**, as shown in the following screenshot:

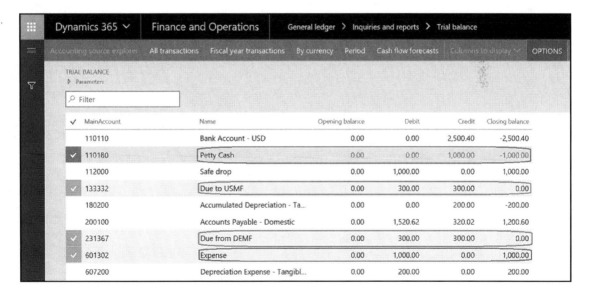

Summary

This chapter covered consolidation and elimination in Microsoft Dynamics 365 for Finance and Operations. We covered consolidation approaches and characteristics, then moved to configuring and setting up a consolidation legal entity, and a subsidiary entity. Finally, we explored consolidation and elimination process execution.

In the next chapter, we will discuss cost management from the inventory perspective, as it is the most significant cost for an organization and requires control and monitoring.

14
Working with Cost Management

The costing function is one of the most critical subjects in the ERP implementation, specifically inventory costing. In the competitive and emerging markets of today, we aim at getting the best usage from the current company resources in order to ensure that they are translated into company profitability and more potential cash flow. On the other hand, the inventory cost affects the company reporting in the balance sheet and income statement, along with the cost of goods sold and cost of production. This function requires intensive workshops during the implementation life cycle to contest the business costing model and how it will be mapped to Microsoft Dynamics 365 for Finance and Operations.

In this chapter, we will cover the following topics:

- Understanding the business costing model
- Configuring inventory costing
- Exploring the inventory costing background (physical and financial update)
- Understanding inventory recalculation and closing
- Working with inventory marking
- Exploring inventory reconciliation

Understanding the business costing model

The highest significant cost of organizations is encountered in the inventory costing. In this sense, one of the main objectives of ERP implementation is to manage, reduce, and control inventory costing. The inventory significantly affects the company's bottom line, and profitability as well. The companies that carry inventory as a raw material for production bear the cost of inventory, which in turn affects the cost of production, in addition to the goods in the process and the **cost of goods sold** (**COGS**), accordingly. The companies that carry inventory as stock for sales bear the inventory cost, which in turn affects the cost of goods sold.

The main driver of inventory cost is the purchase cost from the vendor, in addition to all the costs that are paid until the goods are received into the company's warehouse, such as freight, customs duties, and loading. All these are known as miscellaneous charges, which is a function name in Microsoft Dynamics 365 for Finance and Operations.

The company's profitability is directly impacted by the inventory cost. Therefore, it is essential for the organization to effectively manage the procurement activities and financial cost control that monitors inventory costs. The following diagram shows Microsoft Dynamics 365 for Finance and Operations inventory costing:

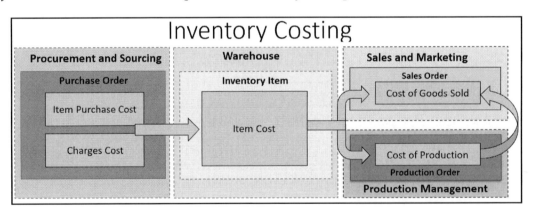

The implementation team ascertains the inventory costing strategy for the company. It is a joint effort between the financial controller, inventory and warehousing manager, and application consultant, during the analysis phase of the implementation. The financial controller sets the inventory valuation method and inventory posting profiles. The inventory and warehousing manager sets the inventory item coding structure and item groups for inventory classifications. The application consultant maps the controller, as well as the inventory and warehousing manager's requirements to Microsoft Dynamics 365 for Finance and Operations.

Configuring inventory costing

The configuration and setup of inventory costing are combined with the integrated modules of inventory and warehousing management, product information management, and financial controls. A collection of all types of setup is shown in the product master form, illustrated in the following figure:

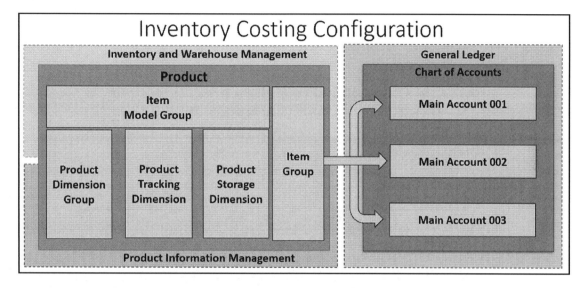

The blocks in the preceding diagram are defined as follows:

- **Item model group**: This identifies the inventory valuation method
- **Product dimension groups**: This identifies the product's attributes
- **Product storage dimension groups**: This identifies the product's location
- **Product tracking dimension groups**: This identifies the product's tracking information

Item model groups

The main configuration and setup of inventory costing in Microsoft Dynamics 365 for Finance and Operations is in **Item model groups**, where we identify the inventory costing valuation method. For inventory model groups, navigate to **Inventory management** | **Setup** | **Inventory** | **Item model groups**. Microsoft Dynamics 365 for Finance and Operations supports the following inventory valuation methods:

- **FIFO**: This is first in, first out
- **LIFO**: This is last in, first out
- **LIFO date**: This is the last-in, first-out date
- **Weighted avg.**: This is the weighted average
- **Weighted avg. date**: This is the weighted average date
- **Standard cost**: This is the standard cost
- **Moving average**: This is the moving average cost

The following screenshot shows all the inventory valuation methods:

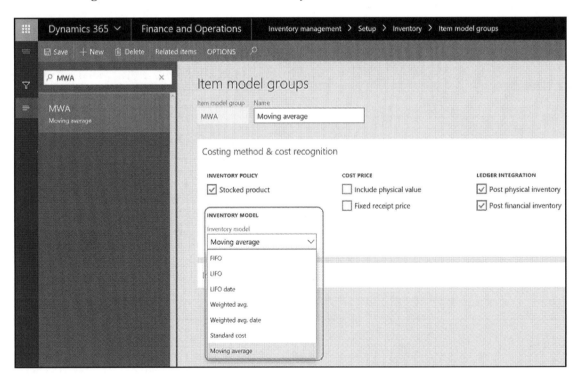

In the following section, we will highlight some of the item module group configurations:

- **Inventory policy**: This indicates whether the item or the service is stockable or non-stockable. Stockability indicates that the item will be tracked in the inventory transaction and included in the inventory costing and its calculation.
- **Physical negative inventory**: This is a control point that prevents the inventory quantities from being issued from the warehouse, if there is no available quantity. If the business needs to issue more quantities than is available in the warehouse, this should be coordinated with the controller and the stock manager, as the inventory balance will be in the negative.
- **Financial negative inventory**: This is allowed, by default, to issue quantities that are not financially updated yet. This is a control point that can prevent issuing inventory quantities from the warehouse without a financial update, which means the final cost must be known before issuing the items.
- **Post physical inventory**: This option posts the physical inventory to the **General ledger** module, and this requires a configuration on the accounts payable parameters and the accounts receivable parameters by checking the **Post product receipt in ledger** checkbox. If the **Post physical inventory** checkbox is unchecked, the physical transactions will not be posted in the ledger, regardless of the configuration in the AP/AR parameter setup forms.
- **Post financial inventory**: This option posts the financial inventory update to the **General ledger** module if this checkbox is checked. The posting will be as follows:
  - **Accrue liability on product receipt**: If this checkbox is checked, the amount of the items cost is posted to the accrual account, this is a mandatory option for stocked products.
  - **Post to deferred revenue account on sales delivery**: If this checkbox is checked, the amount of the items is posted to the accounts receivable not invoice and the accrued sales accounts; otherwise, no posting occurs in the item accrued revenue or the accounts receivable not invoices.

These fields are shown in the following screenshot:

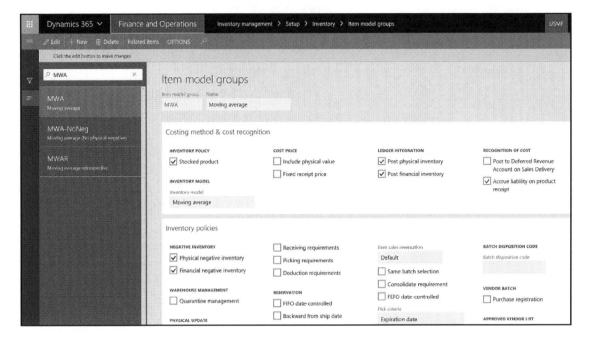

Product dimension groups

Product dimension groups represent the items' characteristics that identify the key differences of each item. For example, a polo shirt item has two dimensions, namely, size and color. The size and color can be small and blue or medium and blue. The following screenshot shows a product dimension group screen that represents the item attributes, **Configuration**, **Size**, **Color**, and **Style**:

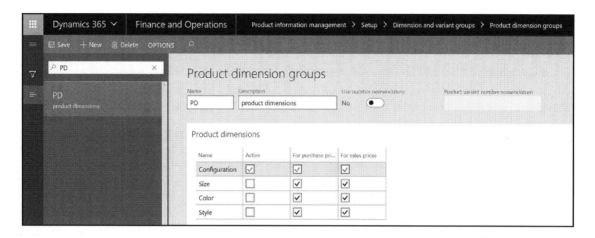

For product dimension groups, navigate to **Product information management** | **Setup** | **Dimension and variant groups** | **Product dimension groups**.

Storage dimension groups

As you can see from the following screenshot, the storage dimension groups screen sorts the required stock, keeping a note of the location, whether it is **Site**, **Warehouse**, **Location**, or **Pallet ID**. This assists in the reporting of inventory quantities and cost:

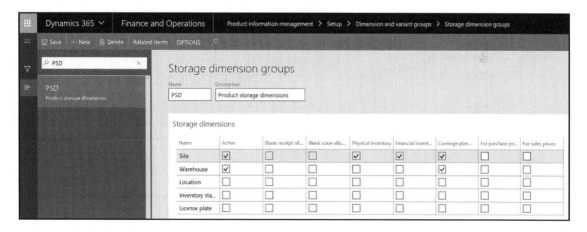

To access the storage dimension window, navigate to **Product information management** | **Setup** | **Dimension and variant groups** | **Storage dimension groups**.

Tracking dimension groups

The tracking dimension is a lower-level assortment of products, irrespective of whether it is a serial number for electronic inventory items or a batch number. For tracking dimension groups, navigate to **Product information management | Setup | Dimension and variant groups | Tracking dimension groups**, as shown in the following screenshot:

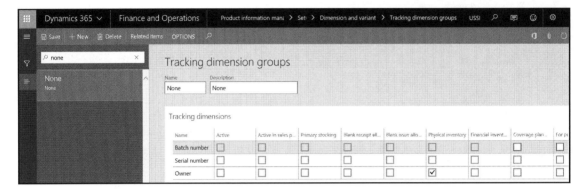

Item groups

As you can see from the following screenshot, **Item groups** is the product classification for inventory items, and it is the integration point between the inventory and financial modules. The classification of **Item groups** should be a joint effort between the stock manager and the controller. To access **Item groups**, go to **Inventory management | Setup | Inventory | Item groups**:

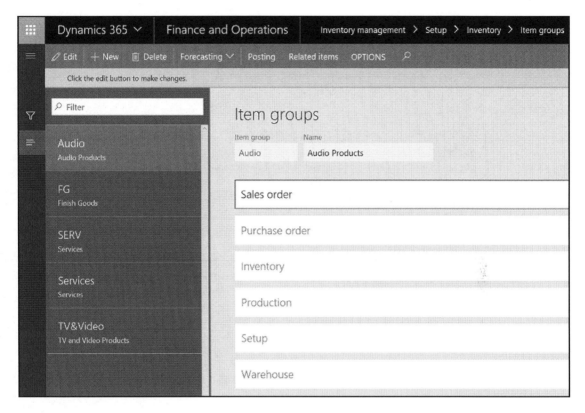

The inventory posting profile consists of the following possible inventory transactions:

- **Sales order**: This is a sales and marketing module transaction
- **Purchase order**: This is a procurement and sourcing module transaction
- **Inventory**: This is an inventory and warehousing management module transaction
- **Production**: This is a production management module transaction

The posting profiles are the integration point between the subledgers and the general ledger. It is a set of ledger accounts that are used to generate the automatic ledger entry in which a transaction occurs. It is possible to select different ledger accounts for each type of subledger transaction. Microsoft Dynamics 365 for Finance and Operations offers flexibility in the setup of posting profiles. The posting can be on four different levels, as shown in the following figure:

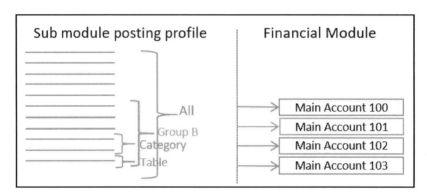

The posting domination levels are **All**, **Group**, **Category**, and **Table**. The preceding diagram can be explained as follows:

- **Group B** dominates over **All**
- **Category** dominates over **Group B** and **All**
- **Table** dominates over **Category**, **Group**, and **All**

If the posting profile is for **All** and there are some groups that have been identified for a specific main account, then these will be excluded from the **All** setup. At the same time, if there is a category relation selected for a specific main account, then these categories will be excluded from the **All** and **Group** posting profiles. If there is a table relation selected for a specific main account, it will apply the **Table** posting profile. To access the inventory posting profile, go to **Inventory management** | **Setup** | **Posting** | **Posting**.

The following screenshot illustrates an example of all of these posting domination levels:

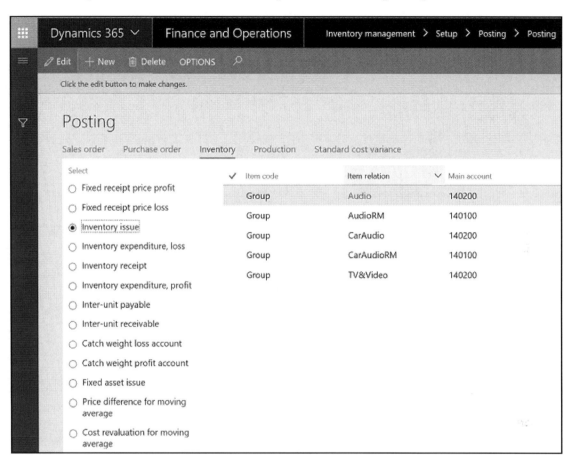

Exploring the inventory costing background

For highlighting the inventory costing model in Microsoft Dynamics 365 for Finance and Operations in order to understand the inventory valuation methods, there are three main concepts—physical and financial update, inventory recalculation and closing, and marking.

Physical and financial updates

The physical and financial update considers real-life business scenarios where there is a difference between the reception costs and invoices. It works in uncertain business environments.

Physical update

The physical update represents the inventory transaction, whether it is a product receipt for a purchase order or a packing slip for a sales order. The reception price inherits from the item purchase price in the purchase order, and identifies the item cost price in the warehouse. The cost of goods sold is retrieved from the inventory cost price and the physical issuance that occurred from the sales order. The following diagram shows the physical and financial updates:

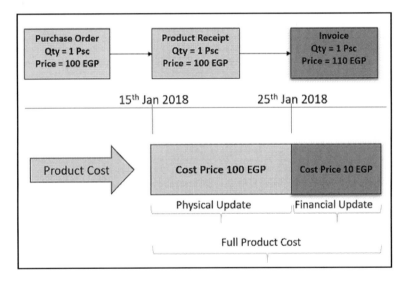

Financial update

The financial update represents the invoice posting, either for a purchase order or a sales order. The sales order invoice only has an effect on sales revenue and cost of goods sold, while, on the other hand, the purchase order invoice affects the inventory cost if there are changes in purchase price, be it an increase or a decrease.

The default mechanism of the financial update for purchase orders in Microsoft Dynamics 365 for Finance and Operations is that the financial update dominates the physical update in order to allocate the final item addition cost that will be reflected in the inventory. The physical update can be considered as an estimated cost, and the final cost is reflected in the purchase order invoice that will affect inventory cost in the warehouse submodule, and the main account in the chart of accounts, as well.

Understanding inventory recalculation and closing

The inventory recalculation is a normal procedure in the Microsoft Dynamics 365 for Finance and Operations environment that calculates the inventory cost in the warehouse and adjusts the inventory issuances, according to the inventory value model (the valuation method).

The inventory cost in Microsoft Dynamics 365 for Finance and Operations is a running average cost. To apply the valuation method, the recalculation process should be run. The normal mechanism of the inventory cost calculation applies the inventory valuation method that is attached to the product master by running the recalculation function. The recalculation function mainly affects two areas: the item cost in the warehouse and the inventory adjustment entries for product issuances from the inventory that generates the inventory financial transaction entries.

The inventory adjustment entries are generated when the issuance cost of the item is different than the current cost of the inventory items in the warehouse, according to the inventory model group (the valuation method). The entries are generated based on the original issuance transactions.

For example, if COGS of the sales order is 100 USD and the current cost in the warehouse is 110 USD, the recalculation process generates an entry by 10 USD (Dr. COGS 10, Cr. Inventory 10).

The commonly applied valuation method is **Weighted Average Cost**, where the inventory issuances are evaluated at the average cost of the items that are received during that period and also the on-hand inventory.

The formula for weighted average is *Weighted average = (Received quantity * Received cost) + (On-hand quantity * On-hand cost) / (Received quantity + On-hand quantity).*

The inventory cost is also considered a tentative cost. The inventory issuances carry the current running average cost. The actual cost is applied after the recalculation process is done, and is based on the inventory valuation method that is configured in **Item model group**. The adjustment transactions represent the difference between the running average cost and the configured costing valuation method. To access the inventory closing window, navigate to **Inventory management** | **Periodic tasks** | **Closing and adjustment**. The following diagram explains the inventory recalculation and closing concept:

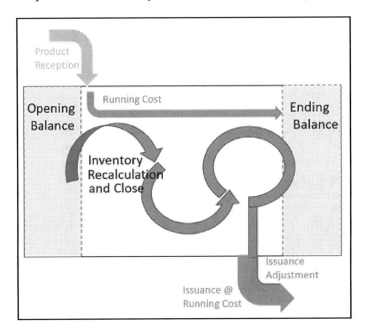

Working with inventory marking

During daily business in inventory management, there are some transactions that need to be returned to the inventory at the same cost at which they were issued. Each inventory transaction is associated to a unique **Lot ID**. Any inventory transaction is assigned to a Lot ID with a unique identification that helps in inventory cost and inventory transaction tracking; this is used to specify the transaction's cost. The marking function can be used with the **Sales order** to specify the cost of goods sold for the marked line in the **Sales order** lines, and it can be used in the issuance return (inventory addition) from the movement journal, production order, and/or the **bill of material (BOM)** journal. The following diagram shows the relationship of the inventory marking to inventory issuance and receptions:

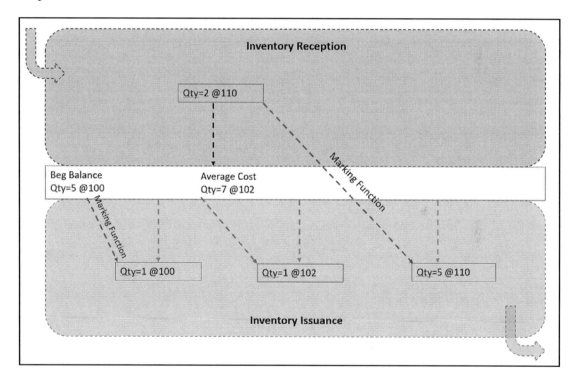

To access the marking function window, navigate to **Sales and marketing** | **Sales orders** | **All sales order**, then go to **Sales order lines**, click on **Inventory**, and select **Marking**. This can be seen in the following screenshot:

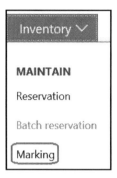

The **Marking** form lists all the relevant transactions for the inventory item, which will be set to mark on. As you can see in the following screenshot, the **Set mark now** checkbox is checked, and the users should click on **Apply** to confirm that the cost will be assigned to the transaction:

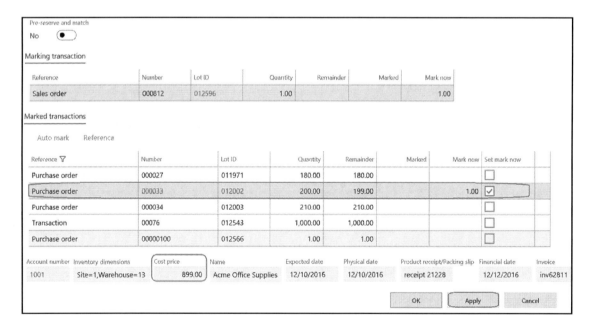

Exploring inventory reconciliation

The inventory reconciliation is a key task that proves system integrity between the general ledger and inventory subledger. This task occurs on a monthly basis as a check point after month close to ensure that everything is properly reconciled with this contentment routine.

In Microsoft Dynamics 365 for Finance and Operations, a set of reports are concerned with inventory and general ledger reconciliation. In the following section, we will explore the inventory value report.

Inventory value report setup

The inventory value report setup gives the option to have versions of the report based on the purpose of the report focus. The report can concentrate on the reconciliation between the inventory and inventory account, the **work in progress** (WIP) account, the **deferred cost of goods sold** (**deferred COGS**) account, and the **cost of goods sold** (**COGS**) account, in addition to the report design for columns and rows.

As shown in the following screenshot, to access the inventory value report setup, go to **Cost management** | **Inventory accounting policies setup** | **Inventory value reports**. To create an inventory report, click on **New** or press *Ctrl + N* and enter the report ID and report description. On the **General** tab, you can predefine the date interval for the report, as this is considered as a proposed value when generating the report in the second stage, and the user can select other date intervals, as per their needs:

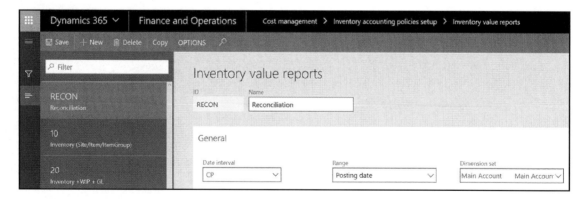

To set up date intervals, go to **General ledger** | **Setup** | **Periods** | **Date intervals**.

Now, identify the report date under the **Range** combobox, whether it is based on **Posting date** or **Transaction time**. Now identify the **Dimension set** that will be used in the report.

To set up a dimension set, navigate to **General ledger** | **Setup** | **Financial dimensions** | **Financial dimensions sets**.

When designing report columns in the **Columns** tab, the first part is the **Financial position** that represents the inventory submodel values for **Inventory**, **WIP**, **Deferred COGS**, **COGS**, and/or **Profit and loss**, which will be shown in the report.

The second part is **COMPARE ON-HAND INVENTORY VALUE TO CUMULATIVE ACCOUNTING VALUES**, which represents the ledger account for **Inventory**, **WIP**, **Deferred COGS**, and/or **COGS**.

The account type must be a total account.

The third part is **Inventory dimension**, which is the inventory breakdown by inventory dimensions and storage dimensions.

The other parts represent the summarization of the report, including transactions not posted to ledger, calculate average cost price, and/or total quantity and value. The following screenshot shows the **Columns** tab:

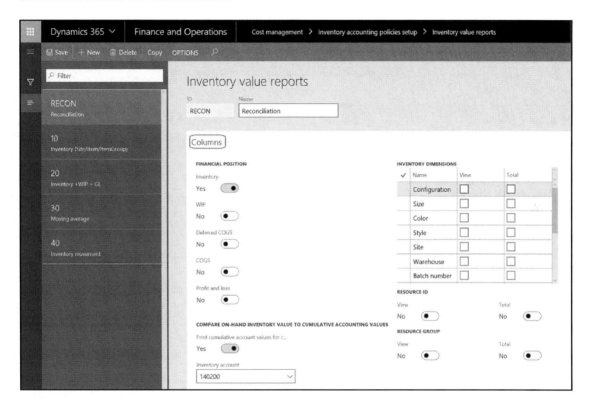

The **Rows** tab, where report rows can be designed, represents the cost elements that are required to be shown in the report row, and also shows whether the level is **Totals** or **Transaction**, as shown in the following screenshot:

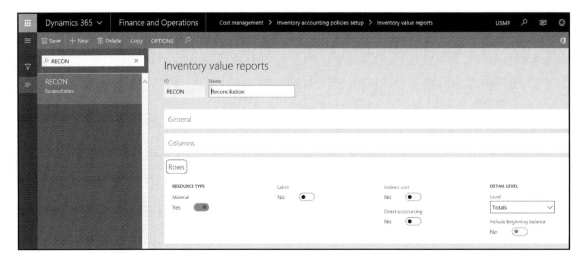

Generating Inventory value report

To generate an inventory value report, go to **Inventory management** | **Inquiries and reports** | **Inventory value reports** | **Inventory value**. The inventory value report form, where we can select the required selection criteria and filtration, is shown in the following screenshot:

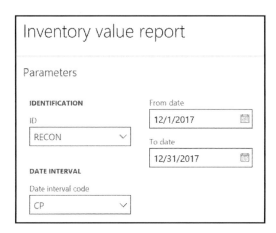

The report is divided into two sections, as shown in the following screenshot of the report printout. The first section represents the inventory submodule values, and the second section denotes the ledger account amount and the difference, if any:

Inventory value
Contoso Entertainment System USA

| From | 12/1/2017 |
| To | 12/31/2017 |

	Reference	Inventory: Financial quantity	Inventory: Financial amount	Inventory: Physical quantity posted	Inventory: Physical amount posted
Material					
	Ending balance	1,410.00	468,590.00	0.00	0.00
Material Totals		1,410.00	468,590.00	0.00	0.00

		Sum Inventory: Financial quantity	Sum Inventory: Financial amount	Sum Inventory: Physical quantity posted	Sum Inventory: Physical amount posted
Report summary					
		1,410.00	468,590.00	0.00	0.00

Inventory

Ledger account	**Account name**	**Amount**	**Percent**
	Total	0.00	
	Discrepancy	468,590.00	100.00

Summary

In this chapter, we covered the business model of inventory costing based on the business domain, the required configuration, and how to set up Microsoft Dynamics 365 for Finance and Operations in the inventory management module, as well as the integration concepts with the general ledger to map business requirements. We also covered the difference between the physical and financial updates model of Microsoft Dynamics 365 for Finance and Operations is the inventory transaction with marking functions, in addition to recalculations and closing processes. And finally, we covered the inventory value report, its setup, and its generation.

In the next chapter, we will discuss fixed assets master data and transactions.

15
Exploring Fixed Assets

The fixed assets module represents tangible assets, intangible assets, and equipment. This module manages and controls the execution of fixed assets transactions. These transactions are based on fixed assets journals or work through other modules such as procurement and sourcing, and accounts receivable.

This chapter will cover the following topics:

- Understanding fixed assets integration with other modules
- Exploring fixed assets master data characteristics
- Exploring fixed assets transactions

Understanding fixed assets integration with other modules

The fixed assets module manages and controls fixed assets transactions, and records fixed assets master information and the basic transactions related to fixed assets acquisition, depreciation, and disposal. The fixed assets function is integrated with other business functions. The first integration function is with the procurement and sourcing business functions, which execute assets acquisition through normal procurement and purchase order processing, then the reception, and finally, the invoice. The second integration is with accounts receivable, which executes fixed assets disposal sales, where there is a transaction document that moves an inventory item to a fixed asset.

The integration of fixed assets documents is shown in the following diagram:

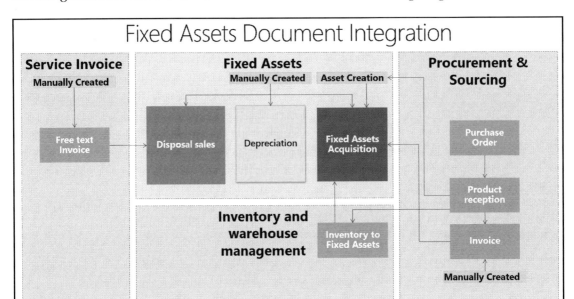

Each transaction is represented in a document type in Microsoft Dynamics 365 for Finance and Operations with the document that contains the details of the transaction. The transaction data, whether inherited from the master data, entered manually, and/or automatically inherited from another transaction, is linked with a specific reference. The integration between fixed assets and other transaction documents gives visibility for tracing the original documents that are related to the asset transactions and who posted it.

There is a list of fixed assets transactions besides the basic transactions of acquisition, depreciation, and disposal sale or disposal scrap. The following screenshot shows fixed assets transactions in Microsoft Dynamics 365 for Finance and Operations. This can be accessed from the fixed assets posting profile under **Fixed assets | Setup | Fixed assets posting profiles**:

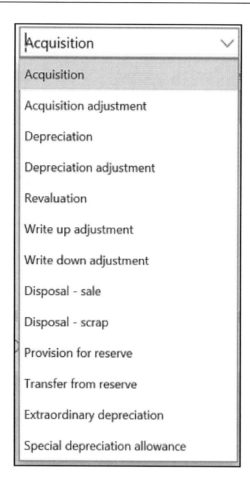

Exploring fixed assets master data characteristics

Fixed assets master data records have essential information that directly affects asset transactions. The following section covers the basic information that should be considered when creating a new fixed asset record. The following diagram shows the basic characteristics of fixed assets. There are more generic and higher levels of assets master data, including the depreciation profile, book, and the asset group that represents the logical grouping of assets.

The fixed asset record is the lowest level, which represents the asset itself:

Depreciation profiles

Depreciation profiles in Microsoft Dynamics 365 for Finance and Operations represent the rules that manage the depreciation principles that will be applied on the fixed assets, for example, the straight line depreciation method or the reducing balance depreciation method. The depreciation profile rules contain the depreciation method, depreciation year, and period frequency. In order to access a depreciation profile, go to **Fixed assets** | **Setup** | **Depreciation profiles**.

Depreciation methods

Depreciation methods represent the method that can be applied for depreciation calculation. The following screenshot shows the supported depreciation methods in Microsoft Dynamics 365 for Finance and Operations:

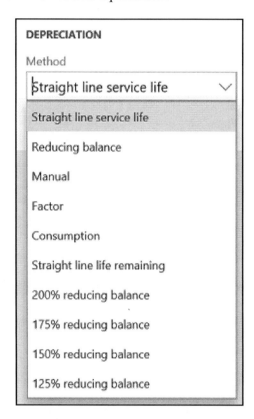

A depreciation method is an accounting principle that identifies the calculation method of distributing the cost of the fixed assets over the service line of the asset. The depreciation method is normally decided based on business requirements that might be founded on law. It is important to understand the business requirements during the analysis and design phases. This requires a close cooperation between the implementation team and financial controller to ensure the proper design, deployment, and operation of fixed assets. The most common depreciation method is called the straight line service life. Consider the following example.

Let's assume that a company acquired a car as a fixed asset costing 20,000 USD, and the service life for this car is 5 years. The depreciation calculation will be as follows:

- There are 60 depreciation months, that is, 5 years multiplied by 12 months
- The depreciation for each month will be equal to its allocation, that is, 20,000 USD divided by 60 months, which is equal to 333.333 USD per month

The form contains two types of field based on the selected depreciation method. The first type is constant fields, which are shared with all the methods, and the second type is dynamic fields, which are activated based on the depreciation method selected.

Constant fields

Constant fields refer to the depreciation year and period frequency. These fields are interrelated, which means that the values in period frequency are based on the depreciation year. The depreciation year represents the basis of calculation of depreciation, whether calendar or fiscal.

The period frequency represents ledger accruals during the calendar year, as follows:

- If the selected depreciation year is a calendar year, Microsoft Dynamics 365 for Finance and Operations assumes that the calendar year starts from January. The available values are yearly, monthly, quarterly, and half-yearly.
- If the selected depreciation year is year, Microsoft Dynamics 365 for Finance and Operations considers the fiscal year setup that might start at July. The available values are yearly and fiscal period.

Dynamic fields

Dynamic fields are activated based on the selected depreciation method:

- **Percentage**: It represents the percentage of the depreciation calculation.
- **Full Depreciation**: It represents that the fixed asset will be fully depreciated when the remaining service life reaches zero.
- **Factor**: It represents the origin of the percentage value that constitutes the depreciation.
- **Interval**: It represents the interval to run the depreciation. This field will be active if the selected depreciation method is factored.

Books

This is a new concept introduced in Microsoft Dynamics 365 for Finance and Operations. The book represents the financial value of the fixed asset that belongs to the book, and it can be the integration point between fixed assets and the general ledger in the posting profile. In order to access the book, go to **Fixed assets** | **Setup** | **Books**. The following screenshot shows the **Books** form:

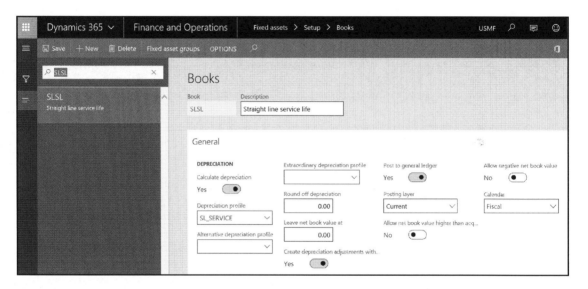

The depreciation profile is attached to the book, and it identifies whether the assets that belong to this book will be depreciated or not. The depreciation can be overridden on a fixed asset level.

The book identifies the control point on the assets belonging to a book, and checks whether to allow the net book value to go higher than the acquisition cost. Let's assume that there is a fixed asset with an acquisition price of 1,200 USD and the depreciation amount is 100 USD. If the user is going to reverse a depreciation transaction and modify the amount to be 150 USD, the system will throw an information log message indicating that the net book value will be higher than the acquisition cost, as shown in the following screenshot:

The second control point on the book denotes whether to allow a negative net book value for assets that belong to this book. Let's assume that there is a fixed asset with an acquisition price of 1,200 USD and the depreciation amount is 100 USD. If the user is going to post a depreciation transaction and modify the amount to be 1,201 USD, the system will throw an information log message to indicate that the net value of the book will be negative, as shown in the following screenshot. If we allow a negative net book value, the net book value will be equal to -1201 USD:

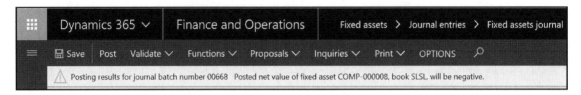

Fixed asset groups

A fixed asset group has three purposes. The first is a logical grouping of fixed assets that is mainly used for reporting and analysis. The second purpose is considered as another integration point between the general ledger and the fixed asset module. The third purpose identifies the asset's service life and depreciation periods. In order to access fixed asset groups, go to **Fixed assets** | **Setup** | **Fixed asset groups**. The following screenshot shows the fixed asset group form:

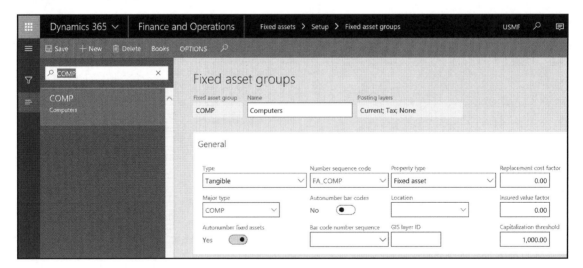

On the fixed asset groups form, identify the asset type and major type, in addition to identifying the auto-numbering of fixed assets, and attach the number sequence that will be used. The capitalization threshold represents the minimum amount of acquisition cost that will be depreciated. If an acquired fixed asset has an amount less than the capitalization threshold, it will not be depreciated.

In order to identify the depreciation period and services life, on the **Fixed asset group** form, click on **Books**. The **Fixed asset group | Book** form will open; here, you have to enter the depreciation period in months and service life in years, as shown in the following screenshot:

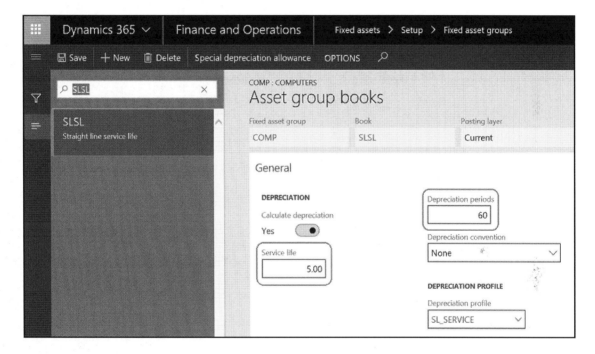

Fixed assets

Fixed assets can be equipment, cars, and/or buildings. They represent the lowest level of assets master data, which contains the fixed asset record, the unique ID, description, grouping, and specific characteristics for fixed assets. There are two ways you can create a fixed asset record. You can either create a record manually or automatically through purchase order posting. The method of creation differentiates the acquisition document. The following diagram shows the creation methods and acquisition documents:

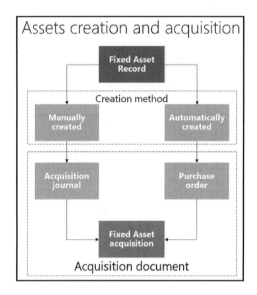

In order to create a new record of fixed assets, go to **Fixed assets | Fixed assets | Fixed assets**, and press *Alt + N* to create a new record. Here, the **Fixed asset group** and **Number** fields are the mandatory fields. When the user selects the **Fixed asset group** value, the number is automatically created. Enter the **Name** and **Search name** of the fixed assets under **Description**, as shown in the following screenshot:

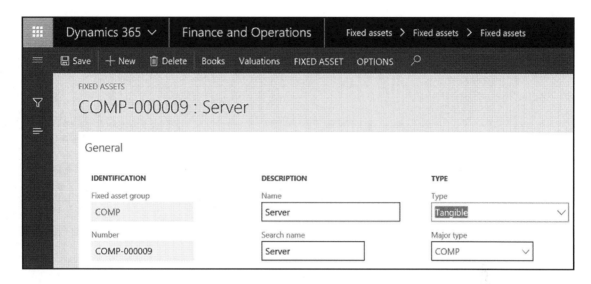

Under **Books**, there are two types of data. The first type of data is populated automatically, which represents the book assigned to the fixed asset group. These fields contains depreciation, service life, and depreciation periods. This is shown in the following screenshot:

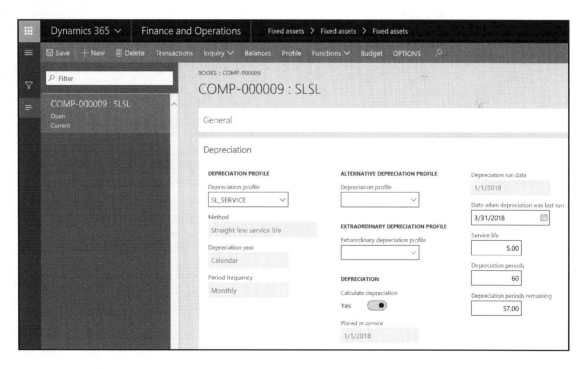

As shown in the preceding screenshot, there is an option to assign alternative depreciation profiles. When using a depreciation method that is based on a percentage, you can use the alternative depreciation profile to automatically switch to the alternative depreciation method from the original depreciation method. You can do this when the amount for the straight line method is higher than for the original method.

The second type of field can be identified manually. For this, navigate to the **General** fast tab to identify the acquisition date and price. These are shown in the following screenshot:

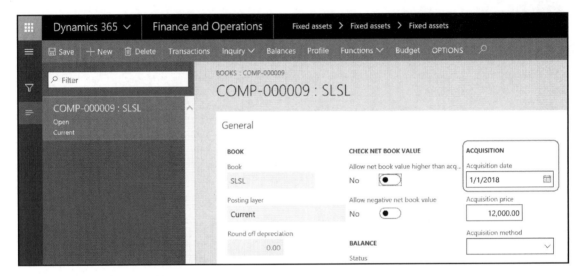

Exploring fixed assets transactions

In this section, we will explore fixed assets transactions starting from acquisition transactions by acquisition journal, acquisition through purchase order, depreciation, disposal scrap, and fixed assets reversal transactions. In order to record and post an acquisition journal, go to **Fixed assets | Journal entries | Fixed assets journal**, as shown in the following screenshot. Create a new journal by pressing *Alt + N* on the journal line, go to **Proposals** and select **Acquisition proposal**, and then go on to select a filter to identify the asset number, which will be acquired, as shown in the following screenshot:

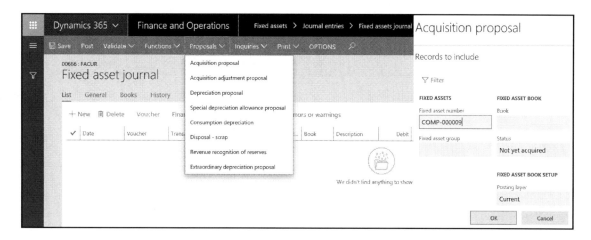

Note that if the acquisition price is not identified, the acquisition proposal will not populate the asset.

In order to acquire fixed assets through a purchase order, a parameter must be activated first. This gives the company the control to acquire the assets through the procurement department and enables it to apply the segregation of duties between the procurement, reception, invoicing, and payment processes. As shown in the following screenshot, go to **Fixed assets** | **Setup** | **Fixed assets parameters** and then click on **Purchase orders**:

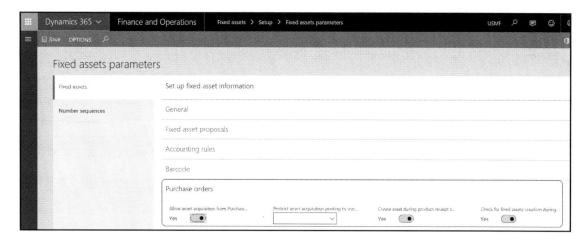

The following options are available under the **Purchase orders** tab:

- **Allow asset acquisition from Purchasing**
- **Restrict asset acquisition posting to user group**
- **Create asset during product receipt or invoice posting**
- **Check for fixed assets creation during line entry**

In the course of the execution of a fixed asset acquisition through a purchase order, go to **Procurement and sourcing** | **Purchase orders** | **All purchase orders**. Then, create a new record by pressing *Alt + N*, select vendor, go to purchase lines, select service item, and then enter warehouse and price details. Now, go to the **Fixed assets** tab, as shown in the following screenshot:

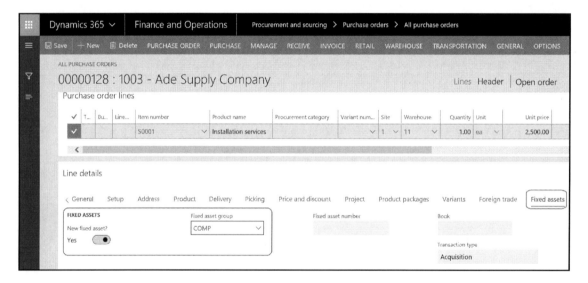

If the fixed asset is new, check the **New fixed asset** checkbox and select a **Fixed asset group**. If this transaction is to capitalize on already created fixed assets, uncheck the **New fixed asset** checkbox, select **Fixed asset group** and **Fixed asset number**, and identify whether the **Transaction type** is **Acquisition** or **Acquisition adjustment**. The **Book** field is populated automatically. The process of the purchase order normally goes from confirmation to product receipt to invoice. After posting the purchase order invoice, the fixed asset record will be created and the asset acquisition transaction will be posted.

An acquisition transaction has the following accounting entry:

- Dr. Fixed assets
- Cr. Vendor balance

As shown in the following screenshot, select the purchase order line after posting the invoice, then go to the Book asset by clicking on the hyperlink on the asset number, and then click on **Books in asset**. Now, click on the **Book** in the fixed asset form:

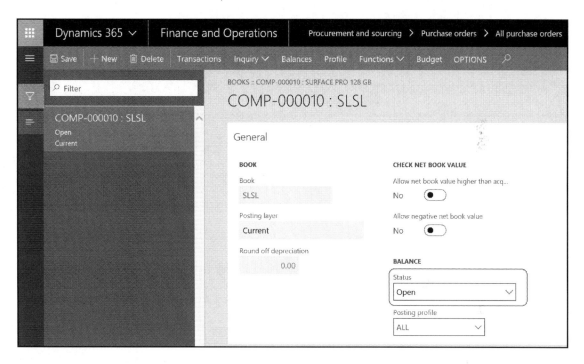

The status changing from **Not acquired yet** to **Open** represents the acquired fixed assets, and this asset will be included in the next depreciation run.

The next step is new to Microsoft Dynamics 365 for Finance and Operations. To create an acquisition proposal journal, go to **Fixed assets** | **Journal entries** | **Create acquisition proposal**; a dialog will open to identify the asset that needs to be acquired.

Then, we move to fixed assets depreciation transactions. As shown in the following screenshot, in order to run fixed assets depreciation, go to **Fixed assets** | **Journal entries** | **Fixed assets journal**, create a new record, and go to **Lines**. Then, go to **Proposals** and select **Depreciation proposal**. Now, identify the depreciation date, find the asset number by clicking on the **Select** button, and decide whether to summarize the depreciation in one line or via separate lines for each month:

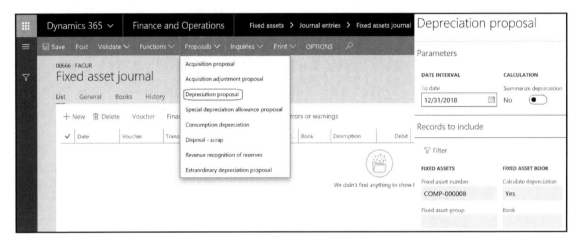

Assume that the acquired fixed assets price is 1,200 USD, the acquisition date is January 1, 2018, and the depreciation period is 12 months. The depreciation for each month is calculated as 1,200 USD divided by 12 months, which is equal to 100 USD. The depreciation will run on till December 31, 2018. The following screenshot illustrates the depreciation for each month:

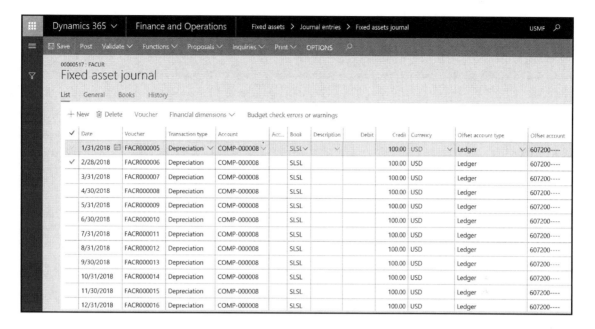

If the **Summarize depreciation** option is set to **Yes**, the depreciation will be created in one line on December 31, 2018 as 1,200 USD.

The depreciation transaction has the following accounting entry:

- Dr. Depreciation expense
- Cr. Accumulated depreciation

Posted transaction of fixed assets are located on the Book, and in order to inquire about a posted transaction, go to **Fixed asset**, select a particular asset ID, go to the **Book** ribbon, and then click on **Transactions**. As shown in the following screenshot, updates have occurred on the **Date when depreciation was last run** field, and the **Depreciation periods remaining** field, which represents the equation. As you can see, depreciation periods minus ran depreciation periods, which is 12 minus 7, equals 5:

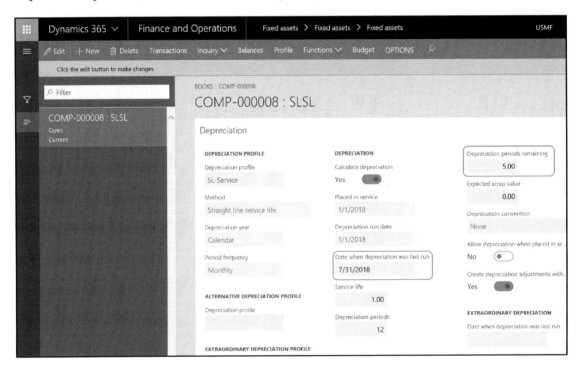

The **Transactions** button shows the posted transactions on the asset depending on whether the transaction type is acquisition or depreciation:

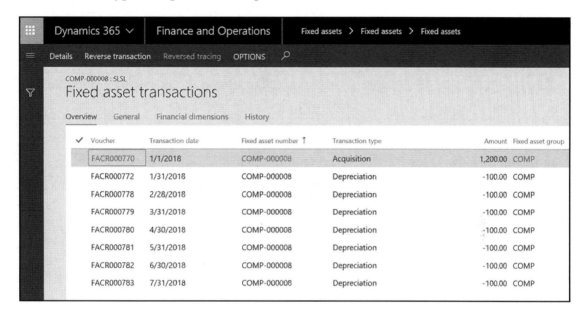

As shown in the following screenshot, the inquiry illustrates the acquisition price, depreciation, and net book value. The net book value represents the equation acquisition price minus depreciation, that is, 1,200 USD minus 700 USD, which equals 500 USD:

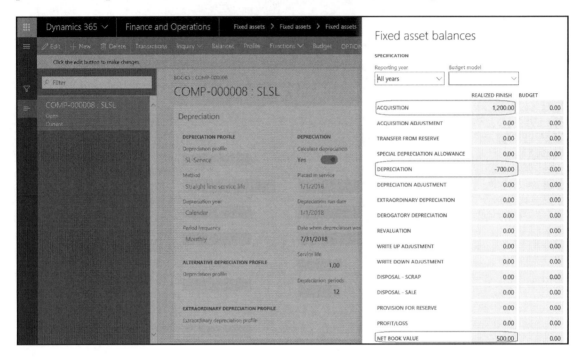

The next feature is new to Microsoft Dynamics 365 for Finance and Operations. You can create a depreciation proposal journal; go to **Fixed assets | Journal entries | Create depreciation proposal**; a dialog will open to identify the asset that needs to be depreciated.

Fixed asset disposal sale

Assume that the disposal sale transaction occurred in a company that decided to sell a car, which is a fixed asset. This transaction of selling a fixed asset occurred through the free text invoice in accounts receivable. The posting profile of a disposal sale considers the following:

- **Depreciation (prior years)**: The total depreciation of prior years will be reversed; the ledger account is the accumulated depreciation account, and the offset account is the fixed assets gain/loss account

- **Depreciation (this year)**: The total depreciation of the current year will be reversed; the ledger account is the accumulated depreciation account, and the offset account is the fixed assets gain/loss account
- **Acquisition value**: The acquisition value will be reversed; the ledger account is the fixed assets account, and the offset account is the fixed assets gain/loss account
- **Net book value**: The ledger account is the fixed assets gain/loss account, and the offset account is also the fixed assets gain/loss account

In order to set up a fixed assets posting profile, go to **Fixed assets** | **Setup** | **Fixed assets posting profile** and select **Disposal** | **Sale**, as shown in the following screenshot:

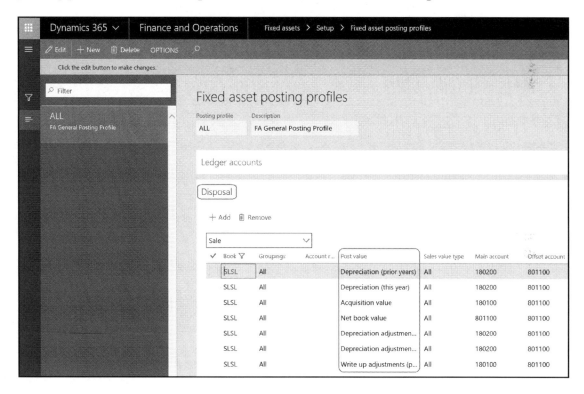

The generated entry will be as follows:

- Dr. Accumulated depreciation account
- Dr. Fixed assets gain/loss account
- Dr. Accounts receivable
- Cr. Fixed assets gain/loss account
- Cr. Fixed assets gain/loss account
- Cr. Fixed assets account

Retrieving fixed asset transactions

There are some scenarios in daily business that require reversing fixed asset transactions. This can be executed from the fixed asset journal, as shown in the following screenshot. Go to **Function** and select **Retrieve fixed asset transactions**. Then, select **New voucher number per transaction** in order to generate a new voucher number, and check **Invert sign** to invert the transaction sign from the original one. To select a particular fixed asset, click on the **Select** button and add the asset number:

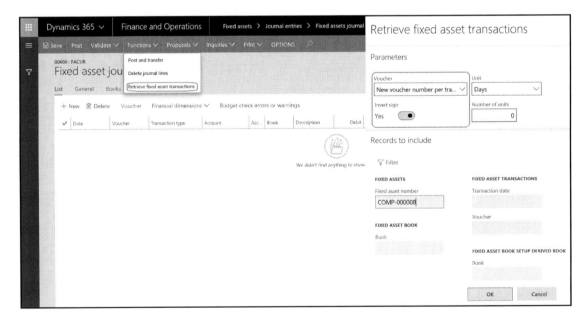

The following screenshot illustrates the retrieved fixed asset transaction with an inverted sign. As you can see, there's a minus sign on the debit side, which means it is a credit. Likewise, if there's a minus sign on the credit side, it is a debit:

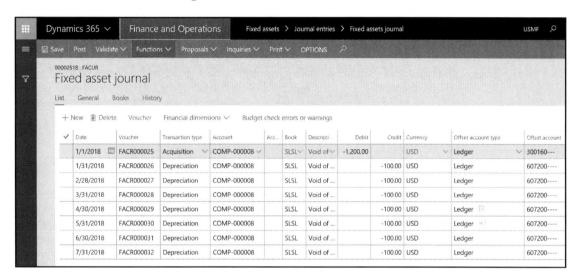

Changing fixed asset groups

Changing fixed asset group functions is commonly used to change the fixed asset group to another group. Let's consider that this function will not reclassify the asset from the accounting point of view. Changing the asset from one group to another may use the same asset ID or rename it, and this does not generate any financial entries. To get to the change fixed asset group path, go to **Fixed assets** | **Fixed assets** | **Fixed assets**, then go to the **Fixed Asset** ribbon, and select **Change fixed asset group**, as shown in the following screenshot:

A dialog box opens to indicate the new group; if you need to create a new fixed asset number, you can do so by renaming the old one. As shown in the following screenshot, a dialog box opens to indicate that you can rename the fixed asset:

Fixed assets reclassification

Now, we will cover the fixed asset reclassification functionality. This function is used to reclassify a fixed asset to another fixed asset from two perspectives; the first perspective is accounting, and the second perspective is the fixed asset group. The reclassification function incorporates changing the asset group by canceling the old one and creating a new fixed asset, and this will generate the necessary financial entries.

Let's assume that there is a fixed asset in an acquired status, and this asset should be reclassified to a new fixed asset ID. The main account, which represents the acquisition, will also be reclassified to another account. The execution of this process will close the original fixed asset, reverse the acquisition entry of the original fixed asset, and create a new entry representing the new asset acquisition.

The following diagram illustrates the reclassification process between the original and new asset:

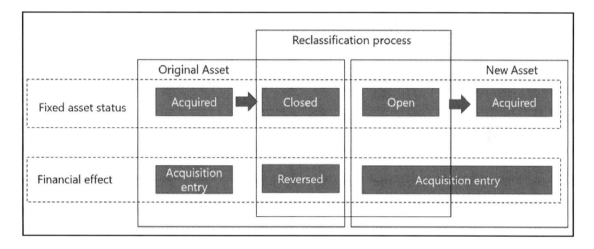

In order to reclassify an acquired fixed asset, go to **Fixed assets | Periodic tasks | Reclassification**. A dialog box will open, as shown in the following screenshot:

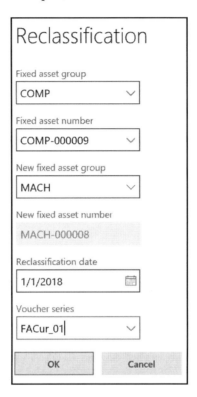

The system will create a new fixed asset record, as shown in the following screenshot:

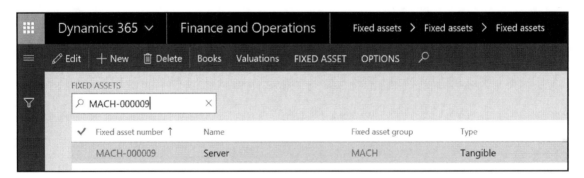

The original fixed asset status is changed to closed, the acquisition entry is reversed, and the newly created fixed asset is acquired. The following screenshot shows the original fixed asset status, under fixed assets book:

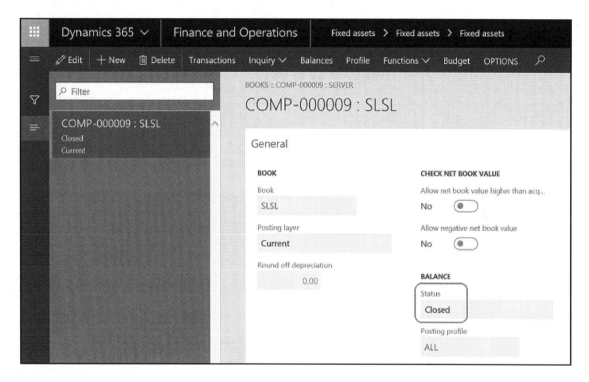

The following screenshot shows the new asset status, under fixed asset book:

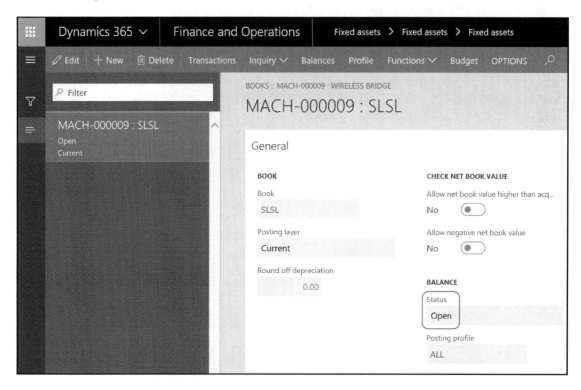

The following screenshot shows the original fixed asset acquisition transaction, and the reversed transaction as well:

The following screenshot shows that the new asset is an acquisition transaction:

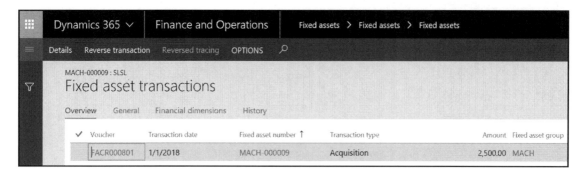

The reversal of the original fixed asset entry and the acquisition entry of the newly created fixed asset are in the same voucher. The debit and credit side are represented as follows: the debit side represents the acquisition account of the newly created fixed asset, while the credit side represents the acquisition account of the original fixed asset:

Fixed assets scrap value

There is a common business requirement for fixed assets where you need to keep a specific amount as a net book value asset. This amount represents the estimated salvage value at the end of the asset's service life, also known as the fixed asset residual value.

In order to consider this business requirement in Microsoft Dynamics 365 for Finance and Operations, it should be identified on the fixed asset book. Let's assume that there is a fixed asset with a depreciation profile called *Straight line service life* with a service life for 1 year, and 12 months as its depreciation period. The asset acquisition date is 1/1/2018 and the acquisition price is 1,200 USD, as shown in the following screenshot:

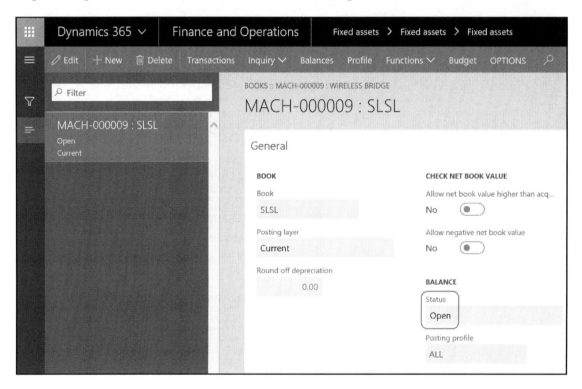

Here, under the **Depreciation** tab, identify the expected scrap value (also known as the salvage or residual value), which represents the estimated scrap value of the fixed assets. In this example, it is 1 USD:

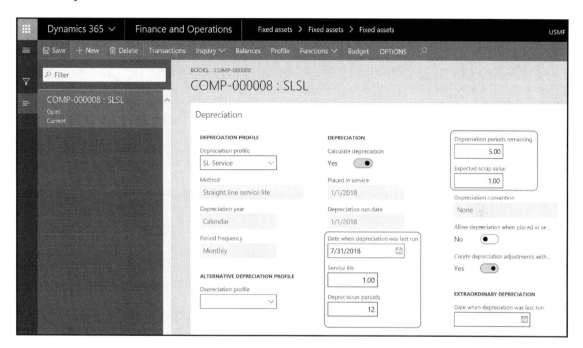

In order to check the monthly depreciation, go to **Inquiry | Profile.**

The depreciation is calculated with the following equation:

Monthly depreciation = (Fixed asset acquisition price – salvage value)/fixed asset useful life
Monthly depreciation = (12000 – 1.00)/12
Monthly depreciation = 1199/12
Monthly depreciation = 99.92

Finally, there is a residual amount of 1 USD, which will be remain in the asset net book value.

Assume that the company needs to dispose of a fixed asset. The execution of disposal scrap can be done by going to **Fixed assets** | **Journal entries** | **Fixed assets journal**. Create a new journal, then move two lines, and then select the fixed asset ID and the transaction type as **Disposal - scrap**; the journal entry should have no amount, as shown in the following screenshot:

The fixed asset status will be changed to **Scrapped**.

Fixed asset statement report

A fixed asset statement is a usable report to give visibility of the fixed assets to a fixed asset accountant. The core of this report is identifying report rows, which will represent a group of fixed assets or a single asset. In order to create a fixed asset statement, navigate to **Fixed assets** | **Setup** | **Fixed asset statement** | **Fixed asset statement row** and create a record, as shown in the following screenshot:

Then, move to **Totals** to identify whether the account relationship is a fixed asset or a fixed asset group, as shown in the following screenshot:

To generate the report, navigate to **Fixed assets** | **Inquiries and reports** | **Transaction reports** | **Fixed asset statement**, and identify the start and end date. Then, filter on the selected row:

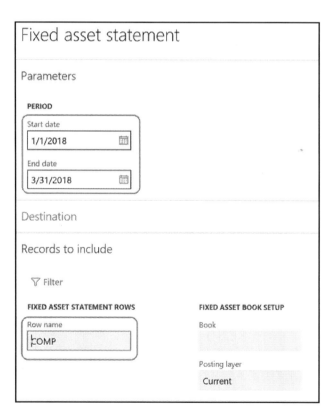

The resulting report shows the acquisition cost of this year, the accumulated depreciation, and the net book value:

Summary

In this chapter, we covered the fixed assets module in Microsoft Dynamics 365 for Finance and Operations. We explored fixed asset characteristics and its integration with other modules. We then explored fixed assets master data and the data required to acquire, depreciate, and dispose of an asset.

Next, we explored fixed asset transactions acquisition, whether through an acquisition proposal journal or through the purchase order, monthly depreciation, disposal sales, and fixed asset transaction reversals. Finally, we covered changing fixed asset groups, fixed asset reclassification, scrap value, posting fixed asset scrap, and fixed asset statement.

In the next chapter, we will explore financial reporting and analysis, planning reporting needs, information source blocks, and discovering Microsoft Dynamics 365 for Finance and Operations financial reporting.

16
Exploring Financial Reporting and Analysis

The main principles of reporting are the reliability of obtaining business information and the ability to get the right information at the right time for the right person. Reports that analyze ERP data in an expressive way represent the output of the ERP implementation. Reporting is considered as the cream of implementation and the next level of value that the solution stakeholders should aim for. This ultimate outcome results from building all reports based on a single point of information. In this chapter, we will cover the following topics:

- Planning reporting needs for ERP
- Understanding the information technology value chain
- Understanding Microsoft Dynamics 365 for Finance and Operations information source blocks
- Discovering Microsoft Dynamics 365 for Finance and Operations reporting
- Reporting options

Planning reporting needs for ERP

The implementation teamwork of Microsoft Dynamics 365 for Finance and Operations should challenge the management's reporting needs in the analysis phase of implementation, with a particular focus on exploring the data required to build reports. These data requirements should then be cross-checked with the real data entry activities that end users will execute to ensure that business users will get vital information from the reports.

On several projects, there are no well-defined reports except the financial reports (trial balance, income statement, and balance sheet) that are in place during analysis. Later, for live operations on such projects, the implementation team determines the need for more data and starts chasing the required information inside the application by completing the missing information fields, and/or redesigning the data entry process. This may lead to an increase in the data entry time due to additional steps for data validation and the surprise discovery that there are not enough end user resources to execute the updated requirements. Hence, there should be a balance between the sum of required data entry values that directly affect the reporting quality, and the total number of end user resources that perform the data entry process.

Another word of caution is that during the operation, the solution architect may recognize that some transactions are performed by one end user, but, typically, these transactions are performed by two or three end users to attain the segregation of duties and control. For example, in the procurement cycle, there is one user who creates the inventory item, purchase order, and reception, but these transactions are normally performed by three different users. In this kind of resource-constrained situation, the segregation of duties and control concepts are breached, and the ERP solution is negatively impacted for the end users and key users. In these situations, the root cause of the concern is not the functionalities of ERP, but the lack of allocated resources.

The two other important models of reporting are as follows:

- **Pulling reports**: The pulling of reports refers to the active requesting of reports by operational managers for the lowest transactional level, such as purchasing, warehousing, sales, marketing, and financial entries. The middle management layer will pull reports to serve procurement, commercial/sales, and controllership.
- **Pushing reports**: The pushing of reports refers to the **business intelligence** (**BI**) capabilities that serve the top management, such as offering KPIs, balance score cards, and analytics/comparison views.

The various reporting levels of Microsoft Dynamics 365 for Finance and Operations are shown in the following diagram:

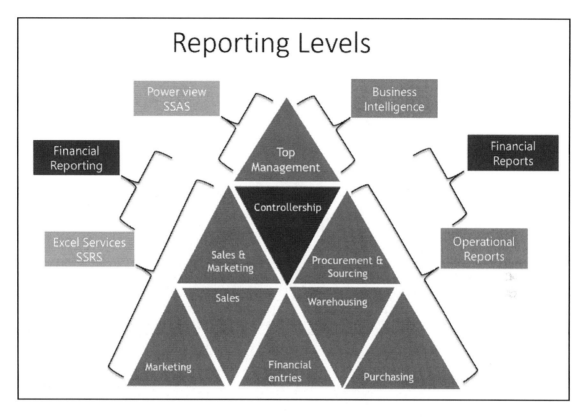

Microsoft Dynamics 365 for Finance and Operations and the supporting Microsoft technology stack offer a diversity of reporting capabilities, including ad hoc reports for the transactional level, developed by Microsoft Excel 2013, Excel Services, and Microsoft **SQL Server Analysis Services (SSAS)**. Microsoft Dynamics **financial reporting** (also known as **management reporter**) offers the controllership in the middle management the ability to create and run financial reports. For the BI solutions built for Microsoft Dynamics 365 for Finance and Operations, customers should begin with **Excel Power View**, SSAS, and Power BI tools. The different levels of management are as follows:

- **Operational management**: The operational managers are involved in monitoring the performance of each business unit and managing employees
- **Middle management**: The middle managers are focused on the internal firm's performance, including revenues and costing management, resource allocation, and the development of short-term plans

- **Top management**: The top managers are focused on strategic business decisions that affect long-term plans, future performance, and the firm's overall objectives

Understanding the information technology value chain

In this section, we will explore reporting and data management in ERP from the management's information system perspective, with its dependent layers.

The model of a management information system is most applicable to the **Information Technology (IT)** manager or **Chief Information Officer (CIO)** of a business. Business owners likely don't care as much about the specifics as long as these aspects of the solution deliver the required results. The information technology value chain is shown in the following diagram:

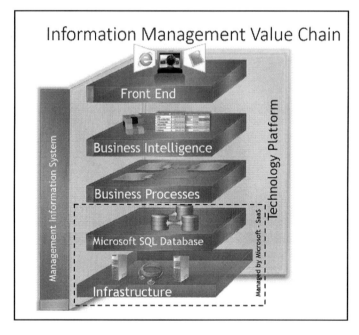

ERP implementations in enterprises have multiple components for successful project delivery. The most common element is addressing business requirements at all enterprise levels, from basic IT infrastructure to user interface technology.

Cloud infrastructure

Infrastructure is vital and ensures the reliability of the solution, assuring the availability of daily business operations. It must also be able to sustain an agreed level of uptime, with cloud SaaS offering that all infrastructure work is managed by Microsoft data centers.

Hardware sizing depends on elements, as well as a number of transactions, users, locations, and the available connectivity for each location. The infrastructure must also meet the architectural requirements of the servers that will ride the application, database, and reporting. All this information is captured during environment provisioning.

Microsoft provides a minimum of three environments, as follows:

- The first is a development environment for testing customizations and new functionalities.
- The second is a **user acceptance test** (**UAT**) environment that is a replication of the live environment and can accept tested updates from the development environment.
- The third is a live production environment for live transactions. It is similarly important to consider clustering and load balancing.

Database management

The relational database (Microsoft SQL Server) that stores all the ERP-related transactions is known as **online transactional processing** (**OLTP**). For BI reporting with a SQL Server, SSAS can store the aggregations, measures, and dimensions. This results in a higher performance in querying reports. It is also important to consider backup and restore strategies.

Reports from Microsoft Dynamics 365 for Finance and Operations are based on the SSRS approach and Financial Reporting.

Business processes

The comprehensive business processes will reflect the data requirements. The design of a business process should identify the data owner, and where and when the data was captured.

Business processes are transformed into business functions in Microsoft Dynamics 365 for Finance and Operations. The applied access rights for users' security ensure the segregation of duties, data ownership, and accuracy of data validation. Similarly, the approval matrix in a workflow will define the control mechanisms in the business processes, such as the required management approvals.

Business intelligence

It is often useful to analyze and measure a company's business results against industry benchmarks and best practices as a technique to develop the most valuable indicators and reports.

The richness of Power View and Excel Services gives the Microsoft Dynamics 365 for Finance and Operations significant power to perform analysis and increase business insights more than any earlier release could.

Frontend

The frontend pinpoints the devices that the organization will need to access the applications that are being used. The most commonly used device in many organizations is still the laptop. More widespread access from numerous locations over the internet may require more planning for mobile devices (cellular phones, handheld devices, and tablets).

Understanding Microsoft Dynamics 365 for Finance and Operations information source blocks

In this section, we will explore the information sources that eventually determine the strategic value of BI reporting and analytics. These are divided into three blocks. The first block is the detailed transaction level, the second is BI, and the third is executive decisions. These three blocks are explained in the following sections.

Detailed transactions block

At its roots, BI depends on capturing accurate transactional data from business processes at the first level of detail and transforming these processes into a regular flow of meaningful entries in an ERP solution, such as Microsoft Dynamics 365 for Finance and Operations. Application consultants should consider the reports that are required by the customers and certify that the required data points are captured through the recording process for daily transactions. Whenever possible, the application consultant has a responsibility to also challenge the business process owners about the process, as it relates to using the data to make changes to optimize the business. The following diagram shows the detailed transactions block:

Business Process Management	Daily Transactions Entries
GL – FA – Banks - Procure To Pay – Sell to Cash – Costing - Budgeting	
Transactions	

In some projects, consultants split their attention between business process workshops during business requirement gathering in the analysis phase, and the establishment of the data structure in forms during the design phase. It is vital to document the business process, including the start point, end point, comprehensive steps of the process (if needed), the data path in each step, and exceptional cases for each process. On the other hand, the forms are a transformation of the business processes into real work activities of employees (fields, grids, buttons, multiple selection, and so on).

The main processes that should be addressed in a typical ERP implementation include banks, fixed assets, procure-to-pay, cash-to-sell, costing, and budgeting, with general ledger integration for each.

Business intelligence block

BI is the second block in the information hierarchy that uses the raw data of transactions to provide valuable information to different levels of the organization. BI adds a layer of aggregation on transactions and makes it possible to create a comparative analysis for key measures such as actual versus budget comparisons.

The consultant should identify the measures needed and how they will be utilized from the transactional level. These measures are raw numbers aggregated from specific fields that result from a definite process or a combination of business processes.

Measures need to be informative, not just as raw numbers, but as a source for analysis at the management level. The consultant should identify the analytic dimensions as well as the dimensions needed by the process owner to analyze numbers. The most common example is sales revenue, which can be analyzed by dimensions such as customer segmentations, geographical locations, warehouses, and customer demographics. The following diagram shows the BI block:

Measures (Operating Profit, Sales amount,…)	Dimensions (segmentations, destinations,…)
Comparative analysis – Aggregations	
Business Intelligence	

Now that we have seen the importance of the structure of reporting blocks based on business processes and daily transaction data, it is worth exploring the common scenarios that consultants may face when the reporting requirements cannot be met by the data that is being captured. This missing data would lead a consultant to revisit the business process that includes the entry of daily transactions, and identify a need for the cleansing of historical data, which may lead to the loss of some information.

Executive decisions block

The third block in the information source is the executive decision support block, where all of the information is summarized and numbers are transformed into KPIs, indicators, analytic views, and dashboards. The following diagram shows the executive decisions block:

KPIs	Indicators	Analytic Views	Dashboard
Executive Decisions			

Executives do not have the luxury of time to drill down to all the comprehensive reports. They need a bird's-eye view of the overall enterprise performance to support them in making critical business decisions. With the right low-level data, the ERP solution should be demonstrating its worth as a true decision support system that offers this visibility.

The conclusion is that when implementing a Microsoft Dynamics 365 for Finance and Operations solution, there is no reliable information for executives without a solid BI platform that is based on a well-defined ERP. The ERP absorbs business processes, such as the daily transactions entered by workers with a high level of clarity.

Discovering Microsoft Dynamics 365 for Finance and Operations reporting

The following section covers the Microsoft Dynamics 365 for Finance and Operations reporting options. The reporting options are inquiry forms and SSRS reports.

Reporting options

Reporting in Microsoft Dynamics 365 for Finance and Operations can be generated through two approaches, namely inquiry forms and predesigned standard reports.

Inquiry forms

Inquiry forms are used for quickly and easily reporting transactions where the transactions are listed. Advanced filtration allows the facility to reduce the inquiry results to a number of specific results. If it is required that you show all the transactions, don't identify any filter.

As you can see in the following screenshot of the inquiry form, navigate to **General ledger** | **Inquiries and reports** | **Voucher transactions**:

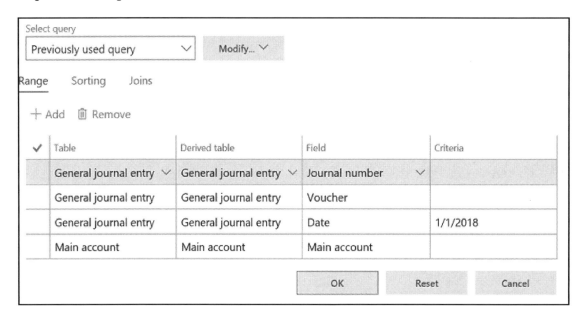

The filters capabilities can be accessed from the inquiry screen by pressing *Ctrl + F3*, as shown in the following screenshot:

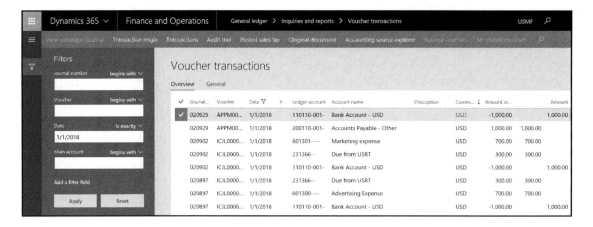

As you can see in the following screenshot, you can save a query by clicking on the **Modify...** button. Now, select **Save as, enter query name** and move to **Joins**, then select **Add table join** to join a data source in the inquiry filtration form. The two join modes here are as follows:

- **1:n**: This represents the relation of one-to-many
- **n:1**: This represents the relation of many-to-one

Under the **Range** tab, we will be able to add tables that are available in the data source, as shown in the following screenshot:

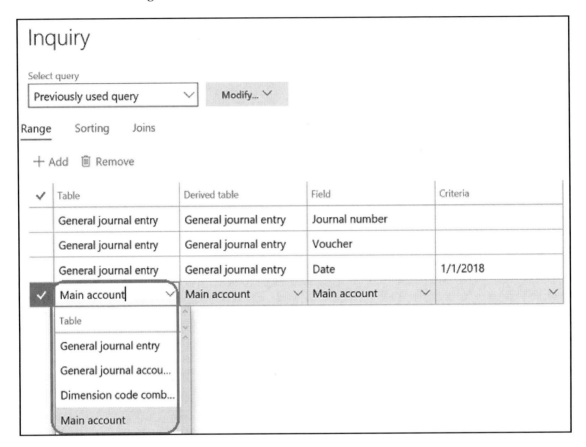

As you can see from the following screenshot, the **Field** column will be used for filtration, and the **Criteria** column will be used to identify values that would be the base for the filtration:

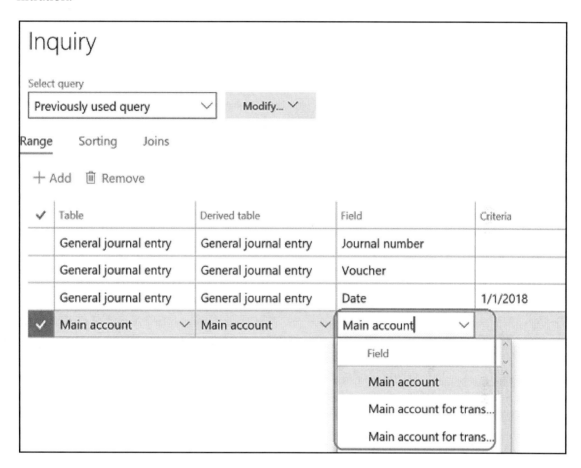

After generating the form, we can use filtration options, and we will see something like what is shown in the following screenshot:

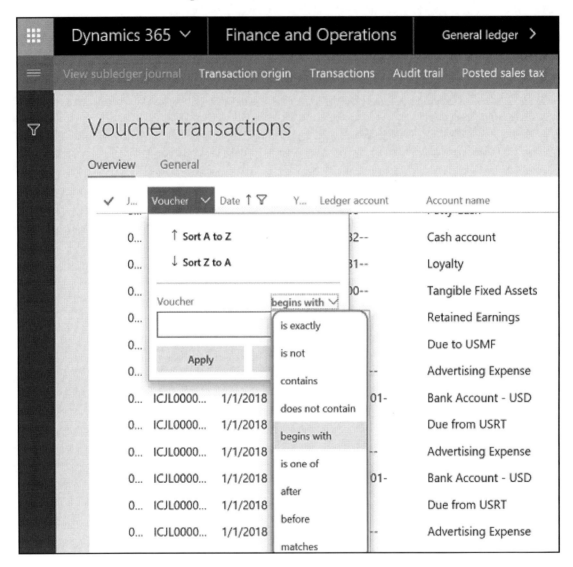

SSRS reports

SSRS reports are used to generate reports in a document format to be printed for filing; these are used as official supporting documents in the company's template or as external official documents. Normal advanced filtration is the base of SSRS report generation, and can sort report results. We can use the tables that are in the data source. We can also specify the fields that will be the base of the sorting and the available sorting option, either **Ascending** or **Descending**.

For the ledger transaction list, navigate to **General ledger | Inquiries and reports | Ledger reports | Ledger transaction list**, and something that looks like the following screenshot should appear:

After completing the selection criteria, click on the **Records to include** and select the **Filter** button and navigate to the **Sorting** tab to identify the report sorting, as shown in the following screenshot:

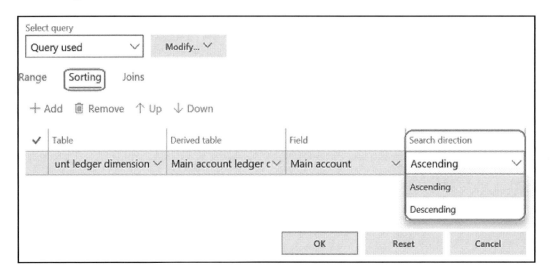

On the ledger transaction form, click on the **Destination** button to access the **Print destination settings**. Now identify the location of report printing, that is, **Print archive**, **Screen**, **Printer**, **File**, or **Email**. Also, select **File format** from the drop-down list, which can be **Microsoft Excel**, **HTML 4.0**, **PDF**, **CSV**, and so on, as shown in the following screenshot:

As you can see in the following screenshot, the generated report is based on SSRS, which gives more flexibility to the report layout:

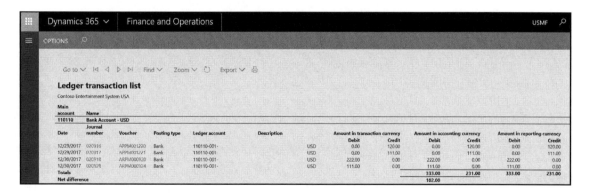

The report can be exported after report generation by the **Export** function, as shown in the following screenshot:

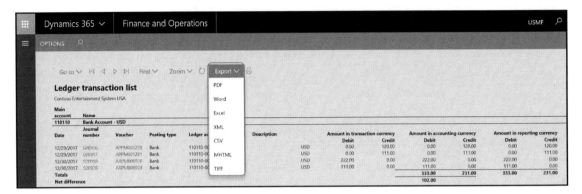

There are three major preferences for financial reporting that Microsoft Dynamics 365 for Finance and Operations users should be familiar with: original transaction, original document, and audit trail, and we will cover all of these in the following section.

The Transaction origin function

The **Transaction origin** function fetches the transaction entries that are posted to the general ledger and their effect on the subledgers. In addition to that, this function can be performed to fetch any transaction entry. It is commonly used when you need to identify the subledger affected by that entry.

For voucher transactions, navigate to **General ledger** | **Inquiries** | **Voucher transactions**. First, you will get an inquiry screen. Here, you do not have to give any criteria, so click on **OK** to see the voucher transactions, then select **Transaction origin**, as shown in the following screenshot:

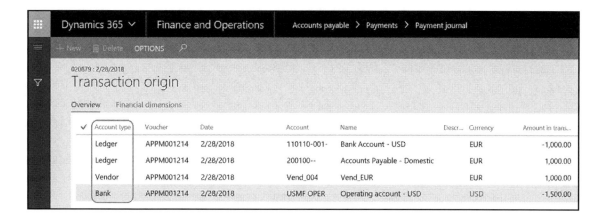

The Original document function

The **Original document** function fetches the transaction entries posted in the general ledger and reaches the original document that generated those entries.

As shown in the following screenshot, the **Original document** function in the voucher transaction inquiry form gives the user the ability to reach the original transaction document regardless of whether it is a general ledger entry, sales order, purchase order, or anything else:

The Audit trail function

The **Audit trail** function in the voucher transaction inquiry form fetches the transaction entries posted in the general ledger and reports. It gives the facility to show who posted the transaction, when, and from which document type. The following screenshot shows the **Audit trail** option of Microsoft Dynamics 365 for Finance and Operations:

 There is a creation date and time that represents the actual date when the transaction was posted. However, this is not the financial posting date, which may be different from the creation date and time.

The main source of the transactions is the transaction database. The transactions are replicated to the cube database or database warehouse every night at midnight. The report information is then pulled out from the cube DB and the DB warehouse. If we are on July 1, the report will get information till the end of July. Let's assume that on July 1, a user posts a transaction dated June 30.

If we run the report again on July 1, which pulls information from cube DB, it will not consider the posted transaction on June 30 since it is not considered in the replication. It will be included with effect from the next replication, which will take place on July 2 at midnight.

Microsoft Dynamics financial reports

Microsoft has introduced Microsoft Dynamics Management Reporter as a financial reporting tool. It gives flexibility and insight in order to represent an organization's financial situation with high-level integration with the ERP. Microsoft Dynamics Management Reporter empowers financial decision-makers with a set of 22 default reports. They are delivered as out-of-the-box reports. Here is a sample list of these reports:

- **12 Month Rolling Single Column Income Statement - Default**
- **12 Month Trend Income Statement - Default**
- **Balance List - Default**
- **Balance Sheet - Default**
- **Cash Flow - Default**
- **Detailed Trial Balance - Default**
- **Expense Three Year Quarterly Trend - Default**
- **Income Statement - Default**
- **Ledger Transaction List - Default**
- **Ratios - Default**
- **Rolling 12 Month Expense - Default**
- **Rolling Quarter Income Statement - Default**
- **Summary Trial Balance - Default**
- **Weekly Sales and Discounts - Default**

In addition to the designing tool used to build financial reports as per company requirements, financial reporting is considered the consolidation tool for Microsoft Dynamics 365 for Finance and Operations where you can report the consolidated company financial reports from the management reports.

Defining the **Financial reporting setup** is a mandatory configuration for running financial reporting. Navigate to **General ledger** | **Ledger setup** | **Financial reporting setup**, as shown in the following screenshot:

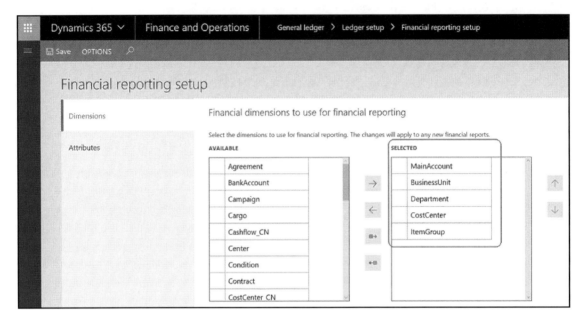

 At the very least, the financial reporting tool requires that **Main Account** is selected in the **Financial reporting setup**.

In Microsoft Dynamics 365 for Finance and Operations, users can access the Management Reporter from the general ledger financial reports menu. To get to the financial reports menu, navigate to **General ledger** | **Inquiries and reports** | **Financial reports**, as shown in the following screenshot:

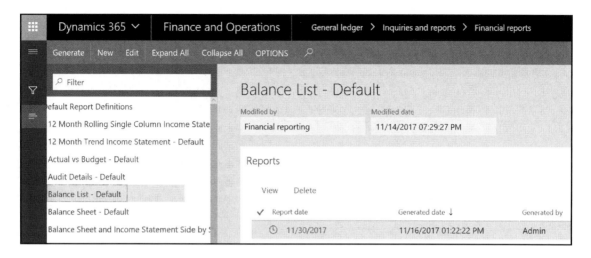

Once the user selects **New** or **Edit**, the **Financial reporting** client will open up; it is a click-once application.

On the **Report Definition** screen, select the report the user wants to generate. Then, click on **Generate**, as shown in the following screenshot:

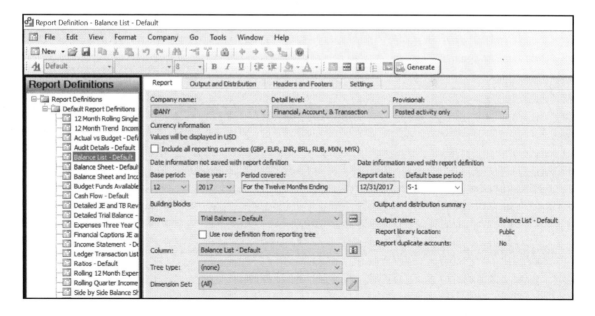

The report generation can also be done from the Microsoft Dynamics 365 for Finance and Operations client, as shown in the following screenshot:

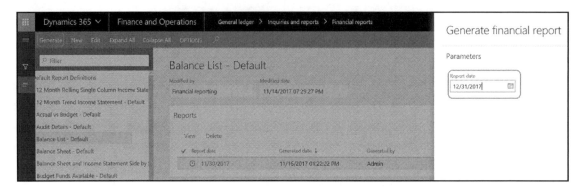

The report will open up. Here is a screenshot that represents the balance sheet as a summarized report:

Microsoft Dynamics Management Reporter provides a drill-down capability to reach the lowest level of transaction and open the ledger entry on the Microsoft Dynamics 365 for Finance and Operations client. In the following example, generate the **Balance List - Default** report title. When we mouse over on an amount, we can drill down to the details of that amount. In the drilled-down transactions, mouse over on the amount and click on **Open in Microsoft Dynamics**:

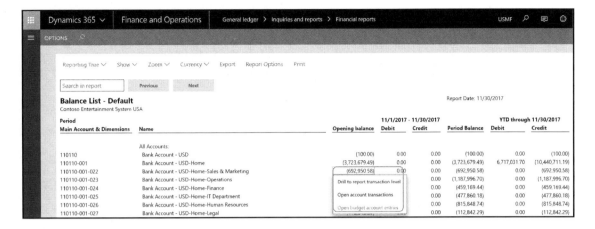

The Microsoft Dynamics 365 for Finance and Operations client will open with the voucher transaction form. In the report header, you will see the function buttons, which is shown as follows:

The function buttons can be summarized as follows:

- **Show**: This shows the report header and footers
- **Zoom**: This presents the users with the zoom-in and zoom-out options for the report
- **Currency**: This represents a function used to convert the report to the selected currency
- **Export**: This represents the download option of the report to Microsoft Office Excel
- **Report Options**: This represents report filtration options

Summary

In this chapter, we covered financial reporting from planning to consideration of reporting levels, where we ensured we gathered the reporting requirements in the early stages of the implementation, and considered the differences of reporting in the different managerial levels.

We covered important points that affect reporting quality by considering the reporting value chain, which consists of the infrastructure, database management, business processes, business intelligence, and the frontend. We also discussed the information source blocks, which consist of the detailed transactions block, business intelligence block, and executive decisions block.

Then, we learned about the reporting possibilities in Microsoft Dynamics 365 for Finance and Operations, such as inquiry forms and SSRS reports and Microsoft Dynamics Financial.

I hope you enjoyed reading this book and that it has given you the required knowledge of the Financial Management module in Microsoft Dynamics 365 for Finance and Operations. Ensure you build your own test environment to practice and advance your career with Microsoft Dynamics 365 for Finance and Operations.

Other Books You May Enjoy

If you enjoyed this book, you may be interested in these other books by Packt:

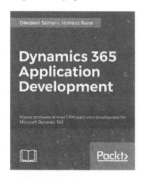

Dynamics 365 Application Development

Deepesh Somani, Nishant Rana

ISBN: 978-1-78839-978-4

- Discover new designers tools included in Dynamics 365 CRM
- Develop Apps using the platform-agnostic Web API
- Leverage Azure Extensions to design cloud-aware applications
- Learn how to implement CRUD operation
- Create integrated real-world apps using Microsoft PowerApps and Flow by combining services such as Twitter, Facebook, and SharePoint
- Configure and use Artificial Intelligence Azure Cognitive Services for Recommendation and Text Analytic services

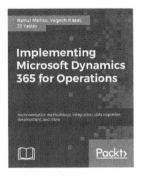

Implementing Microsoft Dynamics 365 for Finance and Operations
Rahul Mohta, Yogesh Kasat, JJ Yadav

ISBN: 978-1-78728-333-6

- Learn about Microsoft Dynamics 365, it's offerings, plans and details of Finance and Operations, Enterprise edition
- Understand the methodology and the tool, architecture, and deployment options
- Effectively plan and manage configurations and data migration, functional design, and technical design
- Understand integration frameworks, development concepts, best practices, and recommendations while developing new solutions
- Learn how to leverage intelligence and analytics through Power BI, machine learning, IOT, and Cortana intelligence
- Master testing, training, going live, upgrading, and how to get support during and after the implementation

Leave a review - let other readers know what you think

Please share your thoughts on this book with others by leaving a review on the site that you bought it from. If you purchased the book from Amazon, please leave us an honest review on this book's Amazon page. This is vital so that other potential readers can see and use your unbiased opinion to make purchasing decisions, we can understand what our customers think about our products, and our authors can see your feedback on the title that they have worked with Packt to create. It will only take a few minutes of your time, but is valuable to other potential customers, our authors, and Packt. Thank you!

Index

Terms of payment field 303

Made in the USA
Lexington, KY
30 April 2019